Protecting National Security

This book contends that modern concerns surrounding the UK state's investigation of communications (and, more recently, data), whether at rest or in transit, are in fact nothing new. It evidences how, whether using common law, the Royal Prerogative, or statutes to provide a lawful basis for a state practice traceable to at least 1324, the underlying policy rationale has always been that first publicly articulated in Cromwell's initial Postage Act 1657, namely the protection of British 'national security', broadly construed. It further illustrates how developments in communications technology led to Executive assumptions of relevant investigatory powers, administered in conditions of relative secrecy. In demonstrating the key role played throughout history by communications service providers, the book also charts how the evolution of the UK Intelligence Community, entry into the 'UKUSA' communications intelligence-sharing agreement 1946, and intelligence community advocacy all significantly influenced the era of arguably disingenuous statutory governance of communications investigation between 1984 and 2016.

The book illustrates how the 2013 'Intelligence Shock' triggered by the publication of Edward Snowden's unauthorized disclosures impelled a transition from Executive secrecy and statutory disingenuousness to a more consultative, candid Executive and a policy of 'transparent secrecy', now reflected in the Investigatory Powers Act 2016. What the book ultimately demonstrates is that this latest comprehensive statute, whilst welcome for its candour, represents only the latest manifestation of the British state's policy of ensuring protection of national security by granting powers enabling investigative access to communications and data, in transit or at rest, irrespective of location.

Phil Glover was born and raised near Belfast, Northern Ireland. Having left school without qualifications, he served in the Royal Ulster Constabulary between 1983 and 2002. He returned to higher education in Scotland in 2008 and obtained an LLB (Honours) from the University of Aberdeen in 2012. He completed a PhD at the University of Aberdeen in 2015 before commencing a career in academia. He now teaches criminal law and conducts comparative national security–related research at Curtin University Law School, Perth, Western Australia.

Protecting National Security

A History of British Communications Investigation Regulation

Phil Glover

Routledge
Taylor & Francis Group
LONDON AND NEW YORK

First published 2022
by Routledge
2 Park Square, Milton Park, Abingdon, Oxon OX14 4RN

and by Routledge
605 Third Avenue, New York, NY 10158

Routledge is an imprint of the Taylor & Francis Group, an informa business

British Library Cataloguing-in-Publication Data
A catalogue record for this book is available from the British Library

Library of Congress Cataloging-in-Publication Data
Names: Glover, Phil, author.
Title: Protecting national security: a history of British communications investigation regulation/Phil Glover.
Description: Milton Park, Abingdon, Oxon; New York,
NY: Routledge, 2021. | Includes bibliographical references and index.
Identifiers: LCCN 2021003239 (print) |
LCCN 2021003240 (ebook) | ISBN 9780815395447 (hardback) |
ISBN 9781032040424 (paperback) | ISBN 9781351183864 (ebook)
Subjects: LCSH: National security–Law and legislation–Great Britain–History. | Great Britain. Investigatory Powers Act 2016. | Criminal investigation–Great Britain. | Electronic surveillance–Law and legislation–Great Britain–History. | Digital communications–Law and legislation–Great Britain–History. | Intelligence service–Law and legislation–Great Britain–History.
Classification: LCC KD8388.G56 2021 (print) |
LCC KD8388 (ebook) | DDC 344.4105/25--dc23
LC record available at https://lccn.loc.gov/2021003239
LC ebook record available at https://lccn.loc.gov/2021003240

ISBN: 978-0-8153-9544-7 (hbk)
ISBN: 978-1-032-04042-4 (pbk)
ISBN: 978-1-351-18386-4 (ebk)

Typeset in Galliard
by Deanta Global Publishing Services, Chennai, India

Contents

Table of cases

Court of Justice of the European Union

Case C26/62 *Van Gend en Loos v Nederlandse Administratie der Belastingen* (1963) ECR 1

Case C–101/01 *Lindqvist* [2003] ECR I–12971

Joined cases C-468/10 and 469/10 *Asociación Nacional de Establecimientos Financieros de Crédito (ASNEF) & Federación de Comercio Electrónico y Marketing Directo (FECEMD) v Administración del Estado* [2011] ECR I-12181

Case C-301/06 *Ireland v European Parliament and European Council* (2009) E.C.R. I-593

C-293/12 *Digital Rights Ireland Ltd* v *Minister for Communications, Marine and Natural Resources* C-594/12 *Seitlinger* (Grand Chamber, 8 April 2014)

Joined Cases C–203/15 and C–698/15 *Tele2 Sverige AB v Post – och telestyrelsen and Secretary of State for the Home Department v Tom Watson and Others*

European Court of Human Rights

Klass and Others v Federal Republic of Germany (1979–1980) 2 EHRR 214

Malone v United Kingdom (1983) 5 EHRR 385, European Commission

Malone v UK (1984) 7 EHRR 14

Leander v Sweden (1987) 9 EHRR 433

Huvig v France (1990) 12 EHRR 528

Halford v UK (1997) 24 EHRR 523

LCB v UK (1998) 27 EHRR 212

Khan v United Kingdom (2001) 31 EHRR 45

Weber and Savaria v Germany (2008) 46 EHRR SE5

Liberty and others v United Kingdom (2009) 48 EHRR 1

Kennedy v UK (2011) 52 EHRR 4

Big Brother Watch and Others v The United Kingdom (Applications Numbers 58170/13, 62322/14 and 24960/15) (Grand Chamber judgment pending as at 30 November 2020)

Republic of Ireland

Digital Rights Ireland v Minister for Communications, Marine and Natural Resources (5 May 2010) High Court, Record No: 2006/3785

United Kingdom

Semayne's Case (1604) 5 Coke Reports 91a
Entick v Carrington (1765) 2 Wilson K B
Attorney-General v Edison Telephone Co (1880) 6 QBD 244
Malone v Commissioner of Police of the Metropolis (No. 2) (1979) Chapter 344
R v Preston (1994) 2 AC 130
R v Effik (1995) 1 AC 309
R v Rasool (1997) 2 Cr App R 190
R v Khan (1997) AC 558
Morgans v DPP (2000) 2 WLR 386
Attorney General's Reference (No 5 of 2002) (R v W) (2003) EWCA Crim 1632
R v E (2004) 2 Cr App R 29
A and others v Secretary of State for the Home Department (2004)UKHL 56
R v S (2008) EWCA Crim 2177
R. *(on the application of Weaver) v London & Quadrant Housing Trust* (2009) EWCA Civ 587
R (Davis and Others) v Secretary of State for the Home Department (2015) EWHC 2092 (Admin)
R *(on the application of Evans) and another (Respondents) v Attorney General (Appellant)* (2015) UKSC 21
R *(National Council for Civil Liberties (Liberty)) v Secretary of State for the Home Department* (2018) EWHC 975 (Admin)

UK Investigatory Powers Tribunal

Jenny Paton and others v Poole Borough Council (2010) (2008) UKIPTrib 09/01/C
Liberty and Others v Security Service, Secret Intelligence Service and GCHQ (2015) UKIPTrib 13/77/H
Privacy International and Others v UK Govt and UKIS (UKIPTrib) 13/92/CH
Privacy International, GreenNet and Others v Secretary of State for Foreign and Commonwealth Affairs and GCHQ, [2014] UKIPTrib 14/85/CH and 14/120-126/CH

Table of legislation

European Union legislation

Consolidated Version of the Treaty on European Union (2012) OJ C 326/01
Charter of Fundamental Rights of the European Union (2012) OJ C326/02

Convention for the Protection of Human Rights and Fundamental Freedoms as amended by Protocols No. 11 and No. 14

Convention for the Protection of Individuals with regard to Automatic Processing of Personal Data Strasbourg, 28.1.1981

Directive 95/46/EC of the European Parliament and of the Council of 24 October 1995 on the protection of individuals with regard to the processing of personal data and on the free movement of such data (2002) OJ L 281/31

Directive 97/66/EC of the European Parliament and of the Council of 15 December 1997 concerning the processing of personal data and the protection of privacy in the telecommunications sector (1998) OJ L 24/1.

Regulation (EC) No 45/2001 of the European Parliament and of the Council of 18 December 2000 on the protection of individuals with regard to the processing of personal data by the Community institutions and bodies and on the free movement of such data (2001) OJ L 008/01

Directive 2002/19 on access to, and interconnection of, electronic communications networks and associated facilities (2002) OJ L 108/07

Directive 2002/20 on the authorisation of electronic communications networks and services (2002) OJ L 108/21

Directive 2002/21/EC of the European Parliament and of the Council of 7 March 2002 on a common regulatory framework for electronic communications networks and services [2002] OJ L108/33

Directive 2002/22 on universal service and users' rights relating to electronic communications networks and services (2002) OJ L 108/51

Directive 2002/58 concerning the processing of personal data and the protection of privacy in the electronic communications sector (2002) OJ L 201/37

Directive 2006/24/EC on the retention of data generated or processed in connection with the provision of publicly available electronic communications services or of public communications networks and amending Directive 2002/58/EC (2006) OJ L 105/54

Council Resolution of 17 January 1995 on the lawful interception of telecommunications (1996) OJ C 329/01

Council Framework Decision 2008/977/JHA of 27 November 2008 on the protection of personal data processed in the framework of police and judicial cooperation in criminal matters (*Data Protection Framework Decision*), (2008) OJ L 350/01.

Council Framework Decision 2006/960/JHA of 18 December 2006 on simplifying the exchange of information and intelligence between law enforcement authorities of the Member States of the European Union (2006) OJ L386/89

European Parliament, Committee on Civil Liberties, Justice and Home Affairs (LIBE), 'Report on the US NSA surveillance programme, surveillance bodies in various member states and their impact on EU citizens' fundamental rights and on transatlantic cooperation in Justice and Home Affairs' (2013/2188 [INI] 21 February 2014)

UK primary legislation

Act 9 Anne, c.10 (Statute of Anne)
Act 1657, c30 Postage of England, Scotland and Ireland setled
Anti-Terrorism, Crime and Security Act 2001
Communications Act 2003
Computer Misuse Act 1990
Criminal Procedure and Investigations Act 1996
Criminal Justice and Police Act 2001
Data Protection Act 1984
Data Protection Act 1998
Data Retention and Investigatory Powers Act 2014
European Communities Act 1972
Electronic Communications Act 2000
Freedom of Information Act 2012
Human Rights Act 1998
Intelligence Services Act 1994
Interception of Communications Act 1985
Interpretation Act 1978
Investigatory Powers Act 2016
Local Government etc. (Scotland) Act 1994
Justice and Security Act 2013
Northern Ireland (Emergency Provisions) Act 1987
Northern Ireland (Emergency Provisions) Act 1991
Northern Ireland Act 1998
Official Secrets Act 1920 Ch75 (10&11 Geo. 5)
Official Secrets Act 1989
Police and Criminal Evidence Act 1984
Police Act 1997
Police (Northern Ireland) Act 2000
Policing and Crime Act 2009
Police Reform and Social Responsibility Act 2011
Police and Fire Reform (Scotland) Act 2012
Post Office (Revenue) Act 1710
Post Office (Offences) Act 1837
Post Office Act 1908
Post Office Act 1953
Prevention of Terrorism Act 2005
Prevention of Social Housing Fraud Act 2013
Prisons (Scotland) Act 1989
Protection of Freedoms Act 2012
Regulation of Investigatory Powers Act 2000

Regulation of Investigatory Powers (Scotland) Act 2000
Scotland Act 1998
Security Service Act 1989
Social Security Administration Act 1992
Social Security Fraud Act 2001
Telegraph Act 1863
Telegraph Act 1868
Telegraph Act 1869
Telephone Transfer Act 1911
Terrorism Act 2000
Terrorism Act 2006
Terrorism Prevention and Investigation Measures Act 2011
Wireless Telegraphy Act 1904 (4 Edw c24)
Wireless Telegraphy 1949 (12, 13, & 14 Geo 6 c54)
Wireless Telegraphy Act 2006

UK secondary legislation

Criminal Justice and Data Protection (Protocol No. 36) Regulations 2014, SI 2014/3141
Data Retention (EC Directive Regulations) 2007, SI 2007/2199
Data Retention (EC Directive) Regulations 2009, SI 2009/859
Data Retention Regulations 2014, SI 2014/2042
Data Retention and Acquisition Regulations 2018, SI 2018/1123
Intelligence Services Act 1994 (Channel Islands) Order 1994, SI 1994/2955
Intelligence Services Act 1994 (Dependent Territories) Order 1995, SI 1995/752
Police and Criminal Evidence (Northern Ireland) Order 1989, SI 1989/ 1341 (N.I. 12)
Policing Protocol Order 2011, SI 2011/2744
Postal Services Act 2000 (Consequential Modifications No. 1) Order 2001, SI 2001/1149
Prevention of Social Housing Fraud (Power to Require Information) (England) Regulations 2014, SI 2014/899
Prevention of Social Housing Fraud (Detection of Fraud) (Wales) Regulations 2014, SI 2014/826
Privacy and Electronic Communications (EC Directive) Regulations 2003, SI 2003/2426
Regulation of Investigatory Powers Act 2000 (Commencement No. 3) Order 2003, SI2003/3140
Regulation of Investigatory Powers (Communications Data) Order 2003, SI 2003/3172
Regulation of Investigatory Powers Act 2000 (Commencement No. 4) Order 2007, SI 2007/2196
Regulation of Investigatory Powers (Communications Data) Order 2010, SI 2010/480

Regulation of Investigatory Powers (Covert Surveillance and Property Interference: Code of Practice) Order 2014, SI 2014/3103
Regulation of Investigatory Powers (Maintenance of Interception Capability) Order 2002, SI 2002/1931
Regulation of Investigatory Powers (Technical Advisory Board) Order 2001, SI 2001/3734
Regulation of Investigatory Powers (Scotland) Act 2000 (Commencement) Order 2000, SSI 200/341
Retention of Communications Data (Extension of Initial Period) Order 2003, SI 2003/3173
Retention of Communications Data (Code of Practice) Order 2003, SI 2003/3175
Retention of Communications Data (Further Extension of Initial Period) Order 2005, SI 2005/3335
Scotland Act 1998 (Commencement) Order 1998, SSI 1998/3178
Security Service Act 1989 (Overseas Territories) Order 1990, SI 1990/238
Telecommunications (Data Protection and Privacy) Regulations 1999, SI 1999/2093
Wireless Telegraphy (Pre-Consolidation Amendments) Order 2006, SI 2006/1391

Table of abbreviations

AFSJ	Area of Freedom Security and Justice
BRUSA	British United States Communication Intelligence Agreement 1946
CD	Communications Data
CD CoP	Acquisition and Disclosure of Communications Data Code of Practice
CFREU	Charter of Fundamental Rights of the European Union
CJEU	Court of Justice of the European Union
CMA	Competition & Markets Authority
CoE	Council of Europe
COMINT	Communications Intelligence
CoP	Code of Practice
CSEC	Communications Security Establishment Canada
DP	Designated Person
DPA 1984	Data Protection Act 1984
DPA 1998	Data Protection Act 1998
ECHR	European Convention on Human Rights
ECtHR	European Court of Human Rights
ELINT	Electronic Intelligence
ENNIR	European Network of National Intelligence Reviewers
GCHQ	Government Communications Headquarters
HRA 1998	Human Rights Act 1998
HUMINT	Human Intelligence
ICO	Information Commissioners Office
IOCA 1985	Interception of Communications Act 1985
IOCC	Interception of Communications Commissioner (1985–99)
IOCCO	Interception of Communications Commissioner's Office
IOCT	Interception of Communications Tribunal
IPA 2016	Investigatory Powers Act 2016
IPCO	Investigatory Powers Commissioner's Office
IPEI	Investigation of Protected Electronic Information
IPT	Investigatory Powers Tribunal
ISA 1994	Intelligence Services Act 1994

ISC	Intelligence Services Commissioner
JSA 2013	Justice and Security Act 2013
LEA	Law Enforcement Agency
LPC	Legislative Programme Committee (UK Parliament)
MoD	Ministry of Defence
NAFN	National Anti-Fraud Network
NCA	National Crime Agency
NCIS	National Criminal Intelligence Service
NCND	Neither Confirm Nor Deny
NSS	(UK) National Security Strategy
NTAC	National Technical Assistance Centre
OSC	Office of Surveillance Commissioners
OSINT	Open Source Intelligence
RCD	Related Communications Data
RIPA 2000	Regulation of Investigatory Powers Act 2000
RIP(S)A 2000	Regulation of Investigatory Powers (Scotland) Act 2000
SIGINT	Signals Intelligence
SIS	Secret Intelligence Service (previously MI6)
SOCMINT	Social Media Intelligence
SPoC	Single Point of Contact
SRO	Senior Responsible Officer
SSA 1989	Security Service Act 1989
SSC	Security Service Commissioner
SST	Security Service Tribunal
TAB	Technical Advisory Board
TIC	Trade and Industry Committee
TPIM	Terrorism Prevention and Investigation Measure
TPIMA 2011	Terrorism Prevention and Investigation Measures Act 2011
UKIC	United Kingdom Intelligence Community (MI5, MI6 & GCHQ)
UKPHAC	United Kingdom Parliamentary Home Affairs Committee
UKPISC	United Kingdom Parliamentary Intelligence and Security Committee
UKUSA	United Kingdom/United States of America Communications Intelligence Agreement

Acknowledgements

Beautiful and eternally patient Amber. Thanks for everything. Not least Mav and ?

My awesome daughters Kristen and Tara, and granddaughter Heidi.

My parents Cecil and Mary Glover, for what they had to put up with.

University of Aberdeen Professor Peter (Pete) Duff, for his unwavering belief in me and for the constant support he provided to me (despite his footballing allegiances). Professors Roddy Paisley and Margaret Ross (University of Aberdeen). Professor Robert Cunningham (Curtin University Perth, WA) for creating the space for me to write.

This work is also in deeply fond and respectful memory of the following people I would have loved to have shown this work off to, but for whom a Higher Power had made alternative plans:

(Aunt) Pearl McCutcheon, latterly of Killaughey, Millisle, County Down, Northern Ireland, for whom 'investigatory powers' would have been 'a load a oul nonsense' but with whom I shared so many laughs.

Former RUC Inspector Derek Monteith, murdered in his kitchen by the IRA in the presence of his family whilst off-duty and defenceless, 22 January 1990. You unknowingly had given my feckless young life new meaning and direction just when I needed it. I see you every waking day and I will never forget you.

Every RUC officer, British soldier, Crown Servant, and innocent member of the public murdered or permanently scarred in the course of trying to maintain peace and public order for the silent suffering majority during Northern Ireland's pointless sectarian conflict.

Henry O'Neill. I never met you, but I first saw your name on a stained-glass window at my little country primary school, O'Neill Memorial, Crossnacreevy, County Down, Northern Ireland (the best place in the world to have grown up).

Under your name it stated:

> 'The pen is mightier than the sword'.

Whilst 'pen' has been replaced by 'keystroke', I understand it now.

Part I

Introductory matters

1 Introductory matters

Introduction

From the outset, precise writing is required to outline what this book seeks to add to the existing academic literature. The area of public law it examines, the 'regulation of investigatory powers', has developed a reputation for tortuous conceptual logic, complex technical definitions, and thus significant difficulties in interpretation.

'Rationalizing' the IPA 2016

This book is neither a practical guide to the Investigatory Powers Act (IPA) 2016 nor an explanation of its main provisions. Others have studied the Act, its Explanatory Notes, and voluminous derivative Codes of Practice, and published important interpretative analysis.[1]

This book primarily aims to 'rationalize' or explain how and *why* the IPA 2016 came to be structured and drafted as it is by illustrating the key historical events, successive governments' policies, and efforts at regulation that preceded it. It thus examines the historical administrative and statutory governance of communications and data investigation in the hope that, by setting the IPA 2016 in its proper context of regulating a 700-year state national security practice, it will be demonstrated as nothing more than a logical progression of that practice.

A legitimate question is why research output such as this might be important or necessary, particularly given the significantly increased level of candour and explicit detail in the IPA 2016, as compared with its regulatory predecessors.[2] The principal reason is that, despite 12 months of parliamentary debate informed by seven parliamentary committee reports containing around 2,400 pages of

1 See particularly Simon McKay, *Blackstone's Guide to the Investigatory Powers Act 2016* (OUP, 2017).

2 The term 'candour' is preferred to the more commonly used 'transparent', because although the IPA 2016 outlines the powers available to the state candidly and with immense detail as to how they should be used, the operational consequences of their practical implementation, of necessity, remain largely unknown.

evidence from technical experts and NGOs,[3] the Act as assented to remains controversial. Despite purportedly providing 'world-leading transparency and privacy protection',[4] it has failed to assuage the longstanding concerns of civil libertarian activism as to the 'scope and magnitude' of the privacy-intrusive powers it contains.[5] Despite limited support and significant public apathy,[6] division remains between the Cabinet, Home and Foreign and Commonwealth Offices, and a well-organised and funded civil libertarian lobby, as to the scope, magnitude, necessity, and proportionality of communications and data investigative powers. The latter's concerns, while undoubtedly genuinely held, can occasionally be articulated in emotive rhetoric, diverting concentration from what should be an objective assessment of necessity and proportionality around powers 'critical to law enforcement and the security and intelligence agencies' ability to counter the threats...[faced]...from terrorism, crime, and state-based threats'.[7]

It is therefore hoped that this work might assist in some way in bridging the current divide, by providing readers with enough relevant historical material, infused with evidence of government policy in this area, to allow a more informed, rational, and objective view of communications and data-investigative powers.

Principal thesis

The history-focused research undertaken for this book sought to test the following thesis statement.

> The IPA 2016 represents the most recent cohesive candid statutory restatement of formerly secretive British state powers, assumed or granted in the interests of national security (broadly construed), aimed at enabling the capability to lawfully access communications and data at rest or in transit wherever located.[8]

3 David Anderson QC, foreword to McKay, *Blackstone's Guide* (n1).

4 Ben Wallace MP, Ministerial Foreword to Home Office, *Investigatory Powers Act 2016 Consultation: Codes of Practice* (February 2017).

5 *Big Brother Watch and Others v The United Kingdom* (Applications Numbers 58170/13, 62322/14 and 24960/15) [3]. This legal challenge, referred to the European Court of Human Rights Grand Chamber, which heard the referral on 10 July 2019, was to aspects of the investigatory powers regime that preceded the IPA 2016 (RIPA 2000). However, the powers in question have been included in the IPA 2016. Judgment remains pending as of 30 November 2020.

6 Ewen MacAskill, 'Extreme Surveillance becomes UK law with barely a whimper' *The Guardian* (London, 19 November 2016) <https://www.theguardian.com/world/2016/nov/19/extreme-surveillance-becomes-uk-law-with-barely-a-whimper> accessed 20 September 2019.

7 HM Government, *Transparency Report 2018: Disruptive and Investigatory Powers* (Cm 9609, 2018) 34.

8 Emphasis added – interpretations of 'national security', 'covert', and 'access' are defined later in the chapter.

Another way of putting this is that this book proceeds on the premise that in creating the IPA 2016, the legislature has aspired to 'cover the field' as regards investigative access to data (including communications) by the state. Consequently, the core question for which an answer is sought herein is whether the IPA 2016, as structured and drafted, can be rationalized by a critical examination of the known history of clandestine communications and data investigation and state regulation thereof. Put another way, and phrased as a question, can history-based research demonstrate that the approach to regulation of investigatory powers within the IPA 2016 is a rational and logical development in state power in response to significant historical events, developments in communications technology, and the needs of the UK Intelligence Community (UKIC)?

National Security (broadly construed) means construing national security (still undefined in UK law) as including protection of the economic wellbeing of the UK and the prevention and detection of serious crime.

Supporting acknowledgements

In order to test the statement in a coherent way and thus 'rationalize' the IPA 2016 as a logical and coherent progression in governance, the following underlying influences require acknowledgement.

The place of secrecy

The doctoral research underpinning this work commenced in 2012.[9] The brief involved critically examining the history of 'investigatory powers' that related to accessing communications. It was thought that this would entail an examination of how the law would be traceable back from the Regulation of Investigatory Powers Act (RIPA) 2000, the human rights-compliant statute governing access to communications, communications data as then defined, and data subject to encryption. RIPA 2000 *appeared* to cover the field of investigative access to communications and data.[10] There was the statute itself, and substantial Explanatory Notes and Codes of Practice for each of the powers regulated. There was also a very useful practitioner's guide.[11] In an area of public law regulating covert investigations, it appeared that any requirement for reform had been addressed by the enactment of RIPA 2000. As such, the research plan moved to examining where it all started. This proved more difficult. The role of secrecy in the history of communications-related investigatory powers rapidly became apparent. This

9 For a useful overview of the UK Civil Service relevance to the early culture in the UKIC, see generally David Vincent, *The Culture of Secrecy: Britain 1832–1998* (Clarendon Publishing 1999).

10 Part II of RIPA regulates covert surveillance and remains in force. As it does not involve dire ctly accessing data or communications, it is not covered in this book.

11 Simon McKay, *Covert Policing* (OUP 2011).

book will illustrate that official policies involving secrecy and 'need to know' have influenced this area of law since at least 1324. Such policies are not unique to the UK, however. States that were considered even more 'privacy-centric', including what was then the Federal Republic of Germany, were practising '*secret* measures of State surveillance'.[12] The very fact that Europe's supreme human rights court referred to communications surveillance in this way evidences the then-prevailing residual Cold War culture. As regards the UK, Christopher Andrew described intelligence matters (including communications investigation) as:

> The [l]ast taboo of British politics...protected from public gaze and parliamentary scrutiny by a bipartisan consensus built around two dubious constitutional principles...the first...that intelligence was wholly undiscussable [*sic*] in public – even in Parliament...and the second...that Parliament must entirely abdicate its powers in this field to the executive.[13]

This aligns with Vincent's observation that the principal concern of successive UK governments, no matter their political persuasion, was the upholding of their contribution to a 'culture of secrecy' in respect of national security matters.[14] This includes the scope and extent of communications investigation through techniques including interception. Even prior to the period covered by Vincent, government secrecy in matters of national security surveillance had evolved from the Bond Association. This document was created by Francis Walsingham, Secretary of State to Queen Elizabeth I, and William Cecil, consequently establishing the infamous 'spy ring' that focused principally on gathering intelligence from a sizeable number of international and domestic informants. The primary ground for doing so was seeking to protect the Protestant British throne from the perceived constant *external* threat, principally from the Catholic Kingdom of Spain.[15] Secrecy in this area undoubtedly became further entrenched following the creation of the now-familiar organizations making up the UKIC in the early 20th century. Although a working relationship wherein the three Directors-General of the UKIC are accountable to Ministers,[16] the 20th century prior to statutification records periods of relative unaccountability based on the very fact

12 A term first coined by the ECtHR in *Klass and Others v Federal Republic of Germany* (1979–1980) 2 EHRR 214, emphasis added.

13 Christopher Andrew, *The Defence of the Realm: The Authorized History of MI5* (Penguin 2010) 753.

14 David Vincent, *The Culture of Secrecy 1832–1998* (OUP, 1999).

15 Although undoubtedly undertaking communications surveillance, Walsingham's Spy Ring was primarily HUMINT focused and falls outside the scope of this work. See generally Alan Haynes, *The Elizabethan Secret Services* (Sutton, 2000) or Steven Alford, *The Watchers: A Secret History of the Reign of Elizabeth I* (Bloomsbury, 2014).

16 Jon Moran and Clive Walker, 'Intelligence Powers and Accountability in the UK', in Zachary K Goldman and Samuel J Rascoff (eds) *Global Intelligence Oversight* (OUP, 2016) 289–314.

of secrecy.[17] However, in overall terms, despite incidents of tension between the Executive and Parliament,[18] their longstanding relationship can be viewed overall as cooperative, even occasionally deferential on the Executive's part. The culture within which they operate has at times involved protracted exposure to variants of established intelligence community information security principles such as 'need to know' and 'responsibility to share'.[19] This, in conjunction with the obligations imposed upon relevantly affected civil servants by the Official Secrets Act (OSA) 1989[20] and the Civil Service Code,[21] has undoubtedly contributed to the maintenance of this culture of secrecy. Despite the post-2015 transition from secrecy to 'transparent secrecy' as part of the wider transparency agenda referred to previously, the influences of 700 years of bureaucratic secrecy are unlikely to have fully dissipated.

This book illustrates these principles on many occasions. It charts the regulation of communication (and more recently data) investigation powers from their commencement in total secrecy, into begrudged 20th-century 'concessions' to candour which ultimately were revealed as disingenuous, to the IPA 2016.

State disingenuousness

Research conducted after July 2013 year led to the unavoidable conclusion that between 1984 and 2016, but particularly between 1997 and 2015, successive UK governments, generally in consensus regarding the regulation of communications and data-investigatory powers, had enacted statutes that in spite of their purported objects were arguably disingenuous. In other words, the statutes purporting to regulate communications (and latterly data) investigation in this time

17 ibid, 294.

18 ibid.

19 Information security is a huge subject of immense importance to the global intelligence community. On the 'need to know' principle, see Dr E G Amoroso, *Fundamentals of Security Technology* (PTR Prentice Hall, 1994) 70. 'Need to know' is also known as the 'principle of compartmentalization'. Since 9/11, it has fallen somewhat out of favour and is being replaced by the 'need to share' or 'responsibility to share' doctrine. On this, see former US Director of National Intelligence James R Clapper, 'How 9/11 Transformed the Intelligence Community: It's No Longer about "Need to Know". Our Guiding Principle is "Responsibility to Share"'. *The Wall Street Journal* (7 September 2011) A15, <www.wsj.com/articles/SB10001424053111904537404576554430822300352> accessed 20 September 2020. For a wider analysis of the principal issues in information security, see Lech J Janczewski and Victor Portougal, '"Need-to-Know" Principle and Fuzzy Security Clearances Modelling' (2000) 8(5) *Information Management and Computer Security*, 210.

20 For extensive restrictions on information disclosure by specified Crown Servants see OSA 1989, ss1–8.

21 On Civil Service confidentiality, see Christopher Jary and Laura Bryant-Smith, *Working with Ministers: A Practical Handbook on Advising, Briefing and Drafting* (6th edn, Crown Office Publishing, 2015) Chapter 7 and the Civil Service Management Code, *GOV.UK* (April 2015) available at <https://gov.uk/government/uploads/system/uploads/attachment_data/file/418696/CSMC-_April_2015.pdf> accessed 24 September 2020.

were drafted and enacted whilst knowledge (perhaps within a very limited circle) existed that these same statutes did not 'cover the field'. Secret power remained, particularly in the developing field of data investigation, and communications metadata in particular. This was despite the growing influence of EU-derived instruments that purported to provide 'data protection', to which the UK had given direct effect since 1984. Whether the retention of secret power was deliberate policy, or the result of negligence or omissions in legislative scrutiny, remains arguably a moot point, but one on which this work invites readers to reach a definitive evidence-based conclusion.

'Transparent secrecy'

The period of statutory disingenuousness referred to may have lasted longer but for events attributable to the Fourth Estate.[22] There can be no doubt as to the contribution to the transition to 'transparent secrecy' observed between 2013 and the present that investigative journalism made.[23] In line with Rachel Noble's term, the IPA 2016 candidly and clearly describes *what* the UKIC, Defence Intelligence (DI), and certain law enforcement agencies (LEA) are empowered to do, but what it continues not to do is outline *how* it is done as that must necessarily remain secret.[24] It also for the first time, in clear language, outlines formerly secret powers enabling communications and/or data-investigation on a 'bulk', as well as 'targeted' basis.

The Fourth Estate

What the IPA 2016's transparent secrecy has done is to finally demonstrate that rigid adherence to Andrew's aforementioned constitutional principles visibly waned after 2013. This was due to two significant contributory factors. The first centres on the inquiries relating to the investigative activities of the Fourth Estate undertaken between 2012 and 2015. The second centres around the increasing number of legal challenges to aspects of the UK's investigatory powers regime, including the IPA 2016, by the civil libertarian lobby, emboldened by the enactment of the Human Rights Act (HRA) 1998. Privacy International, Liberty, and Big Brother Watch have been at the forefront of these challenges, with some

22 A common descriptor for the Free Press: Pippa Norris, *Driving Democracy* (Cambridge University Press, 2008) Chapter 8.

23 Rachel Noble (Director-General Australian Signals Directorate), 'Long Histories, Short Memories – the Transparently Secret Australian Signals Directorate', (presentation to the National Security College, Australian National University, Canberra 1 September 2020) <https://www.asd.gov.au/publication/speech-transparently-secret-asd> accessed 20 September 2020.

24 ibid.

notable successes in the domestic and European courts.[25] The two drivers of change are related, in that a significant amount of evidence tendered in the legal challenges derives from the publication of disclosures made to investigative journalists.[26] Only the first is addressed at this point, however, as the most recent challenge will significantly influence the future direction of investigatory powers regulation in the UK on a number of fronts and is thus examined further in the final chapter.[27]

The Leveson Inquiry

The first, perhaps less cited, influence was the 'inquiry into the culture, practices and ethics of the [UK] press' chaired by the Right Honourable Lord Justice Leveson (Leveson Inquiry), that culminated in the publication in late 2012 of a four-volume report (*Leveson Report*)[28] outlining his Part One findings.[29] The full scope of the Inquiry's terms of reference related to UK press regulation and is thus outside the scope of this work.[30] However, there were numerous references throughout all four volumes of Leveson's report that raised legitimate questions and concerns relative to RIPA 2000, which, with the benefit of hindsight, can be said to have been influential in bringing communications investigation into the public consciousness and in influencing the reviews that would ultimately shape the IPA 2016.[31] A core task of the Inquiry was to investigate the extent of alleged 'phone-hacking' conduct undertaken by sections of the UK press or their agents. 'Phone hacking' euphemistically describes conduct amounting to interception of communications without lawful authority, conduct criminalised by the IPA

25 See generally, Privacy International <https://privacyinternational.org>; Liberty (previously National Council for Civil Liberties) https://www.libertyhumanrights.org.uk; and Big Brother Watch <https://bigbrotherwatch.org.uk> accessed 21 October 2019.

26 See, for example, the procedure section of *Big Brother Watch and Others v UK* (Apps nos 58170/13, 62322/14 and 24960/15) (Grand Chamber Hearing 10 July 2019 – decision pending as of 30 November 2020).

27 *Big Brother Watch and Others v UK* (Apps nos 58170/13, 62322/14 and 24960/15) (Grand Chamber Hearing 10 July 2019 – decision pending).

28 Leveson Inquiry, *An Inquiry into the Culture, Ethics and Practices of the Press Report* (2012–2013, HC 780 – I, II, III, and IV).

29 A residual consequence arising from Leveson is that many criminal investigations into alleged unlawful interception of communications remain ongoing at the time of writing. As they remain *sub judice*, publication of Part Two of his report remains on hold. See his letter to then Prime Minister David Cameron dated 29 November 2012 included as a preface to his report (*Leveson Report* [n13] Vol I).

30 *Leveson* (n28) Vol I, para 1.3, sets out its full terms of reference.

31 Examples include *Leveson* (n) Vol I, Part E, which outlines the relevant criminal and civil law, Vol III, Part H, which explores the relationship between the police and data protection legislation, and Vol IV, Part J as it relates to aspects of press regulation and the relevant criminal and civil legislation.

2016, and by RIPA 2000 (then in force) if undertaken in the UK.[32] While the Leveson Inquiry was significant in inviting focus on the adequacy or otherwise of the UK's then-existing regulatory framework, its significance pales in comparison to the consequences that flowed from *The Guardian* media outlet's headline of 7 June 2013.[33]

The 2013 Intelligence Shock

Loch K Johnson suggests that most lawmakers rarely engage in intensive intelligence accountability, or 'oversight, 'unless a major scandal or failure – an intelligence shock – forces them to pay more attention to the dark side of... government'.[34] *The Guardian*'s publication of unauthorized disclosures made by fugitive US National Security Agency (NSA) contractor Edward Snowden constitutes just such a shock. As this book will show, the 2013 Intelligence Shock constitutes the most significant milestone in the shaping of states' communications and data investigation practices since the tragic events of 11 September 2001 (9/11). It might initially seem distasteful to make this comparison, given that the latter killed thousands of innocent civilians in a matter of one hour. There exists, however, a strong body of opinion that lives were, and will continue to be lost as a direct or indirect consequence of Snowden's decision to approach members of the Fourth Estate with stolen information and their decision to publish his at that point uncorroborated allegations.[35] In a similar way to the fallout from 9/11, media publication of his disclosures forced a hitherto unprecedented and public degree of political scrutiny and intelligence community introspection across many Western liberal democracies including the UK.[36] Views of him remain polarized. Civil libertarians view him as a hero and courageous whistle-blower, worthy of immortalization in print and film.[37] The United States government views him as a fugitive criminal still evading prosecution for 'theft of government property, unauthorised communication of national defence information

32 RIPA 2000, s1(1). It shall be an offence for a person intentionally and without lawful authority to intercept, at any place in the United Kingdom, any communication in the course of its transmission by means of – (a) a public postal service; or (b) a public telecommunication system.

33 Glenn Greenwald and Ewen MacAskill, 'NSA Prism Program Taps in to User Data of Apple, Google and Others', *The Guardian* (London, 7 June 2013) <http://theguardian.com/world/2013/jun/06/us-tech-giants-nsa-data> accessed 26 October 2019.

34 Loch K. Johnson, 'Intelligence Shocks, Media Coverage, and Congressional Accountability, 1947-2012' (2014) 13(1) *Journal of Intelligence History* 1. K.

35 See for example *Australian Financial Review*, 'Interview Transcript: Former Head of the NSA and Commander of the US Cyber Command, General Keith Alexander' (8 May 2014) <www.afr.com/technology/web/security/interview-transcriptformer-head-of-the-nsa-and-commander-of-the-us-cyber-command-general-keith-alexander-20140507-itzhw> accessed 27 October 2019.

36 Reviews also took place in the USA and several EU countries.

37 See Luke Harding, *The Snowden Files* (Vintage Books, 2014), and the identically titled film.

and willed communication of classified communications intelligence to an unauthorised person'.[38] As the Independent Reviewer Terrorism Legislation (IRTL) David Anderson QC (now Lord Anderson) observed in 2015 however, whether Snowden's published disclosures could be believed, they could not be ignored.[39] The legal questions they raised undoubtedly indicated significant deficiencies in the then existing RIPA 2000 framework. That hitherto innocuous statute and the broader regulatory framework within which it existed in 2013 thus fell under the spotlight for review over the following two years, with the IPA 2016 representing the statutory manifestation of many of those reviews' recommendations.

Whatever the view taken of Edward Snowden, perhaps the greatest irony of his decision to appropriate the NSA material and disclose it to selected journalists was that no reduction in the scope and magnitude of communications and data investigation in the UK actually resulted. All that happened was that, after various reviews, changes occurred in the *regulation* of communications and data investigation that reflected a policy change wherein secrecy and disingenuousness were substituted by 'transparent secrecy'. The IPA 2016 represents little more than an entrenchment and consolidation of the secret power his disclosures exposed. This work neither pre-judges, denigrates, nor elevates Edward Snowden. As such, the term '2013 Intelligence Shock' is used throughout this work to describe the historical marker put down on 7 June 2013.

Scandal

Prior to 2013, investigatory powers (more specifically interception of communications) had been examined by Parliament only six times in almost 700 years. It will be shown that there was a gap of 520 years between the traceable commencement of the practice and the first inquiry into it (1844), and another 113 years until the second inquiry (1957). Only public scandal and the accompanying media fallout have ever impelled Parliament to review this area of governance, with the 2013 Intelligence Shock marking the latest example. Setting aside for now the comparative transparency demonstrated in the post-2013 reviews, discussed later, each pre-2013 review of the regulation of interception powers will be shown to have been characterized by:

1 Secretive brevity (when set against the seriousness of the scandal at hand);
2 An explicit effort to locate and legitimize a specific power to intercept;
3 An explicit effort to offer reassurance to the British public in the final published document that powers were being exercised with due restraint and propriety;

38 See Peter Finn and Sari Horwitz, 'U.S. vs. Edward J. Snowden Criminal Complaint' (*The Washington Post*, 21 June 2013) <http://apps.washingtonpost.com/g/documents/world/us-vs-edward-j-snowden-criminal-complaint/496/> accessed 31 October 2019.

39 Independent Reviewer of Terrorism Legislation, *A Question of Trust: Report of the Investigatory Powers Review* (Williams Lea Group, June 2015) para 7.10 (IRTL, *RIPR 2015*).

4 An explicit effort to defend the *status quo* as existing at the time of publication and
5 A failure to publicize the total extent to which interception of communications was being undertaken in the UK, including a breakdown of how many instances of interception each state body with particular functions in a particular area (such as the Security Services or the Police) had undertaken.[40]

Scandal, in a prevailing context of secrecy, can therefore be said to have played an important contributory role in the shaping of interception, and broader investigatory powers regulation.

The post-Intelligence Shock reviews

This book benefitted significantly from the contemporaneous research undertaken as part of the principal post-2013 reviews into data-related investigatory powers published in 2015 and 2016. It is highly unlikely that any of them would have ever been undertaken but for the fallout from the publication of Snowden's disclosures.

For reference purposes, the reviews in question are:

1 The UK Parliamentary Intelligence and Security Committee, *Privacy and Security: A Modern and Transparent Legal Framework* (UKPISC, *Privacy and Security Report 2015*);[41]
2 Independent Reviewer of Terrorism Legislation (IRTL), *A Question of Trust: Report of the Investigatory Powers Review* (IRTL, *Investigatory Powers Review 2015*);[42]
3 Royal United Services Institute for Defence and Security Studies, *A Democratic Licence to Operate: Report of the Independent Surveillance Review* (*RUSI Review 2015*);[43]

40 Despite the nascent transparency agenda, a recent, pre-IPA 2016 example is the Interception of Communications Commissioner's Office (IOCCO), *Report of the Interception of Communications Commissioner March 2015 (covering the period January to December 2014)* (2014–2015, HC 1113, SG/2015/28, 12 March 2015) para 6.41. This shows the total number of interception warrants issued etc. and a breakdown of their purpose, but no information is provided as to the division of warrants amongst the public authorities entitled to apply.

41 UK Parliamentary Intelligence and Security Committee (UKPISC), *Privacy and Security: A Modern and Transparent Legal Framework* (HC 2014–2015, 1075-I). UKPISC is utilised throughout this work instead of the perhaps simpler ISC, to distinguish it from what was, until the enactment of the IPA 2016, the Intelligence Services Commissioner.

42 IRTL, *Investigatory Powers Review 2015* (n39) – David Anderson QC was Independent Review of Terrorism Legislation at the time of enactment of the Data Retention and Investigatory Powers Act (DRIPA) 2014, s7 of which required him to undertake his review.

43 Royal United Services Institute for Defence and Security Studies, *A Democratic Licence to Operate: Report of the Independent Surveillance Review* (Stephen Austin and Sons Ltd, July

4 IRTL, *Report of the Bulk Powers Review* (IRTL, *Bulk Powers Review 2016*).[44]

Whilst each made a distinct contribution to the final content and drafting of the IPA 2016, this work will evidence how the diligence, independence, and objective findings of both the IRTL-led inquiries were the most influential.

Technology and investigatory powers

This book will additionally outline how, since the practice of communicating using technology (including quills and pens) saw humanity progress from *homo loquens* via *homo scriptor* through to *homo somnians*,[45] the state has assumed for itself, or been granted, investigatory powers enabling access to that technology. It will illustrate how prerogative, common law, and statutory powers have been used to enable lawful executive access to communications and data since the inception of the UK postal service, expanding to embrace each new development in wired and wireless communications technology. The most recent example is the controversy surrounding the executive's desire to secure, in regulation, access to internet connection records (ICR).

Technology neutrality

As regards the idea of 'technology neutrality' in this area of public law, it will become apparent herein that when framing policy or legislation, a principle of 'technology neutrality' has been, and remains adhered to, by successive UK governments. An example is its application in the drafting of RIPA 2000.[46] The principle was reaffirmed in 2014 by James Brokenshire (then Home Office Minister for Security and Immigration) who stated that, as regards 'surveillance law' generally, the UK government would continue to recognise the importance of it remaining 'technology-neutral so as to keep pace with technological change in the communications industry'.[47] Put simply, each new assumption of investigatory powers has sought to keep references to any particular means of communications out of any broad enabling provisions with the perfectly logical aim

---

2015). It was undertaken at the request of the then Deputy UK Prime Minister Nick Clegg (Liberal Democrat).

44 IRTL, *Report of the Bulk Powers Review* (Cm 9326 Aug 2016).

45 Humanity in the ages of speech, manuscripts, and the internet, respectively. See generally Marshall T. Poe, *A History of Communications: Media and Society from the Evolution of Speech to the Internet* (Cambridge University Press 2011).

46 Professor Sir David Omand GCB, Visiting Professor, Department of War Studies King's College London (Director GCHQ, 1996–1997) Written Evidence to UKPISC Privacy and Security Inquiry, para 17 available at <http://isc.independent.gov.uk/public-evidence> accessed 23 October 2019.

47 HC Deb 9 December 2014, vol 589, col 824.

of minimizing the need to return to Parliament for amendments. The principle remains reflected in the IPA 2016.

National security interests and fundamental rights

When reviewing the legal challenge brought in the UK Investigatory Powers Tribunal (UKIPT) by *Liberty and Others v UKIS*[48] Rosalind English observed that the case was 'generated by two of the major catalysts of public law litigation: the government's duty to look after the security of its citizens, and the rapid outpacing of surveillance law by communications technology'.[49] As regards the former, it has been asserted that a government's duty to look after its citizens is 'one of its primary functions and (arguably) a condition of its legitimacy'.[50] The 2010–2015 UK Government National Security Strategy observed that 'in a world of startling change, the *first duty* of the government remains: the security of our country'.[51] The European Court of Human Rights (ECtHR) has held that 'the existence of some legislation granting powers of secret surveillance over the mail, post and telecommunications…[is]…necessary in a democratic society in the interests of national security and/or for the prevention of disorder or crime'.[52] This Court has also held that the margin of appreciation afforded to Member States in this respect is a wide one,[53] adding, however, that the interest of states in protecting their national security 'must be balanced against the seriousness of the interference with the applicant's right to respect for his private life'.[54] Ultimately, however, in any national security-critical balancing exercise, the protection of the rights to life should be prioritised over the protection of rights where death is not a likely outcome of infringement. This is not least because the European Convention on Human Rights (ECHR), Article 2, holds states as being 'under a positive duty to do all required of them to prevent lives being put at risk'.[55] States are also required 'to secure the right to life by putting in place effective criminal law provisions to deter the commission of offences against the person backed up

48 *Liberty and Others v UK Government and UKIS* (2014) UKIPTrib/13/77/H 5 December 2014.

49 Rosalind English, 'Cracking Intercepts: The War on Terror and Difficulties with Human Rights' (UK Human Rights blog, 11 December 2014) <http://ukhumanrightsblog.com/2014/12/11/cracking-intercepts-the-war-on-terror-and-difficulties-with-human-rights/> accessed 23 October 2019.

50 David Miller, 'The Responsibility to Protect Human Rights' in Lukas H Meyer (ed) *Legitimacy, Justice and Public International Law* (Cambridge University Press, 2009) 232.

51 Home Office, *A Strong Britain in an Age of Uncertainty: The National Security Strategy* (Cmnd 7953, 2010), emphasis added.

52 *Klass & Others v Germany* (n12) [48].

53 *Leander v Sweden* (1987) 9 EHRR 433 [59].

54 ibid.

55 *LCB v UK* (1998) 27 EHRR 212 [36].

by law-enforcement machinery for the prevention, suppression and sanctioning of breaches of such provisions'.[56]

While the 'security-v-privacy' debate is sometimes considered a recent phenomenon, this book will help demonstrate that, for as long as regulation of communications-related investigatory powers in the UK has existed, it has *always* afforded primacy to the interests of protecting the national security of the state. The UK's 700-year heritage of prioritizing its national security interests (and since 1945, those of its allies),[57] explains why, despite enacting the Human Rights Act (HRA) 1998 to give effect to the ECHR, the UK legislature continues to prioritise national security interests over individuals' rights-based interests (such as those in privacy of correspondence and freedom of expression).[58] Despite being the first ever British statute to explicitly refer to 'general privacy protections',[59] the overall effect of the IPA 2016's operational considerations,[60] when weighed alongside the privacy-focused duties that must be considered prior to exercising the relevant investigatory powers,[61] is to trump them.[62] As the ECtHR has demonstrated, however, this is not in itself unduly controversial or unusual. All state signatories to the ECHR enjoy not only 'sole responsibility' for national security by virtue of the Treaty on European Union,[63] but also the benefit of the national security qualification applicable to ECHR rights potentially infringed by com-

56 *Osman v UK* (1998) 29 EHRR 245 [115].

57 Principally Australia, Canada, New Zealand, and the United States of America, by virtue of the BRUSA (subsequently UKUSA) communications intelligence-sharing agreement of 5 March 1946. See NSA/CSS 'UKUSA Agreement Release' <https://www.nsa.gov/news-features/declassified-documents/ukusa/> accessed 21 October 2019. This agreement and the national security allegiances significantly predate UK participation in national security intelligence-sharing arrangements with European countries.

58 ECHR Articles 8 and 10 respectively.

59 See generally, IPA 2016, Part I 'General Privacy Protections'.

60 ibid, s2(2) …other considerations may, in particular, include (a) the interests of national security or of the economic well-being of the United Kingdom, (b) the public interest in preventing or detecting serious crime.

61 ibid, s2(4) A public authority must have regard to: (a) whether what is sought to be achieved by the warrant, authorization or notice could reasonably be achieved by other less intrusive means, (b) whether the level of protection to be applied in relation to any obtaining of information by virtue of the warrant, authorization or notice is higher because of the particular sensitivity of that information, (c) the public interest in the integrity and security of telecommunication systems and postal services, and (d) any other aspects of the public interest in the protection of privacy.

62 McKay (n1) 2.08–2.10.

63 Treaty on European Union (TEU), Article 4(2), emphasis added:

> [t]he Union shall respect the equality of Member States before the Treaties as well as their national identities, inherent in their fundamental structures, political and constitutional, inclusive of regional and local self-government. It shall respect their essential State functions, including ensuring the territorial integrity of the State, maintaining law and order and safeguarding national security. *In particular, national security remains the sole responsibility of each Member State.*

munications and communications and data investigation.[64] This book will also demonstrate that the *margin* of primacy afforded by the UK state to the interests of national security over the protection of individuals' human rights interests tends to have been broader than that observable in Europe, thus perhaps justifying some of the legal challenges brought by the civil liberties lobby. This may be because alongside an established 700-year heritage of prioritizing national security interests over individuals' rights, and only 30 years of seeking to protect ECHR rights in UK legislation, the UK has not developed a post-WW2 data privacy-centric culture to the same degree as many of its European neighbours. David Anderson correctly identified that for some of them, 'intelligence-gathering has sinister resonances'.[65] Whilst the IPA 2016 undoubtedly aspires to adhere to international human rights norms, its primary purpose is as a weapon in the UK's formidable armoury of disruptive and investigatory powers.[66]

Communications service providers (CSPs): a vital relationship

This work will also show how the 700-year state practice of accessing communications for investigative purposes has been, and remains, fundamentally contingent on state control of the technological *means* by which communications are stored, sent, or received. Put bluntly, the modern UK's massive telecommunications intelligence production regime simply could not operate without the active cooperation of communications service providers (CSPs) subjected to state regulatory control. This book weaves the relatively recent change in the *form* of that state control into the narrative. It originally involved the Executive exercising *total* control of securing access to communications and related material without any perceived requirement for public-facing enabling powers due to the fact of state ownership of the means of communication and its role as sole and exclusive CSP. This form of control changed to a requirement for public-facing enabling powers as a consequence of denationalization and the fragmentation of postal and telecommunications service provision in the late 20th century. The book will illustrate how the relatively recent privatization of UK communications service provision has done nothing to alter the fact that access to communications and

64 ECHR, Art. 8(2), There shall be no interference…[with]…this right except such as is in accordance with the law and is necessary in a democratic society in the interests of national security, public safety or the economic well-being of the country, for the prevention of disorder or crime, for the protection of health or morals, or for the protection of the rights and freedoms of others. ECHR, Art 10(2) The exercise of these freedoms…may be subject to such formalities, conditions, restrictions or penalties as are prescribed by law and are necessary in a democratic society, in the interests of national security, territorial integrity, or public safety, for the prevention of disorder or crime, for the protection of health or morals, for the protection of the reputation or rights of others, for preventing the disclosure of information received in confidence, or for maintaining the authority and impartiality of the judiciary.

65 IRTL, *RIPR 2015* (n28) 4.

66 See Home Office, *Disruptive and Investigatory Powers* (n7) Chapter 6.

related material by executive agencies remains impossible without the cooperation (willing or otherwise) of the private sector's CSPs, and how the state continues to expend significant public funds to ensure it. It will also highlight how, after a relatively trouble-free period in the years following privatization, the advent of near-universal use of internet communications services, coupled with the growth in the number of CSPs providing communications services in the UK but based beyond its jurisdiction, heightened tensions have arisen in what was a hitherto relatively calm relationship. These centre around the encryption debate but have not unduly affected the day-to-day cooperation required for the effective functioning of the IPA 2016 regime.[67]

Parliamentary consensus

This book will show that British state policy and regulation in the area of national security and communications-related investigatory powers has generally transcended parliamentary party ideological differences. Indeed, until relatively recently, communications-related investigatory powers passed from elected government to elected government without controversy, no matter which political party or coalition assumed power. Where party political disagreement has surfaced, opposition benches have tended to voice their concerns but not vote down nascent legislation, instead abstaining and adding their input via amendments. As such, proposed legislation generally proceeds on a consensual footing. The parliamentary journey of the final IPA 2016 exemplifies this.[68] The outcome of this longstanding overall consensus as achieved has been to ensure that communications access powers have kept pace with new communications technology and that intelligence requirements as articulated by the intelligence-lobby are generally met with the provision of the requisite powers.[69]

The UKUSA Communications Intelligence Agreement

This book will demonstrate that the underlying approach to the UK's approach to regulating communications and data investigation is to ensure that its

67 Discussed in Chapter 6.

68 The UK Labour Party, as the official opposition in 2016, abstained from voting at the Second Reading of the IP Bill, meaning that its passage could not be defeated (it was passed by 281 votes to 15 – see HC Deb 15 March 2016). They eventually voted with the government at Third Reading after working through a significant number of amendments (See speech of Rt Hon Andy Birnham MP, HC Deb 7 June 2016, vol 611, cols 1147–1148). The IP Bill went to the House of Lords by 444 votes to 69. One noteworthy exception to the consensus discussed later in this work is the draft Communications Data Bill 2012, which was abandoned by the Conservative/Liberal Democrat Coalition Government prior to any vote in 2014, due to the withdrawal of Liberal Democrat support for it.

69 The passage of the Data Retention and Investigatory Powers Act (DRIPA) 2014 in only three days is another example analyzed later in this book.

participation in the UKUSA Communications Intelligence Agreement originally signed on 5 March 1946 is given effect.[70] There exists a reasonable volume of literature on this formerly secret alliance, primarily within intelligence studies, that evidence the UKUSA's agreement's undoubted fundamental value to its five principal participants.[71] The UK's commitment to the UKUSA Agreement has been unwavering since the outset, and has outlasted commitments to political alliances such as the EU,[72] as well as other, less publicized intelligence-sharing alliances.[73] In recent years, reflecting perhaps the post-2013 transition from secrecy to candour at Five Eyes level, the participating governments have taken to issuing joint communiques explicitly affirming 'shared values' and policy alignment in addressing 'existing and emerging security threats faced…in…communities, at… borders, or in the cyber space'.[74] There appears to have been less written about how the UK's commitments to the UKUSA agreement have been actually given effect in domestic law in the years since 1946. This book aims to demonstrate that the UK's recent (1985) transition to statutory regulation of communications surveillance involved tacitly incorporating SIGINT and communications intelligence (COMINT) concepts within the relevant provisions with the aspiration to render these commitments lawful. The most obvious example is the inclusion of '*signals* serving either for the impartation of anything between persons, between a person and a thing or between things or for the actuation or control of any apparatus' within the definition of 'communication'.[75] Consequently, military SIGINT acquisition potentially falls within the ambit of civilian communications and data investigation governance. As such, this book, where deemed appropriate, examines the role of Defence Intelligence (DI) along with the roles of the United Kingdom Intelligence Community (UKIC) in utilizing Communications and data-investigation powers. Both form 'an essential part' of the UK's National Intelligence Machinery, but significantly less detail exists in the public domain regarding DI.

70 Originally the BRUSA Agreement (as between Britain and the United States) (n49).

71 See for example, Richard Morgan, 'Oversight through Five Eyes: Institutional Convergence and the Structure and Oversight of Intelligence Activities', in Zachary K Goldman and Samuel J Rascoff (eds) *Global Intelligence Oversight: Governing Security in the Twenty-First Century* (Oxford University Press, 2016) 37–70.

72 The UK was a member of the EU since 1 January 1973 by virtue of the European Communities Act 1972. It left on 31 January 2020.

73 Stephane Lefebvre, 'The Difficulties and Dilemmas of International Intelligence Cooperation' (2003) (16) (4) International Journal of Intelligence and Counterintelligence 529–534.

74 See Australian Government, Department of Home Affairs, 'Five Country Ministerial Communiqué: Emerging Threats, London 2019' (30 July 2019) <https://www.homeaffairs.gov.au/news-subsite/Pages/2019-Jul/joint%20meeting%20of%20fcm%20and%20quintet%20of%20attorneys-general%20-%20communique.aspx> accessed 31 October 2019.

75 IPA 2016, s261(2), emphasis added.

The UK Intelligence Community (UKIC)

Related to the assertion that UKUSA Agreement obligations have influenced the drafting of relevant regulation is the assertion that the UKIC and DI themselves influence the nature and scope of such regulation. There exists evidence that this influence has grown since the latter half of the 20th century. There is, of course, nothing inherently improper or illogical about this; the UKIC have an illustrious history in preventing and detecting threats to the UK's national security and in the critically important field of communications decryption.[76] Consequently, where these institutions deem that additional investigatory powers are required in the interests of the 'efficiency of the Service', they will lobby their relevant Secretary of State accordingly.[77] What this book will demonstrate, however, is that occasionally, governments have perhaps been unduly deferential in their readiness to act on advice from the intelligence lobby as to what direction to take, at the expense of being sufficiently forthcoming to the electorate as to the operational consequences of their choice. An example examined herein is the Ministerial decision to follow the intelligence lobby's suggestion to use powers hidden in plain sight within the Telecommunications Act 1984 providing for a Secretary of State to give directions to CSPs in the interests of national security[78] to compel the retention of communications service use data, a practice conducted in secrecy until avowed in 2015.

Personal data

This book will evidence how, until the advent of the digital communications era, the primary material sought by agents of the UK executive when investigating communications with a view to finding threats to national security was communications *content*, the actual 'what was written or said' part of the communications.[79] This of course makes sense, as until the advent of internet communication, written letters and spoken telephone calls formed the principal methods

76 As regards the Security Service (MI5), see generally Christopher Andrew, *The Defence of the Realm: The Authorized History of MI5* (Penguin 2010). As regards the Secret Intelligence Service (formerly MI6) see Keith Jeffery, *MI6 The History of the Secret Intelligence Service 1909–1949* (Bloomsbury, 2010). As regards GCHQ, see generally Richard J Aldrich, *GCHQ The Uncensored Story of Britain's Most Secret Intelligence Agency* (Harper Press 2010).

77 By virtue of the Security Service Act (SSA) 1989, s2, the Director-General of MI5 is 'responsible for the efficiency of the Service' and is appointed by, and reports to, the Secretary of State for the Home Department (Home Secretary). By virtue of the Intelligence Services Act (ISA) 1994, s2, the Chief of the Secret Intelligence Service is also responsible for the efficiency of the Service and reports to the Secretary of State for Foreign and Commonwealth Affairs (Foreign Secretary). By virtue of section 4 of the same Act, the Director of GCHQ is similarly responsible and also reports to the Foreign Secretary.

78 Telecommunications Act 1984, s94, now repealed. The secret use of s94 was only conceded in 2015.

79 Home Office, *Investigatory Powers Act 2016: Response to Home Office Consultation on the Government's Proposed Response to the Ruling of the Court of Justice of the European Union on 21 December 2016 Regarding the Retention of Communications Data* (June 2018), Introduction, available at <https://assets.publishing.service.gov.uk/government/uploads/system/

of communication using the UK's postal and telecommunications systems. The actual substance of these communications thus provided significantly more intelligence utility than any 'data' logically associated with such communications (such as the address or postal stamp on an envelope or 'metering' information on a paper telephone bill). It will be shown how various regulatory efforts associated with enabling access to communications placed 'communications' at their conceptual core.[80] It will be demonstrated that the ubiquitous use of electronic communications technology in recent years now means that *any* data logically associated with a communication, whether classifiable as content data[81] or metadata derived from or logically associated with electronic communications,[82] is of potential intelligence value to those accessing it.[83] In addition to highlighting the difficulties the UK legislature has had in distinguishing content-data and metadata, the book will chart the rise of personal data 'at rest'[84] or 'in

---

uploads/attachment_data/file/724142/June_2018_IPA_regulations_-_Government_Response_to_consultation_on_response_to_ECJ_judgment.pdf> accessed 31 October 2019.

80 For example, the Interception of Communications Act 1985.

81 Defined as 'speech, music, sounds, visual images or *data of any description*' within IPA 2016, s261(2)(a); RIPA 2000, s81(1), emphasis added, and as 'text, voice, videos, images, and sound' in the European Commission, 'Proposal for a Regulation of the European Parliament and of the Council Concerning the Respect for Private Life and the Protection of Personal Data in Electronic Communications and Repealing Directive 2002/58/EC' (Regulation on Privacy and Electronic Communications) Brussels, 10.1.2017 COM(2017) 10 final (Draft e-Privacy Regulation) (not yet adopted as of November 2019) available at <https://eur-lex.europa.eu/legal-content/EN/TXT/?uri=CELEX:52017PC0010> accessed 12 November 2019.

82 Referred to as the 'who, where, when, how and with whom of a communication' – The Draft E-Privacy Regulation, Article 4(3)(c) states 'electronic communications metadata' means data processed in an electronic communications network for the purposes of transmitting, distributing, or exchanging electronic communications content; including data used to trace and identify the source and destination of a communication, data on the location of the device generated in the context of providing electronic communications services, and the date, time, duration, and the type of communication.

83 Recitals 2 and 3 in the Draft E-Privacy Regulation observe that 'metadata derived from electronic communications may also reveal very sensitive and personal information. These metadata includes the numbers called, the websites visited, geographical location, the time, date, and duration when an individual made a call etc., allowing precise conclusions to be drawn regarding the private lives of the persons involved in the electronic communication, such as their social relationships, their habits, and activities of everyday life, their interests, tastes etc. (3) Electronic communications data may also reveal information concerning legal entities, such as business secrets or other sensitive information that has economic value'.

84 IBM states:

> Data at rest is stored physically, for example, in a database, data warehouse, tapes, off-site backups, or on mobile devices. Organizations can use encryption to fight threats to their data at rest. Encrypting data protects information from disclosure even if that information is lost or stolen.

transit'[85] as an intelligence source of arguably greater value than communications content intercepted in the course of transmission. The EU's highest court has found communications data to enable the creation of 'information that is no less sensitive, having regard to the right to privacy, than the actual content of communications'.[86] The UKPISC have acknowledged the importance of 'non-content' communications data to the UKIS more than once.[87]

Methodology

The methodology for the doctoral thesis forming the basis of this book combined not only standard doctrinal but also reform-orientated research, in that it advocated, amongst other things, for a 'comprehensive single statute regulating the acquisition of expression-related data for investigative purposes by UK public authorities'.[88] With the arguably curious exception of the power to compel disclosure of information protected by encryption,[89] the IPA 2016 represents a comprehensive single statute regulating access to communications and data by relevant UK public authorities. As such, this book does not advocate further reform.[90] Research was primarily doctrinal, studying for the most part the 'privileged voices' of successive UK Parliaments where legislation was concerned, and the judiciary where the courts played a role in shaping regulation.[91] As such, Hansard (particularly parliamentary debates and standing committee records) and Command Papers made available online and in libraries by the Home,

---

IBM Architecture Centre, 'Security to Safeguard and Monitor Your Cloud Apps' <https://www.ibm.com/cloud/garage/architectures/securityArchitecture/security-for-data> accessed 31 October 2019.

85 ibid, data that is moving from one place to another – for instance when it is transmitted over the Internet – is referred to as data in transit or data in motion. Encryption methods like HTTPS, SSL, and TLS are often used to protect data in motion.

86 Judgment of the Court (Grand Chamber) 21 December 2016 – Joined cases C203/15 C-698/15 *Tele2 Sverige AB v 2Post-Och telestyrelsen* and *Secretary of State for the Home Department v Tom Watson & Ors* [99].

87 UKPISC, *Access to Communications Data by the iIntelligence and Security Agencies* (Cm 8514, 2013); UKPISC, *Privacy and Security* (n29) Chapter 4.

88 Philip Glover, 'Reconceptualise Investigatory Powers Again? An Argument for a Comprehensive Single Statute Regulating the Acquisition of Expression-Related Data for Investigative Purposes by UK Public Authorities' (DPhil Thesis, University of Aberdeen, 2015) (embargoed until April 2020) <https://ethos.bl.uk/OrderDetails.do?uin=uk.bl.ethos.680987> accessed 31 October 2019.

89 This investigatory power remains in Part III of the Regulation of Investigatory Powers Act 2000 and as it not a covert investigatory power, but rather one involving access to encrypted data by virtue of the overt consent or compulsion of a suspect, it falls outside the scope of this work.

90 It does develop an argument for greater transparency around the role of Defence Intelligence.

91 Terry Hutchinson, *Researching and Writing in Law* (4th edn, Thomson Reuters Australia 2018).

Foreign, and Cabinet Offices played a significant role in shaping this work. As has been noted however, secrecy, particularly pre-2013 secrecy, played a role in limiting the range of research materials available. Attempts at secrecy were not always fully successful however, and some 'leaked' published materials retained by NGOs such as Statewatch or from investigative journalists were also very useful. Where statutory regulation required analysis, accompanying Explanatory Notes and derivative Codes of Practice were analyzed in order to gain a more rounded understanding of the prevailing policy underpinning the legislation. Where there had been pre-legislative public consultation, consultation responses (where available) were also examined. These were useful for establishing whether a particular government followed the majority's wishes or pursued its own policy agenda. Given the history of executive secrecy in this area of public law, it was only in the last 35 years that courts became involved in examining state communications and data investigative practice, at both domestic and European level. The book will show that these courts have played an increasingly significant role in identifying the acceptable parameters for communications investigation in modern times. The key judgments of the ECtHR, the Court of Justice of the European Union (CJEU) represented an important research resource. The judgments of UK courts, and particularly those of the specialized UK Investigatory Powers Tribunal (UKIPT) also formed important source material. Despite adherence to the tried and tested doctrinal research method, however, the relative novelty of aspects of the IPA 2016 (not least its 'double-lock' safeguard introducing *ex-ante* judicial oversight of formerly exclusive executive conduct in certain circumstances)[92] mean that final judgment as to its overall efficacy is of necessity reserved. The cogency of any conclusions drawn herein remains subject to final judicial resolution of the outstanding legal challenges to the IPA 2016 prevailing at the time of writing.

The structural approach of the book

The book is divided into four parts. Part I includes this introductory chapter and a very short second chapter outlining some key concepts that should be kept in mind when examining the regulatory history of investigatory powers explored in this book. Part II, 'Secretive communications investigation governance', comprises two chapters. These cover the longest historical period, that between the earliest known use of interception of communications in the 14th century up until 1984. In this era, the *content* of postal and telecommunications constituted the primary national security-related intelligence material sought. Chapter 3 (1324–1919) covers the secretive Ministerial governance of the interception of communications (the only communications-related investigative technique then available) through the introduction of postal and telecommunications services

92 In the IPA 2016, Judicial Commissioners are responsible for approving the issue of interception, equipment interference, and bulk warrants.

and systems, developments in wireless telegraphy and ends just before the enactment of the first statutory regulation of external telecommunications in 1920.[93] Chapter 4 (1920–1984) examines the internationalization of communications investigation governance that commenced in 1920 and which expanded significantly in 1946 with the secret signing of the BRUSA Agreement (subsequently UKUSA) communications intelligence-sharing agreement. The chapter ends at the point where the first European Court of Human Rights (ECtHR) intervention in UK governance of interception regulation occurred.[94]

Part III, 'Disingenous statutory governance', comprises four chapters examining what is asserted to be disingenuous statutory governance of communications, and latterly data, investigation. The term is not lightly chosen and is apolitical. It reflects the reality that will be proved herein that the statutes enacted to regulate interception, and subsequently other data-investigative powers were ***deliberately*** drafted to either keep the nature and extent of investigation being undertaken hidden or to pretend that the regulation as drafted 'covered the field' and could not be circumvented. Chapter 5 thus examines the period between 1984 and 1999, where the Interception of Communications Act (IOCA) 1985 purported to comprehensively regulate interception of communications, but was drafted to obscure the fact that what is now understood as 'bulk' interception of communications was being enabled, and that contemporaneously, significant state investigative power was deliberately retained in 'hidden in plain sight' provisions in the Telecommunications Act 1984, thus enabling a nascent *data*-investigation regime to secretly operate in tandem with the communications investigation regime already in place.

The next chapters engage with the ascendancy of personal data as national security-related intelligence material. Although the UK enacted its first data protection statute in 1984, there is little evidence that personal data, as defined therein, constituted useful investigative material, at least not until the late 1990s. This book will show, however, that data was in the ascendancy from that period, quickly becoming equal to communications content as a source of potential intelligence. Chapter 6 examines the Regulation of Investigatory Powers Act (RIPA) 2000, Part I, which purported to regulate interception of communications and access to communications data in a single, human rights-centric statute. The chapter also examines the first legal challenge to the UK's governance of bulk communications interception powers, 'masked' within section 8 of RIPA 2000, in *Liberty and Others v UK*.[95] The Capenhurst Tower scandal that led to the challenge is explored in detail. Chapter 7 examines the controversial history of EU and UK policy as regards the retention of communications metadata for future access by investigators, including the secret provisions in place mandating the retention of such data, and the public-facing voluntary retention provisions established

93 The Official Secrets Act 1920.

94 *Malone v United Kingdom* (1984) 7 EHRR 14.

95 *Liberty and Others v United Kingdom* (2009) 48 EHRR 1.

in the Anti-Terrorism, Crime And Security (ATCASA) 2001 that followed the 9/11 tragedy. As is now common knowledge, this era of disingenuous regulation was relatively short-lived, and the activities of the press, civil liberties activism, and both European courts meant that change was neccesary and inevitable. After revisiting some parliamentary activity that followed the 2013 Intelligence Shock, the chapter closes after covering the Court of Justice of the European Union (CJEU) judgment in *Digital Rights and Seitlinger v Ireland*,[96] which saw the UK having to enact the Data Retention and Investigatory Powers Act (DRIPA) 2014, in three days of parliamentary haste, to ensure that a communications data retention operation remained in effect. Chapter 9 examines the troubled entry into force in 2004 of RIPA Part I, Chapter II, which regulated the access to, and subsequent disclosure of, retained communications data by investigators.

Part IV, 'Candid governance', contains the final two chapters. The first examines the reaction to the 2013 Intelligence Shock, focusing on the three principal reviews commissioned after publication of the Snowden disclosures and the principal related events and legal challenges. Chapter 10 deals with the period commencing 4 November 2015, the publication of the initial draft Investigatory Powers Bill (IPB), relevant debates, and extensive consultation that preceded enactment. The key judicial determinations that influenced the scope and magnitude of the powers in the IPA 2016 are also illustrated. Chapter 11, 'Postscript' briefly examines the bedding in of the IPA 2016, the outcomes of the key legal challenges to aspects of it, and asks whether the initial thesis statement has been proved.

References

Access Now et al., 'Open Letter to GCHQ' (22 May 2019) *Lawfare*, 30 May 2019 <https://www.lawfareblog.com/open-letter-gchq-threats-posed-ghost-proposal> accessed 20 October 2019

R J Aldrich, *GCHQ The Uncensored Story of Britain's Most Secret Intelligence Agency* (Harper Press, 2010)

Steven Alford, *The Watchers: A Secret History of the Region of Elizabeth 1* (Bloomsbury, 2014)

C Andrew, *The Defence of the Realm: The Authorized History of MI5* (Penguin, 2010)

Australian Financial Review, 'Interview Transcript: Former Head of the NSA and Commander of the US Cyber Command, General Keith Alexander' (8 May 2014) <www.afr.com/technology/web/security/interview-transcriptformer-head-of-the-nsa-and-commander-of-the-us-cyber-command-general-keith-alexander-20140507-itzhw> accessed 27 October 2019

Australian Government, Department of Home Affairs, 'Five Country Ministerial Communiqué: Emerging Threats, London 2019' (30 July 2019) <https://www.homeaffairs.gov.au/news-subsite/Pages/2019-Jul/joint%20meeting%20of%

96 Joined cases C-293/12 Digital Rights Ireland Ltd and C-594/12 Seitlinger (Grand Chamber, 8 April 2014).

20fcm%20and%20quintet%20of%20attorneys-general%20-%20communique.aspx> accessed 31 October 2019

Robin Callender Smith, 'Private Fire from the Gods: The Protection of Personal Data – The Data Protection Act 1998 as a Celebrity Privacy Remedy' 2015 <http://papers.ssrn.com/sol3/papers.cfm?abstract_id=2596029> accessed 31 October 2019

T Davis et al., 'Risking it All: Unlocking the Backdoor to the Nation's Cybersecurity' (2014) IEEE-USA Committee on Communications White Paper <https://papers.ssrn.com/sol3/Papers.cfm?abstract_id=2468604> accessed 20 October 2019

R English, 'Cracking Intercepts: The War on Terror and Difficulties with Human Rights' (11 December 2014) *UK Human Rights Blog* <http://ukhumanrightsblog.com/2014/12/11/cracking-intercepts-the-war-on-terror-and-difficulties-with-human-rights/> accessed 23 October 2019

European Commission, 'Proposal for a Regulation of the European Parliament and of the Council Concerning the Respect for Private Life and the Protection of Personal Data in Electronic Communications and Repealing Directive 2002/58/EC' (Regulation on Privacy and Electronic Communications) Brussels, 10.1.2017 COM(2017) 10 final (Draft e-Privacy Regulation) (not yet adopted as at November 2019) <https://eur-lex.europa.eu/legal-content/EN/TXT/?uri=CELEX:52017PC0010> accessed 12 November 2019

P Finn and S Horwitz, 'U.S. vs. Edward J. Snowden Criminal Complaint' (21 June 2013) *Washington Post* <http://apps.washingtonpost.com/g/documents/world/us-vs-edward-j-snowden-criminal-complaint/496/> accessed 31 October 2019

J Gibbs, *Gorbachev's Glasnost: The Soviet Media in the First Phase of Perestroika* (Texas A & M University Press, 2000)

P Glover, 'Reconceptualise Investigatory Powers Again? An Argument for a Comprehensive Single Statute Regulating the Acquisition of Expression-Related Data for Investigative Purposes by UK Public Authorities' DPhil Thesis, University of Aberdeen, 2015 (embargoed until April 2020) <https://ethos.bl.uk/OrderDetails.do?uin=uk.bl.ethos.680987> accessed 31 October 2019

G Greenwald and E MacAskill, 'NSA Prism Program Taps in to User Data of Apple, Google and Others' (London, 7 June 2013) *The Guardian* <http://theguardian.com/world/2013/jun/06/us-tech-giants-nsa-data> accessed 26 October 2019

L Harding, *The Snowden Files* (Vintage Books, 2014)

Alan Haynes, *The Elizabethan Secret Services* (Sutton, 2000)

J Hendry, 'Senate Pushes Encryption Fix for US CLOUD Act Fracture' (17 October 2019) *IT News* <https://www.itnews.com.au/news/senate-pushes-encryption-fix-for-us-cloud-act-fracture-532554> accessed 20 October 2019

HM Government, *Transparency Report 2018: Disruptive and Investigatory Powers* (Cm 9609, 2018)

Home Office, *A Strong Britain in an Age of Uncertainty: The National Security Strategy* (Cmnd 7953, 2010)

Home Office, *Investigatory Powers Act 2016 Consultation: Codes of Practice* (February 2017)

Home Office, *Investigatory Powers Act 2016: Response to Home Office Consultation on the Government's Proposed Response to the Ruling of the Court of Justice of the European Union on 21 December 2016 Regarding the Retention of Communications Data* (June 2018)

T Hutchinson, *Researching and Writing in Law* (4th edn, Thomson Reuters Australia, 2018)
IBM Architecture Centre, 'Security to Safeguard and Monitor Your Cloud Apps' <https://www.ibm.com/cloud/garage/architectures/securityArchitecture/security-for-data> accessed 31 October 2019
Independent Reviewer of Terrorism Legislation (IRTL), *A Question of Trust: Report of the Investigatory Powers Review* (Williams Lea Group, June 2015)
Information Commissioner's Office (ICO), 'Our Role' <https://ico.org.uk/about-the-ico/what-we-do/> accessed 2 September 2019
ITRL, *Report of the Bulk Powers Review* (Cm 9326, August 2016)
K Jeffery, *MI6 The History of the Secret Intelligence Service 1909–1949* (Bloomsbury, 2010)
L K Johnson, 'Intelligence Shocks, Media Coverage, and Congressional Accountability, 1947–2012' (2014) 13(1) *Journal of Intelligence History* 1
S Lefebvre, 'The Difficulties and Dilemmas of International Intelligence Cooperation' (2003) 16(4) *International Journal of Intelligence and Counterintelligence* 529–534
Leveson Inquiry, *An Inquiry into the Culture, Ethics and Practices of the Press Report* (2012–13, HC 780–I, II, III and IV)
I Levy and C Robinson, 'Principles for a More Informed Exceptional Access Debate' (29 November 2018) *Lawfare* <https://www.lawfareblog.com/principles-more-informed-exceptional-access-debate> accessed 20 October 2019
E MacAskill, 'Extreme Surveillance Becomes UK Law with Barely a Whimper' (London, 19 November 2016) *The Guardian* <https://www.theguardian.com/world/2016/nov/19/extreme-surveillance-becomes-uk-law-with-barely-a-whimper> accessed 20 September 2019
S McKay, *Blackstone's Guide to the Investigatory Powers Act 2016* (Oxford University Press, 2017)
D Miller, 'The Responsibility to Protect Human Rights' in Lukas H Meyer (ed) *Legitimacy, Justice and Public International Law* (Cambridge University Press, 2009)
R Morgan, 'Oversight through Five Eyes: Institutional Convergence and the Structure and Oversight of Intelligence Activities' in Zachary K Goldman and Samuel J Rascoff (eds) *Global Intelligence Oversight: Governing Security in the Twenty-First Century* (Oxford University Press, 2016)
P Norris, *Driving Democracy* (Cambridge University Press, 2008)
NSA/CSS 'UKUSA Agreement Release' <https://www.nsa.gov/news-features/declassified-documents/ukusa/> accessed 21 October 2019
D Omand, 'Written Evidence to UKPISC Privacy and Security Inquiry' <http://isc.independent.gov.uk/public-evidence> accessed 23 October 2019
M Phythian, *Understanding the Intelligence Cycle* (Routledge, 2014)
M T Poe, *A History of Communications: Media and Society from the Evolution of Speech to the Internet* (Cambridge University Press, 2011)
Royal United Services Institute for Defence and Security Studies, *A Democratic Licence to Operate: Report of the Independent Surveillance Review* (Stephen Austin and Sons Ltd, July 2015)
C Smith, (Minister for the Constitution 2018) 'Government Transparency and Accountability: Written Statement' (HCWS 1216, 19 December 2018)

UK Parliamentary Intelligence and Security Committee, *Privacy and Security: A Modern and Transparent Legal Framework* (HC 2014–15, 1075–I)
US Naval War College, 'Intelligence Studies' <https://usnwc.libguides.com/c.php?g=494120&p=3381427> accessed 21 October 2019
D Vincent, *The Culture of Secrecy: Britain 1832–1998* (Clarendon Publishing, 1999)

2 Rationalizing the Investigatory Powers Act 2016

Conceptual approach and key definitions

> An Act to make provision about the interception of communications, equipment interference and the acquisition and retention of communications data, bulk personal datasets, and other information; to make provision about the treatment of material held as a result of such interception, equipment interference or acquisition or retention; to establish the Investigatory Powers Commissioner and other Judicial Commissioners and make provision about them and other oversight arrangements; to make further provision about investigatory powers and national security; to amend sections 3 and 5 of the Intelligence Services Act 1994; and for connected purposes.[1]

Introduction

As this book is aimed at a cross-disciplinary audience, including those with no law component, this short context-setting chapter seeks to cover a small number of legal scholarly matters that may assist in rationalizing the Investigatory Powers Act (IPA) 2016 as a logical progression of British state practice. As the preamble shows, the IPA 2016 addresses 'interception of communications' first. This is a logical approach, because as this book will demonstrate, interception is by far the oldest of the investigatory powers now regulated in a statute. An understanding of the conceptual approach to interception, and the core definitions applicable to its authorization and oversight framework, enables an improved understanding of the other communications and data access powers additionally catered for in the IPA 2016. Consequently, this chapter first outlines what should be understood by 'interception' and also sets out some recurring constants relating to its use over centuries as an investigative technique. The legal meaning of interception – as now defined in the IPA 2016 – is then explored. Given that any 'interception' that takes place will be of 'communications', the chapter then examines how postal and telecommunications are conceptualized. This centres on what will be shown to be the 'wicked problem' of distinguishing the 'content' of a communication from 'non-content' data in some way relatable to it, particularly as regards

1 Investigatory Powers Act (IPA) 2016, Preamble.

intangible telecommunications. The cogency of the perceived need to make this distinction, which is founded on a longstanding 'Privacy Impact Assessment' that views accessing content as more 'privacy-intrusive' than accessing non-content, is also critically explored. The chapter then briefly discusses the solutions to the problem as adopted in the IPA 2016, which for the first time offers a definition of communications 'content'. This enables all other 'non-content' data (still problematically referred to as 'communications data' rather than the more logical 'contextual data' or 'metadata') to be defined in alignment with the legislature's perception of the degree of privacy-intrusion associated with accessing it. The sheer volume of communications data now available to public authorities with investigative functions on demand is explored. The chapter closes by asserting the centrality of data in the IPA 2016 and illustrating the Act's relationship with the 21st-century EU-inspired data protection regulatory framework.

Conceptualizing interception for the purposes of this regulatory history

Intercepting communications is by far the oldest of the investigatory powers that enable access to communications and, more recently, personal data. It also has the longest history of statutory regulation, with interception of postal communications regulated in statute since 1657, interception of 'external telecommunications' since 1920, and domestic and external 'public' telecommunications since 1985. In some respects, therefore, the investigative technique now understood as interception of communications can be seen as the 'mother power', wherein its principal constituent definitions ('communications' and 'communications data') 'parent' the more recent, derivative investigatory powers first regulated in statute in the Regulation of Investigatory Powers Act (RIPA) 2000 and the Investigatory Powers Act (IPA) 2016. Consequently, an understanding of the key definitions used in the sections of the IPA 2016 addressing interception allows an understanding of the more recent statutory powers. As the reader progresses through the following chapters detailing the development of interception capability and regulation, 'interception of communications' should be conceived of in the following broad terms.

Regardless of the *means* of communication used, the term can be said to have always described conduct wherein state agents are empowered by the British state,[2] on national security and related grounds, to undertake conduct within the British state[3] that secures access to communications that have left the custody and control of the original communicator, but which have not yet been accessed by the intended recipient(s).

2 This term acknowledges that interception of communications substantially predates the creation of the United Kingdom by the Act of Union 1707.

3 Extra territorial interception etc. and other forms of covert action authorized outside the British Islands by the Intelligence Services Act (ISA) 1994 are outside the scope of this work.

Content

Historically, the primary purpose for undertaking interception of communications was to access their *content*. This chapter will illustrate how, since the advent of intangible forms of communication and the growth in intelligence utility of 'communications data' (CD) and 'personal data', the search by the legislature for a definition of 'content' that meaningfully distinguishes it from CD has proven to be wickedly problematic.

Third-party involvement

As communications in the course of transmission from the original communicator are entrusted to the custody of a third party (i.e. neither the communicator nor the intended recipient), interception can be viewed as generally involving accessing the communication with the cooperation, or at least acquiescence, of that third party. In modern parlance, this will be a Communications Service Provider (CSP).

Ground(s) for interception

Another historical constant has been the grounds on which interception of communications has been authorized by the British state. This book proceeds on the premise that the principal ground has always been that of 'the interests of national security', a phrase still present in the IPA 2016.[4]

The IPA 2016 approach to interception of communications

In Part I of the IPA 2016, as part of a range of 'General Privacy Protections', conduct involving interception of communications in the course of transmission 'without lawful authority'[5] and conduct involving obtaining 'communications data' without lawful authority is criminalised.[6] The latter offence is limited to 'relevant persons', defined as those 'holding an office, rank or position with a relevant public authority (within the meaning of Part 3)'.[7] Unlawful interception can be committed by any person. It is important to note that *unlawful* interception of communications can only occur when the conduct amounting to interception takes place in the United Kingdom.[8] This means that interception

4 IPA 2016, s20(2). Additional grounds include preventing or detecting serious crime and the interests of the economic well-being of the UK so far as those interests are also relevant to the interests of national security.

5 ibid, s3(1) The offence encompasses communications passing over public and private telecommunications systems and via public postal services.

6 ibid, s11(1).

7 ibid, s11(2).

8 ibid, s3(1)(b) read with s4(8).

of communications undertaken outside the territorial jurisdiction of the UK can never amount to unlawful conduct for the purposes of the Act.

As a logical progression from the general prohibitions in Part 1, the next Part of the Act (Part 2) sets out the circumstances in which interception of communications may be authorized upon application and thus take place with 'lawful authority'.[9] Part 3 outlines the circumstances in which authorization to obtain 'communications data' may be sought and granted, thus rendering such conduct as being undertaken with 'lawful authority'.[10] Straightaway, it can be seen that access to 'communications' and access to 'communications data' are governed by different authorization mechanisms. This is the consequence of a longstanding state 'privacy-impact assessment' discussed later in this chapter.

The IPA 2016 definition of interception

Section 4 of the IPA 2016 comprehensively outlines the 'meaning of interception' for the purposes of the criminal offences in section 3 and for seeking an interception warrant under the auspices of Parts 2 or 6. It discloses nothing of the technical means by which the state's agents undertake the interceptions, but some redacted clues are available in the 2015 Reviews.[11]

As regards the interception of telecommunications, 'interception' is achieved by doing a 'relevant act'[12] in relation to the telecommunications system[13] which makes any part of the communication available, at the 'relevant time'[14] to any

9 See generally IPA 2016, Part 2. Part 6 is also relevant if a 'bulk' warrant for interception is contemplated.

10 See generally IPA 2016, Part 3. Part 6 is also relevant if a 'bulk' communications data acquisition warrant is contemplated.

11 See, for example, UK Parliamentary Intelligence and Security Committee, *Privacy and Security: A Modern and Transparent Legal Framework* (HC 2014–15, 1075-I) Chapters 3–5 (UKPISC, *Privacy & Security 2015*).

12 IPA 2016, s4(2)–(3):

> modifying, or interfering with, the system or its operation; monitoring transmissions made by means of the system; monitoring transmissions made by wireless telegraphy to or from apparatus that is part of the system...references to 'modifying'...include references to attaching any apparatus to, or otherwise modifying or interfering with any part of the system, or any wireless telegraphy apparatus used for making transmissions to or from apparatus that is part of the system.

13 ibid, s261(13).

> a system (including the apparatus comprised in it) that exists (whether wholly or partly in the United Kingdom or elsewhere) for the purpose of facilitating the transmission of communications by any means involving the use of electrical or electromagnetic energy.

14 ibid, s4(4) 'relevant time', in relation to a communication transmitted by means of a telecommunication system, means (a) any time while the communication is being transmitted, and (b) any time when the communication is stored in or by the system (whether before or after its transmission).

party other than the intended recipient.[15] The meaning of interception is thus candidly expressed, but any conduct as described undertaken outside the UK by *any* investigative agency, British or otherwise (e.g. the United States National Security Agency [NSA]), whilst still 'interception' in the conceptual sense, will not be interception in the legal sense. This has implications as regards the requirement for warrants and the legality of intelligence-sharing under international agreements.

Conceptualizing 'communication' for the purposes of this regulatory history

Postal communications as two parts

The state's regulatory efforts in respect of communications have historically been to conceptualize them as structurally comprising two distinct parts. For introductory purposes, these can be labelled 'content' and 'non-content'. This approach originates in the postal communications context and the logic therein is uncontroversial. Communications transmitted via the public postal service are *tangible* and have always thus been capable of physical separation. The 'two-part' view involves distinguishing the envelope or packaging from the separate, *substantive expression of the communicator* securely contained within it (the *content*). Taking the envelope or packaging first, this performs two functions. Firstly, it adds a layer of privacy and security protecting the enclosed contents, which are clearly a physically separate part of the whole communication. Secondly, an envelope or other postal packaging has always generally carried non-content 'communications data' (broadly defined) clearly distinguishable from the enclosed content by the fact that it is attached to, or is on, the envelope or package. This data has historically provided intelligence or evidence of the fact of postal transmission or tended to identify the communicator or intended recipient (e.g. their name and postal address or the postmark indicating the location from where the communication entered into the custody of the postal service). For present purposes, therefore, it can be said that the IPA 2016 continues to reflect the state's longstanding and seemingly logical intuitive view, namely that a greater degree of intrusion against the communicator or intended recipient occurs when the investigative conduct involves accessing the *contents* of a postal communication, as opposed to simply reading anything inscribed on the envelope or packaging. Consequently, as the following chapters of this book will demonstrate, the regulation of investigative access to postal communications *content* necessitated an authorization process involving obtaining a Ministerial warrant, whereas access to 'communications data' in the postal context did not. A 'two part' conceptualization of a communication meant a two-part approach to regulation. In the postal context, therefore, distinguishing communications 'content' and other non-content

15 ibid, s4(1)(b).

'communications data' has always been relatively unproblematic. The same cannot be said when attempting to draft an equivalent, operationally sound, 'two part' distinction to ***intangible*** telecommunications, the task Graham Smith has described as the 'contest at the heart of the Investigatory Powers Act'.[16] Before examining this contest, it is necessary to examine the rationale for its very existence, namely the state's longstanding Privacy Impact Assessment regarding access to content and non-content communications data.[17]

Conceptualizing communications data (CD): the CD lifespan

Prior to examining the constituent definitions for communications data (CD) that were created for the IPA 2016 and that have influenced the short history of regulation of access to CD and its retention, it is helpful to view CD firstly as having a lifespan and secondly, as a distinctive form of 'personal data' as defined in data protection legislation. In broad terms, the CD lifespan is as follows:

1 *CD as generated*: This stage sees the initial creation or generation of CD. This can arise from the establishment of a contract or other business relationship between a communication service user (customer) and a communications service provider (CSP). This does not include CD in transit acquired in consequence of the interception of communications in the course of transmission over that CSPs network by a public authority by virtue of an interception warrant. In general, CSPs with a UK presence have perennially been required to handle generated CD in accordance with the various incarnations of UK Data Protection Acts (1984, 1998, and 2018);
2 *CD subject to a state retention requirement*: This too is handled in accordance with EU and UK data protection legislation. Its state does not really change unless accessed by virtue of Stage 3, but such CD is now retained by CSPs at the behest of the state, and includes subscriber, traffic, and location data. This book explores how CD retention to enable future investigative access by intelligence services and law enforcement was, for as long as CD held intelligence utility, *always* a policy of both the EU and the UK. It also explores the still controversial transition from voluntary retention and disclosure by CSPs to compulsory retention in statute. The IPA 2016, Part 4 is the sole regulatory mechanism wherein CD can be subjected to a data retention notice. (Chapter 7 of this volume);

16 Graham Smith, 'The content v metadata contest at the heart of the Investigatory Powers Bill' *Cyberleagle.com* (May 2016) <https://www.cyberleagle.com/2016/05/the-content-v-metadata-contest-at-heart.html> accessed 30 September 2020.

17 It is not suggested that a detailed Privacy Impact Assessment as now understood was ever undertaken; rather the term reflects an arbitrary policy decision that will be ultimately attributable to the Right Honourable Charles Clarke MP in 1999. See Chapter 8 of this volume.

3 *Retained CD acquired or disclosed by CSPs upon application for investigative purposes*: CD is lawfully acquired by intelligence services or law enforcement or disclosed to them by virtue of an authorization or notice issued after a successful application on a number of predetermined grounds. Chapter 8, herein, examines the short history of statutory regulation of the Acquisition and Disclosure of CD that commenced in 2004, ostensibly under the Regulation of Investigatory Powers Act (RIPA) 2000, Part I, Chapter II, but occasionally under other statutory provisions and with judicial approval. The IPA 2016, Part 3, is now the single authorising mechanism for obtaining CD for investigative purposes;
4 *CD management by UK public authorities*: This covers the post-acquisition handling, storage, analysis, dissemination, and disposal of CD by those bodies empowered to have acquired it. Subject to certain exceptions, this remains governed by data protection legislation.

The British state's Privacy Impact Assessment

In tracing the history of communications investigation, and, since the late 20th century, data investigation, this book will illustrate how every historical variant of British state efforts to regulate the relevant investigatory powers has been founded on a 'Privacy Impact Assessment'. Graham Smith succinctly captures its finding 'that intercepting, acquiring, processing and examining the *content* of a communication is…more intrusive than for the "who, when, where, how" contextual data wrapped around it'.[18]

This problematic conceptual view has often been articulated by UK governments of all persuasions and illustrates the 'significant practical consequences of the demarcation between communications content and metadata'.[19] Foremost among these is that the power to intercept communications in the course of their transmission remains subject to distinct, separate, and more rigorous regulation than the power to access retained communications metadata. As recently as 2015, during extensive legislative scrutiny, the Joint Committee on the Draft Investigatory Powers Bill (JCDIPB) reaffirmed the longstanding view that

> accessing communications data has historically been perceived to be a less intrusive investigative tool than accessing the content of a communication.

18 Smith (n16), emphasis added. It is worth pointing out at this point that the British legislature would have done well to follow Mr Smith's use of 'metadata' or 'contextual data' to describe 'non-content' data, rather persevere with the more opaque term 'communications data' in legislation. This is especially the case given that the content of a communication can itself contain data. Unless directly citing UK legislation or discussion of it, this book will use the term 'metadata' to describe data relatable in some way to a communication but which is not content.

19 ibid.

While interception would expose the content of a message, communications data revealed only that a communication had taken place.[20]

The uses of communications data: the problem with the Privacy Impact Assessment

While correct from one perspective, this assessment ignores the modern reality whereby equally severe impacts to personal privacy potentially arise from investigative access to communications metadata, particularly since the advent of UK statutory efforts compelling CSPs to retain it.[21] The risks to personal privacy were creditably articulated in the powerfully argued written evidence tendered by civil liberties NGO Liberty to the JCDIPB. While accepting the need to use 'communications data' as an investigative tool, it was argued that:

> The Government seeks to diminish the importance and sensitivity of communications data by distinguishing it from the content of communications. At one time a firm distinction between communications data and content would have been more credible, for example when much communication was by letter: everything inside the envelope is content, everything on the outside communications data. *However, this distinction has been eroded by the scale of modern internet and mobile phone usage.* As communications have become increasingly digital, the data generated is much more revealing and copious than before, *allowing the state to put together a complete and rich picture of what a person does, thinks, with whom, when, and where.* Often, communications data can be of more use than content: it is expansive, easy to handle, analyse and filter; and, it tends to be collected in a consistent manner.[22]

If it were needed, this submission gained added gravitas by reference to inadvertent parliamentary support for their view. In 2015 the Intelligence and Security Committee (UKPISC) had found themselves 'surprised to discover that the primary value to GCHQ of bulk interception was *not in reading the actual content* of communications, *but in the information associated with those communications*'.[23] This finding should not have been surprising. It is now uncontroversial, as submitted to the JCDIPB by Dr (now Associate Professor) Paul Bernal, that

20 Joint Committee on the Draft Investigatory Powers Bill (JCDIPB), *Draft Investigatory Powers Bill Report* (2015–16, HL 93, HC 651) 41.

21 Chapters 7 and 8 explore the history of powers to retain and to access communications metadata respectively.

22 Liberty, 'Written Evidence to the JCDIPB' (IPB0143) para 30, emphasis added. <http://data.parliament.uk/writtenevidence/committeeevidence.svc/evidencedocument/draft-investigatory-powers-bill-committee/draft-investigatory-powers-bill/written/26430.html#_ftnref35> accessed 21 September 2020.

23 UKPISC, *Privacy & Security Report 2015* (n11) 32, emphasis added.

investigating communications metadata is 'differently intrusive' rather than less intrusive.[24] Liberty additionally, and correctly, submitted that:

> Communications...[non-content]...data...disclose the date, time, duration, and type of communication, the type of communication equipment used, its location, the calling telephone number, and the receiving telephone number. *This can reveal personal and sensitive information about an individual's* relationships, habits, preferences, political views, medical concerns, and the streets they walk.[25]

Privacy impact and the EU influence

Personal privacy, or more precisely 'respect for private and family life, home and *correspondence*' is not an abstract concept, but a human right enshrined in the European Convention on Human Rights (ECHR) to which the UK is a signatory.[26] States may only interfere with this right on limited grounds set out in law, in pursuit of a legitimate aim, and where necessary in a democratic society and proportionate to the legitimate aim.[27] Despite the UK's exit from the EU in 2020, the 'right to respect for his or her private and family life, home and *communications*' is also a fundamental right protected by the Charter of Fundamental Rights of the EU (CFREU).[28]

As such, the Liberty submission's reference to the opinion of the Court of Justice of the European Union (CJEU) as regards access to and investigation of communications metadata was telling:

> [communications meta] data, taken as a whole, may allow very precise conclusions to be drawn concerning the private lives of the persons...such as the habits of everyday life, permanent or temporary places of residence, daily or other movements, the activities carried out, the social relationships of those persons and the social environments frequented by them. In particular, that data provides the means...of establishing a profile of the individuals concerned, information that is no less sensitive, having regard to the right to privacy, than the actual content of communications.[29]

24 ibid.
25 Liberty, 'Written Evidence' (n22) para 28, emphasis added.
26 European Convention on Human Rights (ECHR), Article 8(1).
27 ECHR, Article 8(2):

> There shall be no interference by a public authority with the exercise of this right except such as is in accordance with the law and is necessary in a democratic society in the interests of national security, public safety, or the economic well-being of the country, for the prevention of disorder or crime, for the protection of health or morals, or for the protection of the rights and freedoms of others.

28 Charter of Fundamental Rights of the European Union (CFREU), Article 7.
29 Joined Cases *Digital Rights Ireland (C-293/12) and Seitlinger and Others* (C-594/12) (99).

The views of Smith, Bernal, and the CJEU reflect a more ethical and logical approach to the Privacy Impact Assessment of a particular data-investigative technique, wherein the privacy impact of the *outcome* of its use is assessed prior to authorization, as opposed to an assessment undertaken that examines the impact at the point of use. Despite this, the IPA 2016 continues the longstanding tradition of providing a more stringent regulatory mechanism for accessing communications content than for accessing non-content metadata, albeit with a greater degree of sophistication in its attempts to address the 'two-part' problem associated with conceptualizing communications, and telecommunications in particular.

Telecommunications as two parts

The starting point for telecommunications is that they are intangible and thus not capable of *physical* separation. As such, the Privacy Impact Assessment just discussed in the postal communications context runs into difficulties. At their most elementary, the raw material in telecommunications is 'data'. Indeed, in its 'general interpretation' provision, the IPA 2016 defines 'data' as including 'data which is not electronic data and *any information* (whether or not electronic)'.[30] The IPA 2016 defines 'communication' in the telecommunications context as including, in addition to speech, music, and visual images, '*data of any description*'.[31] This reflects the modern reality that modern telecommunications, whether speech, music, visual images or data *become* data for the purposes of electronic transmission. As such, separating what is most accurately describable as 'content data' from 'non-content' data has amounted to a perennial 'wicked problem'. As mentioned previously, the British legislature has not helped matters by using the vague term 'communications data' to describe any data that can in any way be associated with a communication but which is not data forming part of the substantive intended meaning of the communication (i.e. its content).

The problem initially surfaced in the Regulation of Investigatory Powers Act (RIPA) 2000. RIPA acknowledged that, in the course of intercepting a communication in the course of its transmission, certain 'non-content' data, which the Act termed 'related communications data' (RCD), was also picked up as an inevitable consequence.[32] This fell within the authorization and governance mechanism in Part I, Chapter I of that Act and the data became subject to some, but not all, of the safeguards for intercepted material provided within that chapter. Differentiating RCD from 'other' communications data (principally service use,

30 IPA 2016, s263.

31 ibid, s261(1).

32 RIPA 2000, s20 'related communications data', in relation to a communication intercepted in the course of its transmission by means of a postal service or telecommunication system, means so much of any communications data (within the meaning of Chapter II of this Part) as – (a) is obtained by, or in connection with, the interception; and (b) relates to the communication or to the sender or recipient, or intended recipient, of the communication.

traffic data, and location data)[33] was conceptually and practically problematic, meaning that constructing sufficiently rigorous authorization and governance processes for it was also an extremely difficult task for the JCDIPB.

The IPA's 'multi-part' solution

A definition of 'content'

It is to the credit of those charged with drafting the IPA 2016 that a concerted effort was made to confront the two-part conceptual problem associated with communications head-on. Despite the question mark regarding the respective privacy impacts of accessing content or non-content data, it is indisputable that providing a Ministerial warrant authorization mechanism for requests to access the latter would simply not be feasible.[34] The IPA 2016 solution was quite an achievement given that the JCDIPB had taken some evidence suggesting that 'separating communications data from content was not feasible'.[35] For the first time in the history of regulation in this area, a statutory definition of 'content' applicable to intangible telecommunications was created. Doing so enabled the creation of a group of supporting sub-definitions aspiring to provide a more nuanced approach to 'non-content' metadata. Defining 'content' also allowed the legislature to adhere to the longstanding privacy-impact assessment, but to conceptualize communications as essentially comprising three parts as opposed to two. In addition to content obtained via interception in the course of transmission, 'communications data' acquired as a by-product of, or in the course of, interception was distinguished from service user 'communications data' retained by CSPs. Smith's detailed analysis of the legislature's efforts to address the inherent definitional complexity, an exercise he described as 'metaphysical gymnastics' is instructive, but demonstrates the inherent technical complexity in the gymnastic exercise.[36]

'Content' (telecommunications)

The IPA 2016 definition states:

> 'Content', in relation to a communication and a telecommunications operator, telecommunications service, or telecommunication system, means *any element of the communication, or any data attached to or logically associated*

33 See RIPA 2000, s21(4) and Chapter 7 herein.

34 The Investigatory Powers Commissioner's Office (IPCO) *Annual Report 2018* (HC 67) 114 states that there were 210,755 communications data access requests granted in the 2018 reporting year (not including those to the UKIC) compared to 3,840 interception warrants of all variations.

35 JCDIPB, *Draft Investigatory Powers Bill Report* (n20) 44, citing a submission from F-Secure.

36 Smith (n16).

> ***with the communication, which reveals anything of what might reasonably be considered to be the meaning (if any) of the communication***, but –
>
> (a) any meaning arising from the fact of the communication or from any data relating to the transmission of the communication is to be disregarded, and (b) anything which is *systems* data is not content.[37]

Whilst perhaps a 'least worst' solution to the perennial wicked problem, the adoption of a 'meaning' centred definition remains conceptually problematic. The JCDIPB made the following observations in relation to the written evidence of two experts:

> Dr Paul Bernal questioned the reference to 'meaning' in the definition of content, saying 'It is possible to derive "meaning" from almost any data— this is one of the fundamental problems with the idea that content and communications can be simply and meaningfully separated. In practice, this is far from the case". Graham Smith posed a challenging philosophical and technical question, 'For a computer to computer communication, what is the meaning of "meaning"'?[38]

It may have been simpler to define the 'content' of a telecommunication as the substantive intended 'command, message or expression of the communicator',[39] however, the necessity of including computer to computer communications in the scope of the definition means that difficulties might still remain. As such, the definition as chosen remains. Its utility cannot really be measured to those outside the ring of UKIC and Ministerial secrecy, and of course, the sheer volume and utility of non-content data now retained by CSPs under compulsion renders the legal distinction between it and content arguably of minimal practical value. However, what can be said is that, in addition to defining 'content', the IPA 2016 has also adopted two distinct conduct- and context-dependent approaches to acquiring or accessing non-content 'communications data' (broadly defined), and has sub-divided 'non-content' data more logically than was the case with RIPA 2000.

37 IPA 2016, s261(6), emphasis added.

38 JCDIPB, *Draft Investigatory Powers Bill Report* (n20) 44. Dr Bernal is a Lecturer in Information Technology, Intellectual Property and Media Law at the University of East Anglia Law School and was this author's PhD examiner. His supplementary written evidence as cited (IPB0018) is available at <http://data.parliament.uk/writtenevidence/committeeevidence.svc/evidencedocument/draft-investigatory-powers-bill-committee/draft-investigatory-powers-bill/written/25973.html> accessed 21 September 2020. Graham Smith is an eminent Internet Regulation expert. His supplementary written evidence (IPB0126) as cited is available at http://data.parliament.uk/writtenevidence/committeeevidence.svc/evidencedocument/draft-investigatory-powers-bill-committee/draft-investigatory-powers-bill/written/25973.html.

39 This represents the author's best effort to define 'content' but it has not been peer-reviewed.

Communications data accessed/acquired via technical investigative conduct

The first approach appears designed to serve investigators (principally the UKIC) envisaging conduct *with the potential to secure access to communications content* on a 'targeted' or 'bulk' basis. This will either involve intercepting communications in the course of transmission (IPA 2016, Parts 2 or 6) or accessing communications 'at rest' through Equipment Interference (IPA 2016, Parts 5 or 6). As might be expected, this approach designates a greater proportion of the data inherent in the whole communication as 'non-content' data, meaning that a Ministerial warrant might not be required in order to access it and to produce intelligence from it. Where the conduct involved involves targeted or bulk interception of communications, the 'non-content' data additionally encountered is labelled 'secondary data'. In both the postal and telecommunications contexts 'secondary data' comprises '*systems data* which is *comprised in*, *included as part of*, *attached to* or *logically associated with* the communication (whether by the sender or otherwise)'.[40] In the telecommunications context only (i.e. postal communications are excluded), 'secondary data' can additionally include:

> *identifying data* which (a) is comprised in, included as part of, attached to or logically associated with the communication (whether by the sender or otherwise), (b) is capable of being logically separated from the remainder of the communication, and (c) if it were so separated, would not reveal anything of what might reasonably be considered to be the meaning (if any) of the communication, disregarding any meaning arising from the fact of the communication or from any data relating to the transmission of the communication.[41]

Where the investigative conduct involves either targeted or bulk Equipment Interference, the term 'secondary data' is renamed 'equipment data'.[42] There is no material difference in the two definitions, in that 'equipment data' is also comprised of 'systems' data or 'identifying data' in the same manner as for telecommunications.

Systems data

'Systems data' relates to the functioning of communications systems (thus applying to both postal and telecommunications systems) and will never be considered as being 'content' by virtue of section 261(6)(b).[43] Its full definition is:

40 IPA 2016, s16(4), s16(5), s137(4), and s137 (5), emphasis added.
41 ibid, s16(6) (targeted interception) and s137(6) (bulk interception).
42 ibid, s100 (targeted interference) and 177 (bulk interference).
43 ibid, s261(6)(b) anything which is systems data is not content.

any data that *enables or facilitates*, or *identifies or describes anything connected with enabling or facilitating*; the *functioning* of: a postal service; a telecommunication system (including any apparatus forming part of the system); any telecommunications service provided by means of a telecommunication system; a relevant system (including any apparatus forming part of the system); any service provided by means of a relevant system.[44]

Identifying data

'Identifying data' in the IPA 2016 means data which may be used 'to identify, or assist in identifying: *any person*, *apparatus, system or service*, *any event*, or, the *location of any person, event or thing*'.[45] As regards the identification of events, the next subsection expands the type of identifying data to include 'data relating to the fact of the event; data relating to the type, method or pattern of event; and data relating to the time or duration of the event'.[46]

In an era where Augmented Intelligence (AuI), Machine Learning, and data analytics offer significant intelligence-production benefits to the UKIC,[47] and thus significant privacy-intrusion capability, it is perhaps worth pausing at this point to contemplate the sheer scale and qualitative depth of data falling within the scope of 'secondary data'. It is this definition, perhaps more than any other, that impels the continuing resistance to the IPA 2016 communications data framework by civil liberties groups.[48]

Communications data accessed/acquired via non-technical conduct

This second approach serves investigators in the context where non-content 'communications data' retained by CSPs either freely or under Ministerial direction (IPA 2016, Part 4) is sought for investigative purposes on a 'targeted' or 'bulk' warrant basis (IPA 2016, Part 3 or 6).[49] There is no technical conduct involved in obtaining (i.e. no interception or equipment interference) and little

44 ibid, s263(4), emphasis added.
45 ibid, s263(2), emphasis added.
46 ibid, s263(3), emphasis added.
47 For example, see generally Alexander Babuta, Marion Oswald and Ardi Janjeva, 'Artificial Intelligence and UK National Security' (Royal United Services Institute [RUSI] Occasional Paper, April 2020) available at <https://rusi.org/sites/default/files/ai_national_security_final_web_version.pdf> accessed 29 October 2020.
48 See generally *Privacy International v Secretary of State for Foreign and Commonwealth Affairs, Secretary of State for the Home Department, Government Communications Headquarters, Security Service and Secret Intelligence Service* UKIPTrib 15/110/CH and preliminary reference to the Court of Justice of the European Union (CJEU) Case C623/17.
49 Graham Smith (n16).

prospect of acquiring content. In this operational context, 'communications data'[50] is classifiable either as 'entity data' or 'events data'.

Entity data

An 'entity' is a 'person or a thing'[51] meaning that 'entity data' refers to

> *any data* which is about: a person or a thing; an association between a telecommunications *service* and a person or a thing; or an association between any part of a telecommunication *system* and a person or a thing, (b) consists of, or includes, data which *identifies or describes* the person or thing (whether or not by reference to its location), and (c) is not events data.[52]

As such, it can be seen that there is broad provision enabling the matching of a person (or thing) to the use of a telecommunications service or telecommunications system for investigative purposes without the need for technical interception, Equipment Interference, or application for a Ministerial warrant.

Events data

Events data means *any data* which identifies or describes an event (whether or not by reference to its location) on, in or by means of a telecommunication system where the event consists of one or more entities (i.e. persons or things) engaging in a specific activity at a specific time.[53]

Relevant communications data

All the aforementioned 'data' components of a communication accumulate to constitute the whole. In order to appreciate the magnitude of the communications and data-investigative behemoth that has evolved since the advent of the electronic communications era it has to be appreciated that the state has now awarded to itself, in policy alignment with the EU,[54] power to compel CSPs to retain 'relevant communications data'.[55] This power is explored in detail in

50 IPA 2016, s261(5).
51 ibid, s261(7).
52 ibid, s261(3), emphasis added.
53 ibid, s261(4), emphasis added.
54 As Chapter 7 explores, the EU issued Directive 2006/24/EC of the European Parliament and of the Council of 15 March 2006 on the retention of data generated or processed in connection with the provision of publicly available electronic communications services or of public communications networks and amending Directive 2002/58/EC (Data retention Directive). This was subsequently struck down by the CJEU in the *Digital Rights* case (n29).
55 See generally the IPA 2016, Part 4.

Chapter 7 of this volume, but the definition of 'relevant communications data' for which retention by CSPs can be mandatory is worth highlighting at this point.

> 'relevant communications data' means communications data which may be used to identify, or assist in identifying, any of the following –
>
> (a) The sender or recipient of a communication (whether or not a person);
> (b) The time or duration of a communication;
> (c) The type, method or pattern, or fact, of communication;
> (d) The telecommunication system (or any part of it) from, to or through which, or by means of which, a communication is or may be transmitted; or
> (e) The location of any such system, and this expression therefore includes, in particular, internet connection records.[56]

From a historical starting point wherein the only intrusion into the privacy of the polity's correspondence involved accessing the content of letters to identify threats to the monarchy, it is evident that there now exists the potential for the British state to create an 'intelligence' profile of every person registered as living within its jurisdiction through the analysis and machine processing of personal data and communications data either voluntarily provided to the state by the individuals concerned[57] or compulsorily retained by CSPs.[58] Whether or not the relevant data retained is ever actually accessed, civil libertarian concerns regarding 'dataveillance' are credible and understandable.[59] The ethical controversies inherent in the IPA 2016 as enacted are however beyond the scope of this work. Having examined the inherent difficulties in legislating for interception of communications content and access to non-content data, there now follows a short explanation of the rise of data as key target material for investigators.

The modern centrality of 'data' in the IPA 2016

The above preamble to the IPA 2016 is candid and clearly expressed. It sets the tone for what is, despite its length, a clearly drafted statute that entrenches powers authorizing three broad *forms* of investigative conduct,[60] whilst providing two schemes authorizing the retention of personal data for potential investigation.[61] Even from a wholly objective view, these powers facilitate intelligence production

56 IPA 2016, s87.
57 ibid, Part 7 enables the use of Bulk Personal Personal Datasets (BPD).
58 ibid, Part 4.
59 Benjamin J Goold, 'How Much Surveillance is too much? Some Thoughts on Surveillance, Democracy and the Political Value of Privacy' in DW Schartum (ed) *Overvåkning i en rettsstat – Surveillance in a Constitutional Government* (Fagbokforlaget: Bergen 2010) 38.
60 Interception of Communications (IPA 2016, Parts 2 and 6), Equipment Interference (IPA 2016, Parts 5 and 6), and Access to Communications Data (IPA 2016, Parts 3 and 6).
61 Retention of Communications Data (IPA 2016, Part 4) and Bulk Personal Datasets (IPA 2016, Part 7).

and the potential for the investigation and profiling of individuals on an industrial scale. As such, the Act also makes significant amendments to the pre-existing oversight regime, principally through the creation of the Investigatory Powers Commissioner's Office (IPCO).[62] Whilst possible to perceive the IPA 2016 as enabling the investigation of communications and related material, it is more accurate to revisit the preamble, wherein it becomes apparent that the Act primarily enables investigative access to *data*. Despite the fact that 'communications' for the purposes of the Act includes the broad term 'data of any description',[63] the Act's definition of 'data' is arguably infinite in scope. Section 263 provides that 'data' includes 'data which is not electronic data and *any information* (whether or not electronic)'.[64] The inclusion of non-electronic data enables information on postal communications to be conceptualized as data for the Act's purposes. Viewed holistically, therefore, the IPA 2016 enables the covert investigation of data 'in transit' (interception) or 'at rest' (equipment interference and accessing communications data). Much of this data will have been retained at the direction of the state by CSPs or by the UKIC (bulk personal datasets). As the digital communications technology environment currently appears, the IPA 2016 can thus be viewed as enabling the relevant public authorities to access data *wherever* it rests and/or *whenever* it moves.

The IPA 2016 and the protection of personal data

The preamble's reference to 'treatment of material held as a result' of the exercise of the relevant investigatory powers reflects the policy aspiration of ensuring that such treatment aligns as closely as is feasible with the data protection provisions in the Data Protection Act (DPA) 2018 and the Council of Europe's Modernised Convention for the Protection of Individuals with Regard to the Processing of Personal Data (Convention 108+).[65] Despite the UK having exited the European Union (EU) in 2020, the pre-exit undertaking to enshrine the EU General Data Protection Regulation (GDPR) in UK law was honoured in the enactment of the DPA 2018.[66] However, as a recent newcomer to 'non-EU member' status, the UK government became subject to a requirement to satisfy the European Commission that an adequacy decision in respect of the British data protection regulatory framework is merited. This ensures the continuance of a lawful

62 IPA 2016, Part 8 – see also the IPCO website, <https://www.ipco.org.uk> accessed 15 October 2020.

63 IPA 2016, s261(2).

64 ibid, s263, emphasis added.

65 Council of Europe, 'Modernised Convention for the Protection of Individuals with respect to the Processing of Personal Data', available at <https://search.coe.int/cm/Pages/result_details.aspx?ObjectId=09000016807c65bf> accessed 21 September 2020.

66 DPA 2018, s1.

two-way data flow between the EU and UK.[67] Included in this is data processed for national security-related investigations or operations as a result of the exercise of investigatory powers. In March 2020, as part of a wider 'Explanatory Framework for Adequacy Discussions', the Home Office clarified the UK's position. This is that, despite the processing of personal data for national security purposes falling outside EU competence and thus being expressly excluded from both the GDPR and the Law Enforcement Directive (LED), processing of personal data by the UK Intelligence Community (UKIC) is now stringently regulated in a dedicated Part 4 to the DPA 2018. Part 4 has been drafted so as to give effect to C108+. The same document adds that, 'in addition to the safeguards and limitations provided by the DPA 2018, the IPA applies further protections and restrictions on the acquisition, retention, handling and use of communications and communications data acquired by public authorities'.[68] The processing of personal data for law enforcement purposes is regulated in Part 3 of the DPA 2018 but, again, where the data are communications or communications data, the additional protections within the IPA 2016 apply.[69] This policy recognizes 'communications' and 'communications data' as special *types* of 'personal data' worthy of the additional protection that the IPA 2016 provides.[70]

67 The European Commission states that, by virtue of

> Article 45 of Regulation (EU) 2016/679 of the European Parliament and of the Council of 27 April 2016 on the protection of natural persons with regard to the processing of personal data and on the free movement of such data, and repealing Directive 95/46/EC (the GDPR), the Commission is empowered to determine whether a non-EU country offers an adequate level of data protection. Adoption of an adequacy decision involves (i) a proposal from the European Commission; (ii) an opinion of the European Data Protection Board; (iii) an approval from representatives of EU countries and (iv) the adoption of the decision by the European Commission. At any time, the European Parliament and the Council may request the European Commission to maintain, amend or withdraw the adequacy decision on the grounds that its act exceeds the implementing powers provided for in the regulation. The effect of such a decision is that personal data can flow from the EU (and Norway, Liechtenstein, and Iceland) to that third country without any further safeguard being necessary. In other words, transfers to the country in question will be assimilated to intra-EU transmissions of data.

European Commission, 'Adequacy Decisions' <https://ec.europa.eu/info/law/law-topic/data-protection/international-dimension-data-protection/adequacy-decisions_en> accessed 30 March 2021.

68 Department for Digital, Culture, Media and Sport, 'Explanatory framework for adequacy discussions-Section H: National Security Data Processing (*GOV.UK*, March 2020) <https://assets.publishing.service.gov.uk/government/uploads/system/uploads/attachment_data/file/872239/H_-_National_Security.pdf> accessed 21 September 2020.

69 ibid, Section F: Law Enforcement. <https://assets.publishing.service.gov.uk/government/uploads/system/uploads/attachment_data/file/872237/F_-_Law_Enforcement_.pdf> accessed 21 September 2020.

70 The DPA 2018, s3(2), in line with the EU GDPR it gives effect to, defines 'personal data' as 'any information relating to an identified or identifiable living individual'.

The availability of the data-centred investigatory powers regulated by the IPA 2016

The Act extends to 'public authorities', principally those UK bodies enabled in statute to engage in conduct securing access to communications and data either 'in pursuit of intelligence requirements'[71] (principally the UKIC) or for the purposes of law enforcement (principally law enforcement agencies [LEA]).[72] It has been observed that 'the line between "strategic intelligence" (information obtained by the intelligence services for the purposes of policymaking) and probative evidence in criminal proceedings has become blurred'.[73] Whilst this is undoubtedly true and there is also operational overlap between the UKIC and sections of UK law enforcement, this book steers clear of a theoretical analysis of 'intelligence' and 'evidence' or a detailed examination of individual public authority roles.

The data-centred investigatory powers regulated by the IPA 2016

The IPA 2016 regulates three covert investigatory powers applicable to communications and data at rest and in transit:

1 Lawful interception of communications *in the course of transmission* on a 'targeted' or 'bulk' basis in order to access *content*;[74]
2 Acquiring *non-content* communications metadata retained by CSPs on a 'targeted' or 'bulk' basis;[75]
3 Lawful interference with computer equipment to secure access to *equipment data* (which includes communications as already defined in the Act) stored within equipment on a 'targeted' or 'bulk' basis.[76]

It further provides for:

1 The mandatory retention of relevant *non-content* communications metadata by CSPs for potential future acquisition by investigative agencies;[77]
2 The retention of bulk personal datasets (BPD) for investigative purposes.[78]

71 A descriptive term first avowed in Home Office, *Equipment Interference Code of Practice: Draft for Public Consultation* (TSO, February 2015) para 1.6. Para 1.12 affirms the UKIC 'public authority' status under the HRA 1998, s6.

72 IPA 2016, s263 and Human Rights Act (HRA) 1998, s6(3)(b). See also European Convention on Human Rights (ECHR), Article 8(2) wherein only 'public authorities' can interfere with the substantive right.

73 Alex Conte, *Human Rights in the Prevention and Punishment of Terrorism: Commonwealth Approaches: The United Kingdom, Canada, Australia and New Zealand* (Springer, 2010) 697.

74 IPA 2016, Parts 2 and 6, Chapter 1 (read in conjunction with the General Privacy Protections in Part I and the relevant interpretative provisions in Part 9).

75 ibid, Part 3 (also read with Parts 1 and 9).

76 ibid, Parts 5 and 6 (read in conjunction with Parts 1 and 9).

77 ibid, Part 4 (also read with Parts 1 and 9).

78 ibid, Part 7.

As per its preamble, the IPA 2016 has also created a new independent oversight regime, the Investigatory Powers Commissioner's Office (IPCO).[79] Consequently, the Act covers the field as regards the authorization and oversight of covert investigative access to data at rest and data in transit. Part 2 of this book provides the first part of the history-focused explanation of how the UK ended up with the IPA 2016.

References

Alexander Babuta, Marion Oswald and Ardi Janjeva, 'Artificial Intelligence and UK National Security' (Royal United Services Institute (RUSI) Occasional Paper, April 2020) <https://rusi.org/sites/default/files/ai_national_security_final_web_version.pdf> accessed 29 October 2020

Alex Conte, *Human Rights in the Prevention and Punishment of Terrorism: Commonwealth Approaches: The United Kingdom, Canada, Australia and New Zealand* (Springer, 2010)

Department for Digital, Culture, Media and Sport, 'Explanatory Framework for Adequacy Discussions-Section H: National Security Data Processing' *GOV.UK* (March 2020) <https://assets.publishing.service.gov.uk/government/uploads/system/uploads/attachment_data/file/872239/H_-_National_Security.pdf> accessed 21 September 2020

Benjamin J Goold, 'How Much Surveillance Is Too Much? Some Thoughts on Surveillance, Democracy and the Political Value of Privacy' in DW Schartum (ed) *Overvåkning i en rettsstat – Surveillance in a Constitutional Government* (Fagbokforlaget, Bergen, 2010)

Home Office, *Equipment Interference Code of Practice: Draft for Public Consultation* (TSO, February 2015)

Investigatory Powers Commissioner's Office, *Annual Report 2018* (HC 67)

Joint Committee on the Draft Investigatory Powers Bill, *Draft Investigatory Powers Bill Report* (2015–16, HL 93, HC 651)

Liberty, 'Written Evidence to the JCDIPB' (IPB0143) <http://data.parliament.uk/writtenevidence/committeeevidence.svc/evidencedocument/draft-investigatory-powers-bill-committee/draft-investigatory-powers-bill/written/26430.html#_ftnref35> accessed 21 September 2020

Supplementary Written Evidence of Graham Smith to the JCDIPB (IPB0126) http://data.parliament.uk/writtenevidence/committeeevidence.svc/evidencedocument/draft-investigatory-powers-bill-committee/draft-investigatory-powers-bill/written/25973.html.

'The Content v Metadata Contest at the Heart of the Investigatory Powers Bill' *Cyberleagle.com* (26 May 2016) <https://www.cyberleagle.com/2016/05/the-content-v-metadata-contest-at-heart.html> accessed 30 September 2020

UK Parliamentary Intelligence and Security Committee, *Privacy and Security: A Modern and Transparent Legal Framework* (HC 2014–15, 1075–I)

79 ibid, Part 8 – see generally, the IPCO website <https://www.ipco.org.uk> accessed 29 October 2020.

Written Evidence of Dr Paul Bernal to the JCDIPB (IPB0018) <http://data.parliament.uk/writtenevidence/committeeevidence.svc/evidencedocument/draft-investigatory-powers-bill-committee/draft-investigatory-powers-bill/written/25973.html> accessed 21 September 2020

Part II

Secretive communications investigation governance

1324?–1984

3 Secretive non-statutory regulation

Interception of communications, 1324–1919

Introduction

This chapter explores the early history of British state power to access communications in the course of transmission. Choosing the historical scope of each chapter was difficult, but it was decided to end this one at the point just prior to when the British government decided to enact its first statute regulating the interception of telecommunications,[1] where regulation up to this point had been conducted solely by Ministers. By 1919, communications technology had also reached the point where it is now; post, wired and wireless, but an international outlook had not yet been embedded in regulation.

The IPA 2016 continues what has been a perennial tradition of providing a *dedicated* regulatory framework for interception of communications in the course of transmission undertaken in the UK in order to obtain content. A key question is *why*, given that other investigative conduct *not legally defined as interception of communications* can yield exactly the same result. For example, regulation of wireless telegraphy (and the interception of wireless communications) has existed in wireless telegraphy statutes since 1904, and the statutory regulation of interception of fixed-line international (external) telephone communications since 1920 in the Official Secrets Act (OSA) of that year. There was no statutory regulation of conduct amounting to interception of British *domestic* telephone calls, however, until it replaced administrative regulation in 1985.[2] By that year, however, other investigative techniques capable of producing essentially the same intelligence yield as interception were being used by public authorities. These remained separately regulated by administrative guidelines until the enactment of the Police Act 1997, Part III,[3] the Security Service Act (SSA) 1989, the Intelligence Services Act (ISA) 1994, and, as will be shown, the Regulation of Investigatory Powers Act (RIPA) 2000. What is it about the postal and telecommunications of persons

1 The Official Secrets Act (OSA) 1920.

2 Interception of Communications Act (IOCA) 1985, repealed by RIPA 2000.

3 Which introduced statutory authorisation of police surveillance operations involving the interference with property or wireless telegraphy and was enacted in anticipation of the adverse judgment in *Khan v United Kingdom* (2001) 31 EHRR 45.

present in the UK that for hundreds of years has commanded a policy of quasi-secret governance by successive Home and Foreign Ministries and a refusal, prior to the IPA 2016, to cede any aspect of executive control to the judiciary?

Heritage

It might be argued that, despite the piecemeal nature of the IPA 2016's regulatory evolution, the distinctive regulation of interception of communications in Parts 2 and 6 is easily explained by the very fact of its heritage as the oldest investigative technique by which communications content can be accessed. This in itself is unconvincing, especially since the IPA 2016 now includes other equally intrusive investigatory powers.

Interception and trespass

A perhaps more logical potential reason for interception regulation's separate evolution might be English law's longstanding view of privacy as not amounting to a justiciable right.[4] Consideration of this, alongside the fact that the conduct involved in interception of communications *in the course of transmission by a third party*, at no point involves the ancient tort of trespass to property, thus distinguishing it from conduct involving entering premises for the purposes of search or to plant listening equipment. This distinction was considered in detail by Sir Robert Megarry in the initial (and, as shall be shown, pivotal) case involving interception of communications heard in an English court, namely *Malone v Commissioner of Police of the Metropolis*.[5] Sir Robert cited Lord Camden C J in the famous case of *Entick v Carrington* who stated, 'the eye cannot by the laws of England be guilty of a trespass'.[6] Sir Robert stated, 'I would add, nor can the ear'.[7]

Yet English law has also additionally long held the Englishman's home as sacrosanct, whereby entry on behalf of the state for investigative purposes is permissible only by warrant otherwise trespass *is* committed.[8] It would be reasonable to think, therefore, that regulation of information acquisition in the UK would be predicated on the conceptual view that information acquisition *involving* trespass is *more* deserving of a Secretary of State's control than information acquisition undertaken without it. This has not, however, always been the case. As such, interception has historically commanded a more stringent authorisation

4 Robert Walker, 'The English Law of Privacy – An Evolving Human Right' (speech by Supreme Court Justice Lord Walker of Gestingthorpe to Anglo-Australasian Lawyers Society at Owen Dixon Chambers, Melbourne), 25 August 2010 <www.supremecourt.uk/docs/speech_100825.pdf> accessed 23 October 2020.

5 *Malone v Commissioner of Police of the Metropolis (No2)* [1979] Chapter 344.

6 *Entick v Carrington* (1765) 2 Wilson KB 275.

7 *Malone v Commissioner of Police of the Metropolis* (n5).

8 Traceable to *Semayne's Case* (1604) 5 Coke Reports 91a and *Entick v Carrington*.

process, involving the application for a Secretary of State's warrant, than conduct involving trespass to property, where a simple Magistrate's warrant often sufficed. Given that trespass historically involved a greater intrusion to individual privacy, the distinctive regulatory mechanism for obtaining authorisation to intercept still present in the IPA 2016 cannot be logically or credibly explained by reference to the absence of the tort of trespass.

European impetus

One widely agreed upon trigger for the conversion of regulation of interception of telephone communications from administrative guidelines into a dedicated statutory format was the impetus created by the decision of the European Court of Human Rights (ECtHR) at the end of the *Malone* appellate process.[9] There was nothing in the ECtHR's judgment that demanded the continuance of the pre-existing distinctive regulatory regime. Yet the Thatcher government of the time responded with exactly that. The Interception of Communications Act (IOCA) 1985 was a *de minimis* legislative response undertaken in 'grudging compliance under duress', addressing only partly the specific criticisms raised by the ECtHR in *Malone*.[10] The latter judgment may have provided the impetus to statutory regulation of interception, but does not explain why that regulation continues to require authorisation by a Secretary of State.

The involvement of communications service providers

In the debates preceding the Interception of Communications Act (IOCA) 1985, an indication of the policy underpinning the distinctive treatment of interception of communications became clearer. Then Home Secretary Leon Brittan set out the scope of the then Interception of Communications Bill as encompassing:

> communications in the public system. In telecommunications and the post, people have no option but to entrust information to the care of organisations over which they have no control. The sender and receiver are entitled to believe that the privacy of their communications on these systems will be safeguarded while they are out of their hands.[11]

Whilst on an initial reading a logical statement, when the prevailing operational context is taken into consideration, it can, with hindsight, be seen at best as flawed in its reasoning and at worst, yet another example of the disingenuous nature of proposed legislation at the time. It ignored the legal absurdity that at the time,

9 *Malone v UK* (1984) 7 EHRR 14.

10 Francesca Klug, Keir Starmer, Stuart Weir, *The Three Pillars of Liberty: Political Rights and Freedoms in the United Kingdom* (Routledge, 1996) 59–60.

11 Home Secretary Leon Brittan, HC Deb, 12 March 1985, volume 75 col 158.

communications content could be, and was being accessed via investigative conduct not fitting the IOCA 1985 (and subsequently RIPA 2000) definition of interception.[12] It also conveniently ignored the reality of the depth of acquiescence in the interception of the very organisations mentioned. As such, the distinct regulatory regime for interception is not fully explained by the involvement of CSPs, although it goes some way to explaining it.

'A SIGINT capacity worth protecting': the BRUSA and UKUSA Agreements

The most convincing reason, however, for the UK executive's secretive retention of distinctive regulation of communications-content acquisition power was perhaps inadvertently disclosed by an unnamed GCHQ witness before the UK's Parliamentary Intelligence and Security Committee (UKPISC) in 2008. In a relatively innocuous inquiry into the use of intercept product as evidence, they stated that 'the UK is the only country which has all three of the following things: an adversarial legal system, subordination to [the ECHR] and *a strategic intercept and SIGINT capacity that is worth protecting*'.[13] The capacity referred to related to the UK's still ongoing obligations originally cemented in the 'British-U.S. Communication [*sic*] Intelligence Agreement' concluded on 5 March 1946 (BRUSA).[14] This book will regularly demonstrate that UKUSA Agreement considerations, more than any other, constitute the most significant policy influence on the drafting of each of the three statutes that the UK has so far enacted to regulate interception and associated investigatory powers. As Dittmer asserts:

> The foreign policy apparatuses of the UKUSA states do not make rational decisions on the basis of their national interest; rather, the *cognitive sense-making of their interests is shaped through participation in UKUSA*. This transnational assemblage of bodies, satellites, computers, cables, drones, micro-wave transmitters, undercover agents, and so on is a kind of everyday diplomacy that, in conjunction with other discursive and material

12 i.e. via intrusive surveillance (regulated in RIPA Part 2). For how the domestic courts have dealt with this absurdity see *R v Allsopp and Others* [2005] EWCA Crim 703, (35)–(50) ultimately applying the findings of *R v E* (2004) 2 Cr App R 29. For an informative and cogent analysis of it see Simon McKay, *Covert Policing Law and Practice* (OUP, 2011) 79-87

13 Intelligence and Security Committee of Parliament (UKPISC), *Annual Report 2006–2007* (Cm7299, 2008) 33, emphasis added.

14 Subsequently called the UKUSA Agreement, addressed in more detail in Chapter 4. The United States National Security Agency (NSA) has declassified and released many formerly top-secret documents relating to this longstanding agreement, The BRUSA is available at <https://www.nsa.gov/Portals/70/documents/news-features/declassified-documents/ukusa/agreement_outline_5mar46.pdf> accessed 29 October 2020.

> connections between foreign policy apparatuses, enables emergent agencies to reshape global politics.[15]

This demonstrates the importance of the UKUSA Agreement to its participants' international relations. It is no surprise therefore that, leaving aside the mythology that has materialised in conjunction with increased public awareness of the 'Five Eyes' UKUSA Agreement, their conceptual approach, definitional drafting, authorization, and oversight of communications and data investigation is similar and convergent.[16] The importance of the UKUSA Agreement and its influence on the UK's post-war regulation of communications and data investigation thus cannot be overstated. Interception as British state practice dates well prior to the UKUSA Agreement.

In the beginning

In providing a background to modern intelligence gathering, Herman observed that 'intelligence as a set of permanent institutions dates back only to the second half of the nineteenth century',[17] whilst the practice of 'intercepting messages...is as old as governments' use of writing and their protection of it by...cryptography'.[18] He additionally notes that 'the first surviving document on cipher-breaking is said to be an Arabic one from the ninth century'.[19] Communications content acquisition as an investigative state practice can therefore be stated to have existed for over 1,000 years. As regards the British state, however, the following extract from a letter dated 18 December 1324 is instructive.

> [To the] Constable of Dover and Warden of the Cinque Ports, the Mayor and Sheriffs of London, the Bailiffs of Bristol, Southampton and Portsmouth, and the Sheriffs of Hants, Somerset, Dorset, Devon, and Cornwall [who] ...are commanded to...*stop all letters concerning which sinister suspicions*

15 Jason Dittmer, 'Everyday Diplomacy: UKUSA Intelligence Cooperation and Geopolitical Assemblages', (2015) 105(3) *Annals of the Association of American Geographers* 604, 605.

16 As regards homogeneity in conceptual and regulatory approach see Cat Barker, Claire Petrie, Joanna Dawson, Samantha Godec, Holly Porteous, and Pleasance Purser, 'Oversight of Intelligence Agencies: A Comparison of the "Five Eyes" Nations', Parliament of Australia Library Research Paper (15 December 2017) available at <https://parlinfo.aph.gov.au/parlInfo/download/library/prspub/5689436/upload_binary/5689436.pdf> accessed 29 October 2020. As regards convergence, see Richard Morgan, 'Oversight Through Five Eyes: Institutional Convergence and the Structure and Oversight of Intelligence Activities' in Zachary K Goldman and Samuel J Rascoff, *Global Intelligence Oversight: Governing Security in the 21st Century* (OUP 2016) 37–70.

17 Michael Herman, *Intelligence Power in Peace and War* (10th edn, Cambridge University Press 2007) 9.

18 ibid, 11, citing D Kahn, *The Codebreakers* (London: Sphere Books, 1973) 80.

19 ibid.

> *might arise, and their bearers….and to transmit the letters so intercepted* to the King.[20]

This command is founded on a writ issued by King Edward II in the same year. With thanks to Tony Comer, recently retired Departmental Historian at GCHQ, there is agreement that it currently represents the oldest documentary evidence of a 'British' authorization to intercept communications.[21] The instructions to the Constable and Warden are interesting, in that they authorize what would now be construed as port or border control measures, wherein *communications arriving from overseas*, and their bearers (a perceived *external threat*) are to be stopped, and the relevant intelligence brought to the Monarch. This is evidence that early state practice prioritized interception of *external communications* in the interests of protecting British national security. The letter forms part of a treasure trove of 'Documents Specially Relating to the Search and Examination of Letters' contained in an Appendix to the report of the very first parliamentary inquiry into regulation of the interception of communications undertaken over 500 years later. This was undertaken by a secret committee constituted by an Order of the House of Commons dated 2 July 1844, ordering:

> That a Committee *of Secrecy* be appointed 'to inquire into the State of the Law in respect to the detaining and opening of Letters at the General Post-office, and into the Mode under which the Authority given for such detaining and opening has been exercised, and to Report their Opinion and Observations thereupon to the House'.[22]

At this point, the requirement for a secret committee is telling and demonstrates the then-prevailing bureaucratic culture. The consequently established 'Secret Committee on the Post Office' (Commons Committee) published their report on 5 August 1844.[23]

The first interception scandal: Giuseppe Mazzini

In support of the assertion that such reviews were only undertaken following a public scandal, the Commons Committee's Report, supplemented by a similarly titled (but not published) report into the same matter compiled by the House of Lords,[24] represented Parliament's grudging response to the persistent petitioning

20 Emphasis added. Letter contained in an Appendix to the Home Office, *Report from the Secret Committee on the Post Office* (C582, 1844).

21 The author remains open to correction!

22 Emphasis added. The Order is contained in a further Appendix to the Report of the Secret Committee.

23 Home Office, *Report from the Secret Committee on the Post Office* (n20)12.

24 House of Lords, *Report from the Secret Committee of the House of Lords Relative to the Post Office* (C601, 7 August 1844). This report was not made public.

of the Right Honourable Thomas Slingsby Dunscombe, MP, for such an enquiry. Dunscombe alleged under privilege in Parliament that the then Home Secretary, Sir James Graham, had ordered the GPO to intercept and transcribe the written communications of exiled Italian nationalist Giuseppe (Joseph) Mazzini along with the communications of a number of other prominent exiles.[25] Vincent also outlines how, 'in a series of set-piece debates which lasted until February 1845, an increasingly embattled government was subjected to a more extensive interrogation of official secrecy than was to be permitted again for well over a century'.[26]

The General Post Office: GPO

Prior to exploring the Commons Committee's research and conclusions, it is worth recalling the assertion in the introductory chapter that the massive data-investigation regime now regulated in the IPA 2016 simply could not operate without the active cooperation of communications service providers (CSPs). In 1844, there was only one CSP proper. This was the 'General Post Office' (GPO) referred to by the House of Commons. It is impossible to overstate the contribution made to the UK's communications investigation architecture by this institution, variants of which enjoyed a monopoly in UK telecommunications between 1896 and 1981, and in UK postal communications until as recently as 2003.[27]

The origin of communications service providers as protectors of national security

Despite the GPO's innocuous title, Spencer has observed that it was originally actually created with the 'express aim of enabling the government to spy on its citizens by opening and reading their correspondence…this was candidly stated in the preamble to the Protectorate Ordinance of 1657 by which the General Post Office was set up'.[28] The statute referred to is Cromwell's 'June 1657 An Act

25 David Vincent, *The Culture of Secrecy: Britain 1832–1998* (Clarendon Publishing 1999) 1. Vincent describes how the then Prime Minister Sir Robert Peel, feeling intense pressure as a consequence of Dunscombe's allegations, was forced to set up the Select Committee to consider them.

26 ibid, 2.

27 See generally Duncan Campbell-Smith, *Masters of the Post: The Authorized History of the Royal Mail* (Penguin 2012). An alternative comprehensive history of the British postal institution, including its role in the intercepting communications on behalf of State agencies such as the police is provided in K Ellis, *The Post Office in the Eighteenth Century* (2nd edn, Oxford University Press, 1962). For a synopsis of the history of telecommunications service provision see <https://www.bt.com/bt-plc/assets/documents/about-bt/our-history/history-of-bt.pdf> accessed 20 September 2020.

28 J R Spencer, 'Telephone-Tap Evidence and Administrative Detention in the UK' in Marianne Wade and Almir Maljevic (eds) *A War on Terror? The European Stance on a New Threat; Changing Laws and Human Rights Implications* (Springer Publishing, 2010) 375.

for Setling the Postage of England, Scotland and Ireland'.[29] The full preamble indeed states:

> Whereas it hath been found by experience, That the Erecting and Setling of one General Post-Office, for the speedy Conveying, Carrying, and Re-carrying of Letters by Post, to, and from all Places within England, Scotland, and Ireland, and into several parts beyond the Seas, hath been, and is the best means, not onely to maintain a certain and constant Intercourse of Trade and Commerce betwixt all the said Places, to the great benefit of the People of these Nations, but also to *discover and prevent many dangerous and wicked designs* which have been and are daily contrived *against the peace and welfare of this Commonwealth, the intelligence whereof cannot well be communicated but by letter of escript.*[30]

The explicit reference to 'intelligence' in Cromwell's Act marks perhaps the first statutory acknowledgement of the value and utility attached by the British state to communications content acquisition in the interests of national security. The preamble establishes what became an inextricable link between the GPO as established and interception of communications on behalf of the British state, and one which fell to the Commons Committee to investigate. They found the birth of a British postal service of sorts to actually predate 1657, observing that, 'it does not appear at what precise period the Crown undertook to be the regular carrier of letters for its subjects…[but]…in course of time a Master of the Posts was appointed…Brian Tuke, Knight, who held that office in 1516'.[31] It appears there were royally appointed runners known as 'posts' even prior to that date.[32] The Committee went on to find that none of the post office-related statutes following that of 1657 continued the practice of making explicit reference to national security considerations.[33] However, it appears from their research that a state-recognised belief in the existence of a *right of a Secretary of State* to intercept postal communications *on the grounds of national security* had now been assumed. They referred to a number of proclamations and leases to Postmasters-General in the period between 1657 and the Statute of Anne 1710, wherein section 40 provided that:

> whereas abuses may be committed by wilfully opening, embezzling, detaining and delaying of Letters or Packets, to the great discouragement of trade, commerce, and correspondence…no person or persons shall presume wittingly, willingly, or knowingly, to open, detain or delay or cause, procure,

29 'June 1657: An Act for Settling the Postage of England, Scotland and Ireland', in C H Firth and R S Rait (eds) *Acts and Ordinances of the Interregnum, 1642–1660* (London, 1911) 1110–1113.

30 ibid, emphasis added.

31 Home Office, *Report from the Secret Committee on the Post Office* (n20) 3.

32 ibid, 7.

33 ibid.

permit or suffer to be opened, detained or delayed, any letter or letters, packet or packets...*except by an express warrant in writing, under the hand of one of the Principal Secretaries of State.*[34]

The origin of communications service providers as protectors of 'economic wellbeing'

Two significant points of interest arise in section 40 that point towards the policy rationale underpinning the regulation of interception of communications (and derivative data-investigation powers) that has existed ever since that era. Firstly, the mischief the provision seeks to counteract extends beyond external national security threats as envisaged by the court of Edward II and Cromwell to encompass threats to trade, commerce, and correspondence. For the first time, therefore, a UK statute includes the protection of the 'economic wellbeing of the nation' to the grounds for authorizing the interception of communications, a ground that has continued to exist through to the IPA 2016.[35] Secondly, the statute renders the interception of communications in the UK (as the British state became after 1707) unlawful except where authorized by a Secretary of State's warrant. This statutory reflection of policy also remains present in the IPA 2016.[36]

The origin of communications service providers as investigative assistants

As mentioned previously, by 1844 (and indeed until 1969) the GPO was a 'Department of State under the direct control of a Minister (the Postmaster-General)'[37] and possessed a monopoly in the delivery of written communications. As such, the Secret Committee took evidence that interceptions were undertaken by Department (GPO) staff rather than by agents of an investigative body representing the state. This is clear evidence of the longstanding active cooperation or acquiescence of CSPs in pursuing the state's intelligence requirements.

Interceptions were conducted covertly by virtue of either a 'criminal warrant' or a 'discretionary warrant'. Criminal warrants were applied for by the investigatory body (usually the police), with the application requiring the Permanent Under-Secretary's approval before being signed off by the Secretary of State. These warrants were for the purpose of 'obtaining a clue to the hiding place of some offender, or to the mode or place of concealment of property criminally abstracted'.[38] Discretionary warrants were 'issued for the purpose of discovering

34 1710 Act 9 Anne, c10, s40.
35 IPA 2016, s20(2)(c).
36 ibid, Part 2, Chapter 1, 'Interception and Examination with a Warrant'.
37 *Malone v United Kingdom* (1983) 5 EHRR 385, Report of the European Commission 391.
38 Home Office, *Report from the Secret Committee on the Post Office* (n20) 14.

the designs of persons known or suspected to be engaged in proceedings, ***dangerous to the State, or…deeply involving British interests, and carried on in the United Kingdom or in British Possessions beyond the seas***'. Unlike criminal warrants, these warrants 'originate[d] with the Home Office. The Principal Secretary of State, of his own discretion, determines when to issue them'.[39] It appears therefore that long before the advent of official security services, the Home Office felt it had an unfettered discretionary power to authorize interceptions and other covert actions, both domestically and internationally, on grounds of national security.

The origin of the security versus privacy debate

The Mazzini matter ignited what Stone has described as 'a firestorm of controversy over government surveillance and the right to privacy…[which]…[f]or several decades…significantly shaped British domestic policy on government surveillance of private citizens'.[40] Stone, writing before the advent of the publication of Edward Snowden's unauthorized disclosures, presciently parallels the impact of the Mazzini scandal with the post-2013 debate as to how best to regulate access to communications-related data, observing that:

> [I]t brought to the fore conflicts between the individual and the state shaped by an increasingly international world order and the rise of a mass information society with increasingly modernized communications systems…[as well as playing]…a key role in the histories of surveillance and privacy…Indeed [the] case strikingly anticipate[d] the debates that citizens…grapple with today over 'securitizing' the state and 'renditions' of information in the wake of…9/11 in the US and 7/7 in the UK…[a]nd most obviously, of course, [the]controversy…speaks to debates over changing standards and protocols for privacy, as well as diplomatic secrecy, that seem increasingly fraught today with the transformations wrought by electronic media and the hacking of phones…emails, and government documents.[41]

The origin of 'neither confirm nor deny'

The Secret Committee Report provides a fascinating insight into the regulatory history of the UK Postal Service and its predetermined role as a facilitator for communications investigation. It additionally provides candid and detailed insight

39 ibid, 14–15, emphasis added.

40 Marjorie Stone, 'Joseph Mazzini, English Writers and the Post Office Espionage Scandal 1844: British and Italian Politics, Privacy and Twenty-First Century Parallels' (2010) *BRANCH: Britain, Representation and Nineteenth-Century History*. Ed. Dino Franco Felluga. Extension of *Romanticism and Victorianism on the Net*. <http://branchcollective.org/?ps_articles=marjorie-stone-on-the-post-office-espionage-scandal-1844> accessed 23 October 2019.

41 ibid, 3.

into the position the British ruling class, namely the monarchy and Parliament, had hitherto adopted in respect of the acquisition of the content of their subjects' communications. The level of apparent detail provided makes it initially tempting to view their report as both authoritative and comprehensive. Indeed, the Commons Committee reported that it had been empowered to send for 'persons, papers and records'[42] and had before it:

> [E]very person now living who has held the seals of Secretary of State, for Home or Foreign Affairs, since the year 1822...two noblemen who have discharged the office of Lord Lieutenant of Ireland...several persons who have held confidential positions under them...the present Postmaster-general, the Secretaries of the Post Office for England and Ireland, together with several of the most confidential officers in every branch of the Foreign Office ...[who]...without exception...made...the most full and unreserved disclosures; so much so as to have rendered it superfluous ...to examine any other witnesses.[43]

The last line of that statement, however, offers a clue as to the true attitude adopted by the majority of the 1844 government (including the nine Secret Committee members) to the whole Mazzini inquiry. Despite the undoubted experience, import, and standing of the aforementioned witnesses, the arbitrary decision to restrict the summoning of witnesses to just representatives of the state demonstrates an underlying reluctance to fully explore and engage with the issues raised. An immediate consequence was that their published findings were not well received by the original petitioner.[44] Indeed Dunscombe described the Report as 'the greatest take-in I have ever known'.[45] He also challenged the Committee's view, as expressed in the *prima facie* comprehensive report, that they had 'not found it necessary to follow the warrant from the time of its reception at the Post Office to that of its execution'.[46] He asserted under parliamentary privilege that for the Committee to have done so would have meant confirming the existence of the 'secret office' within the general post office and that they had sought to avoid doing so. The existence of that secret office is now of course a historical fact.[47] Home Secretary Graham's robust defence of his actions in the matter, however, neither confirmed nor denied the existence of the secret office.[48] This

42 Home Office, *Report from the Secret Committee on the Post Office* (n20) 2.
43 ibid, 9.
44 HC Deb 18 February 1845, volume 77, cols 668–691.
45 ibid, 668.
46 Home Office, *Report from the Secret Committee on the Post Office* (n20) 16.
47 Richard Aldrich, *GCHQ The Uncensored Story of Britain's Most Secret Intelligence Agency* (Harper Press, 2010) 14.
48 HC Deb 18 February 1845, volume 77, cols 607–709.

stance provides an early example of the 'Neither Confirm Nor Deny' (NCND) policy occasionally still deployed in the UK.[49]

Spencer observes (citing Lord Chancellor Lord Campbell) that all parties were pleased 'to have the matter hushed up by the appointment of a Select Committee'.[50] It is Vincent however who best encapsulates the state's approach to the matter, an approach which, as will be shown, that established a precedent and retains parallels with the prevailing state attitude to public discussion of intelligence matters in modern times:

> Cabinet secrecy was guaranteed by the Privy Councillor's Oath, which supplied the only constitutional definition of a government minister. The Councillor was sworn to 'keep secret all matters committed and revealed unto you, or that be treated of secretly in Council. This was the basis of [Home Secretary] Graham's refusal to answer questions on postal espionage.[51]

The 1844 Report's conclusions as regards the interception of communications were, even on the most objective analysis, cautious. Despite its provision of a detailed history of the practice and the resort to a considerable amount of documentary evidence, it examined the arguments for and against retaining the power to intercept UK residents' communications in only the most general terms. It made no recommendations whatsoever, instead batting the question of statutory regulation of the Secretary of State's power to secure interception of communications back to Parliament, cautioning that legislation might indirectly sanction increased deployment of the power. In its final paragraph, the Report ultimately endorsed the prevailing *status quo* and implicitly backed the discretion and judgment of the Secretary of State to use interception powers sparingly and appropriately.[52]

Policy: maintaining a culture of secrecy regarding interception

As mentioned previously, the very fact that the Committee sat in secret offers telling evidence of the prevailing culture within the government of the day as regards the interception of communications. It also presciently indicates how the culture of state secrecy surrounding interception and broader national security matters

49 A detailed exposition of the government's NCND policy and the rationale underpinning it is provided in the Respondents' (UK Government and UKIS) Open Response to the Investigatory Powers Tribunal in *Privacy International and Others v UK Govt and UKIS* [UKIPTrib] 13/92/CH, (5)–(10). See also Home Office, *Reform of Section 2 of the Official Secrets Act 1911* (Cm 408, 1988) paragraph 43.

50 Spencer (n28) 376, citing M S Hardcastle (ed) *Life of John, Lord Campbell* (John Murray, London 1881), volume 2 187–188.

51 Vincent, *The Culture of Secrecy* (n25) 6.

52 Home Office, *Report from the Secret Committee on the Post Office* (n20) 19.

would evolve and endure until 2013.[53] Home Secretary Graham defended the Committee taking their evidence in secret on the grounds that it was:

> [In] order that its Members might obtain a full and unreserved disclosure from the Ministers of State, and those who acted with the Ministers of State, of everything within their knowledge connected with the subject of the inquiry. The Members of the present Government and of the late Government solicited from Her Majesty permission to make a disclosure of every fact that came within their knowledge. They received that permission on the statement to Her Majesty…[Queen Victoria]…that the Committee was to be secret, and that they could, *without prejudice to the public interests*, disclose the facts which had come within their knowledge. The permission was given on that assurance.[54]

The stated need to solicit the permission of the Monarch for a secret hearing is interesting, given Parliament's supposed supremacy following the Reformation. Equally as interesting is that Queen Victoria saw fit to involve herself in parliamentary matters by granting the request. Three very familiar 21st-century issues manifest themselves in this part of Home Secretary Graham's defence: (i) the soliciting or proffering of secret Royal influence on government policy and decision-making;[55] (ii) the pre-2013 widely held government belief that some aspects of UK government policy are best conducted in secret[56] and (iii) the idea of 'public interest' restrictions on freedom of information.[57] Indeed, Vincent, with reference to the context of the 1844–1845 Mazzini affair, observes that:

53 See generally Vincent, *The Culture of Secrecy* (n25). On the state's relationship with an occasionally irksome investigative media, see Nicholas John Wilkinson, *Secrecy and the Media: The Official History of the United Kingdom's D-Notice System* (Routledge, 2009). On the idea of state secrecy as a privilege of class distinction, see Christopher Moran, *Classified: Secrecy and the State in Modern Britain* (Cambridge University Press, 2012).

54 HC Deb 18 February 1845, volume 77, col 727, emphasis added.

55 *cf* Prince Charles' 'Black Spider Memos' controversy, involving 'lobbying' correspondence between him and various UK government departments. See generally the appellate chain of *R (on the application of Evans) and another (Respondents) v Attorney General (Appellant)* (2015) UKSC 21 which paved the way for publication of the memos, which successive UK governments had vigorously resisted.

56 See for example UKPISC *Annual Report 2012–2013* (HC 547, 10 July 2013) para 131, which asserts that

> unlike other parts of Government, intelligence and security matters cannot be effectively scrutinised in Parliamentary debates, or by a normal departmental Select Committee, the media, academia or pressure groups. Only a body with powers to access highly classified information can fulfil such a role.

57 The modern take on 'public interest' is found in the Criminal Procedure and Investigations Act (CPIA) 1996, s21(1), which introduced a new statutory framework relating to disclosure of certain categories of state information in the public interest. See also the categories of

> [T]he pre-Reform tradition of dealing with criticism by attempting to silence it...had now been abandoned...yet, in the uncertain years of the 1830s and 1840s it was by no means self-evident to successive governments that it was either inevitable or desirable that all controls over official communication be abandoned.[58]

The Mazzini scandal installed the battleground for a sporadic conflict between state and civil libertarian activism that persists in the context of state security and regulation of investigative access to communications-related data to this day.

A robust defence of the policy

Home Secretary Graham's response to Dunscombe is also worthy of inclusion. It not only explicitly grabbed new powers widening the grounds for seeking the interception of communications beyond those of national security, but also presciently set the tone for the defensive position of future governments until very recently as regards covert investigative privacy intrusion more generally:

> The question [of interception of communications] affects the character and conduct of...Government...it is you, the House of Commons, who... placed in our hands this instrument *for maintaining internal tranquillity and preserving general peace.* For no less than 150 years this power has been exercised by the Executive Government...In the year 1735...it was expressly admitted by the Resolutions of the House of Commons, when it was declared to be a breach of privilege of any postmaster, or agent, to open any letter of a Member of the House of Commons, *unless under a warrant from the Secretary of State*...it has been exercised by Secretaries of State the most remarkable for their knowledge of constitutional privileges, and for their defence of civil liberty...if the House of Commons is ignorant of what passed in 1745, what does it say to its own recorded acts in 1837? In that year you were parties to an Act of Parliament which expressly recognised the existence of the power in the hands of the Secretary of State. I do not say that that Act, in express terms and for the first time, gave the power; but as a legal Member denies that Parliament recognised the power, I refer him to the Act of 1837, which subjects to a penalty any officer of the Post Office for delaying, opening, or detaining the post letter of any person, *except in obedience to an express warrant in writing*...You hold us responsible for the *maintenance of public tranquillity and the preservation of internal peace.* This is one of the instruments which you have committed to our hands.[59]

---

information currently exempted from disclosure in the Freedom of Information Act (FOIA) 2000, Part II, and the effect of those exemptions as set out in section 2 of that Act.

58 Vincent, *The Culture of Secrecy* (n25) 6.

59 HC Deb 18 February 1845, vol 77, col 728, emphasis added.

That defence of the state's interception power is interesting when seeking a theoretical justification for the assumption of 'investigatory powers', and, in particular, the purposes for which the state felt it could exercise such powers. As outlined earlier, Cromwell's Act of 1657 had initially expressed the need to gather 'intelligence' from postal interceptions on national security grounds, although explicit references to this were absent from subsequent parliamentary legislation. The rudimentary criminal offence of unlawfully intercepting communications in the absence of the authority of an interception warrant issued by a Secretary of State did however appear in all parliamentary legislation dating back to the Statute of Anne 1710.[60] It would be reasonable to assume that this particular preserved power was, at that stage, palatable to those in government and the wider UK public *for that singular purpose.*

Widening the grounds for interception powers: 'public order' and 'public interest'

The Mazzini scandal, however, seems to have prompted some governmental scrabbling around for not only national security justifications for intercepting UK residents' communications, but also some broader grounds that could assuage both parliamentary and public angst and legitimise Home Secretary Graham's conduct as discovered. As outlined, the Home Secretary appears to have sought and received Royal endorsement to hold the investigation secretly 'in the public interest'. Having sold this public interest immunity to Parliament, in the debates that followed the publication of the Secret Committee Report (and no doubt brimming with the confidence injected by its conclusions) the Home Secretary felt able to respond directly to the criticisms expressed in the House by asserting that his predecessors had actually been afforded wider powers by that House to intercept communications on the grounds of 'maintaining internal tranquillity and preserving the general peace'.[61] Within the context of what was an otherwise eloquent and well-crafted response to Dunscombe, the assumption of the existence of such broad and unfettered extra powers from the Post Office Act 1837 appears to be without foundation. The relevant provision stated:

> If any officer of the Post Office, contrary to his duty, opens...any postal packet in course of transmission by post, or wilfully detains or delays...any such postal packet, he shall be guilty of a misdemeanour...Provided that nothing in this section shall extend to the opening, detaining or delaying of a postal packet returned for want of a true direction, or returned by reason that the person to whom it is directed has refused it, or has refused or neglected to pay the postage thereof, or that the packet cannot for any other reason be delivered, or to the opening, detaining or delaying of a postal packet under

60 Home Office, *Report from the Secret Committee on the Post Office* (n20) 7.
61 HC Deb, 18 February 1845, volume 77, col 728.

> the authority of this Act *or in obedience to an express warrant in writing under the hand of a Secretary of State.* [62]

There is plainly nothing in this provision's creation of a misdemeanour that expressly or impliedly authorized interception on the grounds asserted by Graham. Somewhat ingeniously, the Home Secretary managed to convince the majority of Parliament that it was by *their* hand that he now possessed powers that effectively enabled interception to be sought on grounds of maintaining public order. This is a considerable extension to 'national security' and 'economic wellbeing' as commonly understood. Spencer acknowledges Graham's oratorical masterpiece, noting that a subsequent motion to make interceptions illegal was successfully opposed, effectively subduing debate and ending the Mazzini affair.[63]

The Mazzini legacy: a culture of secrecy regarding state interception powers

Home Secretary Graham's defence also set the precedent for a policy of limiting public discussion and disclosure about interception on the pretext of protecting the 'public interest'. This requires factoring into any critical assessment of the UK's regulatory approach to interception and associated data-investigation powers prior to 2013, wherein it had been observed that 'ever since…[Mazzini]…the *leitmotif* of governmental reaction to the interception of communications has been the supreme importance of keeping the existence of the practice secret'.[64] There appears no evidence, however, that Parliament's ultimate acceptance of Home Secretary Graham's actions (and his defence of them) led to any increase in the discretionary use of powers to intercept. Indeed, Stone observes the converse to be true, summarising the short- to medium-term effects of the Mazzini affair as bringing about a 'relatively restrained policy regarding State surveillance of private letters' and the 'closure of the "Secret" branch of the Post Office'.[65] Despite this, however, Graham's masterful parliamentary defence of the policy rationale underpinning it bequeathed future Home Secretaries the same largely unfettered discretionary administrative powers and an extended range of grounds on which to defend using them.[66] All the post office statutes that followed the 1844 inquiry maintained the criminal misdemeanour first outlined in the Statute of Anne 1710 (which rendered interception of postal communications unlawful except where

62 Post Office Offences Act 1837, s25, emphasis added.
63 Spencer, 'Telephone-Tap Evidence' (n28) 377.
64 ibid, 377.
65 Marjorie Stone (n40) 18.
66 The IPA 2016, s20(2), s138(1), and (2) permit interception in the interests of national security, the economic wellbeing of the UK, and the prevention and detection of serious crime. The public order ground is absent. A case might be made that serious public disorder threatens national security.

an express warrant was issued by the Secretary of State).[67] All included provisions for a scenario whereby intercepting mail would in fact be rendered lawful if an appropriate warrant from a Secretary of State authorized it, thereby implicitly acknowledging the continuance of the power of the Secretary of State to authorize interception. Simultaneously, no co-existing statute expressly set out that power or fettered the discretion of the Secretary of State as to where or on what grounds it could be deployed. A Secretary of State could, in the unlikely event of challenge, cite a common law power of interception existing since the beginnings of written communications, whilst also arguing that as the various post office statutes recognized the existence of this power, it could not, therefore, be one which was unlawfully exercised.[68] In searching for a firm legal origin of the Home Office's power to intercept communications, the two Reports of 1844 fail to offer reliable assistance, instead bequeathing a legacy that directly contributes to a perception of pre-statutory interception of communications as the subject of arbitrary Ministerial power, obscured by secrecy and founded on extremely dubious legality.[69] Both reports are brief and devote a disproportionate amount of their content to searching for a justification for interception. This forms part of a wider policy precedent wherein a government publication seeks to reassure a potentially anxious citizenry that the power to intercept their communications is being used sparingly and with great propriety. The tone of the reports suggests that its authors feel that matters such as those investigated are best left to those who know best as regards what is good for the nation.[70] The possibility of judicial or other independent checks and balances was not considered in either report.

'Wired telegraphy' and the state's regulatory approach

Even as the Mazzini scandal was occupying the UK Parliament and its Secret Committee, communications technology, having been limited to written letters entrusted to the GPO, began to experience what would be seismic change. Sconce reports how, on 28 May 1844, 'friends and observers gathered with Samuel B Morse at the Supreme Court, Washington, D.C. to participate in the first test

67 See Home Office, *Report of the Committee of Privy Councillors Appointed to Inquire into the Interception of Communications* (Cmnd 283, 1957) (*Birkett Report 1957*) 35, which observes that section 58 of the [Post Office] Act 1953 reproduces section 56 of the Post Office Act, 1908 which reproduces section 25 of the Post Office (Offences) Act 1837, which in return re-enacted without material amendment section 40 of the Post Office (Revenue) Act of 1710 (Statute of Anne c.10). There are also certain (strictly limited) exculpatory circumstances whereby the interception will not be unlawful.

68 *Birkett Report 1957* (n67) paragraph 17. The Committee observed that 'none of the [Post Office] statutes contain clauses conferring the power to intercept communications, but recognize the power as an existing power which it is lawful to exercise'.

69 Spencer (n28) 376 refers to the 'supposed power' to intercept letters; this author concurs with that view.

70 This reinforces the suggestion that government secrecy formed a constituent part of governance by class; see Moran (n53) *ante*. This tone also permeates the UKPISC statement (n56).

of an electromagnetic telegraph line...with a reliable line reaching England by 1866'.[71] The first commercial telegraph service, the Electric Telegraph Company, commenced service provision in the UK in 1846 in competition with other companies, some of which amalgamated, or were taken over or collapsed, with the strongest and fittest survivors eventually transferred to state control under the Post Office.[72] Statutory regulation in England swiftly followed in the form of the Telegraph Act 1868, described as an 'Act to enable Her Majesty's Postmaster General to acquire, work, and maintain Electric Telegraphs'.[73] This also allowed the Postmaster-General or authorized delegate potential access to the contents of any communications made using electric or 'wired' telegraphy. The potential for *unlawful* acquisition of the contents of messages communicated by telegraph was obviously recognized at this early stage, as the 1868 Act provided that:

> Any person having official duties connected with the [Post Office], or acting on behalf of the [Post Office], who shall, contrary to his duty, disclose or in any way make known or intercept the contents or any part of the contents of any part of the contents of any telegraphic messages or any message intrusted to the [Post Office] for the purpose of transmission, shall in England and in Ireland be guilty of a misdemeanour, and in Scotland of a crime and offence.[74]

As can be seen, the provision was restricted to the state's post office employees and agents. Unlike the Post Office Act 1837, it made no mention of providing lawful authority for intercepting telegraphic communications (essentially Morse code signals) under a Secretary of State's warrant. Neither did it criminalise unlawful interception of telegraphic messages by the public at large. It also refers to messages 'entrusted for the purpose of transmission' rather than 'in the course of transmission', though this may be attributable to either broad drafting (to include the interception of messages left, like letters, for later transmission) or to the fact that it was not thought technically possible for unauthorized interception of telegraphic communications in the course of their transmission to take place. The Act also demonstrated an emerging precedent, wherein, the state, in the form of the officeholder of Postmaster-General, would arbitrarily assume the power to access service users' communications in response to mainstream use of the new technology enabling that service provision.

71 Jeffrey Sconce, *Haunted Media: Electronic Presence from Telegraphy to Television* (2nd edn, Duke University Press, 2000) 21.

72 British Telecommunications PLC, 'Our History' <https://www.bt.com/bt-plc/assets/documents/about-bt/our-history/history-of-bt.pdf> accessed 20 September 2020.

73 Telegraph Act 1868, c110.

74 ibid, s20. This offence remained on the statute book until 26 March 2001, when it was repealed by the Postal Services Act 2000 (Consequential Modifications No. 1) Order 2001/1149 sch. 2 paragraph.1.

Wired telephony and the state's regulatory approach

Briggs records that electric telegraphy was nationalized (badly) by the Post Office in 1870,[75] before describing the next advancement in communications technology, the fixed-line telephone (i.e. the version patented by Alexander Graham Bell)[76] which entered general use around 1870. He further describes how the initially small service offered by the General Post Office (GPO) was absorbed, along with a number of other small companies, into the National Telephone Company, whose monopoly on fixed-line telephony was ultimately nationalized by the Postmaster-General in 1912.[77] Records show 5,900,000 UK trunk calls recorded in 1898 and 36 million trunk calls in 1913.[78] This gives an indication of the exponential growth in wired telecommunication usage even at this early stage. No consideration appears ever to have been given to licensing telephone usage, a prospect not as ridiculous as it might first seem, given the subsequent licensing of wireless telegraphy apparatus discussed shortly. In addition, no statutory provision was made that criminalized the interception of wired telecommunications without lawful authority by the general public. Most importantly for present purposes, no effort was made to place the state's power to intercept telephone communications in statutory form. It thus remained as it did post-Mazzini, generally secret and without any form of independent oversight.

Wireless telegraphy and the state's regulatory approach

This differs somewhat from the state's approach to the next, hugely significant development in communications technology, that of wireless telegraphy. In July

75 Briggs asserts that the Telegraph Act 1869 'gave the Postmaster-General the exclusive privilege of transmitting telegrams within the United Kingdom, and a year later the telegraphs were taken over by the Post Office'. Asa Briggs, *The History of Broadcasting in the United Kingdom, Volume I* (OUP,1995) 87. Neither Hansard nor the principal legislative data bases contain the Telegraph Act 1869, however, The Telegraph Act 1870 (c88, 33, and 34 Vict) mentions 'the Acts of 1868 and 1869', and requires their provisions, insofar as not expressly repealed by the 1870 Act to be construed along with it (s2) and to extend the provisions of the two preceding Acts to all the Channel Islands and the Isle of Man (s3), through the purchase by the Postmaster-General of the Jersey and Guernsey Telegraph Company (s4) and the Isle of Man Electric Telegraph Company (s5). Interestingly, s3 of the 1870 Act remains in force, drawing parallels with the term 'British Islands' found in RIPA 2000 and the Intelligence Services Act 1994.

76 It has now been officially recognized that Bell did not invent the telephone. In fact, determining its inventor has been controversial and mired in litigation. See generally, for example, A Edward Eveson, *The Telephone Patent Conspiracy of 1876: The Elisha Gray-Alexander Bell Controversy and its Many Players* (McFarland and Co, 2000) and Lewis Coe, *The Telephone and Its Several Inventors: A History* (McFarland and Co, 1995) The US Congress credit Antonio Meucci with its invention. See also US Congressional Record-House, 11 June 2002, volume 148, Part 7, 9905–9908.

77 Telephone Transfer Act 1911. See generally, *BT, Archives Information* at <www.btplc.com/thegroup/btshistory/btgrouparchives/> accessed 23 October 2020

78 Donald Read, *The Age of Urban Democracy: England 1868–1914* (2nd edn, Routledge, 2014) 66.

1897, Guglielmo Marconi 'was granted his famous British patent (No. 12039) and founded the Wireless Telegraphy and Signal Company Ltd'.[79] 'Radiotelegraphy',[80] as Ashley initially described it, evolved as the superior wireless signal transmission method after early experimental induction and conduction methods were rejected in favour of the 'principle of electromagnetic radiation',[81] which allowed the transmission of messages of electromagnetic energy 'over paths not provided by any material substance constructed or arranged for that purpose'.[82] For non-technical scholars (including this author) unable to grasp physics, this perhaps smacks of witchcraft. Collins however explains that wireless *telegraphy* refers to the transmission of messages by means of a telegraph key transmitter, whereas the transmission of conversation and music over the same paths using a microphone transmitter constitutes wireless *telephony*.[83] Taken together, the two terms make up wireless telegraphy as now understood, but, as will shortly be discussed, wireless *telephony* (the transmission of voice and music) only became viable after the end of World War I.

Regulatory divergence

In its infancy, wireless telegraphy involved the use of a key transmitter to enable the transmission of coded messages (rather than speech and music) which largely replicated those sent by Morse's wired (cable) telegraph. Three principal wireless signalling codes came to be in regular use,[84] and were transmitted via systems of radiotelegraphic apparatus constructed by pioneering enterprises such as Marconi, Fessenden, and Telefunken.[85] Bruton records that by 1904, wireless telegraphy had become 'widely recognised as an essential means of modern communication

79 See generally, Elizabeth Bruton, 'Marconi Collection: History' (Museum of History of Science, Oxford, undated) <www.mhs.ox.ac.uk/marconi/collection/history.php> accessed 24 October 2020.

80 Radiotelegraphy and wireless telegraphy are interchangeable terms.

81 Charles Grinnell Ashley, *Wireless Telegraphy and Wireless Telephony: An Understandable Presentation of the Science of Wireless Transmission of Intelligence* (Chicago American School of Correspondence, 1912) 69.

82 See WTA 2006, s116. The definition of wireless telegraphy has remained relatively constant since the inception of the technology.

83 A Frederick Collins, *The Radio Amateur's Handbook* (15th edn, Harper & Row, 1983) Chapter 1 (sourced from Project Gutenberg <www.gutenberg.org/ebooks/6934> accessed 21 October 2020. The distinction between wireless communications and landline or wired telephony is important. Collins helpfully distinguishes wireless *telegraphy* and wireless *telephony* by analogy with Morse's telegraph (which involved keying *signals* along a physical telegraph cable) and the telephone, which enabled voice and music etc. to be transmitted by cable.

84 Ashley, *Wireless Telegraphy* (n81) 69–85. The codes were Naval, Continental, and Morse Code.

85 ibid. Ashley notes that the Fessenden system underpinned the National Electric Signalling Company's groundbreaking transatlantic wireless communication between their two purpose-built stations at Machrihanish, Mull of Kintyre, Scotland, and Brant Rock, Massachusetts.

and was used by both sides in the Russo-Japanese War'.[86] Despite the fact that the transmission of communications by wireless telegraphy represented just another form of telecommunication like the new technologies preceding it, there appears to have been no desire to assimilate regulation of it into existing telegraphy or telephone communications regulation. Instead, the Wireless Telegraphy Act (WTA) 1904 became the first statute in the world to regulate the ownership and use of communications technology, with all transmitters or receivers of wireless signals requiring a license,[87] 'the terms and conditions of which were dictated by the Post Office'.[88] In stark contrast to the secrecy surrounding state interception of fixed-line telecommunications and the absence of statutory regulation, the WTA 1904 explicitly empowered the state to use wireless telegraphy apparatus 'to obtain information as to the contents, sender or addressee of any message (whether sent by means of wireless telegraphy or not)' by criminalizing the obtaining of such information by persons acting 'otherwise than under the authority of the Postmaster-General or in the course of their duty as a servant of the Crown'.[89] Thus, a dichotomy wherein the same communication could be made wirelessly and intercepted under statutory powers, whilst an identical communication could be made by telephone and be intercepted in secret without statutory powers was created. At this stage in the development of communications investigation regulation a distinction had been created that regulated access to communications content according to the *means* by which it was communicated, rather than on the nature of the information. The question therefore arises as to why the government chose to award itself clear statutory powers to intercept wireless communications, but to maintain a policy of keeping powers to intercept UK residents' telephone communications off the statute book at this point in history.

National intelligence machinery

One possible answer might be the undoubted utility of wireless telegraphy to the UK's then-nascent national intelligence machinery.[90] This cannot be understated.[91] The Armed Services undoubtedly exerted the greatest influence in the post office's management of wireless telegraphy.[92] Wireless telegraphy was additionally

86 Bruton (n79).

87 Peter Walker, 'Oftel's Five-Minute Guide to the History of Telecommunications Regulation in the UK', Ofcom <www.ofcom.org.uk/static/archive/oftel/publications/news/on61/5min0903.htm> accessed 26 October 2020.

88 Briggs, *The History of Broadcasting* (n75) 44.

89 WTA 1904, s5.

90 Principally MI5, MI6, and GCHQ. See generally *GOV.UK*, 'National Intelligence Machinery' <https://www.gov.uk/government/publications/national-intelligence-machinery> accessed 31 December 2019.

91 Ashley, *Wireless Telegraphy* (n81). See generally Chapter 5.

92 Briggs, *The History of Broadcasting* (n75) 45. He states that the Wireless Telegraph Board was the most important services committee concerned with wireless, and refers also to the Imperial Communications Committee. BT Archives note that this Committee was

proving its worth in the still-perilous arena of sea travel.[93] Military (including naval and intelligence) influence probably provides the principal reason underlying the enactment of a dedicated statute regulating, licensing, and registering all transmitters and receivers of wireless telegraphy apparatus.

The limited electromagnetic spectrum

The *nature* of wireless communication technology provides another reason for the immediate statutory regulation of it and associated explicit interception provisions. By this is meant the finite availability of viable transmission frequencies available on the electromagnetic spectrum that facilitates wireless communications. These are vital for the UK's defence.[94] The law of demand and supply means that there is a need to regulate the allocation of wireless communication frequencies not previously reserved for military or intelligence-related activity, thus preventing spectrum conflicts and harmful electronic interference.[95] The wireless communication channel has been described as 'an unpredictable and difficult communications medium'.[96] From the outset, therefore, 'the crucial issue was that of wavelengths...[and how]...to allocate the limited number of wavelengths available between commercial broadcasting stations, experimenters, ships at sea, wireless telegraphy companies, and, above all, the Services'.[97] In modern times, 'most countries have government agencies responsible for allocating and controlling the radio spectrum...with commercial spectral allocation...governed in Europe by the European Telecommunication Standards Institute and globally by the International Telecommunications Union (ITU)'.[98] The allocation of civilian use frequencies on the spectrum is a hugely valuable[99] internationally

constituted to advise the government on technical questions, and international and Commonwealth issues and comprised representatives of the defence services, the post office, and the Commonwealth, and was chaired by a cabinet minister. In 1944, it was renamed the Commonwealth Communications Council and became the Commonwealth Telecommunications Board in 1949. <www.btplc.com/thegroup/btshistory/1912to1968/1929.htm> accessed 23 October 2020.

93 Bruton (n79) notes how in January 1909, wireless telegraphy saved over 4,000 lives when it was used to call for rescue when the SS Republic collided with the SS Florida off the shores of Nantucket. It also proved invaluable following the Titanic disaster of 1912.

94 See generally Ministry of Defence, 'Electromagnetic Spectrum Blueprint 2019 Version 1' <https://assets.publishing.service.gov.uk/government/uploads/system/uploads/attachment_data/file/833094/Electromagnetic_Spectrum_Blueprint_V1-O.pdf> accessed 20 October 2020.

95 The problem of electromagnetic interference has dogged wireless telegraphy since its invention. See, for example, HC Deb, 8 February 1938, volume 331, cols 865–866W.

96 Andrea Goldsmith, *Wireless Communications* (Cambridge University Press, 2005) 8.

97 Briggs, *The History of Broadcasting* (n75) 88.

98 Goldsmith, *Wireless Communications* (n96) 17.

99 Estimated in 2014 at £50 billion to the UK economy, Department for Culture, Media & Sport. 'The UK Spectrum Strategy Ministerial Foreword' (*GOV.UK*, 10 March 2014) 4. <www.gov.uk/government/uploads/system/uploads/attachment_data/file/287994/UK_Spectrum_Strategy_FINAL.pdf> accessed 26 October 2020.

harmonized matter,[100] with the Office of Communications (Ofcom) representing the latest UK incarnation of statutory regulation and oversight.[101]

The outbreak of the First World War saw governments suspend the activities of amateurs in the field, with the Admiralty assuming control of production at Marconi's UK works. The interception of wireless transmissions for military purposes on the government's behalf rapidly became a very considerable business.[102] In contrast to the ongoing secret interception of telephone communications, there appears to have been no concomitant culture of secrecy surrounding the interception of wireless telegraphy – neither is there any record of a Mazzini-type public disquiet surrounding it. Of course, by this stage, the requirement for a licence, coupled with public awareness of the criminal offence of unlawfully obtaining the contents of wireless messages, goes some way to explaining this.

The ubiquity of the telephone

Another reason might be that by the end of World War I (WWI), fixed-line wired telephone communication, providing *prima facie* secure communications between two individuals, had become increasingly common under the post office monopoly then in place. Private vocal communication made by *wireless* telephony simply did not concern the masses, as it was not available to them to the same extent. Although it had become technically feasible after the end of WWI and the reinstatement of permission for civilian use of wireless telegraphy apparatus under licence, wireless telephony at that point in time could not seriously threaten the ubiquity of the relatively regulation-free, secure, fixed-line telephony. Confidentiality and practicality considerations also played their part. These included technical limitations on the ability to hold two-way conversations, such as the range over which voice transmissions could be made as well as the fact that wireless telegraphy transmission and reception apparatus required a licence. Furthermore, as regards confidentiality, Collins presciently observed that anyone with suitable receiving apparatus, such as a scanning receiver and aerial, could tune in and receive (or otherwise 'intercept') transmitted wireless communications.[103] An example of how easy and thus persistently problematic the unlawful interception of wireless telegraphy could

100 The Geneva-based International Telecommunications Union (part of the UN) manages, inter alia, international spectrum allocation-see generally ITU website <www.itu.int/en/Pages/default.aspx> accessed 26 October 2015. Ofcom represents the UK's interests at international level and regulates the use of the electromagnetic spectrum in the UK, see generally OFCOM, <www.ofcom.org.uk/> accessed 26 October 2020.

101 See generally the Communications Act 2003. This is a huge statute. Part I sets out a significant range of functions and duties of the regulator. Part II has two chapters: Chapter I regulates networks, services, and the radio spectrum. Chapter II governs spectrum use, including provisions on spectrum trading wireless telegraphy licensing and use.

102 Briggs, *The History of Broadcasting* (n75) 34.

103 Collins, *The Radio Amateur's Handbook* (n83) Chapter I.

be, is reflected in the emergency legislation that had to be enacted and periodically renewed during the Northern Ireland 'Troubles', whereby the security forces had to be empowered to stop and search persons for 'munitions, radio transmitters and scanning receivers'.[104] To this day, secure, private wireless communication remains significantly more difficult to achieve than with cable communication.[105]

Perceptions of confidentiality

The decisive factor for consumers however lay in their perceptions of the confidentiality of their communications. Those users of wireless telegraphy apparatus who had perhaps gone to the trouble of registering themselves and obtaining a licence under the WTA 1904 could not reasonably expect to communicate in confidence. No matter what their allotted or chosen frequency, they would be unavoidably transmitting their communications to an indeterminate audience of indeterminate numbers, as opposed to communicating a conversation with just one person in the reasonable expectation of confidentiality. Put another way, their licensed transmission of communications by wireless telegraphy amounted to *casting* those communications to a *broad* audience; i.e. broadcasting. This was a key difference between fixed-line and wireless communication media at the beginning of the 20th century, which saw wireless telegraphy remaining the preserve of the military, a nascent public service broadcasting industry (BBC), and 'hams',[106] with fixed-line telephony progressing to become virtually omnipresent in UK households. Of course, as will be shown later, wireless communication by handheld telephone would return almost 100 years later to usurp its fixed-line rival in terms of popularity. In the early 1920s, however, the public and disparate nature of communications being broadcast under licence by wireless telegraphy meant that the relevant statutory interception regulation (still the WTA 1904) was concerned more with preventing endangerment of life at sea, the unlawful disclosure of messages, and the interception of communications from stations 'not regarded by the Postmaster-General as authorised broadcasting stations'.[107]

104 Northern Ireland (Emergency Provisions) Act 1987 (repealed 27.8.1991) s7 and Northern Ireland (Emergency Provisions) Act 1991, s19.
105 Goldsmith, *Wireless Communications* (n96) 6.
106 A colloquialism for amateur radio enthusiasts.
107 The WTA 1949, s5, stated that,

> Any person who (a) by means of wireless telegraphy, sends or attempts to send, any message which, to his knowledge, is false or misleading and is, to his knowledge, likely to prejudice the efficiency of any safety of life service or endanger the safety of any person or of any vessel, aircraft or vehicle, and, in particular, any message which, to his knowledge, falsely suggests that a vessel or aircraft is in distress or in need of assistance or is not in distress or not in need of assistance; or
>
> (b) otherwise than under the authority of the Postmaster General or in the course of his duty as a servant of the Crown, either (i) uses any wireless telegraphy apparatus with intent to obtain information as to the contents, sender or addressee of any mes-

This had primacy over preventing threats to UK national security, UK economic wellbeing, or of serious crime posed by individuals communicating privately with each other by telephone. It was this difference in the perceived *type* or nature of communications being transmitted by wireless telegraphy that probably led the government to feel that transparent statutory regulation of wireless telegraphy communications posed no threat to their national security interests at that time. Statutory regulation also did not inhibit access to information from wireless telegraphy communications for intelligence purposes, as this practice was already in the public domain and, as has been shown, post office agents and Crown Servants were explicitly empowered to obtain information from wireless telegraphy messages.[108] Consequently, the relatively uncontroversial WTA 1904, section 5 provisions were not only renewed in 1949, but remained principally unchanged until the advent of the Regulation of Investigatory Powers Act (RIPA) 2000. It appears that UK public perception of the state's interception of wireless telegraphy communications was that it was being undertaken as necessary for national security purposes throughout WWII and indeed into the Cold War, and for the regulation of broadcasting in the UK. The lack of widely available wireless telegraphy apparatus, other than radio and television reception apparatus, meant that seditious or criminal communications on that medium were not really contemplated. The 1949 Act was only finally and comprehensively replaced in 2006.[109] In conclusion, therefore, the policy reasons for the creation of the regulatory dichotomy in respect of wireless and wired communications interception regulation can be said to have been military and intelligence-led, with the technical differences and consumer preferences as regards the two communication formats also exerting a degree of influence.

Conclusion

As regards the central thesis of this book, by 1919 there was regulation of investigation of postal, wired, and wireless telecommunications, meaning that the policy of ensuring powers to access all known forms of communication, if needed in the interests of national security, was being fulfilled, albeit not fully in the public domain. The next chapter explores the 'internationalization' of state interception

sage (whether sent by means of wireless telegraphy or not) which neither the person using the apparatus nor any person on whose behalf he is acting is authorised by the Postmaster General to receive; or (ii) except in the course of legal proceedings or for the purpose of any report thereof, discloses any information as to the contents, sender or addressee of any such message, being information which would not have come to his knowledge but for the use of wireless telegraphy apparatus by him or by another person, shall be guilty of an offence.

See also HC Deb, 18 November 1948, vol 458, cols 609–612 as regards early problems with interpretation.

108 WTA 1904, s5.

109 WTA 2006.

of communications. Whilst this is often conceived of as 1946, the year that the UK entered into the BRUSA Agreement, the chapter will illustrate that international telecommunications-based intelligence production had already been enabled in statute over a quarter of a century earlier.

References

Richard Aldrich, *GCHQ The Uncensored Story of Britain's Most Secret Intelligence Agency* (Harper Press, 2010) 14

Cat Barker, Claire Petrie, Joanna Dawson, Samantha Godec, Holly Porteous and Pleasance Purser, 'Oversight of Intelligence Agencies: A Comparison of the "Five Eyes" Nations' (Parliament of Australia Library Research Paper, 15 December 2017) <https://parlinfo.aph.gov.au/parlInfo/download/library/prspub/5689436/upload_binary/5689436.pdf> accessed 29 October 2020

F Bauer, 'Cryptanalysis' in van Tilborg HCA (eds) *Encyclopedia of Cryptography and Security* (Springer, Boston, MA, 2005)

Asa Briggs, *The History of Broadcasting in the United Kingdom, Volume I* (OUP, 1995)

Elizabeth Bruton, 'Marconi Collection: History' (Museum of History of Science, Oxford, undated) <www.mhs.ox.ac.uk/marconi/collection/history.php> accessed 24 October 2020

British Telecommunications PLC, 'Our History' <https://www.bt.com/bt-plc/assets/documents/about-bt/our-history/history-of-bt.pdf> accessed 20 September 2020

'British-U.S. Communication (sic) Intelligence Agreement' (BRUSA) <https://www.nsa.gov/Portals/70/documents/news-features/declassified-documents/ukusa/agreement_outline_5mar46.pdf> accessed 29 October 2020

Duncan Campbell-Smith, *Masters of the Post: The Authorized History of the Royal Mail* (Penguin, 2012)

Lewis Coe, *The Telephone and Its Several Inventors: A History* (McFarland & Co, 1995)

A Frederick Collins, *The Radio Amateur's Handbook* (15th edn, Harper & Row, 1983)

Gordon Corera, *Intercept: The Secret History of Computers and Spies* (Orion Publishing, 2015)

Jason Dittmer, 'Everyday Diplomacy: UKUSA Intelligence Cooperation and Geopolitical Assemblages' (2015) 105(3) *Annals of the Association of American Geographers* 604

K Ellis, *The Post Office in the Eighteenth Century* (2nd edn, Oxford University Press, 1962)

A Edward Eveson, *The Telephone Patent Conspiracy of 1876: The Elisha Gray-Alexander Bell Controversy and Its Many Players* (McFarland & Co, 2000)

C H Firth and R S Rait (eds) *Acts and Ordinances of the Interregnum, 1642–1660* (London, 1911)

Andrea Goldsmith, *Wireless Communications* (Cambridge University Press, 2005)

Charles Grinnell Ashley, *Wireless Telegraphy and Wireless Telephony: An Understandable Presentation of the Science of Wireless Transmission of Intelligence* (Chicago American School of Correspondence, 1912)

M S Hardcastle (ed) *Life of John, Lord Campbell* (Vol 2, John Murray, London, 1881)

Michael Herman, *Intelligence Power in Peace and War* (10th edn, Cambridge University Press, 2007)
Home Office, *Reform of Section 2 of the Official Secrets Act 1911* (Cm 408, 1988)
Home Office, *Report from the Secret Committee on the Post Office* (C582, 1844)
Home Office, *Report of the Committee of Privy Councillors Appointed to Inquire into the Interception of Communications* (Cmnd 283, 1957)
D Kahn, *The Codebreakers* (Sphere Books, London, 1973)
Francesca Klug, Keir Starmer, Stuart Weir, *The Three Pillars of Liberty: Political Rights and Freedoms in the United Kingdom* (Routledge, 1996) 59–60.
Simon McKay, *Covert Policing Law and Practice* (OUP, 2011)
Ministry of Defence, 'Electromagnetic Spectrum Blueprint 2019 Version 1' <https://assets.publishing.service.gov.uk/government/uploads/system/uploads/attachment_data/file/833094/Electromagnetic_Spectrum_Blueprint_V1-O.pdf> accessed 20 October 2020
Christopher Moran, *Classified: Secrecy and the State in Modern Britain* (Cambridge University Press, 2012)
Richard Morgan, 'Oversight Through Five Eyes: Institutional Convergence and the Structure and Oversight of Intelligence Activities' in Zachary K Goldman and Samuel J Rascoff (eds) *Global Intelligence Oversight: Governing Security in the 21st Century* (OUP, 2016) 37–70
Corey Pfluke, 'A History of the Five Eyes Alliance: Possibility for Reform and Additions' (2019) 38(4) *Journal of Comparative Strategy* 302
Project Gutenberg <www.gutenberg.org/ebooks/6934> accessed 21 October 2020
Donald Read, *The Age of Urban Democracy: England 1868–1914* (2nd edn, Routledge, 2014)
Jeffrey Sconce, *Haunted Media: Electronic Presence from Telegraphy to Television* (2nd edn, Duke University Press, 2000)
J R Spencer, 'Telephone-Tap Evidence and Administrative Detention in the UK' in Marianne Wade and Almir Maljevic (eds) *A War on Terror? The European Stance on a New Threat; Changing Laws and Human Rights Implications* (Springer Publishing, 2010)
Marjorie Stone, 'Joseph Mazzini, English Writers and the Post Office Espionage Scandal 1844: British and Italian Politics, Privacy and Twenty-First Century Parallels' (2010) *Branch: Britain, Representation and Nineteenth-Century History*. Ed. Dino Franco Felluga. Extension of *Romanticism and Victorianism on the Net*. <http://branchcollective.org/?ps_articles=marjorie-stone-on-the-post-office-espionage-scandal-1844> accessed 23 October 2019.
The UK-US Communications Intelligence Agreement (UKUSA Agreement) <https://www.nsa.gov/Portals/70/documents/news-features/declassified-documents/ukusa/new:ukusa_agree_10may55.pdf> accessed 29 October 2020
UK Parliamentary Intelligence and Security Committee, *Annual Report 2006–2007* (Cm7299, 2008)
UK Parliamentary Intelligence and Security Committee, *Annual Report 2012–2013* (HC 547, 10 July 2013)
US Congressional Record-House, 11 June 2002, vol 148, part 7, 9905–9908
David Vincent, *The Culture of Secrecy: Britain 1832–1998* (Clarendon Publishing, 1999)
Peter Walker, 'Oftel's Five-Minute Guide to the History of Telecommunications Regulation in the UK', *Ofcom* <www.ofcom.org.uk/static/archive/oftel/publications/news/on61/5min0903.htm> accessed 26 October 2020

Robert Walker, 'The English Law of Privacy – An Evolving Human Right' (Speech by Supreme Court Justice Lord Walker of Gestingthorpe to Anglo-Australasian Lawyers Society at Owen Dixon Chambers, Melbourne, 25 August 2010) <www.supremecourt.uk/docs/speech_100825.pdf> accessed 23 October 2020

Nicholas John Wilkinson, *Secrecy and the Media: The Official History of the United Kingdom's D-Notice System* (Routledge, 2009)

4 Secretive partial statutory governance

Interception of communications, 1920–1984

Introduction

As regards the central thesis of this book, the UK was, by 1919, regulating postal services, wired and wireless telephony, and wired and wireless telegraphy. These constituted the field of communications technology at the time. Powers to access communications made using any of these forms of communications technology were overseen by Ministers. Entities with investigative functions remained able, with Ministerial permission, to access communications on any of these networks.

Telecommunications as intelligence

Alongside the technological advances ongoing in the theatre of communications in the early 20th century, there was a commensurate evolution in the production of intelligence for the state by the organizations now termed the United Kingdom Intelligence Community (UKIC).[1] Two of them, the Security Service (MI5) and the Secret Intelligence Service (SIS),[2] 'began operations in 1909 as a single organization, the Secret Service Bureau',[3] ostensibly to counter the perceived increasing external threat posed by agents and activities of imperial Germany. The third, and to this day most influential, of the services in terms of policy advocacy, the Government Code and Cipher School (GC&CS) (now GCHQ), commenced operations on 1 November 1919.[4] They are inextricably linked to the principal CSPs of the time.

1 The Security Service (MI5), the Secret Intelligence Service (SIS, formerly MI6), and Government Communications Headquarters (GCHQ). All three host websites outlining their respective roles and also providing a summarized history of their activities. See <www.mi5.gov.uk/>; <www.sis.gov.uk/>; and <www.gchq.gov.uk/Pages/homepage.aspx> respectively, accessed 26 October 2020.

2 Formerly MI6.

3 Christopher Andrew, *The Defence of the Realm: The Authorized History of MI5* (Penguin 2010) 3.

4 Richard Aldrich, *GCHQ The Uncensored Story of Britain's Most Secret Intelligence Agency* (Harper Press 2010) 15.

Aldrich describes how, by the time World War I ended, 'the means by which Britain collected its intelligence was changing…from overhearing military wireless messages…to undertaking more work on enciphered diplomatic telegrams sent by cable'.[5] Offering additional evidence of the already entrenched state/CSP cooperation and interception capability, he further refers to a 'private arrangement' whereby all the commercial cable companies secretly handed their traffic to GC&CS for copying'.[6] His next point is probably the most crucial for understanding how and why the controversial practice of 'bulk interception' as now undertaken by GCHQ with the agency of major CSPs, evolved to become regulated as it is within the IPA 2016.[7] He notes how:

> British dominance of international telecommunications networks meant that many of the world's messages travelled over British cables at some point. Private companies such as Standard Cable & Wireless Ltd were almost an integral part of the worldwide British SIGINT system…[a]…secret state-private network [that] remained hidden until exposed by journalist Chapman Pincher in 1967.[8]

Origin of 'bulk' interception: 'external communications'

What appears less well known in the available histories of communications investigation is that this 'private arrangement' actually was not really private at all. It has occasionally been posited that the Royal prerogative, 'quasi-legislation', or administrative regulation governed the interception of UK residents' telephone communications and that the Interception of Communications Act (IOCA) 1985 marked the first statutory regulation of the practice.[9] This is not strictly true. As will be shown, the IOCA 1985 was the first statute to regulate the interception of UK residents' *domestic* telecommunications; i.e. 'landline' telecommunications on public telecommunications systems that at no point left UK territory. This requires refinement, in that Aldrich's 'private arrangement' reflected the reality of statutory interception 'hidden in plain sight' in the Official Secrets Act (OSA) 1920, 'an Act to amend the Official Secrets Act 1911':[10]

> Where it appears to a Secretary of State that such a course is expedient in the public interest, he may, *by warrant under his hand*, require any person who owns or controls *any telegraphic cable or wire*, or *any apparatus for wireless*

5 ibid, 16.
6 Aldrich, *GCHQ* (n4), 17.
7 IPA 2016, Part 6 deals with bulk warrants. See generally Simon McKay, *Blackstone's Guide to the Investigatory Powers Act* (OUP, 2017) Chapter 7.
8 Aldrich, *GCHQ* (n4) 17. Pincher's famous expose is covered later in this chapter.
9 See, for example, Colin Turpin and Adam Tomkins, *British Government and the Constitution: Text and Materials* (7th edn, Cambridge University Press, 2012) 499.
10 Official Secrets Act 1920, Chapter 75 (10 & 11 Geo. 5), Preamble.

> *telegraphy*, used for the sending or receipt of telegrams to or from any place *out of the United Kingdom*, to produce to him, or to any person named in the warrant, the originals and transcripts, either of all telegrams, or of telegrams of any specified class or description, or of telegrams sent from or addressed to any specified person or place, sent or received to or from any place out of the United Kingdom by means of any such cable, wire, or apparatus, and all other papers relating to any such telegram as aforesaid.[11]

In providing assistance with interpretation, the section further provided that 'telegram' shall have the same meaning as that in the Telegraph Act 1869, and that the expression 'wireless telegraphy' shall have the same meaning as in the Wireless Telegraphy Act 1904'.[12] The former defined 'telegram' as 'any message or other communication transmitted or intended for transmission by a telegraph',[13] and defined 'telegraph' as: 'in addition to the meaning assigned to it in the Telegraph Act 1863,[14] to mean and include *any apparatus* for transmitting messages or other communications by means of electric signals'.[15] By virtue of the seminal decision of Justice Stephen and Brother Pollock in *Attorney-General v Edison Telephone Co*,[16] 'the telephone, even if it were not in a scientific sense a telegraph, was yet a telegraph within the definition of the Telegraph Act of 1863'.[17] Consequently, the power awarded to a Secretary of State to intercept *telegrams* included the power to secure the interception by a CSP of *telephone* communications. What was then clause 4 of a purportedly 'short and simple'[18] Official Secrets Bill quickly became, along with some of its other provisions, highly controversial. Sir Donald Maclean presciently spoke of the allocation of 'war powers in peacetime to destroy the liberties of the subject'.[19] The Attorney-General tried to assuage such concerns by stating that clause 4 was:

> not a power to stop telegrams…[but]…merely a power to compel the production of the originals and transcripts sent to, or received from, any place

11 ibid, s4(1), emphasis added. s4(2) provided heavy penalties for non-compliance.
12 ibid, s4(3).
13 Telegraph Act 1869, c73 (32 & 33 Victoria) s3.
14 Telegraph Act 1863, c112 (26 &27 *Victoriae*) defined 'telegraph' as 'a wire or wires used for the purpose of telegraphic communication, with any casing, coating, tube or pipe enclosing the same, and any apparatus connected therewith for the purpose of telegraphic communication'.
15 Telegraph Act 1869, s3.
16 *Attorney-General v Edison Telephone Co* (1880) 6 QBD 244.
17 Lawrence Lewis, John Houston Merrill, Adelbert Hamilton, William Mark McKinney, James Manford Kerr, John Crawford Thomson (eds) *American and English corporation cases, a collection of all corporation cases, both private and municipal (excepting railway cases), decided in the courts of last resort in the United States, England, and Canada 1883–1894, Vol 11* (2nd edn, Reinkl, 2015) 589.
18 Attorney-General Sir Gordon Hewart, HC Deb 2 December 1920, volume 135, col 1537.
19 HC Deb, 2 December 1920, volume 135, cols 1545 and 1546.

> out of the United Kingdom...the main purpose...[being]...to enable the authorities to detect and deal with attempts at spying by foreign agents.[20]

This supports the central thesis herein. The policy underpinning this stated purpose was that of ensuring that the state was empowered to access externally focused communications being made by every available medium at that point in time in the interests of national security.

The Attorney-General's statement either ignored or played down the practical effect on clause 4 of the decision in *Attorney-General v Edison* as regards the judicial interpretation of 'telegram'. It also represents the source of what would eventually become a controversial and problematic conceptual distinction between intra-UK (internal) and 'external communications'. Whilst the conceptual and practical distinction was easy to make in the early years of public telephone usage, it became more difficult to defend as mass usage of telephone service provision burgeoned in the latter 20th century. As will be shown, distinguishing external telecommunications meant that 'bulk interception' of them in the interests of collecting 'foreign' intelligence was more palatable and an easier 'sell' than avowing domestic interception. Indeed, in this modern era of routine global digital communication, it seems inconceivable that access to electronic communications for intelligence purposes might be regulated according to whether or not such communications leave the UK or not. It might be reasonably assumed that it is the content of the communication or data that is attached to it that would guide the nature of powers to access it, rather than the direction of travel it takes. However, the IPA 2016 still provides a regulatory distinction for 'overseas-related' communications in the context of bulk interception warrants.[21]

Despite the controversy surrounding it, clause 4 was enacted as originally drafted and ultimately remained in force until replaced by the IOCA 1985, s3(2), which largely replicated the former's provisions. In the parliamentary debate accompanying what was an equally controversial section, then Home Secretary Leon Brittan removed any residual doubt as to how successive governments had interpreted the OSA 1920, s4 when he advised that 'warrants under clause 3(2) will replace those issued under the Official Secrets Act 1920 for the interception of external *telecommunications*'.[22] From the little acorn of this innocuous provision, the oak tree of bulk interception eventually grew. The growth was undoubtedly influenced by the UKIC.

20 ibid, col 1539.

21 IPA 2016, s136(3) 'In this Chapter "overseas-related communications" means (a) communications sent by individuals who are outside the British Islands, or (b) communications received by individuals who are outside the British Islands'.

22 HC Deb, 12 March 1985, volume 75, col 161, further stating that external telecommunication interception powers been regularly exercised by Labour and Conservative governments since the OSA 1920 came into operation. The government believes, like their predecessors, that they should continue to be available.

Policy: distinguishing internal and external communications – the rationale

The OSA 1920 also required every person involved in the business of receiving for reward letters, telegrams, or other postal packets, to register with their local police chief, who would maintain a register of the names and addresses of such persons.[23] This assists in showing that the policy underpinning the enactment of the OSA 1920[24] reflects a genuine post WWI concern of the government of the day as regards 'the ingenuity of spies, and...the elaboration of the systems and the methods of spying'.[25] UK national security was of paramount concern. Any perusal of the separate histories of what is now the UKIC reveals a common theme in the early 1920s, wherein the majority of perceived threats to UK national security were external in nature.[26] This may go some way to explaining the policy decision to adopt explicit statutory powers to intercept *external* communications and demonstrate strength in the face of threatened adversity whilst keeping the less palatable and distasteful practice of intercepting UK residents' domestic communications away from the statute book and therefore away from independent or public scrutiny as to their scope, extent of usage and oversight. Furthermore, as a consequence of the UK's dominance of international telecommunications referred to earlier, it was technically much easier to physically separate (and thus obtain the communications content) of 'external' telephone communications from domestic calls at what were then analogue UK telephone exchanges and switchboards. It appears that as a sovereign state pursuing a realist national security posture,[27] the UK legislature deliberately drafted its post-WWI statutory regulation of interception of communications to differentiate 'persons outside the British Islands'.[28] Having done so, regulation of intercepting UK residents' internal communications remained with the national CSP, namely the GPO.

BRUSA, UKUSA, and 'foreign' intelligence collection

The creation of a statutory definition of external telecommunications proved beneficial throughout the Second World War until the present-day. The 'British-U.S.

23 OSA 1920, s5(1).
24 See generally HC Deb, 2 December 1920, volume 135, cols 1537–1583
25 Attorney-General Sir Gordon Hewart, HC Deb, 2 December 1920, volume 135, col 1537
26 See for example Aldrich, *GCHQ* (n4) 15-21 reference the perceived threats from Bolshevik Russia and the Axis and Keith Jeffery, *MI6 The History of the Secret Intelligence Service 1909–1949* (Bloomsbury, 2010) 172–208.
27 Barbara von Tigerstrom, *Human Security and International Law: Prospects and Problems* (Routledge, 2007) 8–9 where she outlines the realist international relations conceptualisation of 'national security' as being chiefly concerned with defending the all-important sovereign state, defined by its military prowess against *external threats*.
28 OSA 1920, s4(1). See also the Intelligence Services Act (ISA) 1994, ss1 and 3, Regulation of Investigatory Powers Act (RIPA) 2000, s16 and the IPA 2016, s136.

Communication [*sic*] Intelligence Agreement' concluded on 5 March 1946 (BRUSA) marked the 'official' commencement of communications intelligence sharing between these two post-war allies.[29] As of that date, although codebreaking practices and intelligence sharing were taking place long prior to that,[30] both parties agreed to the largely unconditional 'exchange of the products of the following operations in relation to foreign communications'.[31] These included (and continue to include):

1 Collection of traffic;[32]
2 Acquisition of communication documents and equipment;[33]
3 Traffic analysis;[34]
4 Cryptanalysis;[35]
5 Decryption and translation;
6 Acquisition of information regarding communication organizations, practices, procedures, and equipment.[36]

'Foreign communications' were defined as:

> All communications of the government or of any military, air or naval force, faction, party, department, agency, or bureau of a foreign country, or of any person or persons acting or purporting to act therefor [*sic*] and shall include [***] communications of a foreign country which may contain information of a military, political or economic value.[37]

'Foreign country' meant 'any country, whether or not its government was recognized by the US or the British Empire, *excluding only the US, the British Commonwealth of Nations, and the British Empire*'.[38]

29 The United States National Security Agency (NSA) have declassified and released many formerly top-secret documents relating to this longstanding agreement, The BRUSA is available at <https://www.nsa.gov/Portals/70/documents/news-features/declassified-documents/ukusa/agreement_outline_5mar46.pdf> accessed 29 October 2020.
30 Gordon Corera, *Intercept: The Secret History of Computers and Spies* (Orion Publishing, 2015) 48–52.
31 BRUSA (29) paragraph 3.
32 Despite not stating 'all traffic', there appears no limitation to the amount of type of traffic to be collected.
33 'Communications data' and 'systems data' as set out in the IPA 2016 are thus not new phenomena.
34 Traffic data is thus not as recent a phenomenon as might be thought.
35 Bauer describes this as the discipline of deciphering a ciphertext without having access to the key text. See F Bauer, 'Cryptanalysis' in van Tilborg HCA (eds) *Encyclopedia of Cryptography and Security* (Springer, Boston, MA, 2005) 87.
36 ibid.
37 ibid.
38 ibid, emphasis added.

Despite being agreed almost 75 years ago, the products for exchange were already vast in their scale and thus in potential intelligence utility. It is also plain that despite the express categories of communication set out in the agreement, it would be necessary to monitor or screen *all* communications traffic entering or leaving the UK and US in order to establish whether or not they contained 'information of military, political or economic value'. The redaction suggests that declassifying words along the lines of 'all external' might still be too controversial, however it is suggested that such a phrase would make a logical fit.[39]

The NSA archives evidence a number of variations to the original BRUSA. It is now uncontroversial however that the 'Top Secret' UK-US Communications Intelligence Agreement (UKUSA Agreement) dated 10 May 1955[40] established the now avowed and ongoing communications intelligence (COMINT) sharing relationship between 'the US and UK as a whole' (i.e. their respective governments) as opposed to merely between their agencies.[41]

As regards the nature of products to be exchanged under the auspices of the UKUSA Agreement, these were a *verbatim* restatement of the BRUSA's third paragraph as previously outlined.[42] Despite being regularly referred to as a signals intelligence (SIGINT) sharing agreement, the 1955 text, in distinguishing COMINT[43] and electronic intelligence (ELINT)[44] as sub-categories of SIGINT,[45] expressly limits the cooperation to the field of COMINT.[46] That said, as the British legislature's definitions of 'communication' since 1984 have included

39 This is merely an educated guess, however all statutory regulation in the UK since the original Interception of Communications Act (IOCA) 1985 included a specific definition for 'external communications'. This aligns with the UKUSA Agreement 'foreign communications' definition and a clear need to monitor all traffic in order to find traffic of COMINT value.

40 The UK-US Communications Intelligence Agreement (UKUSA Agreement) is attached to the London Signals Intelligence Board (LSIB) Document 141/55 'Amendment No4 to the Appendices to the UKUSA Agreement' 10 May 1955 (UKUSA Agreement) available at <https://www.nsa.gov/Portals/70/documents/news-features/declassified-documents/ukusa/new_ukusa_agree_10may55.pdf> accessed 29 October 2020.

41 Document 141/55, para 4A(b).

42 UKUSA Agreement, paragraph 4.

43 ibid, Appendix A,

> All processes involved in, and intelligence information and technical material resulting from, the interception and study of (a) foreign communications passed by wire, radio and other electromagnetic means (except press, propaganda and public broadcasts) and (b) of selected foreign communications sent by non-electromagnetic means.

44 ibid, 'ELINT' is information obtained by intercepting and analyzing non-communications transmissions.

45 Document 141/55, para 4B(b). In Appendix A, 'SIGINT' is defined as 'both COMINT and ELINT'.

46 UKUSA Agreement, paragraph 2. It then states, 'However the exchange of such collateral material as is applicable for technical purposes and is not prejudicial to national interests will be effected between the National Communication Intelligence Agencies of both countries'.

'signals', this UKUSA Agreement limitation appears meaningless.[47] Canada, as a former British Dominion, was admitted to the Agreement in 1948, with Australia and New Zealand being accepted as full partners in 1956.[48]

At this point in history, the UK public had no clue as to the existence of a post-war SIGINT agreement or its implications. They had little idea of the scale of telegram interception that was expanding in line with increased usage of the telephone system and network. Interception of communications simply did not feature in parliamentary or public discourse. Despite what was now a significantly larger interception regime involving Home Secretarial warrants for domestic telephone-tapping and postal intercepts, and Foreign Secretarial/Defence Secretarial oversight of the external communications and military SIGINT obligations, nothing appears to have leaked into the public domain. Investigative journalism had not yet become the norm. As with the Mazzini affair, it would take a grave error on the part of a Home Secretary and a public controversy to reopen the discourse and force a review. Even then, UKUSA would not feature in the discussions.

The second interception scandal: the Marrinan Case

The assertion of the creation of a policy precedent in the 1844 Commons and Lords reports is supported by scrutiny of the protracted efforts some 112 years later to establish a firm legal basis for the interception of telephone communications. Space precludes a detailed description of the 'Marrinan Case'. It is sufficient for present purposes to state that, for the first time in the history of interception of communications, a UK Home Secretary (Gwilym Lloyd George) had seen fit to disclose transcripts of intercepted communications involving a subsequently disbarred and discredited barrister (Marrinan) to the Bar Council, who were investigating him regarding allegations of serious criminality published by Beaverbrook Newspapers.[49] Lloyd George's indiscretion brought interception of telephone communications back into the public domain and the government

47 IPA 2016, s261(2)(b) 'signals serving either for the impartation of anything between persons, between a person and a thing or between things or for the actuation or control of any apparatus'.

48 Corey Pfluke, 'A History of the Five Eyes Alliance: Possibility for Reform and Additions' (2019) 38 (4) *Journal of Comparative Strategy* 302.

49 J R Spencer, 'Telephone-Tap Evidence and Administrative Detention in the UK' in Marianne Wade and Almir Maljevic (eds) *A War on Terror? The European Stance on a New Threat; Changing Laws and Human Rights Implications* (Springer Publishing, 2010). The National Library of Wales holds 'letters and papers, 1956–61, pertaining to the libel action brought in 1957 by Patrick Marrinan, a barrister, against Gwilym Lloyd-George and Beaverbrook Newspapers Limited. They include transcripts of intercepted telephone conversations between Marrinan and a client, extracts from Hansard reports and newspaper cuttings relating to telephone tapping, a copy of the writ and statement of claim served by Marrinan, and a letter, 1961, to Gwilym Lloyd-George from Harold Macmillan. See <https://archives.library.wales/index.php/gwilym-lloyd-george-and-marrinan-case> accessed 20 September 2020.

of the day constituted and convened a Committee of Privy Counsellors chaired by Lord Birkett (the Birkett Committee) in response.

The Birkett Report: compounding the 112-year retention of secret executive power

Given the sizeable time period that had elapsed since Parliamentarians had last examined the issue, including two world wars, the creation of three intelligence agencies, the entry into a top-secret communications intelligence-sharing agreement, and significant advances in communications technology, it would have been reasonable to expect the Birkett Committee to produce a sizeable tome providing in-depth analysis of the prevailing interception regulatory framework and perhaps recommending change. Unfortunately, this was not the case. Much of the Birkett Committee Report simply replicated the precedent set in the 1844 Reports.[50] The first indication that their investigation would follow entrenched policy considerations appeared almost immediately. This was the opening blunt assertion that '[F]ollowing the example of the Secret Committee[s]...1844...we decided not to publish the evidence and so informed those who gave evidence before us'.[51] No reasoning behind this decision was provided. It is reasonable to assume, however, that the 1844 justification was equally applicable in 1957, namely that an *in camera* hearing would be most likely to ensure maximum disclosure. The Committee also confined its inquiry to the previous 20 years, looking back no further than 1937. No reason was provided for this decision either, but it aligns with the introduction of Ministerial warrant-backed interception discussed shortly.[52]

The arrival of 'communications' in the discourse

The 1844 approach involving a detailed search for credible origins of the power to intercept communications was revisited in the Birkett Report.[53] Interestingly, it marks the first time that 'communications' as a definitive descriptive term is explicitly used in a publication scrutinizing a Secretary of State's powers in this area. Descriptively speaking, the term is obviously broader than terms used hitherto; namely 'telegraph', 'telegram', or 'message'. Its introduction subtly introduces to the report's readership the factual reality of the view of successive governments that, rather than possessing *specific* powers to intercept specific *types* of communication (such as telegrams etc.), successive Secretaries of State felt empowered to intercept *all* types of communications, whether or not there existed explicit statutory provision.

50 Home Office, *Report of the Committee of Privy Councillors Appointed to Inquire into the Interception of Communications* (Cmnd 283, 1957) (*Birkett Report 1957*).

51 ibid, paragraph 7.

52 ibid, paragraph 5: 'This period covers pre-war and post-war practice and the practice under both the Administrations that have held office since the war'.

53 ibid, paragraphs 9–51.

Maintaining precedent: the search for a clear legal basis for domestic interception

The Reports of 1844 had explicitly dealt only with the opening of letters (the only form of communications susceptible to practical interception then in existence). Despite the subtle adoption of the term 'communications' into their analysis, it appears that the Birkett Committee knew they might be on flimsy legal ground as regards the absorption of a power to intercept *telephone* communications *made in the UK* into a statutory legal framework that had hitherto expressly regulated only the postal service and the interception of 'telegrams'.[54]

The Committee correctly noted that there had never been a judicial pronouncement on the source of the power,[55] a matter which should have perhaps been of greater concern for a nation that relies (in consequence of an unwritten constitution) on judicial checks and balances to Parliament's actions. The Committee examined three principal viewpoints regarding the source. The first was 'that the power of the Secretary of State to issue his warrant for the interception and opening of letters was in exercise of a prerogative right of the Crown'.[56] The second, alternative view, was that the origin of the Secretary of State's power to intercept communications 'lay in a common law right which was not a part of the Prerogative',[57] and the third stated,

> that from the earliest times the power to intercept and open letters had been in existence. Throughout many centuries the practice had continued. How it arose can only be conjectured because historical records are wanting, but that the power existed and was used permits of no doubt whatsoever.[58]

In fairness to the Birkett Committee, these three viewpoints were investigated in some depth. Having done so however, they stated firstly,

> The power to intercept letters and postal packets and to disclose their contents and otherwise to make use of them had been used and frequently used through many centuries…such a power existed and was exercised widely and publicly known as the debates in the House of Commons and the House of Lords plainly showed…at no time had it been suggested with any authority that the exercise of the power was unlawful.[59]

One hundred and seventeen years after the Secret Committee Reports, and after similarly protracted deliberations, the Birkett Report had contrived to reach

54 Official Secrets Act 1920, s4.
55 *Birkett Report 1957* (n50) para 10.
56 ibid, para 19.
57 ibid, para 27.
58 ibid, para 30.
59 ibid, para 39.

virtually identical findings in respect of the opening of mail. Having done so, they acknowledged, however, that their principal *raison d'etre* was the Marrinan-related 'controversy...concerned with the interception of telephone messages'.[60] They observed that, between 1879 (when the first telephone exchange became operational in the UK)[61] and a 1937 meeting between the Postmaster General and the then Home Secretary,[62] the GPO (then still the only provider of what we would now understand to be a telecommunications service) had:

> acted upon the view that the power, which the Crown exercised in intercepting telephone messages, was a power possessed by any other operator of telephones and not contrary to law. *No warrants by the Secretary of State were therefore issued*, and any arrangements for the interception of telephone conversations were made directly between *the Security Service* or the Police Authorities and the *Director General of the Post Office.*[63]

The introduction of Ministerial warrants for domestic interception

This is a questionable view for the Postmaster-General (head of a government department) to have reached. There were no 'other operators of telephones' in the UK between 1879 and 1937 as a consequence of the GPO's nationalization in 1911. It seems clear from the record a very settled and comfortable cooperative relationship existed between the intelligence services, law enforcement, and the UK's principal service provider. The Birkett Report records that, following the Home Secretary and Postmaster-General's review, it was decided that

> *as a matter of policy*...it was undesirable that records of telephone conversations should be made by Post Office servants and disclosed to the Police or to the Security Service without the authority of the Secretary of State... the Home Office was of [the] opinion that the power on which they had acted to intercept letters and *telegrams* on the authority of a warrant issued by the Secretary of State, *was wide enough in its nature to include the interception of telephone messages also...it has since been the practice of the Post Office to intercept telephone conversations only on the express warrant of the Secretary of State.* that is, upon the authority which had already been recognised in the statutes to which we have referred dealing with letters and telegrams.[64]

60 ibid, para 40.
61 ibid, para 46.
62 The Birkett Report does not state which of the two Home Secretaries that served in 1937 were at the review. Sir John Simon (Liberal National) served as Home Secretary between 7 June 1935 and 28 May 1937, succeeded by Sir Samuel Hoare until 3 September 1939.
63 *Birkett Report* 1957 (n50) para 40, emphasis added.
64 ibid, para 41, emphasis added.

Maintaining precedent: continuing secrecy

The reference to telegrams is interesting, because nowhere else in the Birkett Report is express or implicit mention made of the Secretary of State's existing powers to secure the interception of *external* communications (telegrams) under the OSA 1920.[65] The existence of this power would have been easily locatable to anyone undertaking even cursory parliamentary research and was publicly available via Hansard since the OSA 1920s enactment on 23 December 1920. Given the apparent diligence of the search for a power to intercept telephone communications as a whole, the only plausible explanation as to why this Committee of Privy Counsellors did not mention it was that it consciously decided not to publicize it. This is a firm example of the arbitrary maintenance of a culture and policy of executive secrecy whilst purporting to be transparently seeking the truth. The decision not to discuss the statutory power to intercept external communications also meant successfully avoiding potentially difficult questions as to the legitimacy or legality of non-statutory (administrative) regulation of domestic interception powers. It seems inconceivable, given the evidence placed before them and the experience of the witnesses attending, that the Committee would have been unaware of the state's exercise of this power.[66] The Committee, despite considering the decision in *Attorney-General v Edison*, rejected the idea that, by virtue of that decision, the Telegraph Act 1868, s20 left it

> open to the Postmaster-General to instruct Post Office officials and those acting on his behalf to listen in, to record and disclose telephone conversations, just as he had the power to intercept, disclose and make known the contents of a telegram.[67]

They expressed unhappiness that such an important power should rest on those grounds.[68] Given the parallel (but unmentioned) extrapolation of a power to intercept external telephone communications from the power to require the production of telegrams and transcripts facilitated by a broad construction of the OSA 1920, s4, this is a strange decision. Instead, they reached a significantly more opaque conclusion by a different route, preferring instead the idea that the power to intercept telephone communications rested 'upon the power plainly recognized by the Post Office statutes as existing before the enactment of the statutes, by whatever name the power is described'.[69] This appears to have been

65 OSA 1920, s4(1).

66 *Birkett Report* 1957 (n50) para 3. The Committee heard evidence from all Home Secretaries since 1939, the Permanent Under-Secretary of State at the Home Office, and those in charge of those authorities that use interception of communications as part of their work.

67 ibid, para 48.

68 ibid, para 50.

69 ibid.

because the relevant Post Office statutory provisions as drafted in 1953 possessed longer lineage, being traceable to at least 1710.[70] The Post Office Act 1953[71] provided that:

> [A]ny officer of the Post Office who, contrary to his duty, opens, or procures or suffers to be opened, any postal packet in course of transmission by post, or wilfully detains or delays, or procures or suffers to be detained or delayed, any such postal packet, he shall be guilty of a misdemeanour...Provided that nothing in this section shall extend...to the opening, detaining or delaying of a postal packet under the authority of this Act *or in obedience to an express warrant in writing under the hand of a Secretary of State.*[72]

This was read alongside its interpretative provisions, wherein 'postal packet' included, *inter alia*, a telegram.[73] The Committee then took the interpretation of 'telegram' to include a 'telegraphic message' as found in the Telegraph Act 1869, section 3.[74] Somewhat strangely, though, they did not take the next logical step and use the *Attorney-General v Edison* decision to legitimize the interception of telecommunications.

As such, the Home Secretary's 'administrative fiat' of 1937 was upheld 20 years later by the Birkett Committee.[75] This assumption of power at least matches Home Secretary Graham's assumption of wider powers of interception before Parliament in 1845 in terms of its brazenness. It was undertaken without any parliamentary debate or scrutiny at all and appears never to have been tested by the courts of that time. From 1937 until Birkett (1957), the operational practices surrounding the interception of domestic telephone communications replicated that which would ultimately be enshrined in the IOCA 1985, RIPA 2000, and now the IPA 2016. This was that such interception would be unlawful if not authorized by a Secretary of State's warrant.

70 ibid, para 35:

> Section 58 of the Act of 1953 reproduces section 56 of the Post Office Act 1908 which reproduces section 25 of the Post Office (Offences) Act 1837, which in return re-enacted without material amendment section 40 of the Post Office (Revenue) Act of 1710.

The Committee was slightly erroneous here as it was section 41 of the 1710 Act that set out the offence described.

71 Post Office Act 1953 c36, 1&2 Eliz 2.

72 ibid, s58(1), emphasis added.

73 ibid, s87.

74 *Birkett Report 1957* (n50) para 37.

75 David Barnum, 'Judicial Oversight of Interception of Communications in the United Kingdom: An Historical and Comparative Analysis' (2016) 44(2) *Georgia Journal of International and Comparative Law* 237, 261.

The first 'written conditions' for issue of Ministerial interception warrants

The Committee observed that principles on which the Home Office would grant applications for the 'inherently objectionable' practice governed by interception warrants were first issued in writing by way of letters 'in similar terms sent to the Metropolitan Police and Customs' in September 1951.[76] The following conditions had to be satisfied:

(a) The offence must be really serious.[77]
(b) Normal methods of investigation must have been tried and failed, or must from the nature of things, be unlikely to succeed if tried.
(c) There must be good reason to think that an interception would result in a conviction.[78]

1951–present day: interception warrants for 'preventing or detecting serious crime'

The reference to, and definition of, 'really serious' offending set the tone for the issue of interception warrants on grounds of 'preventing and detecting serious crime' provided for to this day in the IPA 2016,[79] which similarly defines 'serious crime' as

> crime where – (a) the offence, or one of the offences, which is or would be constituted by the conduct concerned is an offence for which a person who has reached the age of 18 (or, in relation to Scotland or Northern Ireland, 21) and has no previous convictions could reasonably be expected to be sentenced to imprisonment for a term of 3 years or more, or (b) the conduct involves the use of violence, results in substantial financial gain or is conduct by a large number of persons in pursuit of a common purpose.[80]

1951–present day: interception warrants for 'protecting the UK's economic wellbeing'

As regards what is now Her Majesty's Revenue and Customs (HMRC), the granting of interception warrants was to be limited to those in cases involving 'a substantial and continuing fraud which would seriously damage the revenue or

76 *Birkett Report 1957* (n50) para 64.
77 ibid, para 65: 'serious crime' meant offences 'for which a man with no previous record could reasonably be expected to be sentenced to three years' imprisonment, or offences of lesser gravity in which a large number of people were involved'.
78 ibid.
79 IPA 2016, s20(2)(b).
80 ibid, s263(1).

the economy of the country if it went unchecked'.[81] This also sets the tone for the IPA 2016 ground for interception 'in the interests of the economic well-being of the United Kingdom so far as those interests are also relevant to the interests of national security'.[82]

1951–present day: interception warrants 'in the interests of national security'

Although traceable in statute as far back as Cromwell's Postage Act of 1657 for mail, and to the Official Secrets Act 1920 for external telecommunications, there appears to have been no written guidance to the Security Service (MI5) in terms similar to that issued to the Metropolitan Police and HMRC for *national* telecommunications. As a consequence of what must have been a deliberate policy to maintain secrecy, the Birkett Committee observed, after hearing secret evidence, that as regards domestic telephone interceptions by or on behalf of MI5,

> The Home Office considers each case. The principles governing the issue of warrants…can be stated in these terms:
>
> (a) There must be a major subversive or espionage activity that is likely to injure the *national interest.*
> (b) The material likely to be obtained by interception must be of diced [*sic*] use in compiling the information that is necessary to the Security Service in carrying out the tasks laid upon it by the State.[83]

The reference to injury to the 'national interest' equates directly to the IPA 2016 ground for issue 'in the interests of national security'.[84] All three grounds for issue of *domestic* interception warrants in 1951 therefore relate directly to those some 70 years later in the IPA 2016. Their issue was unaccompanied by any form of independent oversight, and without the Marrinan affair surfacing it can only be guessed at as to when the matter would have come under parliamentary scrutiny. Having failed to either mention or consider the existing statutory powers to intercept external telecommunications and thus maintaining the distinction between national and international telecommunications interception regulation, the Birkett Committee's ultimate position was that:

1 The power to intercept letters has been exercised from the earliest times, and has been recognized in successive Acts of Parliament;
2 This power extends to telegrams;

81 *Birkett Report 1957* (n50) para 66.
82 IPA 2016, s20(2) (c).
83 Birkett Report 1957 (n50) para 67 'diced use' appears a typographical error and means 'direct use'.
84 IPA 2016, s20(2) (a).

3 It is difficult to resist the view that if there is a lawful power to intercept communications in the form of letters and telegrams, then it is wide enough to cover telephone communications as well.[85]

Their view that it was difficult to resist the addition of a power to intercept telephone communications was not adequately explained. The next paragraph acknowledges the inherent weakness in their argument by conceding that

> if it should be thought that the power to intercept telephone messages was left in an uncertain state that was undesirable, it would be for Parliament to consider what steps ought to be taken to remove all uncertainty if the practice is to continue...so far as letters and telegrams are concerned...the Post Office Act 1953 appear[s] to have worked...without difficulty...a suitable amendment to [it] would remove doubts.[86]

History now records that no such amendments were ever implemented. As in 1844, the public disquiet over the state's interception regime receded and the Home Secretary's administration of domestic interception carried on, regulated only by the letters sent to the Metropolitan Police and HMRC and by unwritten arrangements with MI5. Interestingly, there is no reference to the UK's other two intelligence services whatsoever in the Birkett Report. Despite there being no limitation to interceptions of national or domestic telecommunications in the terms of reference,[87] bringing external or foreign intercept into the public domain of the inquiry would have meant involving the Foreign Secretary, the Foreign and Commonwealth Office, and the uncomfortable proposition of trying to avoid referring to what were then top-secret UKUSA Agreement obligations to collect 'foreign communications'. Despite Appendix 2 to the Report carrying the *prima facie* transparent title 'Authorities That Intercepted *Communications* Between 1937 and 1956'[88] the failure to reference any foreign communications intelligence activity evidences the secretive and ultimately disingenuous governance of the era.

Maintaining precedent: assuaging public disquiet

The next sizeable part of the Birkett Report was devoted to highlighting the provisions of the prevailing Home Office guidelines on intercepting communications, which set out, for the benefit of a concerned populace, all the contingent 'safeguards' that accompanied the application, grant, cancellation, and supervision

85 *Birkett Report 1957* (n50) para 51.
86 ibid, para 52.
87 ibid, para 1: to consider and report upon the exercise by the Secretary of State of the executive power to intercept *communications.*
88 ibid, Appendix 2, emphasis added.

of interception warrants. These safeguards were found to be largely satisfactory.[89] This section of the Report follows the precedent set in the 1844 Reports, wherein significant effort is undertaken to ensure an anxious public (who have been reminded by a public scandal or media controversy that interception as a practice exists) that the state exercises the power with the greatest restraint and with honour and propriety. It unfortunately also reinforces the precedent set in 1844 wherein the opportunity afforded by a public scandal for proper public consultation and debate regarding interception powers was eschewed.

Was there a culture of executive deference to the UKIC?

Birkett's failure to fully engage with and publicize the scope and extent of powers to intercept the telephone communications of persons in the UK provides supporting evidence of adherence to a culture of secrecy. It also tends to reflect the existence of an entrenched culture of post-war deference on the part of successive UK governments to the UKIC as they were then constituted. The government–UKIC relationship had been critically examined before Birkett in the Findlater Report 1945.[90] Lomas notes that Findlater 'made recommendations about oversight of the [Secret] Service, its post-war remit and activities'. He further asserts that Findlater work was 'remarkably forward thinking in that it considered the protection of civil liberties' and 'included suggestions that MI5's archive should be regularly weeded of matter not necessary for the Service's investigative work', whilst most importantly perhaps, outlining 'the apolitical nature of its activities'.[91] Lomas convincingly argues that:

> claims that [Clement] Attlee was suspicious of MI5 are predicated upon popular views of Labour's relationship with Britain's intelligence agencies, a stance that has been increasingly questioned by archival research…Ministers…[were not only]…aware of MI5's value…[but] eager to use their information in 'Defence of the Realm'.[92]

Put another way, the culture of government deference to the post-war UKIC had infiltrated all political persuasions. The apolitical governance of MI5 also formed part of the subject-matter of the 1952 Maxwell-Fyfe Directive.[93] This

89 ibid, para 90.

90 National Archives, 'The Findlater Stewart Report and Prime Minister's Directive to the Director General of the Security Service (MI5)' *National Archives* <http://discovery.nationalarchives.gov.uk/details/r/C13430286> accessed 26 October 2020.

91 Daniel W B Lomas, '…*the Defence of the Realm and Nothing Else': Sir Findlater Stewart, Labour Ministers and the Security Service, Intelligence and National Security* (Routledge, 2014) 2.

92 Lomas (n91), 4.

93 The Directive is reproduced in full in Laurence Lustgarten & Ian Leigh, *In from the Cold: National Security and Parliamentary Democracy* (Clarendon Press, 1994) Appendix 1, 517.

six-paragraph paper rendered the Director-General of MI5 personally responsible to the Home Secretary. It also reaffirmed the 'well-established convention that ministers would not concern themselves with the details within particular MI5 cases, but would be furnished only with information deemed necessary when seeking guidance on any particular matter'.[94] Lomas points out that, in addition to the breadth of the discretion it conferred on MI5, the Directive, being administrative in nature and therefore subject to alteration without consulting Parliament, also contained no legal mechanisms to deal with complaints about abuses and violations of rights and there were no formal limits or controls.[95] In modern times, the notion of such unfettered discretion and absolute power on the part of a public authority responsible for national security might seem unthinkable. However, this regime actually remained in place until 1989.[96] The fact that this situation was allowed to happen, particularly in the face of further public disquiet, surely serves to reinforce the assertion of the existence of a culture of deference on the part of the government to the UKIC. It will be shown later in this chapter, however, that the UK's statutory interception of communications regimes that precede the IPA 2016, viewed holistically, actually continued to reflect the existence of analogous unbridled powers available to the Home and Foreign Secretaries.[97] Given the nature of the state's relationship with the security services as then existing, the Birkett Committee's publicized reassurances ring somewhat hollow. Their reapplication of the 1844 policy (wherein a largely secret investigative process, involving only those within a ring of secrecy, rubber-stamps the arbitrary exercise of unfettered, unaccountable state power) makes their failure to find fault or recommend the statutification of such powers unsurprising.

Justifying the continuing administrative governance of domestic interception

It is not clear whether deference to the UKIC constituted a sufficient reason for not moving to a system of statutory regulation of interception of domestic communications. There appears no evidence of the UKIC (in 1957) taking any particular policy position on what they felt to be the most effective governance model, or of any lobbying on their part for a particular regulatory framework. Of course if the suggestion of a culture of executive deference to the UKIC is accepted, it is quite likely that the Birkett Committee would not wish to 'rock the boat' of administrative governance, but instead only diplomatically suggest

94 Simon Chesterman, '"Ordinary Citizens" or a Licence to Kill? The Turn to Law in Regulating Britain's Intelligence Services' (2010–2011) *Buffalo Public Interest Law Journal* 5,6.

95 Lomas, '...the Defence of the Realm and Nothing Else' (n91) additionally citing Ian Leigh, 'Accountability of Security and Intelligence in the United Kingdom' in H Born, Loch K Johnson, and Ian Leigh (eds) *Who's Watching the Spies: Establishing Intelligence Service Accountability* (Potomac Books, 2005) 79–80.

96 The Security Service Act 1989 placed MI5's functions etc. in statute.

97 By this is meant RIPA Part 1, Chapter 1, the WTA 2006, and the TA 1984 powers.

a return to Parliament. It is possible to use the evidence that is available to posit other reasons why the post-Birkett regulation of interception did not change.

The devil in the definitions

For instance, and to be fair to the Committee, to recommend change would have meant introducing the matter to Parliament for a fresh debate. If the debate accompanying the path to enactment of the OSA 1920 provides a yardstick, the passage of a bill to place the interception of domestic telecommunications in statute would by no means have been trouble-free.[98] It would also have meant drafting definitions that might inadvertently restrict or limit the ability of the security services to apply for authorization to intercept communications, or the power of a Secretary of State to grant authorization in all circumstances.[99] Whilst potential definitional hurdles would of course turn out not to be insurmountable, the creation of a statute for the first time is probably more difficult than amending an existing one.

The avoidance of 'judgment'

Furthermore, eschewing legislation at this point kept any prospect of judicial interference in interception of communications in abeyance. Support for this proposition is assisted by the fact that until the 1979 proceedings in *Malone v Commissioner of the Metropolis*,[100] the very *fact* of interception of any person's communications in the UK by a public authority had never become readily apparent to any member of the UK public. As such, the state's power to intercept had never been challenged in court. The significant impact of such a challenge, and the judicial interference in the interception regime that it brought about, would not become manifest until the completion of the *Malone* litigation chain some three decades after Birkett. However, the consequences of the *Malone* proceedings – as now known – almost excuse the post-Birkett policy stance of maintaining almost total secrecy as regards the scope and extent of domestic and external interception, whilst publishing some internal administrative guidelines.

Policy: intercept product as intelligence, not evidence

Spencer notes that another consequence of Birkett was the further entrenchment of the convention that 'in the criminal justice context, intercepts should only ever

98 See HC Deb, 02 December 1920, vol 135, cols 1537–1583 for a heated debate.

99 Having been drafted in consequence of ECtHR compulsion, the IOCA 1985 quickly provided evidence as to the difficulties of maintaining a legal framework regulating the power to intercept communications in line with communications technology advances. Similar issues affected the drafting of RIPA 2000 and the IPA 2016.

100 *Malone v Commissioner of Police of the Metropolis (No2)* (1979), Ch 344.

be used for operational purposes, and that the resulting evidence should not be used in court'.[101] The reason the Home Office provided for this at the time was that criminals would be made aware of the existence of the practice, therefore undermining its utility.[102] Spencer's view of this argument is that:

> it has been repeatedly recycled in the 50 years that followed [Birkett]...At the time of the Birkett Report, a further reason might well have been an official fear that, if an attempt were made to use such evidence in court, this would lead to a legal challenge on the ground that it had been unlawfully obtained-and this challenge, if upheld, would have exposed the fact that there was no legal basis for interception as things stood.[103]

There is certainly merit in this analysis. Birkett's rubber-stamping of the interception *status quo* in 1957 demonstrated that successive Secretaries of State had been able to arbitrarily assume and maintain an administrative power to intercept the domestic communications of persons in the UK, and that no new statutory provision necessarily required to be made whenever a new technological means of communication came along. Whilst interception remained outside the statute book and occupying an area of secretive administrative quasi-legality, successive governments did not have to concern themselves with either regular reviews or ensuring the continual adaptation of regulation of interception by appropriate parliamentary procedures. The regime established and maintained by Findlater, Maxwell-Fyfe, and latterly endorsed by Birkett managed to keep interception powers (and the true scope extent of their use) secret for the time being. This was achieved by a combination of using Birkett's conclusions to shelve any notion of creating an appropriate statutory framework or to subject interception powers to judicial review. It was further achieved through Birkett's endorsement of the policy of excluding intercept evidence and indeed excluding the very fact of interception from domestic courts, a policy still maintained in the IPA 2016.[104]

Interception of domestic telecommunications: no offence

Birkett's conclusions set the context for British policy on interception that was to continue largely unchallenged until the early 1980s. The Committee's conclusions and recommendations included the entrenchment of the policy that 'in no circumstances should...[intercepted material]...be made available to any body or person outside the public service'.[105] There were also recommendations regarding

101 Spencer 'Telephone Tap Evidence' (n49) 378.
102 *Birkett Report 1957* (n50) para 152.
103 Spencer, 'Telephone-Tap Evidence' (n49) 379.
104 RIPA 2000, ss17, 18.
105 *Birkett Report 1957* (n50) para 154.

the validity, review, cancellation, and record-keeping of warrants.[106] The Report also recommended (and consequentially legitimized) the policy of not publishing full statistics as to the extent of interception.[107] Analogously to their rather weak referral to Parliament of the question of whether or not to legislate to empower interception,[108] the Committee observed that it was also a matter for Parliament 'to consider whether legislation should be introduced to make the unauthorized tapping of a telephone line an offence'.[109] The Committee appear to have weighed the Home Office evidence as regards the extent or potential for unauthorized telephone interception and found it wanting.[110] This would have aligned unauthorized telecommunications interception with its postal counterpart. Yet Kynaston records how, in the late 1950s, 'the end of hire purchase restrictions and reductions in purchase and income tax' meant that 'one in two homes owned a telephone'.[111] Although low statistics by today's standards, this level of subscription to what was still a public service would surely have been sufficient to justify criminalization of unauthorized interception. The three-paragraph discussion of the issue within the Report suggests that the perceived threat from unauthorized 'tapping' was not really taken seriously by government officials of the day.[112] The price for maintaining the *status quo* as regards interception of domestic telecommunications, therefore, was that (in the face of exponentially increasing telephone use) a statutory lacuna remained present, potentially allowing anyone with the relevant desire and expertise to interfere with telephone communications.

Conclusions on the Birkett Report: the dampest of damp squibs?

It is appreciated that a significant amount of space has been devoted to Birkett, and the context in which his Committee reviewed communications interception. However, this is because it represented a significant opportunity to afford statutory legality, or at least provide improved legal certainty, to the authorization of what was simply one, extensively undertaken investigative technique. The Birkett Committee singularly failed to do so. Although it is with hindsight viewed as 'the dampest of damp squibs',[113] it contains one final point of significant interest to this author that has received little coverage in any other academic writing examining the interception of communications in the UK. It reassumes significant

106 ibid, paras 159–163.
107 ibid, para 165.
108 ibid, para 52.
109 ibid, paras 131 and 167.
110 ibid, paras 129–131.
111 David Kynaston, *Modernity Britain: Opening the Box, 1957–1959* (Bloomsbury, 2013) 337.
112 *Birkett Report 1957* (n50) paras 129–131.
113 Spencer, 'Telephone-Tap Evidence' (n49) 378.

weight in light of the multiplicity of reviews of communications content access powers that took place post-2013.

Walker's dissent

The Birkett Committee's conclusions were not, in fact, unanimous. Of its three Privy Councillor signatories, Gordon Walker largely concurred with the findings but offered the following noteworthy (and prescient) reservations. He concluded firstly that 'the purposes for which warrants are issued should…be judged by new and stricter standards particularly in regard to the detection of crime'.[114] In the five paragraphs that followed he made extremely cogent arguments for effectively removing access to the power to intercept from the police and customs on the grounds of preventing or detecting serious crime (except in cases where there exists extreme or urgent reason).[115] He argued that such a move was, *inter alia*, 'in closer accord with…general ideas in [the UK] about the methods we permit the police to use'.[116] He further observed that 'a restriction on the purposes for which interception…is used in the detection of crime would be in accord with the general trend of policy since the war',[117] that 'public repugnance to interception…[had]…increased'[118] and that there was a potential consequent risk of weakening 'popular support and approval of methods used by the police'.[119]

If it is thought that it was the post-2013 reviews of the overall UK communications investigation regime were the first to offer novel critical thinking as regards who should be enabled to undertake covert access to communications in transit, he even more presciently argued that:

> A distinction must…be drawn between the interception of communications for the detection of crime and for security purposes. As my colleagues point out, 'even if some criminals do escape justice the injury to the State cannot compare with the kind of injury the Security Service seeks to prevent'. A far larger proportion of the information that the Security Service must discover is obtained by interception of communication than in the case of the Police or the Customs. A great deal of this vital information could be discovered by no other means. There cannot…be the same sharp restriction of the use of the interception of communications by the Security Service as I recommend in regard to…the detection of crime.[120]

114 *Birkett Report 1957* (n50) para 170.
115 ibid, para 174.
116 ibid, para 171.
117 ibid, para 173.
118 ibid, para 174.
119 ibid, para 172.
120 ibid, para 176.

Walker went on to recommend limiting the power to intercept communications even by the Security Service to 'direct counter-espionage and protection of high secrets of State'[121] and (of somewhat less relevance in modern times) 'the prevention of the employment of Fascists or Communists in connection with work, the nature of which is vital to the State'.[122] Whilst the roles of the UKIC and LEA's (particularly as regards the UK's approach to combating terrorism) have blurred somewhat in recent years,[123] Walker's idea that the communications access powers of the UKIS be regulated separately from other public authorities exercising investigative functions actually resurfaced in the findings of the UKPISC Privacy and Security Inquiry.[124]

Birkett's legacy

Similarly to the aftermath of the Mazzini scandal, the aftermath of the Marrinan affair, wherein the Birkett Report's limited recommendations were adopted, ensured that the interception of communications *status quo* in the UK remained largely unchanged for another lengthy period. Despite the continuation of a 117-year doctrine of 'managing down' public concerns about secret, unfettered, quasi-legal communications access undertaken by the state, a combination of events were going to ensure that these post-Birkett arrangements would not last.

The third interception scandal: 'cable vetting sensation'

Price describes how *The Daily Express* tabloid newspaper of 21 February 1967 carried the above headline and an accompanying report by defence correspondent Chapman Pincher that Harold Wilson's Labour government 'was able to spy on thousands of cables and telegrams sent abroad by ordinary citizens'.[125] The report, some 12 years after Birkett, highlighted the longstanding existence of the powers enacted in the OSA 1920, s4(1) already discussed, but which were 'hidden in plain sight' by virtue of opaque drafting. Wilson's

121 ibid, para 177.

122 ibid.

123 See the UK government's descriptions for national intelligence machinery: the central intelligence machinery based in the Cabinet Office; the UKIC; Defence Intelligence (DI), part of the Ministry of Defence (MOD); and the Joint Terrorism Analysis Centre (JTAC). Other parts of government also contribute to intelligence collection and/or analysis and assessment, e.g. the Serious Organised Crime Agency (SOCA), HMRC, and the Home Office Cabinet Office 'National Intelligence Machinery' 20 *GOV.UK*<www.gov.uk/government/uploads/system/uploads/attachment_data/file/61808/nim-november2010.pdf> accessed 9 September 2020.

124 UK Parliamentary Intelligence and Security Committee, *Privacy and Security: A Modern and Transparent Legal Framework* (HC 2014–15, 1075-I) 118, Recommendation XX.

125 Lance Price, *Where Power Lies: Prime Ministers v the Media* (Simon & Schuster Ltd, 2010) 183.

handling of the allegations probably gave them more publicity than they would otherwise have had, and in 1971, he described 'the D-Notice Affair', as it came to be known, as one of Labour's costliest mistakes.[126] The scandal surrounding it, and Wilson's allegations in Parliament that Pincher and his employer had breached two 'Defence Notices' prompted an investigation and subsequent confidential report. Creevy describes how the 'Radcliffe Report', compiled by the former Conservative Foreign Secretary, Selwyn Lloyd, former minister of Defence Emmanuel Shinwell, and the eminent jurist and authority on security matters Radcliffe, 'though couched in emollient language, represented nonetheless a repudiation of the government standpoint'.[127] It ultimately exonerated Pincher from any wrongdoing, thus invoking the wrath of Wilson.[128] Despite unusually finding against a prevailing government, the confidential report unsurprisingly brought about no changes to the UK's post-Birkett interception regulation regime. However, Pincher's reporting represented a prescient example of how increasingly courageous investigative journalism would begin to challenge the longstanding culture of secrecy and 'need to know'.

The fourth interception scandal: 'bugging and burgling across London'

Goodrich, writing in 1981, noted that 'it again required an outcry bordering on scandal before a recalcitrant government was prepared to re-examine the extent of, and regulations governing, telephone tapping'.[129] The outcry referred to was sparked by a number of revelations made in *The New Statesman* magazine by the ultimately very courageous investigative journalist Duncan Campbell. Campbell was one of three defendants in the now infamous 'ABC' Official Secrets trial in 1978, the collapse of which had caused no little embarrassment to the government and the UKIC at the time. His published allegations were unprecedented in their daring at that time and included, *inter alia*, the existence of a 'national telephone tapping centre' (now avowed as NTAC) located in Chelsea,[130] and 'evidence of snooping technologies employed by Britain's free-booting intelligence agencies: phone-taps, mail interception, elaborate bugging devices'.[131] These and many other

126 Matthew Creevy, 'A critical review of the Wilson Government's handling of the D-Notice Affair 1967' (1999) 14 (3) Journal of Intelligence and National Security 209.

127 ibid.

128 A detailed examination of Pincher's investigative journalism, general irritation to the Establishment, and the D Notice Affair is provided in Christopher R Moran, 'Never To Be Disclosed: Government Secrecy in Britain 1945–1975' (DPhil Thesis, University of Warwick, 2008) Chapter 3.

129 P Goodrich, 'Freedom of the Phone' (1981) 3(2) Liverpool Law Review 92.

130 Duncan Campbell, 'Big Buzby is Watching You' *The New Statesman* (1 February 1980) 158.

131 Duncan Campbell, Bruce Page, and Nick Manning, 'Destabilizing the Decent People', *New Statesman* (15 February 1980) 234.

exposes might well have been written off as little more than sensationalist journalism of the day, except for the fact that most of them turned out to be largely true.[132] Such was the furore generated this time around that the Right Honourable Bob Cryer MP raised a Private Members Bill in Parliament to try and have the matter debated.[133] He used parliamentary privilege to restate some of the allegations and emphasize the need for proper debate and the institution of some form of legal framework to regulate interception.[134] Private Bill 149 was repeatedly ordered for Second Reading on various dates throughout 1980 but was never enacted.

The Telecommunications Bill

Mr Cryer's name surfaces again in the context of interception, this time at the Second Reading of what on 29 November was a massive Telecommunications Bill purporting to regulate the denationalization of the state's telecommunications monopoly. This of course had significant implications for the British state's interception regime, both domestic and external. The very infrastructure by which all interceptions other than those conducted on wireless telegraphy under the Wireless Telegraphy Act 1949 was going to be transferred to a new Office of Telecommunications (OFTEL) whose Director-General would still be accountable to the Secretary of State. The privatization of a telecommunications behemoth valued at around £15 billion at that point was divisive and controversial. Implications for a longstanding national security policy of ensuring investigative access to all forms of communications technology then in existence played a distinct second fiddle to employment and cost implications. However, Mr Cryer appears to have been more observant than many:

> The Bill hands over *virtually unfettered powers to the Secretary of State*...because *British Telecom provides a telephone tapping service for the nation*...a massive operation is already carried out by BT, and the...[Post Office Engineers Union]...has expressed deep concern about it. It has published a document entitled 'Tapping the Telephone' and has made four proposals. It states that there must be legislation to provide an express legal authority for the official interception of communications. We accept the need for mail to be opened and telephones to be tapped on limited occasions by specified authorities... However, we believe that the present lack of an express legal provision for official interception which we have described is unacceptable in a democratic society...Second, there should be stricter criteria for the issue of warrants... Third, there needs to be an independent check upon the judgment of the Home Secretary in deciding upon applications for a warrant or alternatively,

132 See, in general, Duncan Campbell's website and archive <http://duncancampbell.org/content/phone-tapping> accessed 27 September 2020.

133 HC Deb, 20 February 1980, vol 979, cols 474–478.

134 ibid.

> the decisions should be taken elsewhere…Fourth, there should be annual published reports to Parliament detailing the number of interceptions authorised in the previous year and commenting on the effectiveness of the interceptions and any changes in policy or procedure. We believe that the present lack of any meaningful kind of political accountability for the interception of communications if fundamentally wrong and that the minimum requirement is that all MPs know the broad picture as it unfolds from year to year.
>
> Clause 49 wants some reading to be believed, because the Secretary of State can tell the new Director General, who will be a powerful man indeed: 'If it appears to the Secretary of State to be requisite or expedient to do so in the interests of national security or relations with a government' and so on, he can or cannot do 'a particular thing'. Clause 49(3) states: 'The Secretary of State shall lay before each House of Parliament a copy of every direction given under this section unless he' – the Secretary of State – is of opinion that disclosure of the direction is against the interests of national security or the commercial interests of any person. In other words, the Secretary of State decides in secret to give secret instructions to the Director General, who by virtue of clause 49(4) is not allowed to reveal those directions. This is a massive power to the Secretary of State, and on that ground alone the House would be right to reject such a handover of power.
>
> It means that a quasi-private enterprise organisation, which in due time the Secretary of State wishes more and more to hand over to private enterprise, will be operating in total secrecy without any accountability to the House of Commons. That is totally and utterly wrong in any sort of democracy.[135]

His remarks on interception and the view of the Labour Party are interesting, as they demonstrate a growing impetus for statutory regulation among government and opposition figures, supported by union members. In a clear sign of the prevailing culture of Ministerial secrecy at the time, Home Secretary Patrick Jenkin simply did not respond to Mr Cryer. Perhaps more surprisingly, no one else engaged with clause 49 at Second Reading. It would ultimately become section 94 of the TA 1984 without further meaningful debate or scrutiny in either House.

Detective Sergeant Ware: *Malone v UK* (1983) 5 EHRR 385

Goodrich also observes that 'as the wheels of state were grinding towards a most peremptory official discourse'[136] (in the form of a White Paper),[137] the interception of domestic telecommunications on behalf of the UK state was coming under

135 Bob Cryer, HC Deb, 29 November 1982, vol 33, cols 88–90.

136 Goodrich, 'Freedom of the Phone' (n129) 92.

137 Home Office, *The Interception of Communications in Great Britain* (Cmnd 7873, April 1980).

detailed scrutiny for the first time before the European Commission[138] (which would eventually refer its findings to the ECtHR).[139] The UK's accession to what is now the European Union (EU) in 1972 meant that willful blindness on the government's part to any adverse findings by Europe's top courts would not make tenable policy. As such, efforts to cover the field of communications technology with suitable investigatory powers were going to have to take account of European jurisprudence, despite tensions between those and the implementation of a domestic and UKUSA-focused interception regime. On 28 February 1979 in *Malone v Metropolitan Police Commissioner*,[140] Sir Robert Megarry issued a sizeable judgment which dismissed all the heads of the plaintiff's claim against the Metropolitan Police after it had been admitted, during the course of his trial for handling stolen goods, that at least one of his telephone conversations had been intercepted.[141] It appears the diligence of a certain Detective Sergeant Ware in completing his police officer's notebook brought about the grudging admission that interception under a Home Secretarial warrant had taken place. It is nothing short of astonishing that in pre-disclosure times a notebook entry detailing the fact of interception had actually been compiled. It was even more astonishing that it was disclosed to the court. Had it not been, the Malone litigation, which proceeded all the way to Strasbourg, might never have taken place. As a result of the truly excellent arguments of the time, submitted to Sir Robert by Colin Ross-Munro QC, the judge had felt it necessary to examine the potential impact of the European Convention on Human Rights (ECHR) and the then-West German seminal interception of communications case of *Klass v Germany*.[142] He split his consideration into two limbs. Firstly, he considered the ECHR itself, and 'the direct rights conferred' by it.[143] He determined (correctly at that time) that despite the UK having been a High Contracting Party to the ECHR (having ratified it on the 8 March 1951) and therefore having 'long been under an obligation to secure [the relevant Convention rights] to everyone...that [the] obligation [was] under a treaty...[and therefore]...not justiciable in the courts of this country'.[144] More tellingly, however, Sir Robert then turned to examine the *Klass* case, noting that the 'West German system that came under scrutiny in [it] was laid down by statute, and it contained a number of statutory safeguards'.[145]After outlining those, in a damning three-page critique of the prevailing UK position he found as follows:

> it is impossible to read the [*Klass* judgment] without it becoming abundantly clear that a system which has no legal safeguards whatever has small chance

138 *Malone v UK* (1983) 5 EHRR 385 (European Commission).
139 *Malone v UK* (1985) 7 EHRR 14.
140 *Malone* v *Commissioner of Police of the Metropolis (No2)* (n100).
141 ibid, (349).
142 *Klass and Others v Federal Republic of Germany* (1979–80) 2 EHRR 214.
143 *Malone v Commissioner of Police of the Metropolis (No2)* (n100) (378).
144 *Malone v Commissioner of Police of the Metropolis (No2)* (n100) (378).
145 ibid (379).

> of satisfying the requirements of [the European Court] whatever administrative provisions there may be...even if the system were to be considered adequate in its conditions, it is laid down merely as a matter of administrative procedure, so that it is unenforceable in law...in law any 'adequate and effective safeguards against abuse' are wanting. In this respect English law compares most unfavourably with West German law: this is not a subject on which it is possible to feel any pride in English law. I therefore find it impossible to see how English law could be said to satisfy the requirements of the Convention.[146]

There could be no wilful blindness to this. The writing was on the wall for the UK government's post-Birkett quasi-legal policy regulating the interception of domestic telecommunications. Long before the Human Rights Act (HRA) 1998 would give direct legal effect to the ECHR and to the interpretation of ECtHR jurisprudence,[147] the *Malone* legal proceedings were forming a growing cloud on a wilfully blind Conservative government's administrative regulatory horizon.

Pre-statutory White Papers

Prior to the final decision in the slow-moving Malone proceedings, Margaret Thatcher's administration published two White Papers in the space of one year (1981) on the subject. This was an indication (after two examinations of the subject in the preceding 140 years) that a *prima facie* more diligent scrutineering exercise was going to be required to assuage the concerns of the media, the public at large, and Parliamentarians such as Cryer. The first was an eight page paper simply entitled 'The Interception of Communications in Great Britain'.[148] This represented a clever move on the part of the Thatcher administration in that it quietly avoided including any discussion of the interception of communications in Northern Ireland. The province was of course at that time the theatre for an intelligence-led counterinsurgency being waged on many fronts, including 'listening devices, phone taps, hidden cameras, motion detectors, and technologies that intercepted communications traffic'.[149] The full extent of interception conduct undertaken in the Northern Ireland conflict has never been officially disclosed.

Maintaining precedent: retaining secrecy

This command paper's approach appears to have been identical in its policy objective to the 1844 and 1957 official reports. There was no mention of public

146 ibid (380).
147 HRA 1998, s2(1) (a).
148 Home Office, *The Interception of Communications in Great Britain* (Cmnd 7873).
149 Brian A Jackson, 'Counterinsurgency Intelligence in a "Long War": The British Experience in Northern Ireland' (2007) 87 (1) *Military Review*.

anxiety, the pending European decision in the *Malone* litigation, or the factual circumstances of that litigation. The paper merely reiterated the administrative procedures covered in Birkett. Goodrich concludes that

> were it not for the alarming nature of [the] extrinsic evidence...[i.e. the matters raised by the Right Honourable Bob Cryer, Duncan Campbell et al.'s *New Statesman* investigations and the ongoing *Malone* litigation]...the skilfully reassuring message sent would obviate any comment.[150]

Consequently, the 'paper exercise' of this White Paper achieved nothing and served no effective purpose. There is no evidence of any substantive change to the prevailing regulatory framework. However, its release was followed up by an announcement from that Lord Diplock was to be appointed as a Commissioner to oversee the use of interception in the UK and that he would report to the Prime Minister on a regular basis.

Maintaining the precedent: reassuring the public

Lord Diplock is perhaps best remembered for his successful contribution to Northern Ireland's criminal justice system (Diplock Courts) introduced in 1973 during the civil emergency (1969–1998), wherein suspected terrorism offenders were tried without a jury, with the aim of preventing intimidation of jurors and corrupt/sectarian bias in outcomes.[151] He published his first White Paper, the second on the subject of interception of that year, in March 1981.[152] Goodrich observes how this first-ever attempt at demonstrating some semblance of oversight or accountability in respect of interception matters simply restricted itself 'to examining case histories behind the applications for warrants', before superficially concluding that 'where...granted, the "public weal" had not been unduly disturbed'.[153] He further opines that both the 1981 White Papers adopted 'the format of a strident assertion of the stringency of the [administrative] regulations and the administrative care applied in the granting of warrants...to [which was] added an economic argument and...statistics on the success of tapping'.[154] Lord Diplock's approach regrettably once again replicated the policy reflected in all previous inquiries dating back to 1844, thus indicating little desire for meaningful change on the part of the state. Goodrich most tellingly notes that in both papers, 'the omission of any reference to possible legislative measures...

150 Goodrich, 'Freedom of the Phone' (n129) 92.

151 See generally Jean Jackson and Sean Doran, *Judge Without Jury: Diplock Trials in the Adversary System* (Clarendon Press 1996).

152 Right Honourable Lord Diplock, *The Interception of Communications in Great Britain* (Cmnd 8191, March 1981).

153 Goodrich, 'Freedom of the Phone' (n129) 95.

154 ibid.

[seemed]...to deny the legitimacy or relevance of opposing views'.[155] This left 'unofficial or unlawful tapping by government agencies...subject to administrative self-regulation at most'.[156] It appeared that despite all the then-existing external pressure on the government, statutory regulation of the interception of domestic telecommunications was no closer. It took the seminal ECtHR ruling in *Malone* three years later to finally force the UK government's hand in the matter.

Conclusion

This chapter examined the internationalization of secretive UK communications investigation governance. This saw the enactment of statutory governance of external telecommunications via the Official Secrets Act 1920, section 4, the continuation of statutory governance of wireless telegraphy,[157] and the continued administrative governance of postal communications and of the interception of intra-UK telecommunications. All known *forms* of communications technology (post, wired, and wireless) were subject to regulation and the state had powers rendering access to any communications sent or received by means of them in the interests of national security (broadly construed) lawful. None of these powers were subject to independent oversight, but remained overseen by the relevant Secretary of State. The next chapter explores the UK's first-ever statute purporting to regulate what was still the only known (or at least declared) investigatory power, enacted in response to the Malone decision, the Interception of Communications Act (IOCA) 1985. It would not become apparent until 2013, but this statute marked the commencement of what would be almost 30 years of arguably disingenuous statutory governance in this area of law. While readers are invited to draw their own conclusions, the evidence is tendered in the two chapters forming the next part.

References

Richard Aldrich, *GCHQ The Uncensored Story of Britain's Most Secret Intelligence Agency* (Harper Press, 2010)

Christopher Andrew, *The Defence of the Realm: The Authorized History of MI5* (Penguin, 2010)

David Barnum, 'Judicial Oversight of Interception of Communications in the United Kingdom: An Historical and Comparative Analysis' (2016) 44(2) *Georgia Journal of International and Comparative Law* 237

F Bauer, 'Cryptanalysis' in van Tilborg HCA (eds) *Encyclopedia of Cryptography and Security* (Springer, Boston, MA, 2005)

155 ibid.

156 ibid, 96.

157 Wireless Telegraphy Act 1904 and 1949.

Cabinet Office 'National Intelligence Machinery' 20 *GOV.UK* <www.gov.uk/government/uploads/system/uploads/attachment_data/file/61808/nim-november2010.pdf> accessed 9 September 2020

Duncan Campbell, Website <http://duncancampbell.org/content/phone-tapping> accessed 27 September 2020

Duncan Campbell, 'Big Buzby is Watching You' *New Statesman* (1 February 1980) 158

Duncan Campbell, Bruce Page and Nick Manning, 'Destabilizing the Decent People' *New Statesman* (15 February 1980) 234

Simon Chesterman, '"Ordinary Citizens" or a Licence to Kill? The Turn to Law in regulating Britain's Intelligence Services' (2010–11) *Buffalo Public Interest Law Journal* 5

Matthew Creevy, 'A Critical Review of the Wilson Government's Handling of the D-Notice Affair 1967' (1999) 14(3) *Journal of Intelligence and National Security* 209

Right Honourable Lord Diplock, *The Interception of Communications in Great Britain* (Cmnd 8191, March 1981)

P Goodrich, 'Freedom of the Phone' (1981) 3(2) *Liverpool Law Review* 92

Home Office, *Report of the Committee of Privy Councillors Appointed to Inquire Into the Interception of Communications* (Cmnd 283, 1957)

Home Office, *The Interception of Communications in Great Britain* (Cmnd 7873, April 1980)

Brian A Jackson, 'Counterinsurgency Intelligence in a "Long War": The British Experience in Northern Ireland' (2007) 87(1) *Military Review*

Jean Jackson and Sean Doran, *Judge Without Jury: Diplock Trials in the Adversary System* (Clarendon Press, 1996)

Keith Jeffery, *MI6 The History of the Secret Intelligence Service 1909–1949* (Bloomsbury, 2010)

David Kynaston, *Modernity Britain: Opening the Box, 1957–1959* (Bloomsbury, 2013)

Ian Leigh, 'Accountability of Security and Intelligence in the United Kingdom' in H Born, Loch K. Johnson & Ian Leigh (eds) *Who's Watching the Spies: Establishing Intelligence Service Accountability* (Potomac Books, 2005)

Lawrence Lewis, John Houston Merrill, Adelbert Hamilton, William Mark McKinney, James Manford Kerr, John Crawford Thomson (eds) *American and English Corporation Cases, a Collection of All Corporation Cases, Both Private and Municipal (Excepting Railway Cases), Decided in the Courts of Last Resort in the United States, England, and Canada 1883–1894* (Vol. 11, 2nd edn, Reinkl, 2015)

Daniel W B Lomas, *'...The Defence of the Realm and Nothing Else': Sir Findlater Stewart, Labour Ministers and the Security Service, Intelligence and National Security* (Routledge, 2014)

Simon McKay, *Blackstone's Guide to the Investigatory Powers Act* (OUP, 2017)

Christopher R Moran, 'Never To Be Disclosed: Government Secrecy in Britain 1945–1975' (DPhil Thesis, University of Warwick, 2008)

National Archives, 'The Findlater Stewart Report and Prime Minister's Directive to the Director General of the Security Service (MI5)' *National Archives* <http://discovery.nationalarchives.gov.uk/details/r/C13430286> accessed 26 October 2020

Corey Pfluke, 'A History of the Five Eyes Alliance: Possibility for Reform and Additions' (2019) 38(4) *Journal of Comparative Strategy* 302

Lance Price, *Where Power Lies: Prime Ministers v the Media* (Simon & Schuster Ltd, 2010)

J R Spencer, 'Telephone-Tap Evidence and Administrative Detention in the UK' in Marianne Wade and Almir Maljevic (eds) *A War on Terror? The European Stance on a New Threat; Changing Laws and Human Rights Implications* (Springer Publishing, 2010).

The Directive is reproduced in full in Laurence Lustgarten & Ian Leigh, *In from the Cold: National Security and Parliamentary Democracy* (Clarendon Press, 1994)

Barbara von Tigerstrom, *Human Security and International Law: Prospects and Problems* (Routledge, 2007)

Colin Turpin and Adam Tomkins, *British Government and the Constitution: Text and Materials* (7th edn, Cambridge University Press, 2012)

UK Parliamentary Intelligence and Security Committee, *Privacy and Security: A Modern and Transparent Legal Framework* (HC 2014–15, 1075–I)

'UKUSA Agreement' 10 May 1955 UKUSA Agreement <https://www.nsa.gov/Portals/70/documents/news-features/declassified-documents/ukusa/new:ukusa_agree_10may55.pdf> accessed 29 October 2020

Part III

Disingenuous statutory governance

1984–2015

5 Disingenuous statutory regulation

Interception of communications, 1984–1999

Introduction

This chapter is the first of four examining the regulation of communications and data investigative powers in an era of arguably 'disingenuous' statutory governance that would endure from 1984 until the 2013 Intelligence Shock. It begins with the enactment of the Telecommunications Act (TA) 1984, which purported to provide for the de-monopolization of the UK's state-owned public telecommunication system, but which also in fact contained significant and secretly exercisable Ministerial powers 'hidden in plain sight' within its many provisions. The practical effect of the use of these powers would remain secret, despite hints as to their purposes, until 'avowal' some 31 years later.[1] The chapter will show how the TA's telecommunications definitions would underpin the first statute in British history regulating the interception of UK residents' national or domestic telecommunications on public telecommunications systems, the Interception of Communications (IOCA) 1985. The chapter also examines the factors that contributed to the UK being 'forced' to enact the IOCA 1985, principally the legal challenge to the interception of antique dealer James Malone's domestic telephone calls. The chapter also contextualizes the enactment of the IOCA 1985 and examines its place within the context wherein the UK government had to ensure the continuing implementation of the UK's broader UKUSA Agreement obligations. As regards the central thesis of this work as outlined in Chapter 1,[2] the introduction of statutory governance of intra-UK telecommunications did not alter the underlying policy of 'covering the communications technology field' as regards enabling powers, but policymakers appear to have recognized that in order to make regulation palatable to the UK public, a regime of independent oversight of investigatory powers would require to be established. Consequently, this chapter also covers the introduction of an Interception of Communications

1 In the initial Home Office, Draft Investigatory Powers Bill (Cm9152, November 2015) 20.
2 That the IPA 2016 represents the most recent restatement 700 years of formerly more secretive British state powers assumed or granted in the interests of national security (broadly construed), whereby access to communications and data, however transmitted or stored, is made lawful.

Tribunal (IOCT) and Interception of Communications Commissioner (IOCC), the forerunners to what is now the Investigatory Powers Tribunal (IPT) and the Investigatory Powers Commissioner's Office (IPCO). It also examines the 'statutification' of the UK's civilian-focused intelligence services that occurred in the 1990s. The broad information acquisition powers afforded to what is now the UKIC (UK Intelligence Community) complemented the interception powers in the IOCA 1985. The Commissioners and Tribunals established under the Security Service Act (SSA) 1989 and Intelligence Services Act (ISA) 1994 are also examined. The chapter concludes at the point in history where the UK was reviewing the scope of the IOCA 1985 regime in light of the challenges brought by Assistant Chief Constable Alison Halford and broader challenges to other surveillance regimes still under administrative governance in 1999, while the Regulation of Investigatory Powers Act (RIPA) 2000 was being contemplated. This is because RIPA was going to regulate more than simply the single power to intercept communications.

Interception of communications consultation period

In February 1985, Margaret Thatcher's Conservative government produced a third, characteristically terse and succinct White Paper, this time more precisely entitled 'The Interception of Communications in the United Kingdom'.[3] After once again outlining the legitimacy of the existing arrangements governing interception,[4] it was expressly conceded that the 'European Court of Human Rights...judgment in August 1984 in the *Malone* case...concluded...that the law did not indicate with reasonable clarity the scope and manner of exercise of discretion conferred on the public authorities'.[5] The stated aim in introducing legislation was 'to provide a clear statutory framework within which the interception of communications on public systems will be authorized and controlled in a manner commanding public confidence'.[6] Abandoning longstanding executive precedent, the White Paper 'exceptionally'[7] published limited statistics on interception, citing 'powerful arguments against regular disclosure',[8] and justifying the exclusion of statistics relating to Northern Ireland on 'public interest' grounds.[9] This reflects the assumption in Graham's period as Home Secretary that the public interest was a relevant consideration in interception governance. In a welcome development that would become common practice, the Command Paper included the draft provisions of the proposed Interception of Communications

3 Home Office, *The Interception of Communications in the United Kingdom* (Cmnd 9438, February 1985).
4 ibid, para 5.
5 ibid, para 6.
6 ibid, para 7.
7 ibid, para 11.
8 ibid.
9 ibid.

Act (IOCA) 1985 as regards the grounds on which warrants authorizing interception could be sought,[10] as well as the application, duration, revocation, cancellation, and record-keeping procedures to be followed in relation to them.[11]

Telecommunications Act 1984: unfettered Ministerial power

The Telecommunications Bill discussed in the previous chapter received Royal Assent on 12 April 1984. Its lengthy Preamble made no reference to the existence or retention of *any* communications-related investigatory powers.[12] As regards the central thesis of this book, section 94 marked a breathtakingly broad assurance of continuing state power in the field of communications and data investigation. Section 94 entered force on 5 August 1984.[13] There can be little doubt that in denationalizing the sole instrument facilitating not only all of the nation's telephone calls, but also the massive interception operation alleged by Cryer, there would have significant trepidation within the executive about ceding control. The principal way to ameliorate this was to ensure that the Director of the new entity understood from the outset that, as regards national security matters (including interception), Ministers remained in charge. That said, the unfettered discretion retained by the government, thus ensuring the continuation of the ability, if required, to enable investigative access to *any* communications or data traversing the newly privatized network, was breathtaking in scope and merits restatement in full;

> The Secretary of State may, after consultation with a person to whom this section applies,[14] give to that person such directions of a general character as

10 ibid.

11 ibid.

12 'An Act to provide for the appointment and functions of a Director-General of Telecommunications; to abolish British Telecommunications' exclusive privilege with respect to telecommunications and to make new provision with respect to the provision of telecommunication services and certain related services; to make provision, in substitution for the Telegraph Acts 1863 to 1916 and Part IV of the Post Office Act 1969, for the matters there dealt with and related matters; to provide for the vesting of property, rights and liabilities of British Telecommunications in a company nominated by the Secretary of State and the subsequent dissolution of British Telecommunications; to make provision with respect to the finances of that company; to amend the Wireless Telegraphy Acts 1949 to 1967, to make further provision for facilitating enforcement of those Acts and otherwise to make provision with respect to wireless telegraphy apparatus and certain related apparatus; to give statutory authority for the payment out of money provided by Parliament of expenses incurred by the Secretary of State in providing a radio interference service; to increase the maximum number of members of British Telecommunications pending its dissolution; and for connected purposes'.

13 Telecommunications Act 1984 (Appointed Day) (No. 2) Order SI 1984/876.

14 ibid, s94(8). This section applies to the Director and to 'any person who is a public telecommunications operator or approved contractor' (whether in his capacity as such or otherwise); and in this subsection 'approved contractor' means a person approved under section 20 above, emphasis added.

> appear to the Secretary of State to be *requisite or expedient* in the interests of national security or relations with the government of a country or territory outside the United Kingdom.[15]
>
> If it appears to the Secretary of State to be *requisite or expedient* to do so in the interests of national security or relations with the government of a country or territory outside the United Kingdom, he may, after consultation with a person to whom this section applies, give to that person a direction requiring him (according to the circumstances of the case) to do, or not to do, a particular thing specified in the direction.[16]
>
> A person to whom this section applies shall give effect to any direction given to him by the Secretary of State under this section notwithstanding any other duty imposed on him by or under this Act.[17]
>
> The Secretary of State shall lay before each House of Parliament a copy of every direction given under this section *unless he is of opinion that disclosure of the direction is against the interests of national security or relations with the government of a country or territory outside the United Kingdom, or the commercial interests of any person.*[18]
>
> A person shall not disclose, or be required by virtue of any enactment or otherwise to disclose, anything done by virtue of this section if the Secretary of State has notified him that the Secretary of State is of the opinion that disclosure of that thing is against the interests of national security or relations with the government of a country or territory outside the United Kingdom, or the commercial interests of some other person.[19]
>
> The Secretary of State may, with the approval of the Treasury, make grants to public telecommunications operators for the purpose of defraying or contributing towards any losses they may sustain by reason of compliance with the directions given under this section.[20]
>
> There shall be paid out of money provided by Parliament any sums required by the Secretary of State for making grants under this section.[21]

As such, section 94 empowered a Secretary of State to give such directions of a general character so as compel public telecommunications operators to do *anything* the Secretary of State thought necessary on national security or diplomatic relations grounds. It even allowed the Secretary of State the discretion to withhold their activity from Parliament on national security grounds, despite the fact that it empowered a Secretary of State to use funds from the Treasury to give

15 ibid, s94(1), emphasis added. Later replaced by the words 'necessary' and 'proportionate' by the Communications Act 2003.
16 ibid, s94(2), emphasis added.
17 ibid, s94(3).
18 ibid, s94(4).
19 ibid, s94(5).
20 ibid, s94(6).
21 ibid, s94(7).

effect to their secret directions. It also demanded secrecy from any party affected by a direction. Interestingly, in what had been a longstanding culture of CSP cooperative compliance, the provision perhaps foresaw that private CSPs might not always be so cooperative, and as such, compliance was compelled through the use of the non-discretionary 'shall' in s94(3). This provision remains the most empowering in the UK's history of communications and data-investigation regulation.

Section 94 aligns with the central thesis that, despite the fragmentation of communications networks envisaged under the TA 1984, the state would ensure that 'non-state' public telecommunications operators would continue to provide to the executive the ability to enable access by investigators to communications and data being transmitted or stored therein. Alongside the postal architecture, the field of interception (and, as it would transpire, data acquisition) remained covered.

Interception of Communications Act (IOCA) 1985

The following year, the IOCA 1985 entered force on 25 July 1985 with no significant changes to the bill as published in the Command Paper. In line with the UK's longstanding policy underpinning administrative regulation of interception as outlined in the Birkett Report 1957, the IOCA 1985 set the statutory precedent still visible in the Investigatory Powers Act (IPA) 2016, wherein the grounds for issuance of warrants for interception were listed as follows;

> The Secretary of State shall not issue a warrant under this section unless he considers that the warrant is necessary –
>
> (a) in the *interests of national security*;
> (b) for the purpose of preventing or detecting serious crime; or
> (c) for the purpose of safeguarding the economic well-being of the United Kingdom.[22]

Maintaining the precedent: entrenching unfettered Executive power

For anyone hoping to see a groundbreaking, ECHR-compliant piece of legislation putting the fundamental human rights of UK citizens to the fore, there was only disappointment. Apart from the fact that an express offence of unlawful interception of communications was created, Spencer summarized the IOCA 1985 as an Act which 'just gave statutory authority to the informal [administrative]

22 Interception of Communications Act 1985, s2(2), emphasis added. See also RIPA 2000, s5(3), and the IPA 2016, s20 (as regards targeted intercept), s138 (as regards bulk intercept).

arrangements that had existed heretofore',[23] with interception authorization powers remaining with the Secretary of State in cases of both national security and crime investigation.

Maintaining precedent: retaining secrecy whilst feigning transparency

It is important to note the relationship between the IOCA 1985's interpretation section and the TA 1984.[24] The former, perhaps unsurprisingly, drew a number of definitions from the latter. There was a hidden depth to the relationship, however. The IOCA 1985 afforded a greater degree of legitimacy to interception of UK residents' communications by avowing the powers in a public-facing statute. The *fact* of domestic interception of communications could now be said to be out in the open. However, the very enactment of a very limited IOCA 1985 also had the effect of diverting attention, if any existed at the time, from the reality that substantial communications intelligence relating to UK residents was accessible via the UK's telecommunications services by virtue of the residual unfettered power 'hidden in plain sight' in section 94 of the TA 1984.

The origin of independent oversight: the Interception of Communications Tribunal and the Interception of Communications Commissioner

The IOCA 1985 introduced a Tribunal (the forerunner to what is now the Investigatory Powers tribunal (UKIPT)),[25] which for the first time provided a dedicated forum whereby 'any person…[believing that]…communications sent to or by him…[had been]…intercepted in the course of their transmission by post or by means of a public telecommunication system' could apply to have their suspicions investigated.[26] The Act also introduced a Commissioner tasked with keeping under review

> the carrying out by the Secretary of State of the functions conferred on him…[relating to the granting, scope, modification, issue and duration of interception warrants]…and the adequacy of…any safeguards implemented limiting access to material accessed via the use of warrants]…and (b) to give

23 J R Spencer, 'Telephone-Tap Evidence and Administrative Detention in the UK' in Marianne Wade and Almir Maljevic (eds) *A War on Terror? The European Stance on a New Threat; Changing Laws and Human Rights Implications* (Springer Publishing, 2010) 375, 382.

24 IOCA 1985, s10(1) refers to 'the 1984 Act'.

25 Interception of Communications Act 1985, s7(1). The IPT provides more detail as to 'who we are' and 'what we do' on its website <https://www.ipt-uk.com/content.asp?id=10> accessed 10 January 2020.

26 ibid, s7(2).

> to the Tribunal all such assistance as the Tribunal may require for the purpose of enabling them to carry out their functions under this Act.[27]

Sir Anthony Lloyd (later Lord Lloyd of Berwick), a senior judge at the time of his appointment performed this role between 1985 and 1992, being replaced by the late Sir Thomas Bingham (Lord Bingham of Cornhill) who held the role until 1994. The late Lord Nolan held the role until early 2000, whereupon the last Commissioner under the IOCA 1985, and the first under the Regulation of Investigatory Powers Act (RIPA) 2000 was Sir Swinton Thomas. During the existence of the IOCA 1985, the oversight role of these independent Commissioners' extended only to aspects of the IOCA 1985 itself, as the existence of the TA 1984, section 94 directions, if there were any in operation at the time, remained secret. Leigh's comprehensive review of the IOCA 1985 noted how the Act repealed section 4 of the Official Secrets Act 1920, whilst continuing to distinguish international telephone calls from domestic telephone calls.[28] He also proffered the prescient view that the government of the day was 'already engaged in large-scale interception of international calls, telegrams and post'.[29] Leigh ultimately concluded that the Act's 'system for review of interception still prevents judicial or effective parliamentary scrutiny of what is done in the name of the Government' but that it probably did enough to comply with ECHR Article 8 by addressing the deficiencies highlighted in *Malone*'.[30] The IOCA 1985 is generally remembered as the *de minimis* response to the compulsion felt in government circles to legislate after the *Malone* censure. This probably contributed to the Act having a shorter than expected shelf-life as a consequence of the surge in litigation it brought about.[31] Lloyd's assessment of the IOCA 1985 was that it deserved a 'somewhat muted welcome...[in that]...its formulation of legal controls over interceptions and... establishment of [a] Commissioner and Tribunal... clearly improves the lot of the individual'.[32] He additionally noted however that 'the effectiveness of these bodies may be doubtful...[and that] in restricting itself...[to interception of telecommunications in the course of transmission over

27 ibid, s8.

28 ibid, s10(1) defined 'external communication' as one 'sent or received outside the British Islands' a definition carried over into RIPA 2000.

29 Ian Leigh, 'A Tappers' Charter?' (1986) (Spring) Public Law 13.

30 ibid, 18.

31 Ormerod and McKay cite 'the repeated visits to the House of Lords: *R v Effik* [1995] 1 AC 309 (cordless phone outside scope of IOCA 1985); *R v Preston* (1994) 2 AC 130 (no disclosure of intercepts as evidence); *Morgans v DPP* (2000) 2 WLR 386, (overruling *R v Rasool* [1997] 2 Cr. App R 190, holding that intercepts under IOCA, s.1 were inadmissible even if they were conducted on the basis of consent); *R v Sargeant* (2001) 3 WLR. 992 (engineer 'engaged' in running system). See David Ormerod and Simon McKay, 'Telephone intercepts and their admissibility' (2004) (1) *Criminal Law Review* 16.

32 Ian J Lloyd, 'Legislation – The Interception of Communications Act 1985' (1986) 49 *Modern Law Review* 86, 95.

a public telecommunications system]...[the Act] may...promise more than it delivers'.[33]

A fait accompli for the Executive

In addition to reaffirming a statutory power to intercept external telecommunications first seen in the Official Secrets Act 1920, and introducing Ministerial certificates to specify categories of intercepted material that could be examined,[34] the IOCA 1985 also enshrined in statute the ban on the use of evidence acquired through interception in the courts, which still remains.[35] It can be said that in one fell swoop, while the Act assuaged (to the least possible extent) the concerns expressed by the ECtHR in *Malone* as regards the UK's administrative regulation of interception, it simultaneously retained and enshrined the full range of pre-existing executive power in statutory form. The Act additionally consolidated much of the then 150-year policy of secrecy surrounding the use and extent of interception powers, and, by keeping the fact of interception out of the courts in any shape or form, effectively prevented judicial or public scrutiny of the practice (and its extent). This, coupled with the subtle retention of powers within section 94 of the TA 1984 marked something of an executive *fait accompli* as regards the exercise of powers to access UK residents' communications.

The origin of transparent secrecy: the statutification of UKIC functions

Vincent's 'culture of secrecy' accurately describes the longstanding bureaucratic culture within the UK executive in 1985.[36] He subsequently highlighted a point in history where nascent change in national security and related policy was becoming evident. This was perhaps influenced by the European imperative in judgments such as *Malone*. In any case, he asserts that 'between 1985 and 1995 more legislation was passed relating to the secret behaviour of the state than at any time since...just before the First World War'.[37] In addition to the IOCA 1985, statutes included the Security Service Act (SSA) 1989, a revised Official Secrets Act (OSA) 1989, and the Intelligence Services Act (ISA) 1994. A consequence of this was that the UKIC triumvirate all became enabled in statute to continue undertaking their hitherto secret functions. These of course included giving effect to the UKUSA Agreement. Vincent provides several reasons for statutification: 'the final decline of Britain's moral ascendancy in Europe and its empire'[38] (in which

33 ibid.
34 IOCA 1985, s3(2) (b).
35 ibid, s9, RIPA 2000 ss17–18, and IPA 2016, s56(1).
36 See generally David Vincent, *The Culture of Secrecy: Britain 1832–1998* (Clarendon Publishing 1999) 288.
37 ibid, 289. This included IOCA 1985, the SSA 1989, the OSA 1989, and the ISA 1994.
38 Vincent, *The Culture of Secrecy* (n36) 289.

he includes the *Malone* judgment as a contributory example); a 'changed society which…was as much a consequence of the increased deployment of information technology as a cause of the growing unease about its misuse';[39] and the 'striking combination of ineffective repression and specialist reporting'.[40] This is a reference to unsuccessful, and politically embarrassing government attempts to silence participants in the ABC trial and to ban the Channel 4 programme *MI5's Official Secrets*.[41] The latter programme was truly courageous and groundbreaking, in that it featured witnesses prepared to breach the Official Secrets Acts in the public interest. It included allegations that MI5 were undertaking surveillance of organizations that dissented from mainstream political opinion but which were not illegal, citing trade unions and the Campaign for Nuclear Disarmament (CND), as examples.[42] Vincent describes how the best-informed commentators on state secrecy of the time (Duncan Campbell, in particular) created the perception that state surveillance was burgeoning out of control, observing that 'the more journalists wrote about the organization of the system, the less acceptable became the state's silence about the rules for its use'.[43] The Channel 4 broadcast directly contributed to the statutification of the UKIC, an important development discussed in greater detail later in this chapter.

Maintaining the precedent: consensus against change

However, whilst there was widespread media pressure and a definitive, condemnatory judgment from Strasbourg to focus the state's mindset, support for real reform within either of the main political parties in the UK appears to have been 'patchy at best'.[44] In understanding the reluctance of the state to proactively and effectively cover the field in regulating telephone communications interception, it is critical to realize that *neither* of the alternately governing UK parties was very enthusiastic. Vincent's 'culture of secrecy' was probably the principal determinant of the approach the legislature adopted not only in drafting the IOCA 1985, but also, as will be shown, in drafting its successor, RIPA 2000. Analysis such as that provided by Vincent is vital, in that before critically evaluating British investigatory powers regulation and understanding the policy foundations underpinning it, we are reminded of the dominance of secrecy that resulted from the establishment of Westphalian systems of government. This led to a need for the legal protection of state secrets that emerged in the 19th century, as the media started to

39 ibid, 290.
40 ibid, 291.
41 ibid.
42 The original version of Channel 4's 20/20 *MI5's Official Secrets* featuring investigative journalist Hugo Young, an anonymous female informant, and the MI5 whistle-blower Cathy Massiter, '20/20 Vision, MI5's Official Secrets (C4 1985)' remains available on YouTube <https://www.youtube.com/watch?v=qRuAzSDhZXk> accessed 20 September 2020.
43 Vincent, *The Culture of Secrecy* (n36) 292.
44 ibid, 290.

realize the commercial value of publishing state secrets.[45] A near 660-year culture of secrecy could not and would not be simply shrugged off.

Maintaining the precedent: consensus for secrecy

Vincent additionally notes the prescient observation made by Jim Callaghan, who, like Theresa May years later, served as both Home Secretary prior to also becoming the UK Prime Minister, replaced by Margaret Thatcher in 1979. Callaghan had stated that 'any attempt to codify the powers of the Home Office in the field of the secret services was likely…to raise as many problems as it solved'.[46] His analysis of the reasons for this is as fascinating as it is damning of politicians. He cites the 'central difficulty'[47] in moving interception of communications onto the statute book as being the 'shared history'[48] of Conservative and Labour governments of using the prevailing administrative interception framework whilst in office for their own purposes. The Conservative government's demands for telephone surveillance conducted against the miners during their bitter 1984/1985 strike,[49] and the Labour Party's extensive use of interception powers in the Grunwick Strike in 1978 are given as examples.[50] Indeed Vincent observes that:

> From the mid-1960s onwards, the Labour Party was as much the cause as the vehicle of the growing sense of unease about the interception of communications, and had just as much to lose [as the Conservatives] from the release of Secret Service documents into the public domain. The volume of complaints from trade unions and pressure groups about interference with their calls and correspondence increased sharply during the 1974–1979 Labour Government and formed the basis of the campaign against the Conservative administrations in the first half of the 1980s.[51]

Another interlinked reason was that:

> the legitimacy of informal controls was conditional on the maintenance of a particular political culture. The problem in 1985 was not so much the intrinsic weakness of the current arrangements [but] the erosion of the

45 Hitoshi Nasu, 'State secrets law and national security' (2015) 64(2) *Journal of International Comparative Law* 365, 368.
46 Vincent, *The Culture of Secrecy* (n28) 292.
47 ibid, 293.
48 ibid.
49 HC Deb, 7 February 1985, vol 72, col 1126. Rt Hon Dennis Skinner asked for the Home Secretary's categorical assurance from the Dispatch Box that none of the trade union leaders involved in the miners' strike had their phones tapped during the past 11 months…to which Home Secretary Leon Brittan responded by invoking the Neither Confirm Nor Deny policy!
50 Vincent, *The Culture of Secrecy* (n28) 293.
51 ibid.

> constitutional conventions in which they were encased. By deliberately setting out to destroy the post-war consensus, Margaret Thatcher had undermined the trust which the exercise of unwritten powers required. In the absence of consensus over the aims of government policy there could be no confidence in the hidden exercise of the means.[52]

These realities coupled with frequent Campbell-led media pressure and the ECtHR's *Malone* judgment meant that, with the enactment of IOCA 1985, the UK entered the modern era of statutory 'investigatory powers' regulation with a law 'framed so as to offer the least possible concession to the broader arguments for civil liberties, and the smallest opportunity to MPs and electors wishing to monitor the work of the Secret Services'.[53] In what can only be viewed now as a bemusing example of the illogical nature of some of the aspects of the culture of secrecy, Vincent reminds us that:

> the extent to which the concession of statutory regulation implied no necessary alteration of the traditional mindset was confirmed at the end of the debate on the Interception of Communications Bill, when the junior Home Office Minister David Waddington announced the appointment of a new Head of MI5 *but refused to name him*. He further declined to answer any questions about individual cases of phone tapping.[54]

Almost immediately after the enactment of the IOCA 1985, Jim Callaghan's prescient views regarding the perils of statutification came home to roost. The *de minimis* approach adopted in drafting the IOCA 1985 meant that the criminal offence of interception without lawful authority was territorially limited to the UK and the provisions rendering it lawful where a Ministerial warrant was granted extended only to postal services and, crucially, to '*public* telecommunications systems'.[55] Yet despite the brevity of the statute, it appears that interpretation was rapidly going to become problematic and opaque, an issue that plagued this area of law until rectified in the IPA 2016. Cynics would be forgiven for asserting that the roundabout and opaque technical nature of the drafting employed was a manifestation of policy, almost a policy of revenge due to having been forced to legislate. The jury remains out on this question. Any interceptions undertaken outside the narrow regulatory ambit of the IOCA 1985 would remain unregulated and subject only to secret Ministerial oversight. These included interceptions of wireless telegraphic 'messages' under the Wireless Telegraphy Act 1949[56] and communications content access via listening devices.

52 ibid.
53 ibid, 294.
54 ibid, 295, emphasis added.
55 Interception of Communications Act 1985, particularly sections 1 and 2, emphasis added.
56 Wireless Telegraphy Act 1949, s5.

'Certificated warrants': enabling UKUSA Agreement obligations

At the point of the IOCA 1985's enactment, the UK's UKUSA obligations (outlined in Chapter 4 of this volume) remained secret. Section 3(2) of the new Act enabled a successful applicant to conduct

> the interception, in the course of their transmission by means of a public telecommunication system, of (i) such *external communications* as are described in the warrant; and (ii) such other communications (if any) as it is necessary to intercept in order to intercept such external communications as are so described.[57]

This opaquely enabled the interception of a *class* or *tranche* of communications leaving the British Islands, with the qualification that the Secretary of State had to append a certificate to the warrant 'certifying the descriptions of intercepted material the examination of which he considers necessary' on any of the now-standard grounds.[58] Certificates were not published. Section 3 thus implicitly gave effect to the UK's UKUSA Agreement obligations as secretly agreed. The state of affairs existing since the signing of the original BRUSA, whereby its very existence remained secret, and regulation, such as it was, was overseen by the Foreign and Home Secretaries, was enabled to continue. The scope, magnitude, and legality of the IOCA 1985's certificated warrant provisions would ultimately be challenged in the ECtHR after the Capenhurst Tower scandal exposed in 1999. As this lengthy legal challenge occurred following the enactment of the IOCA 1985's statutory replacement, it is addressed in the next chapter.

Regrettably, due to the continuing influence at this point on history of a culture of secrecy, it cannot be authoritatively asserted that the IOCA 1985 was *deliberately* drafted to ensure the ability to continue UKUSA obligations without revealing them. Most commentators view the Act as a hastily drafted response to *Malone*. The failure to draft dedicated definitions would tend to support this. With the benefit of post-2013 hindsight, the continued secrecy surrounding UKUSA obligations and the failure to incorporate them, even in veiled form, into the IOCA 1985 seems naïve and politically risky. However, the hitherto bipartisan consensus on secrecy, as well as the broader societal context, must be factored in. With no internet or social media, no one involved in policy or drafting legislation would likely have contemplated disclosures based on a high-level breach of secrecy and trust such as those made public in 2013. As such, confidence in the culture of secrecy probably made a contribution to the brevity and narrow regulatory ambit of the IOCA 1985.

57 IOCA 1985, s3(2), emphasis added. Section 10 defined 'External communication' as 'communications sent or received outside the British Islands'.

58 ibid, s2(2) (a) in the interests of national security, (b) for the purpose of preventing or detecting serious crime; or (c) for the purpose of safeguarding the economic well-being of the United Kingdom.

IOCA 1985: the devil in the definitions

Despite its brevity, interpretation of the IOCA 1985 could not be said to be straightforward. By way of an example, its 'Interpretation' provision provided that 'public telecommunications system' had the same meaning as 'in the 1984 Act'.[59] This meant the Telecommunications Act 1984, from which many of the IOCA definitions were appropriated.[60] It appears the appropriation was not scrutinized in great depth. The TA 1984 as enacted carried no definition of 'public telecommunications system'.[61] To put one together it was necessary firstly to read the definition of 'telecommunications system', defined as

> a system for the conveyance, through the agency of electric, magnetic, electro-magnetic, electro-chemical or electromechanical energy, speech, music and other sounds; visual images;...signals serving for the impartation (whether as between persons and persons, things and things or persons and things) of any matter otherwise than in the form of sounds or visual images; or signals serving for the actuation or control of machinery or apparatus.[62]

The broad and commendably technology-neutral section 4 then had to be read in conjunction with a very lengthy section 7 (power of a Secretary of State to licence the running of telecommunications systems), section 8 (special provisions relating to a telecommunications system operators licence), and finally section 9 (Secretary of State's designation of certain telecommunications systems as 'public'). Section 9 provided that:

> The Secretary of State may by order designate as a public telecommunication system any telecommunication system the running of which is authorized by a licence to which section 8 above applies; and any reference in this Act to a public telecommunication system is a reference to a telecommunication system which is so designated and the running of which is so authorized.[63]

IOCA 1985: the questionable absence of 'communication'

Another distinctly odd consequence from the relationship between the TA 1984 and the IOCA 1985 that was definitionally dependent on it was the fact that, despite the latter's title and clear regulatory intent, neither statute actually defined 'communication'. As was the case for 'public telecommunication system',

59 ibid, s10.
60 ibid.
61 The definition examined here was eventually repealed as part of the enactment of the Communications Act 2003.
62 Telecommunications Act 1984, s4(1).
63 ibid, s9(1).

a legally certain meaning had to be inferred from the TA 1984 definition of 'telecommunications system'. Consequently, a 'communication' constituted

> speech, music and other sounds; visual images;...signals serving for the impartation (whether as between persons and persons, things and things or persons and things) of any matter otherwise than in the form of sounds or visual images; or signals serving for the actuation or control of machinery or apparatus.[64]

The only reference to a 'communication' in the IOCA 1985, was to 'external communication', which served only to define 'external'. While it might initially appear that the lack of a specifically drafted meaning for 'communication' in a statute specifically drafted to enable interception of them was of no practical consequence, there was actually one crucial related consequence, one which led to the divergence in the authorization mechanisms for communications investigation that flowed from the IOCA 1985's enactment, and which remains in the IPA 2016.

IOCA 1985: the questionable absence of 'data'

1984 was a big year for communications and data. As the year that saw the enactment of the TA 1984 and also the drafting of the Interception of Communications Bill, 1984 also saw the UK legislature's first-ever foray into 'data protection' legislation. The Data Protection Act (DPA) 1984 purported to 'regulate the use of automatically processed information relating to individuals and the provision of services in relation to such information'.[65] It defined 'data' as 'information recorded in a form which can be processed by equipment operating automatically in response to instructions given for that purpose'.[66] It further introduced what is now a fundamentally important precursor definition of 'personal data' as including 'data consisting of information *which relates to a living individual who can be identified from that information* (or from that and other information in possession of the data user)'.[67] During scrutiny, Lord Elton told the Lords that the DPA 1984 aspired to protect individuals from use or misuse of information held about them and to provide data protection in a form satisfying the Council of Europe Convention on Data Protection so as to enable the UK's data processing industry to participate freely in the European market.[68] At the risk of

64 ibid, s4(1).
65 DPA 1984, Preamble.
66 ibid, s1.
67 ibid, s2, emphasis added.
68 Lord Elton, Parliamentary Undersecretary of State, Home Office, HL Deb, 5 July 1983, vol 443, col 509. The reference to the Convention is to the Convention for the Protection of Individuals with regard to Automatic Processing of Personal Data (ETS No. 108) modified in 2018 and now known as 'Convention 108+'.

appearing cynical, the latter was the prime motivator. This level of awareness of the requirement to protect individuals' data in UK legislation, prevailing at least since the UK's signature on 14 March 1981 to the original Convention for the Protection of Individuals with regard to Automatic Processing of Personal Data 1981 (Convention 108+), begs the question as to why there was no provision in the IOCA 1985 for the protection of *data* from interception in the course of its transmission, that is, in the process of being *communicated.* This is not least because the UKIC, GCHQ in particular, would, from interception, readily be able to identify living individuals from any relevant data they came across. As things stood, personal data would be protected at rest, but not in transit.

It seems highly unlikely that when drafting the IOC Bill, whether as a hasty response to *Malone* or otherwise, the concept of 'data' as a commodity requiring to be 'communicated' to and from Europe would not have been envisaged. This begs the question as to why 'data' (as conceptualized for the DPA 1984) was not either added by amendment to the otherwise future-proof definition of 'communication' inferable from the future-proof definition of 'telecommunications system' in the TA 1984, or added in a brand new, dedicated definition of 'communication' purpose-built for the IOCA 1985. As will be seen, the IOCA 1985's replacement, RIPA 2000, created a dedicated definition for 'communication' by adding 'data of any description' to 'speech, music and visual images' etc.[69] This appears to have been 15 years overdue. The question of why 'data' was not factored into the IOCA 1985 becomes even more pertinent given that, in their adverse judgment in *Malone*, the European Court, in addition to examining the UK's regulation of interception, had examined the associated process of 'metering' (the forerunner to the retention of communications metadata by CSPs) and clearly found as follows:

> The process...involves the use of a device...which registers the numbers dialled on a particular telephone and the time and duration of each call. In making such records, the Post Office – now British Telecommunications - makes use only of signals sent to itself as the provider of the telephone service and does not monitor or intercept telephone conversations at all. From this, *the Government drew the conclusion that metering, in contrast to interception of communications, does not entail interference with any right guaranteed by Article 8*...By its very nature, metering is therefore to be distinguished from interception of communications, which is undesirable and illegitimate in a democratic society unless justified. The Court does not accept, however, that the use of *data obtained from metering*, whatever the circumstances and purposes, cannot give rise to an issue under Article 8...*The records of metering contain information, in particular the numbers dialled, which is an integral element in the communications made by telephone.* Consequently, release of that information to the police without the consent of the subscriber also

69 RIPA 2000, s81(1).

> amounts, in the opinion of the Court, to an interference with a right guaranteed by Article 8...There has accordingly been a breach of Article 8 (art 8) in the applicant's case as regards *both interception of communications and release of records of metering to the police.*[70]

A deliberate exclusion of metadata?

Yet despite these findings, the Thatcher government of the day *deliberately* chose to maintain the conceptual view of interception of communications argued before Strasbourg by drafting the IOCA 1985 to only encompass investigative access to communications 'in the course of transmission'. Access to communications metadata was left off the statute book. The then-prevailing culture of secrecy means that a definite conclusion on the reasons for this is problematic. The Hansard records of the IOC Bill sessions evidence emotionally charged debates that seem inordinately focused on theorizing as to the level of spying on Ministers and many references to the recent screening of the Channel 4 programme *MI5's Secrets* referred to earlier.[71] Despite repeated references by Opposition speakers to the *Malone* judgment, these contain no mentions of 'metering' or 'data'. With the benefit of hindsight and the post-2013 increase in state candour, it is possible to suggest some explanations.

A flawed Privacy Impact Assessment?

The first is the most obvious and follows the argument made in Strasbourg. It is based on the conceptual view of the fixed-line telephony that dominated British telecommunications systems as defined in the TA 1984 at the time. This was the belief, articulated by Home Office Minister David Waddington in a 'fundamental difference between the disclosure of the contents of a communication and the disclosure of so-called metering information...[hence the reason]...why metering is dealt with separately from interception'.[72] So it can be said that at that point in time, in conceptual terms, it never occurred to the legislature or executive that the privacy implications of accessing billing and location information could potentially yield intelligence material of at least equivalent value to content.

Keeping data investigation secret?

Despite the simplicity of the government's privacy-impact assessment, it belies their awareness of personal data as warranting protection in contexts other than communications, as demonstrated by the enactment of the DPA 1984. Given

70 *Malone v UK* (1985) 7 EHRR 14 (83)–(84) and (89), emphasis added.
71 See generally, HC Deb, 12 March 1985, vol 75, cc151–244, and *MI5's Official Secrets* (n33).
72 HC Deb, 3 April 1985, vol 76, col 1310.

that UKUSA Agreement cooperation had become embedded over the previous 40 years, such cooperation would have undoubtedly involved exchanges of not only SIGINT/COMINT, but investigative best practice and knowledge exchange on optimal data processing techniques for intelligence purposes. Cerruzi refers to GCHQ's Five Eyes counterpart, the US National Security Agency (NSA), as being at the forefront of computing research in the 1960s.[73] Fuster outlines how the US government had experienced concerns circulating over proposals for 'databanks' at Federal level 'centralising information about individuals already in the hands of Federal authorities' as far back as 1965.[74] Citing Westin, she articulates the publicly debated concerns that massive quantities of information could be easily stored and made readily available to the state.[75] It appears unarguable therefore that, even if not developing similar practices as quickly as the NSA, Defence Intelligence, and GCHQ would, by 1984, have developed significant capacity to acquire datasets, aggregate the data therein, and construct intelligence assessments and profiles based on data analytics. Given that military technology advances tend to remain secret until it appears appropriate to introduce derivative technology into the public domain, there may have been a desire to keep the UK's early data-analytical capabilities secret at this point.[76] This would have been justifiable at the time for 'national security capability' reasons.

Those inclined to a sceptical view of this assertion might wish to reflect on the 2015 'avowal' of Equipment Interference. The accompanying explanatory factsheet made it clear that the newly avowed power was not in fact 'new', but as for the secret directions under section 94 of the TA 1984, had been hidden in plain sight in other statutes.[77] It is extremely unlikely that use of this technique only commenced in the year of avowal. As such, by omitting to bring regulation of access to metering or 'communications-related' data onto the statute book, regulation, if there was any regulation at this point in time, could remain out of the public sphere and under the cloak of executive secrecy. Chapter 9 will outline how it was eventually conceded that communications data (CD) was being acquired in bulk by MI5 and GCHQ from 1998 by virtue of section 94 directions. There is nothing on record to prevent the conclusion that the practice, and the directions, commenced much earlier.

Supplementing the deliberate omission to regulate it in the IOCA 1985 was the additional omission (either deliberate or negligent) to insert 'data' into the

73 Paul E Ceruzzi, *Computing: A Concise History* (MIT Press Essential Knowledge Series, 2012) 38.

74 Gloria Gonzalez-Fuster, *The Emergence of Personal Data Protection as a Fundamental Right of the EU* (Springer 2014) 30.

75 ibid, citing Alan F Westin, *Privacy and Freedom* (Atheneum, 1967).

76 See Benjamin DuVal's 'Taxonomy of the Occasions of Secrecy' in Benjamin S DuVal Jr, 'The Occasions of Secrecy' (1986) 47 *University of Pittsburgh Law Review* 579.

77 Home Office 'Investigatory Powers Bill – Factsheet' (2015) <https://assets.publishing.service.gov.uk/government/uploads/system/uploads/attachment_data/file/473740/Factsheet-Targeted_Equipment_Interference.pdf> accessed 29 October 2020.

prevailing definition of 'communication', or to include any reference to 'data' in the IOCA 1985 at all. The beneficial consequence to the UKIC was that any interceptions of data in transit, however made, could not be construed as being 'without lawful authority'. Rather they remained outside the law. As such, neither Ministerial warrant nor meaningful public-facing accountability was required. Accessing, appropriating, acquiring or examining *any* form of communications-related data (including data as content) in pursuit of intelligence requirements, whether in transit over telecommunications systems or at rest in the control of telecommunications service providers, thus remained outside the statute book and behind the longstanding veil of secrecy, *unless* section 94 directions were already in place. Looking back from a 2020 perspective, this state of affairs fell woefully short of satisfying European conceptions of surveillance as requiring to be 'in accordance with law'.[78] However, the fact that national security was (and remains) outside EU competence,[79] that the UKIC had been exempted from the data protection provisions in the original DPA 1984,[80] and that nascent data-investigation practices (including communications-related data investigations) were almost certainly being conducted in secret at this point in an approved culture of secrecy meant that the Thatcher government was able to justify the IOCA 1985 as a necessary minimum response to *Malone*. There seems to have been no adverse reaction to their omission to regulate 'data' investigation from the European angle, academic commentary, politicians or even the civil liberties lobby. Data protection and the concept of non-content communications data as being of intelligence value was 'new'. In societal and cultural terms, it appears that the polity was not yet ready or able to conceptualize fixed-line telephone call data as representing a genuine threat to individual privacy. In this regard the ECtHR deserves commendation for being ahead of its time in its view of 'metering' as articulated in *Malone*. It would be another 15 years before the scope of data-investigation regulation would be seen to broaden in the public domain.

IOCA 1985: other definitional difficulties

The IOCA 1985 additionally had to include the legislature's first attempt to place in statute what secret administrative governance had for a long period ensured, namely that evidence of the very fact that interception had taken place or any reference to material obtained in consequence of interception was inadmissible in any proceedings before any court or tribunal, subject to a strictly limited range of exceptions.[81] As far back as 1957, the Birkett Committee described the ban as

78 ibid, (67)–(68).
79 Treaty on European Union, Art 4(2).
80 DPA 1984, s27 provided the first 'national security' exception to the main provisions of the Act.
81 IOCA 1985, s9.

> the settled policy of the Home Office that, save in the most exceptional cases. information obtained by the interception of communications should be used only for the purposes of detection, and not as evidence in a Court or in any other Inquiry.[82]

Because of the occasional implications for procedural fairness and obligations for disclosure, the issue has not been without controversy. The most recent review, undertaken in 2014 by the incumbent Conservative/Liberal Democrat coalition government observed that the issue had been reviewed on eight occasions since 1993.[83] Each review ultimately reached a variant of the same conclusion reached in 2014, namely that,

> although it is feasible to design a legally compliant intercept as evidence regime it would not be consistent with previous operational requirements, would incur significant costs and risks, and that the benefits would be uncertain. *The Government therefore intends to make no change to the current arrangements which permit intercept material from this country to be used for intelligence purposes only.*[84]

This position undoubtedly informed the continuance of the ban in the IPA 2016.

Ormerod and McKay highlight a significant number of legal challenges testing the scope of the section 9 proscription.[85] A scholarly analysis of their findings is beyond the scope of this work. Spencer describes the testing of section 9 in these cases as spawning 'a body of intricate case law which must rank as one of the most difficult chapters in the history of the law of evidence...[attracting]...the attention of the House of Lords...on no less than four occasions'.[86] These provide one reason for its relatively short shelf-life. Another driver of change was the legal challenges in other areas of covert operations, such as Sultan Khan's appellate litigation in respect of evidence obtained via a police listening device.[87] This meant that covert investigatory powers other than the narrow conduct defined as interception were now becoming ripe for review and statutification. In addition, the post-1997 Labour government were committed to enacting a human rights statute that would give direct effect to the rights enshrined in the ECHR. This would mean that powers used by law enforcement and the UKIC would be required to be exercised by reference to perceived necessity and proportionality. All these factors were pointing towards the need for a new 'Regulation of

82 Home Office, *Report of the Committee of Privy Councillors Appointed to Inquire into the Interception of Communications* (Cmnd 283, 1957) (*Birkett Report 1957*) para 92.

83 Home Office, *Intercept as Evidence* (Cm 8989, 2014) 5.

84 ibid, emphasis added.

85 Ormerod and McKay (n23).

86 Spencer, 'Telephone-Tap Evidence' (n23) 383. In addition to the cases cited by Ormerod and McKay he mentions *R v Khan* [1997] AC 558.

87 *R v Khan* [1997] AC558.

Investigatory Powers Bill' in the late nineties. The final straw as regards the IOCA 1985 however, was that troublesome definition of 'public telecommunications system'.

Rationalizing the IOCA 1985

As part of the historical journey towards rationalizing the Investigatory Powers Act 2016, there is another way to look at the much-criticized and so-called *de minimis* IOCA 1985. Whilst it certainly reflects a *de minimis* response to an adverse European court judgment, it also reflects a policy of continuing to ensure that *all means* of communication are accessible for investigative purposes in the interests of national security broadly construed and to facilitate top secret UKUSA commitments. Importantly however, by establishing the Commissioner and the first of several tribunals the *utility* of providing independent oversight had now been recognized by government, perhaps in response to the early jurisprudence emanating from the ECtHR. Furthermore, the publication of *safeguards*, albeit minimally informative at this juncture, was also significant.[88] Whilst questions of efficacy might remain, the express provisions for independent oversight mechanisms, and safeguards for any product obtained meant that national security-derived investigative practices could be not only continued, but actually expanded in an environment where, on the face of things, the public were protected from abuses of power. Whilst cynics might (in light of section 94) doubt the *bona fides* of the government, the publication of oversight and safeguards in primary legislation represented not only a welcome, but also a politically clever development. The existence of legislative safeguards for material with intelligence potential would become vitally important leverage in European judicial determinations of the rights compliance or otherwise of EU Member States' communications surveillance regimes still to come, including those of the UK. A fairer assessment of the IOCA 1985 is that it represents a first attempt, in an era of national security regulation still defined by 'need to know' and large-scale secrecy, and prior to the enactment of the Human Rights Act (HRA) 1998, to *explicitly* regulate communications-related investigatory powers in the UK arena and *expressly* provide public reassurance via Ministerial and independent oversight mechanisms. Whilst *de minimis* in one respect, the IOCA 1985 was a significant policy development in others. The overall policy of ensuring that all *forms* of communication technology were accessible was unaffected by the IOCA 1985.

ACC Alison Halford: Halford v UK (1997) 24 EHRR 523

It was a police officer (Detective Sergeant Ware) who had unintentionally provided sufficient evidence for a legal team to appeal an interception case the whole way to Strasbourg, thus ultimately bringing about major regulatory change and

88 IOCA 1985, s6.

the introduction of the IOCA 1985. It is perhaps noteworthy, therefore, that it was another police officer, this time the actual subject of legal proceedings, who was going to ultimately impel the next change in interception regulation. Alison Halford's case involved, amongst other things, her office telephone calls being intercepted as part of a 'campaign' against her by other senior officers due to her having brought a sex discrimination case to an Industrial Tribunal over the repeated failure of senior officers at Merseyside Constabulary to recommend her to the Home Office for promotion beyond her Assistant Chief Constable rank.[89] The ECtHR's judgment in her case often receives only passing attention, usually a line or two about its principal finding. However, for present purposes it merits closer examination because it makes a rare public reference, for its time, to the establishment and operation of the Interception of Communications Tribunal (IOCT) and the Commissioner established under the IOCA 1985.[90] This allows a more informed assessment of the IOCA regime and its limitations.

The Interception of Communications Tribunal

The *Halford* judgment describes how the IOCT consisted of five members appointed for five years, all required to have served as lawyers for at least ten years.[91] Any person, for example ACC Halford, 'believing' (they had no way of ***knowing***) 'that their communications may have been intercepted in the course of their transmission by means of a public telecommunications system' could apply to the IOCT to have their allegation 'investigated'. Subject to deciding whether or not the application was 'vexatious', the IOCT was under a duty to determine whether an interception warrant had been issued and, if so, whether it was issued in accordance with the 1985 Act. This was the extent of the 'investigation'. In doing so, the IOCT was to apply judicial review application principles.[92] Barnum makes a good case that the practical effect of this was that the IOCT was to apply the 'Wednesbury unreasonableness' principle[93] meaning that it was prohibited from overturning a Secretary of State's decision to issue an interception warrant unless it believed that the decision was 'so unreasonable that no reasonable Secretary of State could ever have come to it'.[94] The likelihood of reaching such a conclusion seems negligible. If the IOCT found there to be no breach of the 1985 Act, it was required to inform the complainant accordingly, but it was not enabled to confirm to a complainant whether they had found no breach due to no authorized interception having actually taken place, or no breach because

89 *Halford v UK* (1997) 24 EHRR 523, (8)–(16).
90 IOCA 1985, sections 7 and 8, respectively.
91 *Halford v UK* (n89) (30)–(32), citing the IOCA 1985, s7, and sch 1.
92 ibid, (32) citing the IOCA 1985, s7 (2)–(4) of the 1985 Act.
93 Derived from Lord Greene's 1947 decision in *Associated Provincial Picture Houses v Wednesbury Corporation* (1948) 1 KB 223.
94 David Barnum, 'Judicial Oversight of Interception of Communications' (2016) 44 (2) *Georgia Journal of International and Comparative Law* 239, 273.

there *had* been an authorized interception, and it was justified under the terms of the 1985 Act.[95] Where the IOCT had found that a breach of the IOCA 1985 had occurred, it was duty-bound to report its findings to the Prime Minister and had a power to notify the complainant. The IOCT was additionally empowered to order the quashing of the warrant and the payment of compensation to the complainant, but was not required to provide reasons for its decisions and there was no avenue of appeal from an IOCT decision.[96] As the Court noted, Ms Halford had applied to the IOCT seeking an investigation. It appears that the IOCT decided that her application was not vexatious and consequently, in 'a letter dated 21 February 1992...[they]...informed her that its investigation had satisfied it that there had been no contravention of sections 2 to 5 of the 1985 Act in her case'.[97] The Court also noted that 'in a letter dated 27 March 1992, the Tribunal confirmed that it could not specify whether any interception had in fact taken place'.[98] Terse and unreasoned communications such as this characterize the IOCT, which by reason of having to apply 'Wednesbury' principles can be viewed with hindsight as little more than a quasi-judicial rubber stamp for Executive action. This view is supported by the fact that at the end of its operational life, when replaced as part of the revision of investigatory powers regulation that occurred in RIPA 2000, the incumbent Commissioner, Sir Swinton Thomas, who remained in the role in its new RIPA guise, observed that

> [the IOCA Tribunal in place until RIPA's enactment on 2 October 2000] received 60 new applications during 2000 and completed the investigation of 14 of these during the year as well as concluding its investigation of the two outstanding cases from 1999. Forty six cases have been carried over to 2001. ...*on no occasion has the Tribunal concluded that there had been a contravention of sections 2–5 of the Interception of Communications Act 1985.*[99]

The IOCA 1985 Commissioner

This author could locate no documentary evidence in the National Archives or elsewhere of the work of either the IOCT or the Interception Commissioner as originally established under the IOCA 1985.[100] There are limited references to the latter's reports between 1986 and 1992 in evidence before the ECtHR, where they have been used to reassure the reader of statutory safeguards of

95 David Barnum, 'Judicial Oversight of Interception of Communications' (2016) 44 (2) *Georgia Journal of International and Comparative Law* 239, 273.
96 ibid, citing the IOCA 1985, s7(7), and (8).
97 ibid, (19).
98 *Halford v UK* (1997) 24 EHRR 523 (19).
99 Rt Hon Sir Swinton Thomas, *Report of Interception of Communications Commissioner for 2000* (Cm 5296, 2001) 10, emphasis added.
100 IOCA 1985, s8.

intercepted material.[101] In the *Halford* judgment, the ECtHR usefully summarized the Commissioner's functions as:

> reviewing the carrying out by the Secretary of State of the functions conferred on him by sections 2 to 5 of the 1985 Act, reporting to the Prime Minister breaches of sections 2 to 5 of the 1985 Act which have not been reported by the Tribunal and making an annual report to the Prime Minister. This report must be laid before Parliament, although the Prime Minister has the power to exclude any matter from it the publication of which would be prejudicial to national security, to the prevention or detection of serious crime or to the well-being of the United Kingdom.[102]

As for the IOCT, there was a transition in Commissioner that occurred at 12:01 am on 2 October 2000, when the RIPA 2000 replaced the IOCA, and the Human Rights Act (HRA) 1998 also entered force. As previously stated, Sir Swinton Thomas was the final IOCA 1985 Commissioner, and also the first Interception of Communications Commissioner under RIPA 2000. As with his brief synopsis of the role of the IOCT in his first report as RIPA Commissioner, we have him to thank for any clue as to how he and the Commissioners before him (1985–1999) fulfilled their statutory responsibilities.

Typically for the time, there is little in operational detail and much in the way of platitudes and attempts at public reassurance, although in fairness a number of pages are devoted to errors as discovered. His 15-page report cites at least two visits to the Security Service, Secret Intelligence Service, and GCHQ, as well as selected law enforcement agencies, the Home Office, and the Scottish Executive. Interestingly, he also visited CSPs, which he defined as the postal service and the major telephone companies. In a rare insight for that period into how interception was actually effected he highlighted how each of the private enterprises visited 'employ personnel who are engaged solely in the execution of interception of communications warrants'.[103] As for everyone he visited, he expressed himself as 'impressed by their care, expertise and dedication'.[104] This reinforces the evidence of cooperative and fully embedded nature of the executive/CSP relationship by that time. There is a clue as to how seriously the Thatcher and Blair governments viewed the Commissioner's post-hoc oversight of interception between 1985 and 2000. It appears in a lengthy paragraph 20 of the Report, entitled 'Staffing of the Secretariat'. It appears that Sir Swinton had a single Secretary in the role to assist him, and that the staff level would increase to three following the enactment of RIPA 2000, it having been observed that

101 *Liberty and Others v United Kingdom* (Application 58423/00) (26), (31), and (33).
102 *Halford v UK* (n89) (34).
103 Rt Hon Sir Swinton Thomas, *Report of Interception of Communications Commissioner for 2000* (Cm 5296, 2001) 7.
104 ibid.

the workload was 'far too great for one person'.[105] When the number of warrants issued that year is used as an example (and these did not include those for Northern Ireland or the Foreign and Commonwealth Office) this staffing level appears wholly inadequate.[106]

The ECtHR offered no opinion as to the efficacy of the Tribunal/Commissioner oversight mechanism as provided in the IOCA 1985. Barnum notes that many UK academic commentators of the time had serious doubts about it.[107] On the available evidence, it is difficult to argue with their conclusions.

'In accordance with law': a very British problem

Returning to the IOCA 1985 definitional issue that ultimately decided Ms Halford's application, the ECtHR found that

> the 1985 Act does not apply to *internal* communications systems operated by public authorities, such as that at Merseyside police headquarters, and that there is no other provision in domestic law to regulate interceptions of telephone calls made on such systems…*It cannot therefore be said that the interference was 'in accordance with the law' for the purposes of Article 8 para. 2 of the Convention*…since the domestic law did not provide adequate protection to Ms Halford against interferences by the police with her right to respect for her private life and correspondence. It follows that there has been a violation of Article 8…in relation to the interception of calls made on Ms Halford's office telephones.[108]

This finding constituted the final nail in the IOCA 1985's coffin, one that been under construction in consequence of the repeated litigation in respect of interpreting aspects of the Act before the House of Lords. It was fully anticipated by the Blair government. By way of proactive response, and for the first time ever in this area of law, the views of the UK public on the form that legislation regulating the interception of their communications should actually take were sought by means of a Consultation Paper.[109] This is discussed after an examination of the statutification of the UK's three civilian intelligence services that took place and came into effect alongside the important ECtHR judgments of the era driving change.

105 ibid, 9.

106 ibid, in the Statistical Annex to his report, the figure is 1474 IOCA warrants issued for the Home Office to 1 October 2000, and a further 237 for the Scottish Executive.

107 Barnum, 'Judicial Oversight of Interception of Communications' (n94) 273.

108 *Halford v UK* (n89) (51), emphasis added.

109 Home Office, *The Interception of Communications in the United Kingdom: A Consultation Paper* (Cm 4368, 1999).

The statutification of British Intelligence machinery

In addition to the *Malone* and *Halford* judgments in respect of interception, Europe's judicial institutions were proving instrumental in compelling the transfer of administrative governance of the principal *users* of communications and data-investigative powers into statutory format, namely the UKIC. A key government objective at this juncture would be to ensure that UKIC access to communications and data, irrespective of communication means, would be enabled on an uninterrupted basis. It was no surprise therefore that the enabling statutory provisions are broad.

The first of its three civilian intelligence production members to have functions enshrined in statute was the domestic Security Service (MI5). The Security Service Act (SSA) 1989 entered force on 1 February 1991 and marked the UK's anticipatory response to the European Commission's findings in *Hewitt and Harman v UK*.[110]

Patricia Hewitt and Harriet Harman had been members of the National Council for Civil Liberties (now Liberty) and had been among those named by MI5 whistleblower Cathy Massiter as being subject to MI5 surveillance (having been incorrectly labelled 'communist sympathisers' to enable that surveillance) in the Channel 4 *MI5's Official Secrets* broadcast of 1985.[111] The Court examined the administrative governance of the Security Service and noted that it flowed from the published Maxwell-Fyfe Directive of 24 September 1952, whilst also noting that the UK government did not claim the Directive had the force of law.[112] They further found that the Directive did not 'provide a framework which indicates with the requisite degree of certainty the scope and manner of the exercise of discretion by the authorities in the carrying out of secret surveillance activities'.[113] Consequently, and in language very similar to that used in *Malone* and *Halford* the Commission found that 'the interference with the applicants' right to respect for private life was not "in accordance with the law" as required by Article 8 para. 2 (Art. 8–2) of the Convention'.[114]

As with the IOCA 1985, the transfer from administrative to statutory governance was succinct.

In the space of seven sections, the SSA 1989 firstly recorded the continuation, as opposed to creation, of the Security Service.[115] In broad terms, its functions were described as the protection of national security and the protection of the economic wellbeing of the UK, thus dovetailing with the grounds for obtaining interception warrants under the IOCA 1985.[116] Further regula-

110 *Hewitt and Harman v United Kingdom* Application 12175/86 (1989) ECHR 29 (9 May 1989).

111 ibid, (40).

112 ibid.

113 ibid.

114 ibid, (41).

115 SSA 1989, s1(1): 'There shall continue to be a Security Service (in this Act referred to as 'the Service') under the authority of the Secretary of State'.

116 ibid, s1(2), and 1(3).

tory alignment with interception warrant provisions occurred via an addition to its functions brought about by the Security Service Act (SSA) 1996, wherein it became authorized to 'act in support of police forces in the prevention and detection of serious crime'.[117] The Act also provided for the issue of Ministerial warrants authorizing entry onto or interference with property in circumstances where it was thought 'necessary' in order to 'obtain information likely to be of substantial value in assisting the Service to discharge any of its functions and which could not reasonably be obtained by other means'[118] and was satisfied that 'satisfactory' safeguards existed with respect to the disclosure of any information so obtained.[119] These provisions undoubtedly reflected a desire to homogenize safeguarding arrangements for intelligence product by property interference with those for product obtained through interception.[120] The SSA 1989, similar to the IOCA 1985, established a Security Service Commissioner (SSC)[121] and a Security Service Tribunal (SST).[122]

The SSC was required: to have held high judicial office;[123] to report annually to Parliament;[124] to keep under review the issue of Ministerial warrants;[125] and (where requested to do so by the SST following a complaint of alleged prop-

117 SSA 1996, s1(1) creating SA 1989 s1(4).
118 SSA 1989, s3(2) (a), as enacted.
119 ibid, s3(2) (b), as enacted.
120 IOCA 1985, s6(1)–6(3):

> Where the Secretary of State issues a warrant he shall, unless such arrangements have already been made, make such arrangements as he considers necessary for the purpose of securing (a)that the requirements of subsections (2) and (3) below are satisfied in relation to the intercepted material; and (b) where a certificate is issued in relation to the warrant, that so much of the intercepted material as is not certified by the certificate is not read, looked at or listened to by any person. (2) The requirements of this subsection are satisfied in relation to any intercepted material if each of the following, namely (a) the extent to which the material is disclosed; (b) the number of persons to whom any of the material is disclosed; (c) the extent to which the material is copied; and (d) the number of copies made of any of the material, is limited to the minimum that is necessary as mentioned in section 2(2) above. (3) The requirements of this subsection are satisfied in relation to any intercepted material if each copy made of any of that material is destroyed as soon as its retention is no longer necessary as mentioned in section 2(2) above.

121 SSA 1989, s4.
122 ibid, s5.
123 ibid, s4(1) within the meaning of the Appellate Jurisdiction Act 1876, s25: 'The office of Lord Chancellor of Great Britain or Ireland, or of paid Judge of the Judicial Committee of the Privy Council, or of Judge of one of Her Majesty's superior courts of Great Britain and Ireland'. 'Superior Courts' means As to England, Her Majesty's High Court of Justice and Her Majesty's Court of Appeal, and the superior courts of law and equity in England as they existed before the constitution of Her Majesty's High Court of Justice and the Scottish Court of Session.
124 ibid, s4(5) subject to a power to withhold parts of the Report (after consultation with the UK Prime Minister) if prejudicial to the ongoing functions of the Security Service (s4[7]).
125 ibid, s4(3).

erty interference) to investigate whether a property interference warrant had in fact been issued and if so, to review its issue using 'principles applied by a court on an application for judicial review'.[126] Barnum has already noted the inherent problem with such an approach.[127] Paul Scott, citing David Anderson, has discussed the difficulty that Commissioners such as the SSC have had in performing a role where 'potential conflicts between state power and civil liberties are acute, but information is tightly rationed',[128] concluding that they ultimately 'facilitate performance of functions which neither fully legal nor fully political institutions could fulfil'.[129] His conclusions are cogent.

Similarly to the establishment and constitution of the IOCT, the SST was established to investigate complaints about alleged property interference or disclosure of information obtained thereby by the Security Service,[130] establish that such complaints were not vexatious,[131] and to refer the complaint to the Commissioner for investigation before making a determination.[132] Decisions of the SSC and SST were final and carried no right of appeal in any court.[133]

The SSA warrant provisions were repealed and replaced when the functions of the Secret Intelligence Service (SIS) and GCHQ were transferred from administrative governance to statutory governance in the Intelligence Services Act (ISA) 1994.[134] Although not a response to any particular European legal challenge, John Wadham noted how the ISA 1994 was modelled on both the IOCA 1985 and SSA 1989, introducing, for the first time, parliamentary accountability for all three intelligence services.[135] The five-year gap between placing the Security Service on a statutory footing and following suit with the SIS and GCHQ was because the 1989 (Conservative) government 'were still curiously unwilling to acknowledge even the existence of those public agencies', a clear example of the culture of secrecy still prevailing.[136]

126 ibid, sch 1(4).
127 Barnum (n94) and *Associated Provincial Picture Houses v Wednesbury Corporation* (1948) 1 KB 223.
128 David Anderson QC, 'The Independent Review of Terrorism Laws' (2014) *Journal of Public Law* 403, 421 cited in Paul F Scott, 'Hybrid Institutions in the National Security Constitution: the Case of the Commissioners' (2019) 39 (3) *Journal of Legal Studies* 432.
129 Scott (n128).
130 SSA 1989, s5(1), and sch 2.
131 ibid, sch 2(1).
132 ibid, sch 2.
133 ibid, s5(4).
134 ISA 1994, s5 provided for property interference and wireless telegraphy interference warrants for all three UKIC members.
135 John Wadham, 'The Intelligence Services Act 1994' (1994) 57 (6) *Modern Law Review* 916.
136 Lord Lester of Herne Hill, HL Deb, 9 December 1993, vol 550, col 1044, he added that 'Nor, again regrettably, did the 1989 Act subject the agencies to any parliamentary oversight or scrutiny'.

As regards authority for property interference, the new warrant provisions largely replicated those in the SSA 1989, but applied their provisions on 'necessity', 'no other reasonable means', and 'safeguards' to all three services.[137] The ISA 1994 additionally introduced a Ministerial warrant requirement for interference with wireless telegraphy.[138] The absence of Explanatory Notes and the prevailing influence of the Official Secrets Acts means that the rationale for this can only be the subject of conjecture. Clause 5 of the Intelligence Services Bill, as then was, was agreed to in Lords scrutiny without comment on the matter.[139] It had not been mentioned in Commons Standing Committee scrutiny either. The most likely reason for extending the need for a Ministerial warrant for this variant of covert investigative conduct was that doing so put it on a par with governance of interception of postal and telecommunications. Until this point, interception of wireless telegraphy was undertaken with lawful authority only when 'authorized' by the Postmaster-General or when forming part of duties as a Servant of the Crown.[140]

The ISA replicated the SSA 1989 by initially providing for the continuation of the SIS and outlining its functions in very broad terms.[141] The standard 'protection of national security interests' function differed slightly, but logically from that of the Security Service in that national security information access was to be conducted with 'particular reference to the defence and foreign policies of the UK government.[142] As for the Security Service, the other grounds for obtaining information related to the protection of the UK's economic well-being and the prevention and detection of serious crime.[143] The ISA additionally provided for the continuation of the role of Chief of the Intelligence Service (CIS).[144] The CIS became accountable for ensuring that arrangements were in place for securing that no information would be obtained by the SIS other than that 'necessary for the proper discharge of its functions' and that no information would be disclosed by it except where necessary for properly discharging its functions, in the interests of national security or for the purpose of the prevention or detection of serious

137 ISA 1994, s5(2).

138 ibid, s5(1).

139 Lord Skelmersdale, HL Deb, 13 January 1994, vol 551, col 280.

140 Wireless Telegraphy Act 1949, s5(b) (i). The Act makes no mention of a warrant requirement.

141 ISA 1994, s1(1):

> There shall continue to be a Secret Intelligence Service (in this Act referred to as 'the Intelligence Service') under the authority of the Secretary of State…its functions shall be – (a) to obtain and provide information relating to the actions or intentions of persons outside the British Islands; and (b) to perform other tasks relating to the actions or intentions of such persons.

142 ibid, s1(2) (a).

143 ibid, s1(2) (b) and (c), respectively.

144 ibid, s2(1).

crime.[145] This distinguished it from the SSA 1989, where the only expressly permitted purposes for disclosure were the proper performance of the Security Service's functions or the prevention or detection of serious crime.[146] Despite being expressly enabled to obtain information or perform other tasks relating to the actions or intentions of persons outside the British Islands 'in the interests of the UK's economic wellbeing',[147] there was, and remains, no express permission to disclose such information.[148] These differences in the express permissions seem to have evaded discussion during Commons and Lords scrutiny, meaning the rationale underpinning them remains unclear. The ISA 1994 also introduced an express permission to disclose information obtained 'for use in any criminal proceedings'.[149] This applied to both the SIS and to GCHQ and, by way of a consequential amendment to the SSA 1989 section 1 in schedule 4 of the ISA 1994, to the Security Service.[150] As regards the nature of obtained information that the UKIC might seek to disclose for use in evidence, the SSA 1989 carries no 'interpretation' provision and section 10 of the ISA 1994 carries no definition of 'information'. One definite exclusion, however, would be information acquired by interception of communications by or on behalf of any of the UKIC by virtue of the safeguards in the IOCA 1985.[151]

For both the SIS and GCHQ, the ISA 1994 replicated the SSA 1989 proscription on taking 'any action' to 'further the interests of any political party'.[152] Although well-intentioned, there appears a dichotomy given that the UKIC priorities were (and remain) set by the prevailing political party in government, thus potentially (if indirectly) furthering their interests.[153]

145 ibid, s2(2) (a).
146 SSA 1989, s2(2)(a).
147 ISA 1994, s1(1) and 1(2) (b).
148 ibid, s2(2) (a) remains unchanged as of December 2020.
149 ibid, s2(2) (a) for the SIS and s4(2) (a) for GCHQ.
150 ibid, sch 4(1) (1).
151 IOCA 1985 s9 precludes even reference to interception in any proceedings before any court or tribunal.
152 See SSA 1989, s2(2)(b) and the ISA 1994, ss2(2)(b) (SIS), and 4(2) (b) (GCHQ).
153 See Wadham (n135) 920, fn 27, where he observes 'It should be noted, however, that political control via the "tasking" process of the Joint Intelligence Committee does exist', referring to *Central Intelligence Machinery* (London: HMSO, 1993). At the time of writing, Joint Intelligence Committee (JIC) are responsible, inter alia, for contributing to the 'formulation of statements of the requirements and priorities for intelligence gathering and other tasks to be conducted by the intelligence agencies'. See GOV.UK website <https://www.gov.uk/government/groups/joint-intelligence-committee> accessed 20 October 2020. MI5 state that 'the comprises senior officials from Cabinet Office, including the JIC Chairman, the Chief of the Assessments Staff and the National Security Advisor, as well as officials from the Foreign & Commonwealth Office, the Ministry of Defence, the Home Office, the Department for International Development, HM Treasury and the agency heads. Other departments attend as necessary' see <https://www.mi5.gov.uk/national-intelligence-machinery> accessed 20 October 2020.

Given its leading role in communications and data investigation, and in ensuring fulfilment of the UK's UKUSA Agreement obligations, GCHQ's statutory functions at the time of enactment bear *verbatim* restatement:

(a) to monitor or interfere with electromagnetic, acoustic and other emissions and any equipment producing such emissions and to obtain and provide information derived from or related to such emissions or equipment and from encrypted material; and
(b) to provide advice and assistance about – (i) languages, including terminology used for technical matters, and (ii) cryptography and other matters relating to the protection of information and other material, to the armed forces of the Crown, to Her Majesty's Government in the United Kingdom or to a Northern Ireland Department or to any other organisation which is determined for the purposes of this section in such manner as may be specified by the Prime Minister.[154]

Closer regulatory alignment was achieved by limiting the grounds on which GCHQ could undertake its functions to those seen in the SSA 1989, the IOCA 1985 and indeed traceable as far back as the Mazzini Inquiry, namely the protection of national security, the protection of the economic wellbeing of the UK and the prevention and detection of serious crime.[155] As for the Security Service, the ISA 1994 also created a similarly modelled Intelligence Services Commissioner (ISC) whose role, responsibilities and powers equated to those of the SSC.[156] An additional tribunal, the Intelligence Services Tribunal (IST) was also created.[157] It is unclear why, at the point of enactment, it was not thought prudent to amal gamate the IOCT and the SST with the new IST. Neither of the pre-existing tribunals appears to have been snowed under with work and cynicism as regards their efficacy was already present, with Baroness Blackstone observing (as regards the proposed IST) that

> Cases will be heard in secret and without a hearing. The complainant has no access to any information, even if disclosure of information would not affect national security. Without access to any information about the case before the tribunal, the complainant is in a somewhat difficult position to argue his or her case properly. The so-called remedy is therefore of rather dubious value. *It certainly does not comply with the safeguards contained in Article 6 of the European Convention on Human Rights.* In the circumstances, it is perhaps hardly surprising that since the 1989 Act was set up no complaint has ever been upheld by the tribunal. The Interception of Communications

154 ISA 1994, s3(1).
155 ibid, s3(2).
156 ibid, s8 and Sch 1 'Investigation of Complaints'.
157 ibid, s9 and sch 1 and 2.

> Tribunal set up to deal with telephone tapping in 1985, which has provided the model for the tribunal in both this Bill and the 1989 Act, has an equally 'perfect' record.[158]

Her remarks reflect the increasing influence the ECHR was having on the legislature's discourse by the late 1990s. They also reflected John Wadham's perception of 'serious problems' with the tribunal model as adopted.[159] Nonetheless, the IST was established as envisioned.

The Intelligence and Security Committee of Parliament

The ISA 1994 introduced accountability to Parliament for all three UKIC members by establishing the Intelligence and Security Committee of Parliament (UKPISC).[160] At this point in history, its role was to examine only the 'expenditure, administration and policy' of the three services.[161] Wadham observes that 'there was considerable debate at all stages of the Parliamentary process about the extent to which discussions of "operations" could be considered by this Committee and the extent to which the definition of the function of the Committee allowed detailed consideration of the work of the three services'.[162] In limiting its composition to six members chosen by the Prime Minister in consultation with the Leader of the Opposition on grounds of maintaining to the greatest degree possible a 'ring of secrecy', it was observed that that the UKPISC chairperson would be provided with a casting vote, thus meaning that an even number would not be inappropriate.[163] It was further asserted that 'it would be extremely useful if this committee were to act as a committee with a common purpose'.[164] Wadham's cogent analysis of the UKPISC essentially concluded, perhaps pessimistically, that it would only be as effective as the members appointed to it, and that assessing its performance would be difficult, given the secrecy surrounding it.[165] Whilst it has survived in various incarnations since its creation by the ISA 1994, Wadham's measured critical analysis was ultimately listened to when the Justice and Security Bill fell to be scrutinized in 2013.

The passing of the SSA 1989 and ISA 1994 into law meant that, by late 1994, each of the UK's intelligence services had their existence, functions and broad powers enshrined in statute. Their enabling statutes had also created the

158 Baroness Blackstone, HL Deb, 13 January 1994, vol 551, col 298.

159 Wadham (n135) 923–924.

160 ISA 1994, s10 and sch 3. UKPISC is used so as to distinguish the Committee from the Intelligence Services Commissioner (ISC) that operated between 1994 and 2017.

161 Wadham (n135) 925.

162 ibid.

163 Lord Chancellor (Lord James Mackay of Clashfern) HL Deb, 13 January 1994, vol 551, col 299.

164 ibid.

165 Wadham (n135) 927.

initial regulatory effort to provide a degree of independent *post hoc* oversight of communications and data investigation and a degree of parliamentary oversight. Both statutes were drafted in very broad terms however, meaning that secretive Ministerial governance and administrative guidelines still provided for the minutiae of operational practices, procedures and safeguards.

The human rights imperative

As an ECHR signatory since 1951, some final pieces were still missing from the UK's statutory governance of communications and data access outside the ambit of interception as Y2K approached.[166] One required the UK to enshrine and afford primacy to the ECHR in British law, in the same manner that European Community law had been afforded primacy in the European Communities Act 1972 after the UK joined it.[167] This was achieved by enacting the Human Rights Act (HRA) 1998, a statute that would

> incorporate the rights declared by the European Convention on Human Rights and by the First Protocol to the Convention into the law of the land. The Bill authorises British courts to provide speedy and effective remedies to the victims of breaches by the public authorities of the United Kingdom.[168]

Another human rights imperative was the aspiration of Tony Blair's government (or more accurately, perhaps, Home Secretary Jack Straw) to ensure that all covert investigatory powers (including interception of communications) whereby information was obtained by infringing an individual's 'right to respect for private and family life, home and correspondence'[169] became governed by legislation giving effect to the ECHR's principles of necessity and proportionality.

Consultation

The 1999 Consultation Paper followed the traditional line of setting out the perceived benefits to society of having powers to intercept communications retained by the government, but asserting that any new law would subject them to tough and independent scrutiny by a senior judge.[170] This signposted the creation of the IOCT's replacement, the Investigatory Powers Tribunal (IPT). The purported rationale for the Regulation of Investigatory Powers Bill was given as

166 A colloquialism of the time for the year 2000.

167 The rationale and history behind the Human Rights Act 1998 eloquently explained by Lord Lester of Herne Hill, HL Deb, 25 January 1995, vol 560, cols 1136–1142.

168 ibid.

169 European Convention on Human Rights 1950, Article 8(1).

170 Home Office, *The Interception of Communications in the United Kingdom: A Consultation Paper* (Cm 4368, 1999) foreword by then-Labour Home Secretary Jack Straw.

'developments in technology and services'.[171] It was conceded that the drafting of the IOCA 1985 had failed to keep up with technological advances, 'which had taken communications outside the definitions originally borrowed from the Telecommunications Act 1984 (for telephones) and the Post Office Act 1969 (for post)'.[172] Certain email channels also fell outside the interception framework and the deficiencies outlined in the *Halford* judgment regarding private telecommunications networks were also admitted.[173] EU influence was also clear in the reference to Article 5 of the Telecommunications Privacy Directive (TPD), wherein confidentiality of communications was to be protected by Member States.[174] Another reason cited was the need to provide a legal basis for commercial monitoring of calls (such as in call centres) which again were outside the ambit of the prevailing legislation.[175] Rapid advances in communications technology using wireless telegraphy such as mobile telephones (as opposed to physical landlines) were also stated to be outside the scope of the prevailing Act, whilst the former monopoly that was the UK postal/parcel service, after fragmentation under various privatization and competition-enhancing government measures (owing to the definitions employed in the prevailing Act) now required the law on interception to acknowledge the existence of private postal carriers.[176] It did not appear, however, to require the existence of what was being authorized under section 94 of the TA 1984.

The introduction of 'communications data'

Despite the Command Paper's title, it additionally introduced to the British public the concept of 'communications data' as a *sui generis* form of personal data that would require specific protection outside the DPA 1984 (and recently enacted DPA 1998) frameworks. 'Communications data' was described as 'information held by communication service providers relating to the communications made by their customers...[including]...*data* such as itemised billing, routing information and subscriber details'.[177] In a departure from the dismissal of the intelligence utility of 'metering' after the Malone judgment, policy now reflected that 'telephone itemised billing...provides a great deal of information on individuals'

171 ibid, 13.
172 ibid, 14.
173 ibid.
174 Directive 97/66/EC of the European Parliament and of the Council of 15 December 1997 concerning the processing of personal data and the protection of privacy in the telecommunications sector. Article 5 stated Member States shall ensure via national regulations the confidentiality of communications by means of a public telecommunications network and publicly available telecommunications services. In particular, they shall prohibit listening, tapping, storage or other kinds of interception or surveillance of communications, by others than users, without the consent of the users concerned, except when legally authorized.
175 Home Office, *The Interception of Communications in the United Kingdom* (n170) 15.
176 ibid.
177 ibid.

contacts and how they organise their life...[that]...can be used in the planning of operations, the gathering of intelligence and...in the prosecution of criminals'.[178] A dedicated Chapter 10 then informed the reader that

> In recent years, advances in telecommunications have meant that the amount of data held by communications service providers has increased, making the information much more useful as an investigative tool. But so has the potential for privacy infringements. *Although accessing a person's communications data is not as intrusive as interception, it clearly still represents an interference with the privacy of the individual.* The Government therefore believes it is time to put in place a statutory framework for authorising access to communications data.[179]

This again reflected the privacy impact assessment discussed elsewhere herein and ultimately shaped the structure and definitions in RIPA 2000, Part 1. This had two constituent chapters. Chapter One regulated the interception of communications and Chapter Two regulated the acquisition and disclosure of communications data. These are addressed in Chapters 6 and 8 herein, respectively.

Conclusion

As the first chapter of four covering a period in history which saw successive UK governments transfer regulation of the investigatory powers of the intelligence services and law enforcement from secretive administrative governance to statutory format, has this chapter provided proof, or least provided evidential material, for an argument that the legislature's regulatory efforts between 1984 and 1999 were disingenuous?

The principal statutes regulating UKIC and law enforcement access to communications and other 'information' were: the Telecommunications Act 1984; the Data Protection Acts of 1984 and 1998; the Interception of Communications Act 1985; the Security Service Acts 1989 and 1996; the Intelligence Services Act 1994; and Part III of the Police Act 1997.[180] Cumulatively, these gave very broad information (or data in its broadest sense) access, analysis and dissemination powers, previously governed by Ministers in conditions of administrative secrecy. They told the public, whom the ECtHR had stated time and again required the law to be accessible and foreseeable, that covert investigatory powers, whether involving interception or acquiring information by other means, were indepen-

178 ibid.

179 ibid.

180 Part III of the Police Act 1997 introduced a requirement for 'authorisation' for law enforcement agencies to enter onto or interfere with property or wireless telegraphy. Unlike the provision in s5 of the ISA 1994 for Intelligence Services however, entry was authorized by a high-ranking police officer and only on the grounds of preventing or detecting serious crime.

dently overseen and accountable to Parliament. There were Commissioners and Tribunals, and statutory safeguards for data obtained in the exercise of investigatory powers. There was certainly a veneer of benevolent statutory governance and ECHR compliance.

Yet none of these statutes acknowledged the operational reality of communications and data investigation facilitated at the time. Whether it was only governments that knew, or selected individuals within a government 'ring of secrecy', or only the respective intelligence services, the original BRUSA Agreement of 5 March 1946 was underpinning the structure, definitions, and scope of all of these statutes but was mentioned in none of them. In the modern context, that is disingenuous. Judged by the waning culture of post-war executive secrecy of the time, perhaps less so. However, when the unfettered power of a Secretary of State 'to issue directions in the interests of national security' is deliberately slipped into the 94th section of a statute purporting to oversee the denationalization of the state telecommunications monolith and when the significant investigative powers of the UKIC and law enforcement are independently overseen in virtually total secrecy without meaningful access to a remedy it appears that the state's efforts to fend off European criticism were cynical, *de minimis*, and disingenuous. The next chapters assert that, despite the enactment of the HRA 1998 and RIPA 2000, disingenuousness remained at the heart of the legislature in this area of public law.

References

20/20 Vision, 'MI5's Official Secrets' (C4 1985) <https://www.youtube.com/watch?v=qRuAzSDhZXk> accessed 20 September 2020

David Anderson QC, 'The Independent Review of Terrorism Laws' (2014) *Journal of Public Law* 403

David Barnum, 'Judicial Oversight of Interception of Communications' (2016) 44(2) *Georgia Journal of International and Comparative Law* 239

Paul E Ceruzzi, *Computing: A Concise History* (MIT Press Essential Knowledge Series, 2012) 38

Benjamin S DuVal Jr, 'The Occasions of Secrecy' (1986) 47 *University of Pittsburgh Law Review* 579

Gloria Gonzalez-Fuster, *The Emergence of Personal Data Protection as a Fundamental Right of the EU* (Springer, 2014) 30

Home Office 'Investigatory Powers Bill- Factsheet' (2015) <https://assets.publishing.service.gov.uk/government/uploads/system/uploads/attachment_data/file/473740/Factsheet-Targeted_Equipment_Interference.pdf> accessed 29 October 2020

Home Office, *Report of the Committee of Privy Councillors Appointed to Inquire into the Interception of Communications* (Cmnd 283, 1957) (*Birkett Report 1957*)

Home Office, *The Interception of Communications in the United Kingdom* (Cmnd 9438, February 1985)

Home Office, *The Interception of Communications in the United Kingdom: A Consultation Paper* (Cm 4368, 1999)

Ian Leigh, 'A Tappers' Charter?' (1986) (Spring) *Public Law* 13

Ian J Lloyd, 'Legislation – The Interception of Communications Act 1985' (1986) 49 *Modern Law Review* 86, 95

Hitoshi Nasu, 'State Secrets Law and National Security' (2015) 64(2) *International Comparative Law* 365

David Ormerod and Simon McKay, 'Telephone Intercepts and Their Admissibility' (2004) 1 *Criminal Law Review* 16

Paul F Scott, 'Hybrid Institutions in the National Security Constitution: The Case of the Commissioners' (2019) 39(3) *Journal of Legal Studies* 432

J R Spencer, 'Telephone-Tap Evidence and Administrative Detention in the UK' in Marianne Wade and Almir Maljevic (eds) *A War on Terror? The European Stance on a New Threat; Changing Laws and Human Rights Implications* (Springer Publishing, 2010) 375

Rt Hon Sir Swinton Thomas, *Report of Interception of Communications Commissioner for 2000* (Cm 5296, 2001)

David Vincent, *The Culture of Secrecy: Britain 1832–1998* (Clarendon Publishing, 1999)

John Wadham, 'The Intelligence Services Act 1994' (1994) 57(6) *Modern Law Review* 916

Alan F Westin, *Privacy and Freedom* (Atheneum, 1967)

6 Disingenuous statutory regulation

Interception of communications, 2000–2013

Introduction

2 October 2000 marked the entry into force of the Tony Blair-led Labour government's flagship statute, the Human Rights Act (HRA) 1998. On the same day, Part I, Chapter 1 of the Regulation of Investigatory Powers Act (RIPA) 2000, regulating the interception of communications, and Part IV, creating new oversight mechanisms, also entered force. Entry into force of Part I, Chapter II (regulating the acquisition and disclosure of communications data), and Part III (governing the investigation of encrypted data) was substantially delayed due to the controversy surrounding them at the time.[1]

This chapter's structure

As this book seeks to illustrate a regulatory chronology of the evolutionary path to the IPA 2016, this chapter is confined to examining the rationale for, and effect of, Part I, Chapter I of RIPA 2000 and the oversight regime created in Part IV. Furthermore, although these parts of RIPA endured until the enactment of the IPA 2016 in December of that year, the chapter ends just prior to the Intelligence Shock of 7 June 2013, as events following it would impact the UK investigatory powers regime as a whole. RIPA additionally introduced regulation of covert surveillance and the use of Covert Human Intelligences Sources (CHIS) in a dedicated Part II of the Act, with then-Home Secretary Jack Straw explaining that the powers therein were 'not new', but that their use would now be on a statutory basis and 'properly regulated', thus providing (without creating any illegality) that, 'where such actions are authorised properly under...[RIPA's]... provisions, that will be an answer to any subsequent assertion based on article 8 of the European convention that a person's privacy has been invaded without justification'.[2] RIPA Part II however falls outside the scope of this work as

1 Part I Chapter II entered force on 5 January 2004. See Chapter 8 of this book, and Part III (not covered in this book) entered force on 1 October 2007.

2 Jack Straw, HC Deb 6 Mar 2000, vol 345, col 767. See generally RIPA 2000, Part II, still in force.

its provisions relate to the acquisition of 'private information' obtained through investigative techniques not generally involving ***direct*** targeted investigation of communications or data in transit or at rest, but rather of human actors.[3] In conceptual terms, RIPA Part II can be viewed as HUMINT-focused as opposed to COMINT-focused. This assists in explaining why, unlike RIPA's covert communications and data investigative provisions, they were not transferred to the IPA 2016.

RIPA Part I, Chapter I

Part I, Chapter I of RIPA involves only 20 sections. However, their inherent complexity, opacity and the scope and magnitude of communications and data investigation they enabled were perpetually controversial. As such, this chapter, after outlining some of the key changes and definitional improvements, focuses on the myth of 'blanket surveillance' that evolved after they entered force. It initially examines communications and data investigation enabled by the somewhat disingenuously titled 'targeted' interception warrants (hereafter section 8[1] warrants) and how a particularly tenuous definition of 'person' enabled what would become euphemistically termed 'thematic warrants'. It then examines the controversy surrounding 'mass' or 'blanket' communications surveillance arising from RIPA's section 8(4)–(6) 'certificated warrant' regime authorizing the interception and examination of tranches of 'external' communications.[4] As these provisions approximated those in the IOCA 1985,[5] the chapter also explores in detail the facts and issues raised in the first legal challenge brought before the European Court of Human Rights (ECtHR) regarding the scope and use of certificated warrants; that brought by *Liberty and Others v UK*.[6] This challenge occupied both the newly constituted Investigatory Powers Tribunal (IPT) and the ECtHR for the first eight operational years of RIPA 2000. As the IPT constituted a new beginning in *post hoc* independent oversight previously undertaken by three separate tribunals, a short commentary on its role in the RIPA era is also offered. The role and performance of the revamped Interception of Communications Commissioner as regards RIPA Part I, Chapter I is also assessed, as both the IOCCO (as the Commissioner later became known) and the IPT played a role in shaping the oversight framework now offered in the IPA 2016. The chapter concludes by asking if it is fair to label the regulation of interception of communications in RIPA 2000, Part I, Chapter I as disingenuous. Firstly though, some analysis of the overall purpose of RIPA 2000 as a whole is offered.

3 See generally RIPA 2000, s26 and, in particular, s26(10) wherein 'private information' in relation to a person, includes any information relating to his private or family life.

4 RIPA 2000, Part I, Chapter I.

5 IOCA 1985, s3.

6 *Liberty and others v United Kingdom* (2009) 48 EHRR 1. The case can be contrasted with *Malone v UK* (1984) 7 EHRR 14 and *Halford v UK* (1997) 24 EHRR 523 which challenged the *absence* of statutory provisions.

Rationalizing RIPA 2000: the Regulation of Investigatory Powers Bill

In introducing the Regulation of Investigatory Powers Bill (RIPB) at Second Reading, Labour Home Secretary Jack Straw pronounced it 'a significant step forward for the protection of human rights', with human rights considerations having dominated its drafting. In further acknowledging that none of the law enforcement activities it covered were new (having been previously subject to administrative governance), he asserted that

> what is new is that, for the first time, the use of these techniques will be properly regulated by law and externally supervised...[ensuring]...that law enforcement and other operations are consistent with the duties imposed on public authorities by the European convention on human rights and by the HRA 1998.[7]

He then placed the RIPB in context as 'one of a series of measures aimed at securing a better balance between law enforcement and individual rights', additionally referring to, amongst the UKIC enabling statutes and others covered in the previous chapter, the Police and Criminal Evidence Act (PACE) 1984, further noting that the RIPB would 'in conjunction with existing legislation, consolidate the law on the use of investigatory powers'.[8] It is thus fair to state that RIPA 2000 primarily aspired to assure the public that the 'relevant investigatory powers were used in accordance with human rights'.[9] In terms of rationalizing the IPA 2016, RIPA 2000 purported to be the final statute that covered the remainder of the field of investigatory powers, those that were conducted without the knowledge of the subject(s) under investigation.

Distinguishing 'investigatory powers'

Mr Straw's references to PACE 1984 and 'consolidation' are interesting and, on one view, somewhat ironic. Writing in 2005, John R Spencer highlighted the fact that in 1981, a Royal Commission on Criminal Procedure (Philips Commission)[10] had recommended a single statute governing the 'coercive powers of public authorities to gather evidence'.[11] This had largely become manifest in PACE 1984, but contrary to the Philips Commission's recommendation, 'covert evidence-gathering by the police' had been omitted from the ambit of

7 Jack Straw, HC Deb, 6 Mar 2000, vol 345, col 767.
8 ibid.
9 Explanatory Notes to RIPA 2000, para 3.
10 Professor Sir Cyril Phillips, *Report of the Royal Commission on Criminal Procedure*, (Cmnd 8092, 1981).
11 J R Spencer, 'Prosecution Powers to Gather Evidence: The Case for Reform' (2005) *Archbold News*.

PACE.[12] Spencer further lamented the subsequent 'walk-away' by successive governments from the unity of the original PACE scheme, viewing it as having been thoroughly destroyed by 'raft upon raft of new coercive and invasive powers of evidence-gathering', including RIPA 2000.[13] He noted that as a consequence, 'covert evidence-gathering' by the police was now regulated 'in two different Acts (Part III of the Police Act 1997 and RIPA 2000)[14] and consisted of 'three separate schemes: one for telephone-tapping,[15] one for bugging and burgling',[16] and one for other covert practices[17]...all...[differing]...radically from the scheme contained in PACE'.[18]

Following the Philips Commission recommendations however would have meant separating regulation of covert communications and data-investigative powers conducted by law enforcement from that governing the UKIC, thus aligning with Gordon Walker's dissenting voice in the Birkett Report 1957.[19] A related consequence therefore would have been the introduction of Ministerial warrants for interception and national security considerations into a statute providing for overt responses to 'arrestable offences'[20] and judicial authorization of the most intrusive powers.[21] Consequently it is less surprising that this particular Philips Commission recommendation was not implemented.

A similar question relatable to the concept of consolidation was posed at second reading by Simon Hughes (Liberal Democrat), who asked Mr Straw to explain 'two matters relating to its central proposition'.[22] The first was why the opportunity had not been taken 'to bring all the different authorities to intercept under a common procedure, so that there could be just one', as opposed to 'having nine different sets of powers and sets of authorities'.[23] The second was why the opportunity had not been taken to 'do what many democratic countries have done, and transfer the authority power from politicians or officials to a judicial authority in the first instance'.[24]

His reference to nine powers and authorities referred to the fact that the RIPB (and the subsequent Act) contained: three distinct authorization mechanisms whereby the interception of communications would be considered as conducted

12 ibid.
13 ibid.
14 The Police Act 1997, Part III and RIPA 2000.
15 An early description of interception of communications, regulated in RIPA 2000, Part I, Chapter I.
16 Police Act 1997, Part III.
17 RIPA 2000, Part I, Chapter II and Part II.
18 Spencer, 'Prosecution Powers to gather evidence' (n11) 6.
19 Discussed in Chapter 4 of this volume.
20 PACE 1984, s24.
21 ibid, s8 and schedule 1.
22 Rt Hon Simon Hughes, HC Deb 6 Mar 2000, vol 345, col 769.
23 ibid.
24 ibid.

with lawful authority;[25] two mechanisms enabling the acquisition or disclosure of communications data;[26] three authorization mechanisms relating to directed surveillance, the use of CHIS, and intrusive surveillance respectively;[27] and a power to issue a disclosure requirement in relation to protected information.[28]

RIPA, Part 1: the questionable Privacy Impact Assessments

Mr Straw's response to the first question is instructive in that, in addition to offering a logical response to an inherently illogical question,[29] the somewhat arbitrary Home Office 'Privacy Impact Assessments' in relation to the various investigatory techniques the subject of regulation were again in evidence:

> we are not dealing with matters that are exactly similar. There is a world of difference between the interception of someone's telephone or telecommunications system and, for example, the planting of a covert microphone, and the use of directed surveillance...We need a regime or set of regimes for regulation that are appropriate to the sort of investigatory powers that are used. It would be absurd and impractical if, every time the police wished to use directed surveillance, they had to approach the Secretary of State or a judge for a warrant. Equally, it would be inappropriate – I do not think that it is the subject of any argument in the House – if warrants for telephone interceptions were authorised at a lower level than they are now. Therefore, we have produced bespoke authorisation procedures that are fitted to the particular powers in the Bill.[30]

The 'world of difference' and structure of the 'bespoke authorisation procedures', or more particularly, the privacy impact assessments underpinning them, were not without their critics. Gillian Ferguson and John Wadham, for example, in finding that 'RIPA fails to deal with privacy in a logical or structured way', opined that

25 RIPA 2000, s3 (where one party to the communication consented to its interception, or where it was authorized under the Wireless Telegraphy Act 1949, section 5). See also s4 (interception where the 'interceptor' believes target is outside the UK, interception in prisons etc.) and s5 interception by virtue of a Ministerial warrant. Each provision is explored in depth in Simon McKay, *Covert Policing* (OUP, 2011) 88–91.

26 RIPA 2000, s22 and McKay, *Covert Policing* (n25) 119–133.

27 ibid, ss 28, 29, and 32. See also the Regulation of Investigatory Powers (Scotland) Act 2000, which introduced a replicant of RIPA, Part II for Scotland's devolved jurisdiction in respect of serious crime only (national security and economic wellbeing being reserved matters under the Scotland Act 1998, schedule 5.

28 ibid, s49.

29 The inherent illogicality lies, in addition to Mr Straw's answer, in the fact that applications to acquire communications data, even in the year 2000, numbered in the tens of thousands, thus rendering a single Ministerial or judicial authorization scheme unworkable from the outset.

30 Rt Hon Jack Straw, HC Deb, 6 Mar 2000, vol 345, cols 769, 770.

it would seem logical to expect that 'in every context where privacy was highly valued, the law would provide similar controls and safeguards', before concluding that 'RIPA does not comply with that expectation'.[31] Their illustrative example was that 'although it is a criminal offence to listen in to telephone calls without authorisation, no crime is necessarily committed if a listening device is placed in a bedroom without authorisation'.[32] This view aligns with McKay's critical appraisal of 'RIPA's self-imposed limitation', wherein, although creating authorization regimes for covert conduct, the 'obtuse' drafting of section 80 meant that there was no unlawful act (other than in circumstances of unlawful interception)[33] of failing to obtain or to take steps to obtain one of the authorizations provided for.[34] As McKay witheringly put it, section 80 made RIPA no more than a voluntary code.[35]

As regards Mr Hughes second question, that of 'the long-running debate' regarding the utility of judicial oversight, Mr Straw referred to the 'very careful' exercise of powers by himself and previous Secretaries of State, and to the *post hoc* scrutiny of the Interception of Communications Commissioner (then Lord Nolan), holding that the system is judicially supervised by virtue of the Commissioner having held high judicial office.[36] There was no likelihood, at this stage of the history of interception regulation, of the executive ceding power to the judiciary.

The increasing influence of data as intelligence raw material

In addition to introducing 'communications data' in the RIPB, Mr Straw also made direct reference to the increasing utility of data as intelligence raw material, stating that the RIPB was 'designed to ensure that not only telephone calls, but – subject to proper procedures, when appropriate – data streams can be

31 Gillian Ferguson and John Wadham, 'Privacy and surveillance: a review of the Regulation of the Investigatory Powers Act 2000', (2003) *European Human Rights Law Review Supplement* (Special issue: privacy 2003), 101.

32 ibid.

33 Interception of communications without lawful authority was a criminal offence under RIPA 200, s1. It remains so by virtue of the IPA 2016, s3.

34 McKay, *Covert Policing* (n25) 6. RIPA 2000, s80 provided that nothing in any of the provisions of this Act by virtue of which conduct of any description is or may be authorized by any warrant, authorization, or notice, or by virtue of which information may be obtained in any manner, shall be construed – (a) as making it unlawful to engage in any conduct of that description which is not otherwise unlawful under this Act and would not be unlawful apart from this Act; (b) as otherwise requiring – (i) the issue, grant or giving of such a warrant, authorization or notice, or (ii) the taking of any step for or towards obtaining the authority of such a warrant, authorization or notice, before any such conduct of that description is engaged in; or (c) as prejudicing any power to obtain information by any means not involving conduct that may be authorized under this Act.

35 McKay, *Covert Policing* (n25) 7.

36 HC Deb, 6 Mar 2000, vol 345, col 770.

intercepted', noting that, 'given the current vast scale of data traffic, which was unimagined even 15 years ago...[at the time of the IOCA 1985's enactment]... the possibilities for law enforcement agencies to keep track of that traffic, except for very specific and targeted purposes, is very limited'.[37] The RIPB, and ultimately RIPA 2000, introduced the notion of 'communications' and 'data' as being of equal intelligence or evidential utility.

A clever definition of 'communication'

RIPA 2000 extended the inferable definition of 'communication' in the Telecommunications Act 1984 to encompass:

> anything transmitted by means of a postal service; anything comprising speech, music, sounds, visual images or *data of any description*; and *signals serving either for the impartation of anything between persons, between a person and a thing or between things or for the actuation or control of any apparatus.*[38]

The inclusion of the infinite term 'data of any description' was cleverly technology-neutral and also accommodated Mr Straw's views regarding 'data-streams'.

RCD: a high-value intelligence source

It also acknowledged the reality that what was termed 'related communications data' (RCD) constituted an inevitable by-product of communications intercepted in the course of transmission. RIPA warrants thus not only authorized a limited range of specified applicants to engage in conduct necessary to secure 'the interception in the course of their transmission by means of a postal service or telecommunication system of the communications described in the warrant',[39] but also to engage in 'conduct for obtaining RCD'.[40] RCD was defined as

> so much of any communications data (within the meaning of Chapter II of this Part) as...is obtained by, or in connection with, the interception; and...relates to the communication or to the sender or recipient, or intended recipient, of the communication.[41]

As such, it was distinguishable from CD 'at rest' in the custody or control of communications service providers (CSPs). RCD was eventually acknowledged

37 HC Deb, 6 Mar 2000, vol 345, col 771.
38 RIPA 2000, s81(1), emphasis added.
39 ibid, s5(1) (a).
40 ibid, s5(6) (b).
41 ibid, s20.

as having become of vital intelligence-production importance to the UKIC and LEA's, particularly GCHQ.[42]

Despite its inclusion in the RIPA 2000, Part I, Chapter I intercept regime, RCD did not fall within the definition of 'intercepted material', which was limited to only the content of communications.[43] The effect of this only became clear when examining the associated safeguard provisions.[44] These imposed a duty on a Secretary of State to ensure that safeguard arrangements were in place to ensure that the requirements of section 15 ('general safeguards') and section 16, ('extra safeguards in the case of section 8(4) 'certificated warrants') were complied with.[45] These included, *inter alia*, arrangements to ensure: that the distribution and disclosure of intercepted material and RCD are kept to a minimum;[46] that all copies of any intercepted material and RCD be destroyed as soon as it is no longer necessary to retain it for any of the authorized purposes;[47] and that intercepted material and RCD are stored in a secure manner for as long as they are retained.[48] Therefore, as regards section 15, intercepted material and RCD were subject to the same safeguards. However, RIPA's section 16 adds additional safeguards for 'certificated warrants' (discussed shortly) applied only to 'intercepted material', thus excluding RCD.[49] It seems unlikely that this was accidental, as section 15 expressly included RCD as distinct from 'intercepted material' and if it were not so, there would have been no requirement for a separate definition for RCD. Given the acknowledged 'primary value' of bulk RCD acquisition to the UKIC,[50] the exclusion of RCD from RIPA's section 16 additional safeguards, when considered alongside its additional exclusion from most of the provisions of the Data Protection Act (DPA) 1998 and its associated fair processing principles[51] raises the question of why it was so excluded. The most likely explanation is that the super-computing power and investigative data-analysis techniques already available to the UKIC and LEAs meant that it was operationally impractical to fetter RCD investigation with similar safeguards to those for external communications content.[52]

42 UK Parliamentary Intelligence and Security Committee (UKPISC), *Privacy and Security: A Modern and Transparent Legal Framework* (HC 2014-15, 1075-I) 48–50.
43 RIPA 2000, s20, 'intercepted material', in relation to an interception warrant, means the contents of any communications intercepted by an interception to which the warrant relates.
44 ibid, s15.
45 ibid, s15(1).
46 ibid, s15(2).
47 ibid, s15(3).
48 ibid, s15(5).
49 ibid, s16(1).
50 UKPISC *Privacy and Security Report 2015* (n42) para 80.
51 By virtue of the DPA 1998, ss28, personal data (of which CD is but one strain) is exempted from the data protection provisions of that Act and the schedule 1 processing principles on the issue of a Secretary of State's Certificate.
52 Whilst beyond the scope of this book, investigative data mining is undoubtedly a core business for the UKIC and LEAs. As regards its practical application to investigations, see gener-

Rationalizing RIPA, Part 1, the implicit influence of the UKUSA Agreement

RIPA's definition of communication also cleverly maintained the Telecommunications Act 1984-based inclusion of 'signals', thus enabling the continuing secret acquisition of SIGINT by GHCQ and Defence Intelligence as envisaged under the UKUSA Agreement. This was not referred to in any of the debates or publications relating to RIPA's enactment, a fact explained by the then-prevailing secrecy surrounding the UKUSA Agreement. Another noteworthy aspect of RIPA 2000 was that it corrected the IOCA 1985 provision that enabled a Secretary of State to theoretically address an interception warrant to anyone.[53] Under the new act, a very limited number of applicants were provided for.[54] Notably, military interception of communications was quietly brought into the regulatory ambit with the inclusion of Defence Intelligence (DI).[55] There is little in the public domain about the role of DI in the UK's overall communications and data-investigative machinery, but they were obviously undertaking a sufficient degree of SIGINT production in support of the civilian UKIC around 1999/2000 to warrant inclusion. The annual reports of the Interception of Communications Commissioner's Office, established under s58(1) of RIPA and published between 2000 and 2016, carry no information regarding the role or degree of civilian communications investigation undertaken by DI.[56]

The UKUSA Agreement, 'Echelon', and RIPA 2000

The wall of secrecy amongst the five UKUSA Agreement eyes surrounding the fact of its existence and its ongoing implementation was beginning to experience

ally Colleen McCue, *Data Mining and Predictive Analysis: Intelligence Gathering and Crime Analysis* (2nd edn, Butterworth-Heinemann, 2015). As regards its undoubted value and utility see UKPISC *Privacy and Security Report 2015* (n42) para 90; Independent Review of Terrorism Legislation (IRTL), *A Question of Trust: Report of the Investigatory Powers Review* paras 7.43–7.51.

53 IOCA 1985, ss2–5.

54 RIPA 2000, s6(2)

> (a) the Director-General of the Security Service; (b) the Chief of the Secret Intelligence Service; (c) the Director of GCHQ; (d) the Director General of the National Crime Agency; (e) the Commissioner of Police of the Metropolis; (f) the Chief Constable of the Police Service of Northern Ireland; (g) the chief constable of the Police Service of Scotland; (h) the Commissioners for Her Majesty's Revenue and Customs; (i) the Chief of Defence Intelligence; (j) a person who, for the purposes of any international mutual assistance agreement, is the competent authority of a country or territory outside the UK.

55 RIPA 2000, s6(2) (i) DI remain empowered to apply for interception warrants under the IPA 2016, s18(1) (g).

56 It appears that DI fell outside the oversight of the IOCCO. See generally the archived Annual IOCCO Reports available at the website of the Investigatory Powers Commissioner's Office (IPCO) created by the IPA 2016. <https://www.ipco.org.uk> accessed 30 October 2020.

some cracks around the time of enactment of RIPA Part I, Chapter I. On 5 July 2000, the European Parliament had established a 'Temporary Committee on the ECHELON Interception System'(Echelon Committee).[57] This had followed a debate focused on a Science and Technology Options Assessment (STOA) study investigating allegations made by the by now renowned investigative journalist Duncan Campbell at a Citizens' Freedoms and Rights, Justice and Home Affairs Committee hearing, wherein the existence of the ECHELON system, which in practical terms gave effect to the UKUSA Agreement, was alleged.[58] In September 1998, the European Parliament had been apprised of the contents of a report by the Omega Research Foundation somewhat ominously entitled 'An Appraisal of the Technologies of Political Control' as part of a broader scientific and technological options assessment (STOA) research undertaking. This wide-ranging and prescient document asserted the existence of 'two separate national and international communications interception systems', namely:

1 The UK/USA system comprising the activities of military intelligence agencies such as NSA-CIA in the USA subsuming GCHQ & MI6 in the UK operating a system known as ECHELON.
2 The EU-FBI system links up various law enforcement agencies such as the FBI, police, customs, immigration, and internal security.[59]

The Echelon Committee produced a comprehensive 194-page investigative report (the ECHELON Committee Report), published on 11 July 2001. It included chapters, hitherto unprecedented in their detail, outlining the operations of foreign intelligence services;[60] technical conditions governing the interception of communications;[61] satellite communications technology;[62] and 'clues to the existence of at least one global interception system'.[63] The level of technical detail regarding an area of pre-existing secrecy remains fascinating. Indeed a very good case was made for the argument that the UKUSA parties could, and continued to, intercept every known form of electronic communication then

57 European Parliament, 'Report on the existence of a global system for the interception of private and commercial communications (ECHELON interception system)' (11 July 2001, 2001/2098[INI]). <http://cr.yp.to/export/2001/09.07-europe.html#1> accessed 3 November 2020.
58 ibid.
59 An Omega Foundation Summary and options Report for the European Parliament, 'An Appraisal of the Technologies of Political Control' (September 1998) <https://cryptome.org/stoa-atpc-so.htm#N_32_> accessed 3 November 2020.
60 ECHELON Committee Report (n57) Chapter 2.
61 ibid, Chapter 3.
62 ibid, Chapter 4.
63 ibid, Chapter 5.

in existence.[64] Given the pre-existing general secrecy surrounding the UKUSA Agreement, Chapter 5 of the Echelon Committee report contained a surprising source (among many documentary and testamentary sources) affirming its existence,[65] namely the UK's Parliamentary Intelligence and Security Committee established only six years previously.[66]

The Echelon Committee made a number of conclusions, which included that

> a global system for intercepting communications exists, operating by means of cooperation proportionate to their capabilities among the USA, the UK, Canada, Australia and New Zealand under the UKUSA Agreement…It may be assumed, in view of the evidence and the consistent pattern of statements from a very wide range of individuals and organisations, including American sources, that the system or parts of it were, at least for some time, code-named ECHELON. What is important is that *its purpose is to intercept private and commercial communications*, and not military communications.[67]

In finding that industrial espionage (it had been alleged that huge EU industries such as Airbus had been adversely affected by ECHELON interceptions, and the ECHELON system itself likely contravened EU competition law, as well as fundamental and human rights), the Echelon Committee made a plethora of recommendations, chief amongst which

64 ibid, Chapter 1.6:

> The first such feature attributed to…[ECHELON]…is the capacity to carry out quasi-total surveillance. Satellite receiver stations and spy satellites in particular are alleged to give it the ability to intercept any telephone, fax, Internet or e-mail message sent by any individual and thus to inspect its contents. The second unusual feature of ECHELON is said to be that the system operates worldwide on the basis of cooperation proportionate to their capabilities among several states (the UK, the USA, Canada, Australia and New Zealand), giving it an added value in comparison to national systems: the states participating in ECHELON (UKUSA states) can place their interception systems at each other's disposal, share the cost and make joint use of the resulting information. This type of international cooperation is essential in particular for the worldwide interception of satellite communications, since only in this way is it possible to ensure in international communications that both sides of a dialogue can be intercepted. It is clear that, in view of its size, a satellite receiver station cannot be established on the territory of a state without that state's knowledge. Mutual agreement and proportionate cooperation among several states in different parts of the world is essential.

65 ibid, Chapter 5 at 5.4.2.

66 UKPISC, *Annual Report 1999–2000* (Cm4897, November 2000) para 14, 'GCHQ has continued to provide valuable intelligence for both policymakers and operational deployments of UK forces…the quality of intelligence gathered clearly reflects the value of the close cooperation under the UKUSA Agreement'.

67 ECHELON Committee Report (n57) Chapter 13, emphasis added.

> called upon the Secretary-General of the Council of Europe...to submit to the Ministerial Committee a proposal to protect private life, as guaranteed in Article 8 of the ECHR, brought into line with modern communication and interception methods by means of an additional protocol or, together with the provisions governing data protection, as part of a revision of the Convention on Data Protection, with the proviso that this should neither undermine the level of legal protection established by the European Court of Human Rights nor reduce the flexibility which is vital if future developments are to be taken into account.[68]

The Report's recommendations were adopted by parliamentary resolution on 5 September 2001, only four days before the world-changing terror attacks against the USA.[69] The fact that the UKUSA Agreement was effectively in the public domain by this time strongly suggests that RIPA's drafting, particularly its provisions on certificated warrants and its continuation of the inclusion of 'signals' in the definition of 'communications', had the hitherto secret agreement in mind. RIPA's 'certificated warrant' provisions (section 8[4]–[6]) largely mirrored those in the IOCA 1985 and are examined in detail later in this chapter.

NTAC

The UKPISC 2000 Report also makes reference to its interest in the Regulation of Investigatory Powers Bill (RIPB), which would be RIPA 2000 by the time of publication, noting that its recommendations as to interception warrant applications and the amalgamation of Tribunals had been accepted.[70] A following paragraph introduced the establishment of a National Technical Assistance Centre (NTAC).

> A 24-hour centre operated on behalf of all the law enforcement, security and intelligence agencies, providing a central facility for the complex processing needed to derive intelligence material from lawfully intercepted *computer to computer communications and from lawfully seized computer data*, which are being increasingly encrypted. The NTAC will also support the technical infrastructure for the lawful interception of communications services including internet services...it will be operated by the National Criminal Intelligence Service (NCIS) on behalf of the Home Office, the three Agencies will provide

68 ibid, (n60) Chapter 13.2.

69 European Parliament resolution on the existence of a global system for the interception of private and commercial communications (ECHELON interception system) (2001/2098(INI)) 5 September 2001 available at <http://cryptome.org/echelon-090501.htm> accessed 20 October 2020.

70 UKPISC 2000 Report (n66) paras 96 and 97.

> the NTAC with both some staff and will fund part of its activity. They will also be fully engaged in its operation and will be customers of its product.[71]

To this day, NTAC plays a vital role in the processing of intercepted communications.[72] Consequently, it can be asserted with confidence that RIPA 2000, Part I, Chapter I was drafted to ensure that it fitted seamlessly with the requirements of the NCIS and the UK Intelligence Community at the time. As part of the wider aim to ensure that all forms of communications and data, whether in transit or at rest, were lawfully accessible for investigative purposes.

Meaning of interception

Despite its statutory predecessor's title, the IOCA 1985 had not included a definition of 'interception'. In addition, the territorial or jurisdictional scope of interception had not been circumscribed. RIPA 2000 changed that, and provided a complex and intricate and ultimately narrow definition of the conduct that would amount to interception of a communication for the purposes of that Act alone.[73] The communications the subject of the warrant (or the alleged criminal offence of unlawful interception) were required to be 'in the course of transmission'[74] by a 'public postal system' or a 'telecommunications system'.[75] A consequence of the narrow definition was that conduct acquiring communications content

71 ibid, para 98.

72 UKPISC, *Privacy and Security Report 2015* (n42) paras 29–31.

73 RIPA 2000, s2.

74 See RIPA 2000, s2(2) which states that

> For the purposes of this Act, but subject to the following provisions of this section, a person intercepts a communication in the course of its transmission by means of a telecommunication system if, and only if, he – (a) so modifies or interferes with the system, or its operation, (b) so monitors transmissions made by means of the system, or (c) so monitors transmissions made by wireless telegraphy to or from apparatus comprised in the system, as to make some or all of the contents of the communication available, while being transmitted, to a person other than the sender or intended recipient of the communication.

This is then expanded upon in s2(8) which states that

> for the purposes of this section the cases in which any contents of a communication are to be taken to be made available to a person while being transmitted shall include any case in which any of the contents of the communication, while being transmitted, are diverted or recorded so as to be available to a person subsequently. This encompasses voicemail and pager systems.

The findings in *R v E* (2004) 2 Cr App R 29 provide the leading UK judicial interpretation of this phrase.

75 Defined at RIPA 2000, s2(1) as 'any system (including the apparatus comprized in it) which exists (whether wholly or partly in the United Kingdom or elsewhere) for the purpose of facilitating the transmission of communications by any means involving the use of electrical or electro-magnetic energy'.

(i.e. its substantive expression or meaning) or RCD falling outside this definition would not be construed as interception, meaning that RIPA's provisions could, at least in theory, be circumvented.[76] The fact that Simon McKay's analysis and commentary on the legislative and judicial interpretations of RIPA's 'meaning of interception', and 'in the course of transmission' runs to 11 pages, illustrates the complex and technical nature of section 2.[77] The IPA 2016 has thankfully (albeit counter-intuitively) clarified the term 'in the course of transmission' to mean 'any time while the communication is being transmitted, and any time when the communication is stored in or by the system (whether before or after its transmission)'.[78]

Intercepted material in evidence

RIPA also continued the IOCA 1985's proscription on reference to, or use of, interception or evidence obtained thereof being disclosed in British courts.[79] As discussed in the previous chapter, the merits of easing the proscription had been debated many times, however, the policy remains intact in the IPA 2016.[80]

Grounds for issuing interception warrants

These replicated those in the IOCA 1985 and indeed throughout the history of the practice (and those now in the IPA 2016), namely the interests of national security, the protection of the economic wellbeing of the UK, and the prevention or detection of serious crime. There was an additional provision for issuing a warrant in relation to the prevention or detection of serious crime as part of giving effect to an international mutual legal assistance agreement.[81]

Rationalizing RIPA, Part I, Chapter I, and the myth of 'blanket surveillance'

The myth that the UK legislature enables 'mass' or 'blanket' surveillance has permeated the debate surrounding the communications investigation regulation since at least the time of Pincher's 'cable vetting sensation' outlined in Chapter 4 herein. Even the enactment of the IPA 2016 has failed to fully assuage civil libertarian concerns. Whilst occasionally attributable to civil libertarian or media

76 e.g. by covert surveillance. See McKay, *Covert Policing* (n25) 76–87 for a detailed analysis of the provision and the leading cases interpreting it.
77 ibid.
78 IPA 2016, s4(4).
79 RIPA 2000, ss17–18 and IOCA 1985, s9.
80 IPA 2016, ss57–59 regarding unauthorized disclosures.
81 RIPA 2000, s5(3) (a)–(d).

hyperbole,[82] it cannot be disputed that RIPA's operational architecture, wherein the opaquely drafted requirements for interception warrants (section 8) required to be read with the equally opaque conduct permitted (section 5) and accompanying Code of Practice (Interception CoP)[83] assisted in perpetuating mistrust and misconceptions of the UK's communications investigation regime. Even after such a reading, the sheer magnitude of the communications-related information acquisition being implicitly authorized under RIPA's twin-track approach to interception would have remained unascertainable but for the post-2013 policy of transparent secrecy on the part of the UKPISC.[84] RIPA 2000, section 8(4) replaced the virtually identical provisions of the IOCA 1985,[85] which themselves repealed the OSA 1920 provisions outlined earlier.[86] The UKPISC provided an in some respects painfully detailed[87] (and in others almost comically redacted)[88] exposition of the practical operation of the UK's bulk interception regime in 2015. This was superseded by an arguably more objective version in the same year from the IRTL's Investigatory Powers Review.[89] The best exposition however came in his later Bulk Powers Review 2016, which made a significant contribution to shaping the drafting and scope of bulk powers more generally in the IPA 2016.[90] In a nutshell, RIPA 2000, s8(4) empowered the Secretary of State to issue an interception warrant exempted from the purportedly proportionate 'ordinary' or 'targeted' interception warrant criteria outlined in sections 8(1)[91] and 8(2).[92] It was through that exemption that *implicit* authorization was given

82 See, for example, Liberty, 'Mass Surveillance and Snoopers Charter, <https://www.libertyhumanrights.org.uk/issue/mass-surveillance-briefings-and-reports/> accessed 20 September 2020; AFP, 'Academics Petition for End to Blanket Surveillance' (*SecurityWeek*, 3 January 2014) <www.securityweek.com/academics-petition-end-blanket-surveillance> accessed 9 September 2020; Simon Jenkins, 'Blanket Digital Surveillance is a Start. But How About a Camera in Every Bathroom?' *The Guardian* (17 July 2014). <www.theguardian.com/commentisfree/2014/jul/17/blanket-digital-surveillance-is-a-start-but-how-about-a-camera-in-every-bathroom> accessed 9 September 2020.

83 Home Office, *Interception of Communications Code of Practice* (7th edn, TSO, 2007).

84 UKPISC, *Privacy and Security Report 2015* (n42) para 59,

> The proportion of bearers making up the internet…accessed by GCHQ's 'bulk interception' systems is very small – and certainly far from the 'blanket' coverage of all communications that some are concerned is happening. Nevertheless, the volume of communications…and the number of people those communications relate to, is still extremely large. We therefore consider that 'bulk' remains an appropriate term to use…describing this capability.

85 IOCA 1985 s3(2).

86 OSA 1920, s4(1).

87 UKPISC *Privacy and Security Report 2015* (n42) Chapters 4 and 5.

88 ibid, see particularly paras 58, 60, 61, and 62.

89 IRTL, *RIPR 2015* (n52) paras 6.45–6.59 and 7.20–7.31.

90 IRTL, *Report of the Bulk Powers Review* (Cm9326, August 2016) paras 2.13–2.28.

91 Requiring the interception warrant to name or describe one person or a single set of premises.

92 Requiring that the interception warrant comprise one or more schedules setting out the addresses, numbers, apparatus, or other factors, or combination of factors to be used for identifying the communications to be intercepted.

for what is now understood as 'bulk interception'. Given that the IPA 2016 effectively reaffirmed the scope of RIPA 2000's provisions, it is worth examining whether, in combination, targeted interception warrants (s8[1]) and bulk interception warrants (s8[4]) constituted or facilitated 'blanket surveillance' or provided latent potential to do so.

Section 8(1) Warrants

RIPA 2000, section 8(1) provided that:

> An interception warrant must name or describe either –
>
> (a) *one person* as the interception subject;
> or
> (b) *single set of premises* as the premises in relation to which the interception to which the warrant relates is to take place.[93]
>
> The provisions of an interception warrant describing communications the interception of which is authorised or required by the warrant must comprise one or more schedules setting out the addresses, numbers, apparatus or other factors, or combination of factors, that are to be used for identifying the communications that may be or are to be intercepted.[94]

The s8(1) 'targeted' interception warrant appeared self-explanatory, and, when read in conjunction with the requirements of section 5, that a Secretary of State assess the necessity[95] and proportionality of issue,[96] appeared ECHR compliant. Closer inspection revealed that such warrants, as a consequence of RIPA's drafting style, actually implicitly enabled a potentially huge acquisition of communications-related information on the basis of RIPA's definition of 'person'.

'Thematic warrants': when a 'person' is not a person

This 'included any organisation and any association or combination of persons'.[97] This incredibly broad and little-publicized definition cannot have been an accident

93 RIPA 2000, s8(1), emphasis added.
94 ibid, s8(2), emphasis added.
95 ibid, s5(3)

> in the interests of national security; (b) for the purpose of preventing or detecting serious crime; (c) for the purpose, in circumstances appearing to the Secretary of State to be relevant to the interests of national security, of safeguarding the economic wellbeing of the UK or (d) for the purpose, in circumstances appearing to the Secretary of State to be equivalent to those in which he would issue a warrant by virtue of paragraph (b), of giving effect to the provisions of any international mutual assistance agreement.

96 ibid, s5(2).
97 ibid, s81(1).

of drafting. Indeed, whilst acknowledging that 'the very significant majority of 8(1) warrants relate to one individual', the UKPISC publicly avowed for the first time that 'in some limited circumstances an 8(1) warrant may be "thematic" whilst simultaneously acknowledging that the term was not defined in statute'.[98] The potential scope of 'thematic warrants' was thus troubling, not least on the question of proportionality. They were reviewed after the 2013 Intelligence Shock and are thus revisited in Chapter 9 of this volume.

Thematic warrants and the ECtHR

It is puzzling that, in the comparative analysis undertaken in respect of the *Liberty* case in *Kennedy v United Kingdom*,[99] the ECtHR, after setting out RIPA's section 8(1) to 8(3) targeted warrant provisions in full,[100] appear to have been blind to the disingenuous drafting they were reading, holding that:

> in internal communications cases, the warrant itself must clearly specify, either by name or by description, *one person as the interception subject or a single set of premises as the premises in respect of which the warrant is ordered.* Names, addresses, telephone numbers and other relevant information must be specified in the schedule to the warrant. Indiscriminate capturing of vast amounts of communications is not permitted under the internal communications provisions of RIPA. The Court considers that, in the circumstances, no further clarification in the legislation or the Code of the categories of persons liable to have their communications intercepted can reasonably be required.[101]

Whilst 'indiscriminate' or 'vast' may not accurately describe the amount of intercepted material obtainable under a thematic interception warrant, there certainly, in the case of organizations, existed the potential for significant capture of intercepted material and collateral intrusion that the ECtHR apparently missed. The Court simply did not identify or engage with the RIPA definition of 'person'. Their omission is excusable on the ground that legal counsel for Kennedy, a 'person' in the literal sense, would have had no reason to query RIPA's definition of the term in front of Judge Garlicki et al. and thus have Europe's supreme arbiter explore it in depth. This is unfortunate, because in setting out the section 8(1) provision, but omitting or neglecting to scrutinize the scope of the definition within it, the ECtHR, in addition to upholding the holistic proportionality of RIPA's 'targeted' warrant regime, ultimately sanctioned the use of 'thematic

98 UKPISC, *Privacy and Security Report 2015* (n42) para 42: thematic warrants are examined further in Chapter 9 of this volume.
99 *Kennedy v United Kingdom* (2011) 52 EHRR 4.
100 ibid, (40)–(41).
101 ibid, (160), emphasis added.

warrants' despite the lack of an explicit statutory basis for them. It is difficult to avoid the conclusion that, as regards 'targeted' interception warrants, RIPAs definition of 'person', and the drafting of sections 8(1) to 8(3) that implicitly authorized 'thematic warrants', demonstrated the disingenuousness of the government of the day when enacting RIPA 2000. Intentionally or otherwise, the provisions misled the public and clouded the nature and scope of the interception regime.

RIPA 2000's 'bulk interception' provisions

> S8(4) The provisions relating to interception warrants [in section 8(1) and 8(2)] shall not apply to an interception warrant if – (a) the description of communications to which the warrant relates confines the conduct authorised or required by the warrant to conduct falling within subsection (5); and (b) at the time of the issue of the warrant, a certificate applicable to the warrant has been issued by the Secretary of State certifying – (i) the descriptions of intercepted material the examination of which he considers necessary; and (ii) that he considers the examination of material of those descriptions necessary as mentioned in section 5(3)(a), (b) or (c).[102]
>
> (5) Conduct falls within this subsection if it consists in – (a) the *interception of external communications* in the course of their transmission by means of a telecommunication system; and (b) any conduct authorised in relation to any such interception by section 5(6).[103]
>
> (6) A certificate for the purposes of subsection (4) shall not be issued except under the hand of the Secretary of State.[104]

From these three seemingly innocuous provisions, the drafters of RIPA 2000 enabled what is now commonly acknowledged as 'bulk' communications and RCD access on a mammoth scale. Between 2000 until 2013, this was largely beyond the knowledge or comprehension of the UK public, apart from those who needed to know. Given the regulatory continuation and relationship in terminology between s8(4) and its predecessor, s3(2) of the IOCA 1985 (which in turn replaced s4 of the Official Secret Act 1920), it is likely that bulk interception of communications 'sent or received outside the UK' expanded as investigative practice in direct proportion to the number of external communications being made.

As such, RIPA 2000, s8(4)–(6) can be more accurately and objectively described as authorizing 'bulk interception' as opposed to 'mass surveillance'. This meant that communications exiting or entering the UK could be 'collected' and after a secret 'filtering' process, 'intercepted material' that was deemed to fit

102 RIPA 2000, s8(4).
103 ibid, s8(5).
104 ibid, s8(6).

predetermined (but very broad) criteria,[105] outlined within a Secretary of State-issued certificate[106] accompanying the warrant, could be 'read, looked at or listened to'[107] by appropriately vetted intelligence analysts.

Scope and magnitude of bulk interception

The principal ground for complaint about the UK's electronic surveillance programmes such as 'bulk interception' has perpetually related to their 'scope and magnitude'.[108] Where such a complaint is made to the ECtHR, the Court firstly considers the complaint's admissibility.[109] In broad terms, once an application has been deemed admissible, the Court then makes findings as to whether a particular ECHR right (in intercept cases, primarily Article 8) has been interfered with by the state and, if so, whether the interference was justified. To be justified, the Court will have to find the interference to have been 'in accordance with the law' and considered 'necessary in a democratic society'. Prior to complaining to the ECtHR, 'challengers' are required to have exhausted all domestic avenues for remedy.[110] Given that interception of communications is a covert investigatory power exercised by the UKIC, amongst others, the only avenue open to challengers following the enactment of the IOCA 1985 was the IOCT established under the IOCA 1985, subsequently 'reinvented' as the Investigatory Powers Tribunal (IPT) with effect from 2 October 2000.[111] At that point in time, there was no right or avenue of appeal from an IOCT or IPT finding.[112] It has been shown that, over hundreds of years, the UK created regulatory provisions that sought to ensure that any type of communication made using any form of communication could be accessed if need be for investigative purposes linked to the protection of national security. The British state's policymakers had never been required to question if their regulation was necessary in a democratic society or, more importantly, proportionate to any legitimate aim being pursued. The NGO Liberty was going to change this.

105 The contents of Ministerial Certificates have tended to be secret, however an example of the category of communications to be intercepted is 'Material providing intelligence on terrorism (as defined by the Terrorism Act 2000 [as amended]), including, but not limited to, terrorist organisations, terrorists, active sympathisers, attack planning, fund-raising'.

106 RIPA 2000, s8(6) a certificate for the purposes of subsection (4) shall not be issued except under the hand of the Secretary of State.

107 ibid, s16(1) and 16(2).

108 The phrase used by the complainants in *Big Brother Watch and Others v United Kingdom* (Applications numbers 58170/13, 62322/14, and 24960/15, (3)).

109 ECHR, Article 35.

110 ibid.

111 RIPA 2000, s65(1).

112 A right of appeal has now been inserted with the creation of RIPA 2000, s67A inserted under the IPA 2016, s242.

The fifth interception scandal: Capenhurst Tower

In 1989 the UK Ministry of Defence (MoD) had issued an innocuous press release outlining their purchase of a site adjacent to British Nuclear Fuels at Capenhurst, Cheshire for an Electronic Test Facility (ETF). Its purpose was to 'test electronic equipment being developed for Ministry of Defence use'.[113] Capenhurst Tower was subsequently constructed and remained in use throughout the 1990s before being put up for sale by the MoD in late 1998. Following an inspection of the vacant tower, Mr Richard Lamont was the first to publish what he described as 'overwhelming' circumstantial evidence that it had in fact been 'a secret radio tower which the government used to intercept thousands of trunk phone lines running through Britain to the Republic of Ireland'.[114] He describes how, after first publishing his suspicions, investigative journalist Duncan Campbell 'phoned him up stating "frankly, I'm not convinced", wherein he took "cold feet" and deleted his article on 16 April 1999, before undertaking "a lot more research with Duncan Campbell in the intervening three months"'.[115] Their joint investigation came to the attention of the UK's Channel 4 News. On 15 July 1999, Channel 4 broadcast a five-minute news segment featuring Mr Campbell inspecting the disused facility, during which Mr Lamont's allegations were repeated, with Mr Campbell heard to state 'this proves it'.[116] The broadcast caused a furore; even during the five-minute segment references were made by various interviewees to 'information piracy on a grand scale', and doubts as to the existence of an effective remedy for people who thought their emails, faxes, and telephone calls had been intercepted. The severest criticism was that, in light of the terrorist and public order insurgency continuing in Northern Ireland, the UK was eavesdropping on its neighbour at a time they needed its cooperation.[117] Campbell illustrated the reaction in Republic of Ireland official circles. This included Foreign Affairs Minister David Andrews instructing the Irish Ambassador in London to raise the matter with the British authorities, ex-Taoiseach Albert Reynolds calling the tower an 'outrageous incursion into the sovereignty of the Irish state'; Fine Gael MP Gay Mitchell calling the tower's operation an 'offensive act', and Green MEP Patricia Reynolds calling for an official investigation, claiming that the tower's

113 Duncan Campbell, 'How Embassy Eavesdropping Works' <https://www.duncancampbell.org/embassy-bugging> accessed 29 April 2021.

114 Richard Lamont, 'Ministry of Defence Hid Microwave Phone-Tap Tower inside Nuclear Plant (15 April 1999) available at <http://www.lamont.me.uk/capenhurst/original.html> accessed 20 September 2020. His webpage states that he reinstated the article on 16 July 1999, the day following the Channel 4 News broadcast.

115 Richard Lamont, 'The Capenhurst Tower' (July 1999) available at <http://www.lamont.me.uk/capenhurst/followup.html> accessed 20 September 2020.

116 A recording featuring the original Channel 4 broadcast is embedded in Duncan Campbell's website: see generally Duncan Campbell, 'How Embassy Eavesdropping Works', (*DuncanCampbell.org*) <https://www.duncancampbell.org/embassy-bugging> accessed 29 September 2020.

117 ibid.

operation 'pose[d] alarming consequences not just for the basic civil liberties of the Irish public, but also for the economy'. [118]

Liberty and Others v United Kingdom

The investigation and broadcast led directly to the first legal challenge to the 'bulk' interception of communications brought by a collective of civil liberties advocates in *Liberty and Others v UK*.[119] This challenged the statutory forerunner to the RIPA 2000, s8(4)–(6) regime examined herein, namely that in the IOCA 1985 in operation throughout the nineties.[120] Warrants issued under the IOCA provisions required the interception, in the course of transmission by means of a public telecommunications system, of 'such *external communications* as described in the warrant and such other communications (if any) as it is necessary to intercept in order to intercept such external communications as are so described'.[121] When issuing such a warrant, the relevant Secretary of State also had to issue a certificate describing what intercepted material was permitted to be examined on national security, crime prevention/detection, or UK economic well-being grounds.[122] The *Liberty* collective's application was lodged on 9 September 1999, after the forum for their original complaint, the IOCT as then was, found no contravention of sections 2 to 5 of the 1985 Act.[123] The ECtHR did not publish the judgment until almost nine years later in June 2008, by which time the RIPA framework being discussed here had been in operation for eight years.[124] The long period of time between the application and the judgment was because the ECtHR had effectively postponed hearing the case until the newly constituted IPT had ruled on it. As in the IOCT finding, the IPT failed to uphold Liberty's complaint.[125] Consequently, before the ECtHR, the collective complainants alleged that 'between 1990 and 1997, telephone, facsimile, e-mail and data communications between them were intercepted by the Capenhurst facility, ***including legally privileged and confidential material***'.[126] The Court declared the complaint admissible.[127]

118 Duncan Campbell, 'Bugging Ring around Ireland' (25 July 1999). <https://www.duncancampbell.org/PDF/Bugging%20ring%20around%20Ireland.pdf> accessed 29 September 2020. This article provides significantly more detail on the story than was feasible herein.
119 *Liberty and Others v United Kingdom* (n6).
120 IOCA 1985, ss2–5.
121 ibid, s3(2) (a) 'external communication' meant a communication 'sent or received outside the UK'.
122 ibid, s3(2) (b).
123 *Liberty and Others v United Kingdom* (n6) (7).
124 ibid (69)–(70).
125 ibid, (14)–(15) referring to UKIPTrib PT/01/62 and 77.
126 ibid, (42). An expanded version of their allegation based on the Channel 4 documentary appears at (5).
127 ibid, (55).

'Neither Confirm Nor Deny'

In line with prevailing policy, the UK (Labour) government counsel employed a 'Neither Confirm Nor Deny' (NCND) approach to the proceedings, but indicated they were content for the Court to proceed on the hypothetical basis that the applicants, or indeed any person, could rightly claim that communications sent to or from their offices might have been intercepted at the Capenhurst ETF but that this could only have been under 'an appropriate warrant under section 3(2) of the 1985 Act'.[128] Their approach represents an early example of proceedings based on 'assumed facts' in consequence of the NCND policy, which dates back at least as far as the Mazzini affair. For the purposes of its own proceedings, the IPT has endorsed the NCND policy as it relates to interception of communications as being 'judicially recognized as a legitimate objective in relation to security and intelligence gathering activities and…not in itself incompatible with Convention rights'.[129] The IPT's adoption of 'assumed facts' proceedings has allowed it to hold hearings in public to consider questions of law without (at that stage) deciding whether the facts are true.[130]

The parties' submissions

These warrant examination as they demonstrate the civil libertarian perspective on the prevailing IOCA 1985 'certificated warrant' scheme, and, given the length of time the proceedings took, on its RIPA, s8(4)–(6) replacement. As regards the UK government's position, in addition to the ongoing use of NCND, their submissions demonstrate the prevailing 'defence' or 'respondent' position that would become more familiar as civil libertarian activism gathered the confidence and expertise to bring further legal challenges to aspects of the UK's data-investigation regime after the enactment of the HRA 1998 and RIPA 2000. These are useful statements of policy in a still relatively secret area of law. Thanks to the evidence adduced on Liberty's behalf from Duncan Campbell, now described in proceedings as a 'telecommunications expert', the Court was provided with a detailed description of how the interceptions were actually taking place under the hypothetical warrant.[131]

For the complainants

The complainants submitted that:

> since the…[IOCA]…procedure permitted the interception of all communications falling within the large category set out in each warrant, the only

128 ibid, (47).
129 UKIPTrib 01/62 and 01/77 (54).
130 Sir Rabinder Singh, Kay Everett Memorial Lecture, 'Holding the Balance: National Security, Civil Liberties and the Role of the Investigatory Powers Tribunal' (School of Oriental and African Studies, 20 February 2019) available at <https://www.ipt-uk.com/docs/soas-lecture-20-feb-19-final.pdf> accessed 20 September 2020.
131 *Liberty and Others v United Kingdom* (n6) (43).

> protection afforded to those whose communications were intercepted was that the Secretary of State, under section 6(1) of the Act, had to 'make such arrangements as he considers necessary for the purpose of securing that… so much of the intercepted material as is not certified by the certificate is not read, looked at or listened to by any person' unless the requirements of section 6(2) were met. However, the precise nature of these 'arrangements' were not, at the relevant time, made known to the public, nor was there any procedure available to permit an individual to satisfy him or herself that the 'arrangements' had been followed. The [IOCT] did not have jurisdiction to examine such compliance, and although the Commissioner was authorised under section 8 to review the adequacy of the 'arrangements' in general, he had no power to review whether they had been met in an individual case.[132]

Rationalizing 'bulk interception': for the UK government

The government submissions assist in rationalizing the British state's policy approach to strategic bulk interception as provided for in the IOCA 1985 regime and in RIPA 2000. It was argued that,

> the section 3(2) warrant regime was proportionate and 'necessary in a democratic society'. Democratic States faced a growing *threat from terrorism*, and as *communications networks became more wide-ranging and sophisticated*, terrorist organisations had acquired ever greater scope to operate and co-operate on a trans-national level. It would be a gross dereliction of the Government's *duty to safeguard national security and the lives and well-being* of its population if it failed to take steps to gather intelligence that might allow preventative action to be taken or if it compromised the operational effectiveness of the surveillance methods available to it. Within the United Kingdom the Government had extensive powers and resources to investigate individuals and organisations that might threaten the interests of national security or perpetrate serious crimes, and it was therefore feasible for the domestic interception regime to require individual addresses to be identified before interception could take place. Outside the jurisdiction, however, the ability of the Government to discover the identity and location of individuals and organisations *which might represent a threat to national security was drastically reduced and a broader approach was needed.* Maintaining operational effectiveness required not simply that the fact of interception be kept as secret as appropriate; it was also *necessary to maintain a degree of secrecy* as regards the methods by which such interception might be effected, to prevent the loss of important sources of information.[133]

132 ibid, (44).
133 ibid, (53).

This policy avowal supplemented an initial, and then subsequent Home Office statement made by Mr Steven Boys Smith, a 'Senior Home Office official', in which significant details as to the relevant safeguards regarding the handling of intercepted communications were disclosed. These were largely classifiable as highly technical administrative and procedural guidance and are consequently too numerous to repeat here.[134] An additional, arguably weaker, submission pleaded that the UK was

> not the only signatory to the Convention to make use of a surveillance regime involving the interception of volumes of communications data and the subsequent operation of a process of selection to obtain material for further consideration by government agencies.[135]

In rationalizing the UK's approach to communications investigation and its regulation, the aforementioned submissions to Europe's highest court midway through RIPA's lifespan demonstrate the perception in government of a 'right' to fulfil a 'duty to protect national security and wellbeing' (the economic well-being aspect is implicit) through broad-scale foreign-focused communications screening (an implicit nod to UKUSA). In line with the central thesis herein, all communications made within the UK, whether leaving the jurisdiction or otherwise, are envisaged as potentially accessible for investigative purposes, and the IOCA 1985 and RIPA 2000 were drafted to enable this on national security-related grounds, broadly construed.

The Court's deliberations

The ECtHR examined the relevant IOCA 1985 provisions including those on warrants and safeguards applicable to intercepted material. They additionally made reference to the IOCT procedure and findings, various IOC Commissioner's reports dating between 1986 and 1992, as well as the new regime under RIPA 2000 and the very first Interception of Communications Code of Practice issued under that Act.[136] The Court found there was no dispute that the interceptions were in accordance with law, in that the legal basis was the IOCA 1985.[137] They also held, however, that the law (statutory or administrative) should be compatible with the rule of law and accessible to the person concerned, who must, moreover, be able to foresee its consequences for him.[138]

134 ibid, (47)–(53).
135 ibid, (54).
136 ibid, (40). The Code was issued by virtue of RIPA 2000, s71.
137 ibid, (60).
138 ibid, (60).

The Weber Principles

As regards the foreseeability of consequences, the Court repeated what became commonly known as the 'Weber Principles' (derived from an earlier case, *Weber and Savaria v Germany*).[139] Such has been their importance they are repeated here:

> foreseeability in the special context of secret measures of surveillance, *such as the interception of communications*, cannot mean that an individual should be able to foresee when the authorities are likely to intercept his communications so that he can adapt his conduct accordingly…However, especially where a power vested in the executive is exercised in secret, the risks of arbitrariness are evident…*It is therefore essential to have clear, detailed rules on interception of telephone conversations, especially as the technology available for use is continually becoming more sophisticated*…The domestic law must be sufficiently clear in its terms to give citizens an adequate indication as to the circumstances in which and the conditions on which public authorities are empowered to resort to any such measures.[140]
>
> Moreover, since the implementation in practice of measures of secret surveillance of communications is not open to scrutiny by the individuals concerned or the public at large, it would be contrary to the rule of law for the legal discretion granted to the executive or to a judge to be expressed in terms of an unfettered power. Consequently, *the law must indicate the scope of any such discretion conferred on the competent authorities and the manner of its exercise with sufficient clarity* to give the individual adequate protection against arbitrary interference (see, among other authorities).[141]

Paragraph 95 in Weber and Savaria has been particularly influential in subsequent proceedings:

> In its case-law on secret measures of surveillance, the Court has developed the following…[six]…minimum safeguards that should be set out in statute law in order to avoid abuses of power: *the nature of the offences which may give rise to an interception order; a definition of the categories of people liable to have their telephones tapped; a limit on the duration of telephone tapping; the procedure to be followed for examining, using and storing the data obtained; the precautions to be taken when communicating the data to other parties; and the circumstances in which recordings may or must be erased or the tapes destroyed.*[142]

139 *Weber and Savaria v Germany* (2008) 46 EHRR SE5.
140 ibid (93), emphasis added.
141 ibid (94), emphasis added.
142 ibid (95), emphasis added.

The judgment in Liberty and Others v United Kingdom

After further deliberation, the Court concluded that

> it did not consider that the domestic law at the relevant time indicated with sufficient clarity, so as to provide adequate protection against abuse of power, the scope or manner of exercise of the very wide discretion conferred on the State to intercept and examine external communications. In particular, it did not, as required by the Court's case-law, set out in a form accessible to the public any indication of the procedure to be followed for selecting for examination, sharing, storing and destroying intercepted material. The interference with the applicants' rights under Article 8 was not, therefore, 'in accordance with the law'.[143]

As Benjamin Goold predicted, the UK government did not react to the adverse judgment by Liberty with changes to primary legislation or to the convoluted oversight mechanisms then in place.[144] The RIPA 2000 regime, which was undoubtedly by this stage significantly greater in scope and magnitude than that originally complained of by the Liberty collective continued. This would not be the end of legal challenges to aspects of what is now understood as the 'bulk interception' and 'foreign intercept' aspects of UK data-investigation.[145]

Post-Capenhurst analysis

An initial observation is that, when compared to the scale of bulk interception now avowed in more recent litigation, the state conduct alleged seems almost tame in comparison. That said, the interception alleged, and the volume and content of communications potentially accessible as a consequence, remains significant. It does not, however, amount to 'blanket' surveillance. The resources available to the UK, military and civilian, are insufficient to achieve blanket coverage.

Questions of law

In line with longstanding policy, the existence of a certificated warrant complying with sections 2 to 5 of the IOCA 1985 – authorizing the interception of communications at Capenhurst – was neither confirmed nor denied either in the course of the Liberty proceedings, or subsequently. As regards the fallout from the

143 *Liberty and Others v United Kingdom* (n6) (69).

144 For analysis of the case and the UK government's failure to respond see Benjamin Goold, '*Liberty and others v The United Kingdom*: A New Chance for Another Missed Opportunity' (2009) 1 Public Law 5.

145 See particularly *Big Brother Watch and Others v The United Kingdom (Applications Numbers 58170/13, 62322/14 and 24960/15)* (Grand Chamber judgment pending as of 31 October 2020).

matter, it appears diplomacy prevailed and as Richard Lamont noted, the story disappeared from the public gaze as suddenly as it arrived.[146] He further posits that, if the operation was legal, and a certificated warrant was in place, would British Telecom (as BT was then known) not have undertaken the intercepts themselves, this being much cheaper and more discrete.[147] It is not difficult to agree with that view. However, if there was no IOCA 1985 warrant in place, the mass intercepts would not so much have been illegal, but rather outside statutory regulation and under Ministerial supervision, as in the pre-IOCA 1985 period. It seems unlikely that the MoD would issue a press notice and build the tower and use it for the interceptions alleged without the executive's knowledge. As the operation involved intercepting *external* communications, it would seem likely that the then Secretary of State for the Foreign and Commonwealth Office would have had Ministerial oversight. However, the belated efforts of the Home Office before at the European Court suggest that a certified warrant was in place at the relevant time. This also aligns more closely with the narrow definition of conduct amounting to interception in the then-prevailing IOCA 1985, wherein interception would not amount to an offence if it was undertaken 'in obedience to a warrant issued by the Secretary of State' and the communications are in the course of transmission over a 'public telecommunications system' (the British Telecom system).

National Intelligence Machinery

A more interesting question raised by the Lamont/Campbell investigation, and at Strasbourg, was the fact that the purchase and construction of the tower was by the MoD. When interception is contemplated, it is usually GCHQ that are assumed to be undertaking it. In his press release of 25 July 1999, Duncan Campbell stated that:

> Although ostensibly built for the British Ministry of Defence, the tower was operated by and for...GCHQ...the site was manned 24 hours a day by a team of 2–3 people, until the start of 1998. Communications were sifted by eight floors of high-tech computers and electronics, and then sent on to *intelligence agency* HQs for analysis.[148]

As with most investigative journalists, Mr Campbell provides no information regarding his sources. Without questioning his integrity, however, in the absence of corroboration his statement requires some investigation.

146 Lamont (n114).
147 ibid.
148 Duncan Campbell, 'Bugging Ring around Ireland' (n118).

GCHQ

Although dating to 2010, the UK government's *GOV.UK* continues to provide access to a booklet entitled 'National Intelligence Machinery'.[149] The fact of its presence suggests it remains current. In a section entitled 'The Intelligence and Security Agencies' it states that GCHQ has

> two main missions: ***gathering intelligence through the interception of communications*** (known as 'Signals Intelligence', or Sigint) and providing services and advice as the UK's national technical authority for Information Assurance. ***GCHQ's Sigint work provides intelligence in support of Government decision-making in the fields of national security, military operations and law enforcement.*** It provides essential intelligence in the battle against terrorism and also contributes to the prevention of serious crime. [150]

This is uncontroversial and suggests that it may well have been GCHQ that were operating at Capenhurst under the auspices of an IOCA 1985 'certificated warrant', or, in the absence of such a warrant, under Ministerial supervision. It is worth remembering that GCHQ's functions were not assigned in statute until the entering into force of the Intelligence Services Act (ISA) 1994 on 15 December of that year. Consequently, between 1990 and 1994, GCHQ was accountable only to the UK Foreign Secretary by virtue of mainly secret executive administrative arrangements as the independent Intelligence Services Commissioner and Intelligence Services Tribunals created by the ISA had not come into existence.[151] As regards GCHQ's functions prior to 1994, the statutory language in the ISA 1994 made it clear that 'statutory' GCHQ was a ***continuation*** of 'Ministerial GCHQ' and already possessed functions 'to monitor or interfere with electromagnetic, acoustic and other emissions and any equipment producing such emissions and to obtain and provide information derived from or related to such emissions or equipment and from encrypted material'.[152] Intercepting 'external communications' in the course of transmission going to and coming from the Republic of Ireland would have fallen squarely within this brief.

Defence intelligence

There seems no dispute that it was the MoD who commissioned the building of Capenhurst Tower. If Duncan Campbell is correct, the MoD bought the land,

149 Cabinet Office, 'National intelligence Machinery' (*GOV.UK*) <https://assets.publishing.service.gov.uk/government/uploads/system/uploads/attachment_data/file/61808/nim-november2010.pdf> accessed 20 September 2020.

150 ibid, 8.

151 ISA 1994, s8 and sch 2.

152 ibid, s3(1) (a) (as enacted) 'There shall ***continue to*** be a [GCHQ] under the authority of the Secretary of State', emphasis added.

built the tower, and had GCHQ operate their equipment from within by some internal arrangement. However, since 1964, an integral part of the MoD has been Defence Intelligence (DI). It is comprised of military and civilian intelligence expertise drawn from the three Armed Services. Consequently, such DI do not appear to have entered the mainstream consciousness of politicians, academics, civil liberties groups, or other parties with an interest in the data investigation or communications surveillance of civilians, particularly civilians generally residing in the UK. Even in this post-2013 era of 'transparent secrecy', DI receive significantly less publicity than their UKIC counterparts contributing to the National Intelligence Machinery, where it is described as follows:

> DI…*differs in a number of important ways from the Agencies.* It is not a stand-alone organisation but is *a constituent part of the Ministry of Defence (MOD).* DI conducts all-source intelligence analysis from both overt and covert sources. It provides intelligence assessments in support of policymaking, crisis management and the generation of military capability. In addition to such assessments, DI *collects intelligence* in direct support of military operations, *as well as in support of the operations of the Agencies. This intelligence collection is authorised in accordance with procedures laid down by the Regulation of Investigatory Powers Act 2000.*[153]

Given the broad statutory functions and capabilities of the UKIC as now known, and their known interception capabilities, a question arises as to the nature of the intelligence collection undertaken in support of the operations of the agencies and why agencies with such broad technological capabilities would require intelligence collection support, as opposed to operational support, from intelligence expertise drawn from the British Army, Royal Navy, and Royal Air Force. At the time Capenhurst was initially occupied, the IOCA 1985 'certificated warrant' regime, unlike its successors, had no express limitation stating which persons or bodies could apply for a section 3 warrant. Warrants were simply issued 'to the person to whom they were addressed'.[154] As such, certificated warrant for the interception of communications complained of in *Liberty* could just as easily have been issued to elements of DI. This is actually alluded to by Richard Lamont who states that the 'Defence Estate Organisation' [*sic*][155] indicated that the Capenhurst facility was operated by the RAF's 'Radio Introduction Unit'

153 National Intelligence Machinery (n149) 13, emphasis added.

154 IOCA 1985, s2(1).

155 Possibly meaning the Defence Infrastructure Organisation, or this may have been a previous variant. DIO maintains a website and states it is 'the estate expert for defence, supporting the armed forces to enable military capability by planning, building, maintaining, and servicing infrastructure'. <https://www.gov.uk/government/organisations/defence-infrastructure-organisation> accessed 20 September 2020.

(RIU).[156] The RIU charter states that it is 'a non-executive advisory organisation established to support MOD and other staff with selection and introduction into service of C-E systems' and would appear to fit logically within the DI signals intelligence cohort.[157] Although they investigated Capenhurst together, Lamont's assertion as regards the RIU is contrary to Campbell's assertion that it was GCHQ who operated the tower. Furthermore, Campbell asserted the tower as being in use until 1998, whereas Lamont asserts an earlier abandonment in 1994, coincidentally, the year GCHQ's functions were placed on a statutory footing and independent oversight of the SIS and GCHQ commenced.[158]

If questioning whether the identity of the occupants and operators of Capenhurst were of any meaningful importance in that time period, the answer is that it raises questions of independent oversight and operational function. If, as Lamont asserts, the tower was abandoned in 1994 and it was GCHQ undertaking the interceptions, they would have left before the new independent oversight regime introduced by the ISA 1994 entered force. As such, no one except the Foreign Secretary needed to know what was going on at the tower. If it was DI that had been operating Capenhurst however, it would never be subject to any form of independent oversight and the date of abandonment has less meaning. Their operation of the tower would have been a military operation overseen in secret by the Defence Secretary. A perhaps more serious question arising from Capenhurst and the Liberty collective's legal challenge is that, if it was DI staffing the tower and conducting the interception, why was a military intelligence unit undertaking the investigation of civilian communications?

Military investigation of civilians?

As earlier outlined, when RIPA 2000 was enacted, it replaced the IOCA provision under which a Secretary of State could theoretically address an interception warrant to anyone.[159] Under the new Act, a very limited number of applicants were permitted to apply. DI was listed, in addition to the UKIC, selected UK law enforcement agencies, HMRC, and 'competent authorities' for

156 Lamont (n115). He further asserts that

> the RAF has often acted as a 'front' organisation for GCHQ and its American big brother(!), the National Security Agency. The radio intercept station at nearby Cheadle, Staffs was known as 'RAF Cheadle', and 'RAF Menwith Hill' in Yorkshire is the site of the largest American intelligence gathering base outside the USA itself.

This author is unable to expand on or verify these assertions.

157 Flight Lieutenant Jeff Tremaine, 'From Texas to Cyberspace the Radio Introduction Unit' (unknown date) available at <http://web.archive.org/web/19990508000428/http://www.raf.mod.uk/history/riu1.html> accessed 20 September 2020. (C-E stands for Communication-Electronic).

158 Lamont (n115).

159 IOCA 1985, ss2–5.

the purposes of international mutual legal assistance agreements.[160] Nothing in RIPA 2000 prevented any of these bodies from applying for, or being granted, an s8(4) 'certificated warrant'. As such, it remained theoretically possible for DI, in the UK, to be involved in the interception of communications in the course of transmission 'in support of the Agencies' as outlined in National Intelligence Machinery.

RIPA 2000, Part IV: independent oversight

Jack Straw introduced Part IV of RIPA 2000 as 'in many ways the most important part of the [RIPB, setting out]...who is to scrutinise the use of the six powers and [establishing the Investigatory Powers Tribunal]'.[161] He added that the then-existing Interception of Communications Commissioner, Security Service Commissioner, Intelligence Services Commissioner, and the Surveillance Commissioner would continue in their current roles but that some would receive added powers.[162] He had not thought it appropriate to merge all the separate Commissioner roles but had 'accepted the argument that we should amalgamate the current plethora of tribunals and different avenues available for complaints'.[163] In establishing the new Investigatory Powers Tribunal, he stated 'it will be a serious and powerful tribunal, and will be available as redress in respect of the use of a wide number of techniques by the investigating agencies'.[164] The IPT and IOCCO are briefly reviewed in Chapter 10 herein.

Conclusion: was RIPA 2000's approach to interception of communications disingenuous?

The policy underpinning the RIPA 2000 approach to interception of communications had appeared in the 1999 Consultation paper:

> The Government believes that it should not make any difference how a communication is sent, whether by a public or non-public telecommunication or mail system, by wireless telegraphy or any other communication system. Nor should the form of the communication make any difference; *all interception which would breach Article 8 rights, whether by telephone, fax, e-mail or letter, should all be treated the same way in law. A single authorising framework for all forms of lawful interception of communications will mean that each application will follow the same laid down procedure and will be judged against a*

160 RIPA 2000, s6(2) (i) DI remain empowered to apply for interception warrants under the IPA 2016, s18(1) (g).
161 Jack Straw, HC Deb, 6 Mar 2000, vol 345, col 777.
162 ibid.
163 ibid. The IPT subsumed the previous Interception of Communications Tribunal, Security Service Tribunal, and Intelligence Services Tribunal into its ambit.
164 ibid.

> *single set of criteria*. This will ensure that this type of intrusive activity is used only when justified, necessary and, in the case of criminal investigations, proportional to the offence.[165]

History now demonstrates, however, that this clear statement of policy, effectively replicating a recommendation put forward by the respected civil liberties group JUSTICE,[166] simply did not manifest itself in RIPA 2000. Instead, the new Act sat within a wider legislative maze,[167] wherein communications content, data associated in any way with communications, and other personal data at rest continued to be covertly accessible by investigators without any need to comply with RIPA's 'single authorising framework', a fact ultimately conceded by the UKPISC in 2015.[168] In their commendably comprehensive review, published not long after the enactment of RIPA 2000, Akdeniz, Taylor, and Walker concluded that it

> fell far short of an effective Parliamentary response...[whereby]...the law still does not offer a single legal regulatory system even though one was promised...[furthermore]...the law remains weak in terms of the imposition of regulation and the protection for privacy in electronic communications.[169]

165 Home Office, *The Interception of Communications in the United Kingdom: A Consultation Paper* (Cm4368, 1999) para 4.5, emphasis added.

166 *Under Surveillance: Covert Policing and Human Rights Standards* (JUSTICE, 1998) Recommendation 1.

167 For example, in evidence tendered to the UK Investigatory Powers Tribunal (IPT) in 2013 between *Privacy International* (IPT/13/92/CH); *Liberty* (IPT/13/77/H), and the UK government counsel for the UK in the 'Respondent's Open Response' (15 November 2013) outlined the official view that the legal regime governing the acquisition of extra-jurisdictionally sourced intercepted material encompassed:[t]he Security Services Act (SSA) 1989; the ISA 1994 as read with the Counter Terrorism Act (CTA) 2008; the HRA 1998; the Data Protection Act (DPA) 1998; and the Official Secrets Act (OSA) 1989. In addition, the provisions of RIPA are relevant as regards the scope of the power of UK public authorities to obtain communications and/or communications data from foreign intelligence agencies.

168 UKPISC, *Privacy and Security Report 2015* (n42) para 272 and Recommendation XX – other Acts included the Wireless Telegraphy Acts of 1949 and 2006, and the Telecommunications Act 1984.

169 Akdeniz, Taylor, and Walker, 'Regulation of Investigatory Powers Act 2000' (1): Bigbrother.gov.uk: 'State Surveillance in the Age of Information and Rights' (2001) 2 *Criminal Law Review* 73, 90. They were also of the view that

> the statements by the Home Secretary, Jack Straw, under the HRA that RIPA is Convention compatible and that it is 'a significant step forward for the protection of human rights in this country' may eventually be proven to be more the advocacy of a politician than the judgment of a lawyer.

They were right.

This would remain the position until the arrival of the IPA 2016. Thus, RIPA's theoretically laudable regulatory framework was in practice undermined from the point of enactment. It is the author's view, in the absence of evidence to the contrary, that the unfettered discretion and unlimited secret powers available to the Secretary of State under the Telecommunications Act 1984, s94, were quietly but *deliberately* retained, thus rendering the Blair government's assertions of a comprehensive ECHR-compliant framework regulating communications content information acquisition within RIPA 2000 disingenuous. Communications data retention is the subject of the next chapter.

References

'Academics Petition for End to Blanket Surveillance' (*Security Week*, 3 January 2014) <http://www.securityweek.com/academics-petition-end-blanket-surveillance> accessed 9 September 2020

An Omega Foundation Summary and Options Report for the European Parliament, 'An Appraisal of the Technologies of Political Control' (September 1998) <https://cryptome.org/stoa-atpc-so.htm#N_32_> accessed 3 November 2020

D Anderson, *Independent Reviewer of Terrorism Legislation, A Question of Trust: Report of the Investigatory Powers Review (Anderson Review 2015)* (Williams Lea Group, June 2015)

David Barnum, 'Judicial Oversight of Interception of Communications' (2016) 44 (2) *Georgia Journal of International and Comparative Law* 239

Rt Hon Sir Stanley Burnton, *Report of the Interception of Communications Commissioner Annual Report for 2016* (HC 297 SG/2017/77 20 December 2017)

Cabinet Office, 'National Intelligence Machinery' (*GOV.UK*) <https://assets.publishing.service.gov.uk/government/uploads/system/uploads/attachment_data/file/61808/nim-november2010.pdf> accessed 20 September 2020

CAGE <https://www.cage.ngo> accessed 9 September 2020

Duncan Campbell, 'Bugging Ring Around Ireland' (25 July 1999) <https://www.duncancampbell.org/PDF/Bugging%20ring%20around%20Ireland.pdf> accessed 29 September 2020

Duncan Campbell, 'How Embassy Eavesdropping Works' <https://www.duncan-campbell.org/embassy-bugging> accessed 29 April 2021

Simon Chesterman, *One Nation Under Surveillance: A New Social Contract to Defend Freedom Without Sacrificing Liberty* (Oxford University Press, 2011)

Defence Infrastructure Organisation <https://www.gov.uk/government/organisations/defence-infrastructure-organisation> accessed 20 September 2020

European Parliament Resolution on the Existence of a Global System for the Interception of Private and Commercial Communications (ECHELON Interception System) (2001/2098(INI)) 5 September 2001. <http://cryptome.org/echelon-090501.htm> accessed 20 October 2020

European Parliament, 'Report on the Existence of a Global System for the Interception of Private and Commercial Communications (ECHELON Interception System)' (11 July 2001, 2001/2098(INI)) <http://cr.yp.to/export/2001/09.07-europe.html#1> accessed 3 November 2020

Gillian Ferguson and John Wadham, 'Privacy and Surveillance: A Review of the Regulation of the Investigatory Powers Act 2000' (2003) *European Human Rights Law Review Supplement* (Special issue: Privacy 2003) 101

Benjamin Goold, 'Liberty and Others v The United Kingdom: A New Chance for Another Missed Opportunity' (2009) 1 *Public Law* 5

Home Office, *The Interception of Communications in the United Kingdom: A Consultation Paper* (Cm4368, 1999)

Home Office, *Interception of Communications Code of Practice* (7th edn, TSO, 2007), replaced by the Interception of Communications Code of Practice (March 2018) issued pursuant to Schedule 7 of the IPA 2016 <https://assets.publishing.service.gov.uk/government/uploads/system/uploads/attachment_data/file/715480/Interception_of_Communications_Code_of_Practice.pdf> accessed 31 December 2019

Interception of Communications Commissioner's Office (IOCCO), *Report of the Interception of Communications Commissioner March 2015 (Covering the Period January to December 2014)* (2014–15, HC 1113, SG/2015/28)

Investigatory Powers Commissioner's Office <https://www.ipco.org.uk> accessed 30 October 2020

Simon Jenkins, 'Blanket Digital Surveillance Is a Start. But How About a Camera in Every Bathroom?' *Guardian* (17 July 2014) <http://www.theguardian.com/commentisfree/2014/jul/17/blanket-digital-surveillance-is-a-start-but-how-about-a-camera-in-every-bathroom> accessed 9 September 2020

JUSTICE, *Under Surveillance: Covert Policing and Human Rights Standards* (JUSTICE, 1998)

Richard Lamont, 'Ministry of Defence Hid Microwave Phone-Tap Tower Inside Nuclear Plant' (15 April 1999) <http://www.lamont.me.uk/capenhurst/original.html> accessed 20 September 2020

Richard Lamont, 'The Capenhurst Tower' (July 1999) <http://www.lamont.me.uk/capenhurst/followup.html> accessed 20 September 2020

Liberty, 'Liberty Responds to ISC Report on Mass Surveillance' (*Liberty*, 12 March 2015) <http://www.liberty-human-rights.org.uk/news/press-releases/liberty-responds-isc-report-mass-surveillance> accessed 31 December 2019

Liberty, 'Mass Surveillance and Snoopers Charter' <https://www.libertyhumanrights.org.uk/issue/mass-surveillance-briefings-and-reports/> accessed 20 September 2020

Simon McKay, *Covert Policing* (Oxford University Press, 2011)

NGO Monitor, 'Founding, Structure and Lost Vision' (*NGOMONITOR*) <http://www.ngo-monitor.org/article/23> accessed 9 September 2020

Professor Sir Cyril Phillips, *Report of the Royal Commission on Criminal Procedure*, (Cmnd 8092, 1981)

Royal United Services Institute for Defence and Security Studies, *A Democratic Licence to Operate: Report of the Independent Surveillance Review (RUSI Review 2015)* (Stephen Austin and Sons Ltd, July 2015)

Sir Rabinder Singh and Kay Everett Memorial Lecture, 'Holding the Balance: National Security, Civil Liberties and the Role of the Investigatory Powers Tribunal' (School of Oriental and African Studies, 20 February 2019) <https://www.ipt-uk.com/docs/soas-lecture-20-feb-19-final.pdf> accessed 20 September 2020

JR Spencer, 'Prosecution Powers to Gather Evidence: The Case for Reform' [2005] *Archbold News*

Rt Hon Sir Swinton Thomas, *Report of Interception of Communications Commissioner for 2000* (Cm 5296, 2001)

Flight Lieutenant Jeff Tremaine, 'From Texas to Cyberspace the Radio Introduction Unit' (unknown date) <http://web.archive.org/web/19990508000428/http://www.http://raf.mod.uk/history/riu1.html> accessed 20 September 2020
UK Parliamentary Intelligence and Security Committee (UKPISC), *Privacy and Security: A Modern and Transparent Legal Framework* (HC 2014-15, 1075-I)
UKPISC, *Annual Report 1999–2000* (Cm4897, November 2000)

7 Disingenuous statutory regulation

Communications data retention

Introduction

Chapter 2 of this volume introduced the communications data (CD) lifespan. In line with Stage 1,[1] communications service providers (CSPs) throughout the EU have in recent years become required by European and domestic law to retain and store CD as it becomes generated in the course of business. When testing the central thesis of this work, communications data retention policy *extends* the national security protection policy in place since 1324 by ensuring that not only can the state enable access to communications and data in transit (via interception) and access to communications data at rest, but it has now chosen to compel those in charge of communications networks to *retain* the categories of CD it views as being of potential utility to the UK Intelligence Community (UKIC) and law enforcement. CSPs are thus engaged as intelligence collectors.

Unsurprisingly, as with the bulk interception of communications explored in the previous chapter, efforts to compel the retention of a broad spectrum of CD 'categories' have been controversial and subjected to legal challenges in UK and European courts. Ní Loideáin usefully fleshes out the implications of what investigators can glean from the simplistic CD categories initially termed 'subscriber data', 'service use data', and 'traffic data'; [2]

> the *context* as opposed to the content of a communication...[and]...a rich source of personal information[that] reveals the 'who' (parties involved), the 'when', how long and how often, (time, duration and frequency), the 'what' (type of communication, e.g. phone call, message, e-mail), the 'how' (the communication device used, e.g. landline telephony, smartphone, tablet) and the 'where' (location of devices used) involved in every communication we make.[3]

1 See Chapter 2. Stage 1 refers to CD generation.

2 Joint Committee on the Draft Communications Data Bill, *Legislative Scrutiny: Draft Communications Data Bill (Final Report)* (2012–2013, HL79, HC 479) 13. (JCDCDB, *Final Report 2015*).

3 Nora Ní Loideáin, 'Judicial Review of Mass Metadata Surveillance in the Post-Snowden Era' (2015) *University of Cambridge Faculty of Law Legal Research Paper* 32/2015, 2 <http://papers.ssrn.com/sol3/papers.cfm?abstract_id=2613424> accessed 30 September 2020.

Such CD, subjected to data analytics, can thus be put to many uses and concerns about the detailed profiling of individuals it enables have existed for as long as the EU and UK have sought to ensure in law that it is kept.[4] Privacy International assert the valid point that CD 'storage and access is often indiscriminate and fails to guarantee sufficient safeguards from abuse'.[5]

In the UK, the Investigatory Powers Act (IPA) 2016 Part 4 makes provision for a Secretary of State, by way of a 'Data Retention Notice', to compel CSPs with a UK presence to retain an immense potential range of CD.[6] In just 11 intricately detailed and candid sections,[7] the controversial state policy compelling the retention of CD so as to create a huge data-at-rest treasure trove for investigators manifests itself in the most recent statutory governance of this controversial area of law.

This chapter explores the short but perennially controversial history of CD retention regulation. This evolved separately from the acquisition and disclosure powers initially provided in the Regulation of Investigatory Powers Act (RIPA) 2000, Part I, Chapter II, and now in the IPA 2016, Part 3. This chapter precedes that addressing acquisition and disclosure, because Chapter II of RIPA did not enter force until 2004, some time after statutory CD retention provisions had been enacted in the UK.

The origin of British secret CD retention

The first documentary evidence that British policymakers wanted to see a broad spectrum of CD retained for future investigative access appears not long after the Blair (Labour) government's 1999 pre-RIPA consultation paper was in circulation. After restating that 'accessing a person's communications data is not as intrusive as interception' the consultation signalled the belief and intention that it was 'time to put in place a statutory framework for authorising access to communications data'.[8]

4 See Chapter 2 and Liberty, 'Written Evidence to the JCDIPB' (IPB0143) para 30, emphasis added. <http://data.parliament.uk/writtenevidence/committeeevidence.svc/evidencedocument/draft-investigatory-powers-bill-committee/draft-investigatory-powers-bill/written/26430.html#_ftnref35> accessed 21 September 2020; Court of Justice of the European Union (CJEU) Joined cases C-293/12 *Digital Rights Ireland Ltd* v *Minister for Communications, Marine and Natural Resources* and C-594/12 *Seitlinger* (Grand Chamber), 8 April 2014 [99].

5 Privacy International, 'National Data Retention Laws since the CJEU's *Tele2/Watson* judgment: A Concerning State of Play for the Right To Privacy in Europe' (*Privacy International*, September 2017). <https://privacyinternational.org/sites/default/files/2017-12/Data%20Retention_2017.pdf> accessed 3 November 2020.

6 IPA 2016, s87.

7 ibid, ss87–98.

8 Home Office, *The Interception of Communications in the United Kingdom* (Cm 4368, 1999) 26.

The NCIS Joint Submission

In an initially 'confidential' document, the UKIC,[9] HMRC,[10] ACPO,[11] ACPO(S),[12] and the NCIS[13] articulated a 'joint submission on communications data retention law' (NCIS Joint Submission) articulating the case for mandating the retention of CD in statute and submitted it to the Home Office.[14] Adopted some two months prior to the entry into force of RIPA 2000, the document became public knowledge in December 2000.[15] Had its high-level consensus been tendered earlier, a CD retention scheme might well have been included in RIPA 2000. Constituting 'data' in itself, the leak of the confidential document ironically illustrated the risks associated with ensuring secure storage of data in compliance with the safeguard provisions of the Data Protection Act (DPA) 1998 or RIPA 2000.[16]

How the UKIC and law enforcement view CD

It was asserted in the document that:

> [CD] is *crucial to the business of the Agencies.* It is pivotal to reactive investigations into serious crime and the development of proactive intelligence on matters effecting [*sic*] not only organised criminal activity but also national security. At...lower level, it provides considerable benefit to the detection of volume crime. The four principle [*sic*] requirements for [CD] are [as]: Primary Evidence...often the only evidence to locate the proximity of a mobile phone user to a crime scene and the sole eyewitness account in Hi-Tech crime. Corroborative Evidence, e.g. proof of association between criminal elements through telephone contact; Intelligence, e.g. identifying and tracing associates and locating places of significance; Post-trial Evidence,

9 UK Intelligence Community – The Security Service (MI5), the Secret Intelligence Service, and GCHQ.
10 Her Majesty's Revenue and Customs.
11 Association of Chief Police Officers.
12 Association of Chief Police Officers in Scotland.
13 National Criminal Intelligence Service, since reconstituted as the NCA (National Crime Authority)
14 Roger Gaspar, 'Looking to the Future: Clarity on Communications Data Retention Law' (NCIS Submission to the Home Office on Communications Data Retention Law, 21 August 2000) (NCIS Joint Submission) <https://cryptome.org/ncis-carnivore.htm> accessed 30 September 2020.
15 Kamal Ahmed, 'Secret plan to spy on all British phone calls', *The Observer* (4 December 2000). <www.theguardian.com/uk/2000/dec/03/kamalahmed.theobserver> accessed 26 September 2020.
16 It was leaked to the NGO Statewatch. See Statewatch, 'NCIS Communications Data Retention Law' (1) (Statewatch, 3 December 2000). <https://www.statewatch.org/news/2000/december/ncis-submission-on-communications-data-retention-law-1/> accessed 26 October 2020.

> e.g. accuracy of digital data to support appeals against conviction and investigations into miscarriages of justice. *Short term retention and then deletion of data will have a disastrous impact on the Agencies' intelligence and evidence gathering capabilities.*[17]

A second paragraph offered an alternative, but very clever, argument which never received equivalent publicity;

> Communications data is becoming increasingly important to provide evidence to establish innocence. Premature deletion will seriously compromise the interests of justice. Communications data has a unique value to promoting a safe and free society. This provides the overriding justification for longer-term retention.[18]

Given its authorship, significant weight can be attached to the advocacy within the NCIS Joint Submission. Furthermore, when considered alongside the EU policy imperative that was driving statutory mandatory CD retention (discussed shortly), its views continued to impel a Home Office policy of CD retention 'mission creep' until arrested by the UK Administrative Division of the Court of Appeal in 2015.[19]

9/11: the beginnings of statutory mandatory CD retention

The mass murder perpetrated against US civilians on 11 September 2001 (hereafter 9/11) was described as a 'sudden and critical watershed, not only in Western foreign policy and national security posture, but also in the development of intelligence tradecraft and capability'.[20] As regards foreign policy and national security posture, it had profound consequences for the UK as well as the US, with cross-party consensus quickly achieved on the principle that 'national security' considerations required to assume primacy over many of the perceived privacy rights of citizens. This took the form of both governments 'focusing on the harm coming from terrorist organizations and ill-meaning individuals…[and stressing]…the

17 NCIS Joint Submission (n14), emphasis added.

18 ibid. Illustrative examples of this are the Scottish Criminal Cases Review Commission and its UK equivalent were both 'relevant public bodies' entitled to acquire CD by virtue of the Regulation of Investigatory Powers (Communications Data) Order 2010, reg 2(a) 'to assist investigations into alleged miscarriages of justice'.

19 Mission Creep refers to the creeping expansion in the scope and extent of statutory mandatory CD retention. In *R (Davis and Others) v Secretary of State for the Home Department* (2015) EWHC 2092 (Admin) Bean LJ and Collins J declared that the UK's data retention legal framework (then expressed in section 1 of the Data Retention and Investigatory Powers Act (DRIPA) 2014) was unlawful.

20 Julian Richards, 'Intelligence Dilemma? Contemporary Counter-terrorism in a Liberal Democracy' (27) 5 *Intelligence and National Security* 761.

importance of *information gathering* to mitigate the potential risk of attacks'.[21] With the benefit of hindsight, it can be said that the proportionality of some of the measures adopted in this regard was improperly assessed.

The Anti-Terrorism, Crime and Security Act (ATCASA) 2001

An example is the widely acknowledged low point in UK national security-related legislation, the Anti-Terrorism, Crime and Security Act (ATCASA) 2001, which was hastily enacted as the UK's legislative contribution towards regulating conduct assisting in US President George Bush's self-declared 'War on Terror'.[22] In addition to its infamous 'section 23',[23] it amended the Terrorism Act 2000, itself then only a year old, and provided, *inter alia*, and for the first time in the UK, for a scheme wherein CSPs would retain their CD. Whilst largely superseded by the Prevention of Terrorism Act (PTA) 2005, the 'voluntary' statutory CD retention regime it introduced remained on the UK statute book until repealed by the IPA 2016 in November 2018.

The ATCASA 2001, Part 11, Voluntary CD Retention Regime

The Act made provision for a Secretary of State to issue a Code of Practice (the ATCASA CoP) relating to the retention by CSPs of CD obtained by or held by them,[24] and to enter into such agreements as considered appropriate with CSPs regarding the retention of such CD.[25] It was additionally provided that the ATCASA CoP could contain any provision deemed necessary 'for the purpose of safeguarding national security' or 'for the purposes of prevention or detection of crime or the prosecution of offenders *which may relate directly or indirectly to national security*'.[26] Its voluntary nature meant that a CSP failure to comply with either the CoP or any agreement made with the Secretary of State fell short of being sanctionable by criminal or civil proceedings.[27] The UK Parliament's Joint Committee on Human Rights' scrutiny of the then draft ATCASA CoP expressed

21 Russell B Wilson, 'A New Balance: National Security and Privacy in a Post 9-11 World' (Honours Thesis, Paper 729, 2014) 14–15, emphasis added. <http://digitalcommons.colby.edu/cgi/viewcontent.cgi?article=1738&context=honorstheses> accessed 30 September 2020.

22 US President George W. Bush, Address to the Joint Session of the 107th Congress September 2001, in untitled, 'Selected Speeches of President George W. Bush 2001–2008' Whitehouse Archives, <http://georgewbush-whitehouse.archives.gov/infocus/bushrecord/documents/Selected_Speeches_George_W_Bush.pdf> accessed 28 July 2020.

23 Subsequently 'demolished' by the late Lord Bingham in *A and others v Secretary of State for the Home Department* [2004] UKHL 56 [68].

24 ATCASA 2001, s102(1).

25 ibid, s102(2).

26 ibid, s102(3), emphasis added. This was a late House of Lords amendment designed to narrow the scope of the provision.

27 ibid, s102(4).

what would become depressingly familiar concerns in this area of law. These included: disappointment that the Home Office had not sought their views;[28] that the blanket standard periods for CD retention specified in the CoP would not meet the ECHR, Article 8(2) proportionality requirement,[29] and a lack of clarity and detail regarding the consultation process.[30] These serious concerns were effectively disregarded and the ATCASA CoP entered force on 5 December 2003.[31]

EU developments: Regulation 45/2001

At EU level, the Treaty of Amsterdam had inserted a new Article 286 into the Treaty establishing the European Community[32] providing that community (EU) legislation concerning the protection of individuals on the processing of personal data and its free movement would, with effect from December 1999, apply to EU institutions and bodies.[33] This supplemented the enactments of the Data Protection Directive (DPD)[34] in 1995 and the CD-centric Telecommunications Privacy Directive (TPD) in 1998.[35] Consequently, on 18 December 2000, just after the enactment of RIPA 2000, but well before the entering into force of its Acquisition and Disclosure provisions, Regulation 45/2001 was enacted, purporting to ensure that data processing carried out in the exercise of activities, all or part of which fell within the scope of community law, were brought within the scope of EU law.[36] In line with developing EU policy, which incorporated a tougher anti-terrorism stance following 9/11, Regulation 45/2001 explicitly

28 Joint Committee on Human Rights, *Draft Voluntary Code of Practice on Retention of Communications Data under Part 11 of the Anti-Terrorism, Crime and Security Act 2001* (2002–03, HL 181, HC 1272) 6.
29 ibid, 7.
30 ibid, 12.
31 By virtue of the Retention of Communications Data (Code of Practice) Order 2003, 2003/3175.
32 Now Consolidated Version of the Treaty on European Union (2012) OJ C 326/01, art 16.
33 Gloria González Fuster, *The Emergence of Personal Data Protection as a Fundamental Right of the EU* (2014 edn, Springer, 2014) 144.
34 Directive 95/46/EC of the European Parliament and of the Council of 24 October 1995 on the protection of individuals with regard to the processing of personal data and on the free movement of such data.
35 Directive 97/66/EC of the European Parliament and of the Council of 15 December 1997 concerning the processing of personal data and the protection of privacy in the telecommunications sector (1998) OJ L 024/1.
36 Regulation (EC) No 45/2001 of the European Parliament and of the Council of 18 December 2000 on the protection of individuals with regard to the processing of personal data by the Community institutions and bodies and on the free movement of such data (2001) OJ L 008/01.

protected the DPD and TPD while simultaneously exempting 'public security' related data acquisition and processing from its ambit.[37]

From 'telecommunication' to electronic communication

The 1999 European Commission review of its holistic communications regulatory framework brought about a proposal to update the TPD, as this Directive had rapidly come to evidence the hazards of drafting EU legislation on the basis of what constituted the technological state of the art at the time, as opposed to drafting it on a technology-neutral basis.[38] The objective of the draft proposal was therefore to update the provisions of the TPD to cope with rapid technological evolution, including 'the move from fixed to wireless communications, and from voice to data communications, wherein analogue speech is digitized prior to transmission.[39]

Circuit-switching to packet-switching

Adopting this technology involved a transition to Voice over Internet Protocol (VoIP) technology from the existing circuit-switched public switched telephone network (PSTN) (on which the definitions in the Telecommunications Act 1984, IOCA 1985, and RIPA 2000 principally focused) to using Internet Protocol (IP) packet-switched networks for the provision of voice and associated convergent services.[40] This transition in the form of human expression as communication has been accurately described as 'probably the most significant paradigm shift in the entire history of modern telecommunications since the invention of the telephone'.[41] With the policy aspiration of streamlining technology regulation within the EU, the European Commission enacted five new Directives making up the telecommunications regulatory package in 2002, all of which entered effect in July 2003.[42]

37 ibid, recital 18. This Regulation should not affect the rights and obligations of Member States under Directives 95/46/EC and 97/66/EC. It is not intended to change existing procedures and practices lawfully implemented by the Member States in the field of national security, prevention of disorder or prevention, detection, investigation, and prosecution of criminal offences.

38 Quinten Kroes, *E-Business Law of the European Union* (2nd edn, Kluwer Law International BV, 2010) 13.

39 Eloïse Gratton, *Internet and Wireless Privacy: A Legal Guide to Global Business Practices* (CCH Canadian Ltd, Toronto, 2003) 55.

40 Katrina Dick, 'The Emergence and Regulation of VoIP' (2004) 10(7) *Computer and Telecommunications Law Review* 157.

41 ibid, citing US Federal Communications Commission ('FCC') chairman Michael Powell, at the World Economic Forum in Davos, Switzerland 2004.

42 ibid. Directive 2002/19/EC on access to, and interconnection of, electronic communications networks and associated facilities (2002) OJ L 108/07 (the Access Directive); Directive 2002/20/EC on the authorization of electronic communications networks and services (2002) OJ L 108/21 (the Authorisation Directive); Directive 2002/21/EC on a common regulatory framework for electronic communications networks and services (2002) OJ L108/33 (the Framework Directive; Directive 2002/22/EC on universal service and users'

These established a technology-neutral regime for regulating electronic communications services and networks across the EU, wherein Member States became obliged to adopt an approach to electronic communications regulation providing a level playing field for fixed-line telephony, voice, and data services. The overall framework was given effect in the UK by the vast Communications Act 2003.[43]

The 'E-Privacy' Directive

The most relevant of the five directives for present purposes is the 'E-Privacy' Directive (EPD) 2002, which repealed the TPD in July 2002.[44] It is apparent that in the debates preceding its enactment, and after reflection on the events of 9/11, it was the EU Council of Ministers who began advocating mandatory CD retention provisions that would require CSPs to retain and store logs of all telephone calls, emails, faxes, and internet activity for law enforcement purposes. These proposals were, however, initially strongly resisted.[45] A July 2001 draft of the EPD, approved by the European Parliament's Civil Liberties Committee (LIBE),[46] contained no CD retention provisions, with LIBE expressing itself to be:

> in favour of a strict regulation of law enforcement authorities' access to personal data of citizens, *such as communication traffic and location data*. This decision is fundamental because in this way the EPD blocks European Union States' efforts underway in the Council to put their citizens under generalised and pervasive surveillance following the Echelon model.[47]

---

rights relating to electronic communications networks and services [2002] OJ L 108/51 (the Universal Service Directive) and Directive 2002/58/EC concerning the processing of personal data and the protection of privacy in the electronic communications sector (2002) OJ L 201/37 (the E-Privacy Directive).

43 Its preamble states,

> An Act to confer functions on the Office of Communications [OFCOM]; to make provision about the regulation of the provision of electronic communications networks and services and of the use of the electro-magnetic spectrum; to make provision about the regulation of broadcasting and of the provision of television and radio services; to make provision about mergers involving newspaper and other media enterprises and, in that connection, to amend the Enterprise Act 2002; and for connected purposes.

44 Directive 2002/58/EC concerning the processing of personal data and the protection of privacy in the electronic communications sector [2002] OJ L 201/37.

45 Jody R. Westby, *International Guide to Privacy* (American Bar Association, 2005) 102.

46 At that time referred to as the Committee on Citizens' Freedoms and Rights.

47 Electronic Privacy Information Centre (EPIC) 'Origins of the EU Directive 2002/58/EC'. <https://epic.org/privacy/intl/data_retention.html#history> accessed 30 July 2020, emphasis added. As regards the existence of the Echelon worldwide communications surveillance programme (subject to NCND), see Chapter 5 of this volume and the European Parliament, 'Report on the Existence of a Global System for the Interception of Private

This was the position adopted by the plenary session of the European Parliament in November 2001.[48] However, it appears that when LIBE reconsidered its position at a Second Reading in the face of continuing demands from the Council of Ministers for a CD retention scheme, the PPE group,[49] led by Committee Chair Ana Palacio (Spain), broke ranks and voted against the previously agreed position.[50] Two further votes then took place. The PPE/PSE alliance[51] firstly voted to reject the first reading position, in effect voting against the maintenance of the original TPD provision that data could only be retained for billing purposes and must then be erased. The second vote was in favour of an amendment (by this time agreed with the Council of the EU [the 15 EU governments]) allowing national governments to introduce legislation requiring telecommunications network and service providers to retain data (traffic and location data) and for law enforcement agencies to have access to this data.[52] It has been noted that

> the United Kingdom and the Netherlands, in particular, questioned whether the...[initial rejected draft of the]...proposed privacy rules still struck 'the right balance between privacy and the needs of the law enforcement agencies in the light of the battle against terrorism'.[53]

This marks the beginning of the post-9/11 'privacy-v-security' debate and policymaking based on it that has come to prevail in the wider national security arena in modern times. It seems likely that the UK government of the day, in adopting a policy of strong advocacy for CD retention, were undoubtedly articulating the confidential influence of the NCIS Joint Submission previously outlined. Whilst it had been adopted too late to influence the enactment of RIPA 2000, it seems unlikely that it was not continuing to shape Home Office policy at that time.

The Privacy and Electronic Communications (EC Directive) Regulations 2003

In the UK, as a consequence of the EPD's transposition requirement, the Privacy and Electronic Communications (EC Directive) Regulations (PECR) 2003 were introduced,[54] repealing the Telecommunications (Data Protection and Privacy)

---

and Commercial Communications (ECHELON Interception System)' (2001/2098(INI)) <http://cr.yp.to/export/2001/09.07-europe.html> accessed 30 July 2020.

48 Statewatch, 'EU Surveillance of Telecommunications: The Vote in the European Parliament to Accept Data Retention and Surveillance by the Law Enforcement Agencies: An Analysis' Statewatch (15 May 2002) <www.statewatch.org/news/2002/may/15epvote.htm> accessed 29 July 2020.

49 European Peoples' Party/Christian Democrats grouping – 233 MEPs at that time.

50 Statewatch, 'EU Surveillance' (n48).

51 PSE (Socialist group – 179 MEPs at that time).

52 Statewatch, 'EU Surveillance' (n48).

53 EPIC, 'Origins of the EU Directive 2002/58/EC' (n47) 93.

54 Privacy and Electronic Communications (EC Directive) Regulations 2003, SI 2003/2426.

Regulations 1999. The EPD, as with the TPD it replaced, purported to protect data privacy in general in Article 5.[55] However, in line with what had become settled policy at EU level, it significantly restricted that protection in the form of Article 15.[56] The UK's PECR 2003 demonstrated the inherent dichotomy in providing the privacy-centric requirement to erase traffic data unless consensually storing it for marketing, fraud-detection, or billing-related purposes,[57] while not being required to delete it due to 'certificated' national security[58] or 'law enforcement'[59] exemptions that were analogous to the DPA 1998 provisions regarding all personal data.[60]

55 'Confidentiality of the communications'. 'Member States shall ensure the confidentiality of communications and *the related traffic data* by means of a public communications network and publicly available electronic communications services, through national legislation. In particular, they shall prohibit listening, tapping, storage or other kinds of interception or surveillance of communications and the related traffic data by persons other than users, without the consent of the users concerned, except when legally authorised to do so in accordance with Article 15(1)', emphasis added.

56 'Application of certain provisions of Directive 95/46/EC. Member States may adopt legislative measures to restrict the scope of the rights and obligations provided for in Article 5, Article 6, Article 8(1), (2), (3) and (4), and Article 9 of this Directive when such restriction constitutes a necessary, appropriate and proportionate measure within a democratic society to safeguard national security (i.e. State security), defence, public security, and the prevention, investigation, detection, and prosecution of criminal offences or of unauthorised use of the electronic communication system, as referred to in Article 13(1) of Directive 95/46/EC. To this end, Member States may, *inter alia, adopt legislative measures providing for the retention of data for a limited period justified on the grounds laid down in this paragraph.* All the measures referred to in this paragraph shall be in accordance with the general principles of Community law, including those referred to in Article 6(1) and (2) of the Treaty on European Union', emphasis added.

57 PECR 2003, regs 7 and 8.

58 PECR 2003, reg 28(1).

> Nothing in these Regulations shall require a communications provider to do, or refrain from doing, anything (including the processing of data) if exemption from the requirement in question is required for the purpose of safeguarding national security. (2)...a certificate signed by a Minister of the Crown certifying that exemption from any requirement of these Regulations is or at any time was required for the purpose of safeguarding national security shall be conclusive evidence of that fact.

59 (1)

> Nothing in these Regulations shall require a communications provider to do, or refrain from doing, anything (including the processing of data) – (a) if compliance with the requirement in question (i) would be inconsistent with any requirement imposed by or under an enactment or by a court order; or (ii) would be likely to prejudice the prevention or detection of crime or the apprehension or prosecution of offenders; or
>
> (b) if exemption from the requirement in question – (i) is required for the purposes of, or in connection with, any legal proceedings (including prospective legal proceedings); (ii) is necessary for the purposes of obtaining legal advice; or (iii) is otherwise necessary for the purposes of establishing, exercising or defending legal rights.

60 cf, DPA 1998, s28.

ATCASA 2001 reviewed

In addition to the enactment of the PECR 2003, December 2003 also saw the entry into force of the Retention of Communications Data (Code of Practice) Order 2003, which gave effect to the draft ATCASA CoP previously outlined.[61] The Code provided for CSP's to retain CD for longer than would be required for their ordinary business purposes and outlined the CD retention periods the Secretary of State deemed it necessary to retain CD for national security purposes.[62] Shortly after the ATCASA CoP's entry into force, a Committee of Privy Counsellors – originally invited by Labour Home Secretary David Blunkett in April 2002 to review the ATCASA 2001 as a whole – published their report (the Newton Report).[63] Lord Newton of Braintree's committee undertook a thorough and comprehensive review of the Act's Part 11 provisions ('Communications Data Retention') and paid particular attention to the Home Office's summary of responses to its March 2003 consultation paper on the draft ATCASA CoP.[64] The Committee's analysis and findings effectively drew the battle lines for the debate surrounding mandatory CD retention in statute. Amongst the consultation responses was one from the influential Foundation for Information Policy Research (FIPR), which submitted, *inter alia*, that

> legal opinions given to…the Information Commissioner and elsewhere have concluded that retention would be unlawful given the disparity of purpose between access to traffic data under [RIPA, Part I, Chapter II for all its permitted purposes] and retention only for national security related purposes under the ATCASA. This is a barrier to both voluntary and mandatory retention that could only be addressed through new primary legislation.[65]

In its consultation document, the Home Office had argued that the fact that CD was held by a CSP under the ATCASA CoP for national security (and crime directly or indirectly linked to national security) purposes should not prevent the police or other public authorities from having access to the data for other purposes, when there was a proportionate need. Statewatch's analysis of the Home Office's summary of Consultation Responses[66] observed that it struggled to find

61 Retention of Communications Data (Code of Practice) Order 2003, SI 2003/3175, enabled by the ATCASA 2001, s102(1).

62 Joint Committee on Human Rights (n28) 6.

63 Privy Counsellor Review Committee, *Anti-terrorism, Crime and Security Act 2001 Review: Report* (HC 2003–04, 100-I).

64 Home Office, 'Consultation Paper on a Code of Practice for Voluntary Retention of Communications Data', (March 2003) <www.statewatch.org/news/2003/mar/atcs.pdf> accessed 30 September 2020

65 FIPR, 'FIPR response to the retention of communications data consultation' (2003) <https://www.fipr.org/030530retention.html> 3 August 2020.

66 The author has made numerous attempts to access this document on the GOV.UK archive and the National Archives' websites without success.

any support for that view, holding that, 'on the central issue of whether communications data held for the purpose of "national security" could be used for other purposes...25 of the 35 responses on this question said that "the approach was not appropriate or proportionate"'.[67] In addition, as regards 'the question of the "disparity between the retention and access regimes", 24 of the 25 respondents... "considered the matter as a problem that needed to be resolved"'.[68]

Disparity of purpose

The Newton Committee found the '"disparity of purpose" between retention and access...to be a fundamental difficulty with the framing of these provisions', wryly noting the Home Office's 'spin' on interpretation of the same responses that Statewatch had analyzed, before concluding that 'we believe it would be beneficial both for users and subjects of the data if retention and access were based on a coherent statutory framework', further noting that 'the Home Office have indicated that work in the EU context may, eventually, provide the basis of such a framework'.[69]

Towards mandatory retention in statute

Having further noted the (as yet unused) power of the Home Secretary to issue compulsory directions if not satisfied that the ATCASA CoP was effective,[70] they further observed that this power was subject to renewal every two years, lapsed if not so renewed, and in light of the fact (in their view) that most major CSPs were unlikely to voluntarily adopt the voluntary Code, such a renewal had been made by means of the Retention of Communications (Extension of Initial Period) Order on 13 November 2003.[71]

A new principle of statutory mandatory CD retention

As regards the future direction for policymaking in the area of CD retention, the Newton Committee arrived at the following view:

67 Statewatch, 'Government Trying to Slip through "Voluntary" Data Retention Rejected by Consultation Process' (2003) <https://www.statewatch.org/news/2003/september/uk-government-trying-to-slip-through-voluntary-data-retention-rejected-by-consultation-process/> accessed 3 August 2020.

68 ibid.

69 Privy Counsellor Review Committee, *ATCASA 2001 Report* (n63) 95.

70 Under the ATCASA 2001, s104, the Home Secretary is authorized to do so by affirmative order and for the purposes of safeguarding national security and the prevention and detection of crime or the prosecution of offenders which may relate directly or indirectly to national security.

71 Retention of Communications Data (Extension of Initial Period) Order 2003, SI 2003/3173.

> *We can see the case in principle for requiring communications data to be retained* for a minimum period (which would vary with the type of data) for a defined range of public interest purposes such as helping in the prevention and detection of terrorism and other serious crime. These...should, therefore, be part of mainstream legislation and not special terrorism legislation... *[ATCASA] Part 11 does not provide a sound legislative basis for the retention of communications data because, no matter whether the retention requirements are implemented by a voluntary code or by mandatory order, the legality of access to that data for purposes unrelated to national security will remain contentious*...the Government should accept the logic of the results of its consultation and *replace Part 11 with a mainstream communications data retention regime which limits in primary legislation the longest retention period which the Government can impose to one year*...It would permit data which is of potential use in safeguarding national security to be retained. Access to the data must, however, be subject to strict regulation, and that regulation must be properly enforced.[72]

They further noted the Information Commissioner's view, expressed in response to the Home Office consultation, that he had 'yet to be convinced of the need for a CSP to retain data routinely for the prevention of terrorism, for any longer than the data would be normally retained for its own business purposes'.[73] They concurred with the Information Commissioner's cautious acceptance that 'the twelve month maximum retention period caused considerably less concern from a privacy point of view'[74] taking the view that although the privacy of the individual would be curtailed, it would be curtailed by a maximum of one year.[75] They were additionally of the view that, given the complicated nature of the supervisory framework for retention and access wherein responsibility was then divided between the Interception of Communications Commissioner's Office (IOCCO) (for access) and Information Commissioner (for retention) that 'the whole retention and access regime, including for those access routes not governed by [RIPA] 2000, should be subject to unified oversight by the Information Commissioner'.[76]

NCIS Joint Policy and government policy explicitly align

The Home Secretary's response in February 2004[77] agreed with the Newton Committee on a need for CD retention for the purposes of fighting crime in addition to the purpose of safeguarding national security, noting that that view

72 Privy Counsellor Review Committee, *ATCASA 2001 Review* (n63) 96, emphasis added.
73 ibid.
74 ibid.
75 ibid, (n63).
76 ibid, 96.
77 Home Secretary, *Reconciling Security and Liberty in an Open Society: A Discussion Paper* (Cm 6147, February 2004).

was echoed by the police and other law enforcement agencies.[78] This was almost certainly an implicit reference to the NCIS Joint Submission and, for the first time, expressly aligned government policy with it.[79] The response indicated that the government were considering whether CD retention for the purposes of safeguarding national security (*and* combatting crime)[80] would be better addressed in mainstream legislation as opposed to special terrorism legislation, the insertion of the ATCASA, Part 11 CD voluntary CD retention provisions into RIPA 2000 being one option.[81] The need for primary legislation was dismissed; the view being expressed that 'rapid technical developments within the telecommunications industry' meant that the government required a relatively speedy process (secondary legislation) to add or remove the types of data to be retained and to adjust retention time periods when deemed necessary.[82]

The continued exclusion of the Information Commissioner

Opposition was expressed to the involvement of the Information Commissioner performing an oversight role in the realm of CD acquisition and retention.[83] Their purely reactive role, then limited to 'investigating complaints related to personal access requests for data and access requests made under the Social Security Fraud Act 2001...[and]...complaints into the retention of data including the length of time it is held', was cited as the reason.[84] It appears the idea of granting the Information Commissioner additional powers was not entertained. After expressing satisfaction with the current statutory oversight procedures for both retention of and access to data, the response promoted the IOCCO's pro-active role, including powers to pro-actively inspect and audit all processes and safeguards used by authorities accessing data, to deal with reported errors and to submit their role to Prime Ministerial scrutiny. Consequently, the policy view was that, by transposing the CD retention provisions to a new part of RIPA, both regimes would come under the collective oversight of the Interception Commissioner.[85]

The ATCASA CoP and the Telecommunications Act 1984

The Newton Committee recommendations and the government's reflection on them ultimately withered on the vine, and RIPA 2000 was never expanded to

78 ibid, para 143.
79 NCIS Joint Submission (n14) Chapter 2: Law Enforcement Business Case for Data retention.
80 Home Secretary, *Reconciling Security and Liberty in an Open Society* (n77). The issue of the disparity in purpose was acknowledged at para 141.
81 ibid, para 145.
82 ibid, para 148.
83 ibid.
84 ibid, paras 152–159.
85 ibid, paras 152–159.

embrace CD retention. This may, as indicated earlier in this chapter, have been due to progress at EU level. As far as the UK public were concerned therefore, any CD retention being undertaken in 2004 was on a 'voluntary' basis by CSPs under the auspices of the ATCASA and its CoP. Hedley notes the Code's inherent detail, and how it authorized the retention of subscriber details and telephony for twelve months, email and ISP data for six months, and web activity logs for four days.[86] He additionally noted that the power to make compulsory directions under the ATCASA 2001 had never been invoked but that it had been renewed.[87]

The question of why the power to make compulsory directions was renewed but not used and indeed why it remained in force while remaining unused is an interesting one.[88] When the fact of its renewal is considered along with Hedley's additional evidence as to the 'stormy' nature of the negotiations surrounding government payments to CSPs for CD retention,[89] and the Newton Committee's view that the 'main communications service providers' were likely not going to adopt the ATCASA CoP,[90] a related question arises as to how many of them eventually did actually adopt it, and why. This is further compounded by the legitimate questions asked about CD retention and access to it at the time by Statewatch. They noted how 'in December 2001 the...[ATCASA 2001]...was rushed through parliament on the grounds that the new powers were urgently needed to combat "terrorism"'[91] before asking (in light of the fact that RIPA's Chapter II regime enabling access to CD was still not in force) 'does this mean that [the UKIC and LEAs] are still waiting for access to communication data to combat "terrorism" or does it mean they already had access?' They then asserted that:

> perhaps the reason that the Home Secretary is prepared to ride rough-shod over all the objections by much of the industry and civil society and the law is that he is keen to put in place a measure...[i.e. give effect to RIPA, Part I, Chapter II Acquisition of CD regime]...which will legitimate, and make lawful, the long-standing practice of those 'longer-established' communications providers who have been retaining data at the request of the law enforcement agencies *well prior to* 11 September 2001. *This is confirmed in a submission by the National Criminal Intelligence Service to the Home Office on 21 August 2000.*[92]

86 Hedley, *The Law of Electronic Commerce and the Internet in the UK and Ireland* 118.
87 ibid. Retention of Communications Data (Extension of Initial Period) Order 2003, SI 2003/3173.
88 It was renewed again via the Retention of Communications Data (Further Extension of Initial Period) Order 2005, SI 2005/3335.
89 Hedley (n86) 118.
90 Privy Counsellor Review Committee, *ATCASA 2001 Review* (n64) para 394.
91 Statewatch UK: 'Government Trying to Slip through "Voluntary" Data Retention' (n67).
92 ibid, emphasis added.

This appears to have been good detective work by Statewatch. The NCIS Joint Submission stated:

> From a commercial perspective, the longer-established CSPs wish to ensure that an obligation to retain communications data for an appropriate period is placed equally on every CSP. Otherwise, some of the newer companies may be tempted to delete valuable data and exploit a competitive edge through reduced overheads. Examples of this are already appearing with certain CSPs proposing to delete data after very short periods. This will rapidly undermine *the voluntary agreements* achieved so far which now appear to have an increasingly [*sic*] fragility.[93]

The reference to 'voluntary agreements' strongly suggests the existence of some sort of CSP CD retention and public authority CD acquisition regime prior to the entry into force of RIPA 2000, Part I, Chapter II on 5 January 2004, and indeed prior to the entry into force of the ATCASA CoP on 5 December 2003. The NCIS Joint Submission of August 2000 reinforces this. Crucially, it pointed out to the Home Office that:

> section 94(1) Telecommunications Act 1984 does provide a Minister of State with the power to *direct* CSPs to carry out certain specific activities, which could include directions on data retention periods. If the argument for a statutory basis for the retention of data is accepted; *a necessary interim step prior to the introduction of appropriate legislation would be consideration of the use of Section 94(1) in this way.*[94]

The version of the Telecommunications Act 1984, section 94, in force at that time went further however, by providing that:

> the Secretary of State shall lay before each House of Parliament a copy of every direction given under this section unless he is of opinion that disclosure of the direction is against the interests of national security or relations with the government of a country or territory outside the United Kingdom, *or the commercial interests of any person.*[95]

This would certainly have included the significant commercial interests of the major CSPs consulted prior to the confidential NCIS Joint Submission.[96] Indeed, section 94 was amended by the Communications Act 2003 to provide for 'grants

93 NCIS Joint Submission (n14) para 3.3.3, emphasis added.
94 ibid, emphasis added.
95 Telecommunications Act 1984, s94(4).
96 NCIS Joint Submission (n14) para 3.1.1, emphasis added. These included BT PLC, BT Cellnet (now o2) NTL/Cable and Wireless, Vodafone, One 2 One, and Orange. They certainly amount to significant commercial interest.

to providers of public electronic communications networks'[97] and to OFCOM[98] following the implementation in the UK of the E-Privacy Directive.

It is now of course public knowledge that the 'necessary interim step' confidentially recommended to the then Home Secretary was indeed adopted, with the use of section 94 as advocated in the NCIS Joint Submission finally avowed on 4 November 2015.[99]

It can thus be confidently asserted that the secret use of section 94 directions explains the non-enactment of compulsory directions under the controversial ATCASA, section 104, and also the minimal uptake of the ATCASA voluntary CoP by any of the main CSPs referred to in the Newton Committee Report.

Statutory mandatory data retention: the EU takes the lead

Vilasau describes how the European Council had made clear its belief in the retention of electronic data communications in its declaration on the fight against terrorism on 25 March 2004 and again at an extraordinary session of 13 July 2005 that followed the London terrorist attacks.[100] This ultimately led to the enactment of what would be an ill-fated Data Retention Directive (DRD).[101] She further outlined how the road to enactment was not free of controversy, with the draft proposal preceding the DRD receiving severe criticism from the Article 29 Working Party,[102] the European Data Protection Supervisor, the European Parliament, and the European Economic and Social Committee, all of whom objected to it in the belief that CFREU fundamental rights at stake were not sufficiently protected.[103] This view would of course ultimately be found to be correct.

The Data Retention Directive

The DRD called for Member States to adopt laws requiring CSPs to retain, for a minimum of six months and a maximum of 24 months, all traffic and location data generated by them in the course of providing their services. This included a

97 Telecommunications Act 1984, s94(6).

98 ibid, s94(8).

99 Home Office, *Draft Investigatory Powers Bill* (Cm 9152, November 2015) 20.

100 Monica Vilasau, 'Traffic Data Retention v Data Protection: The New European Framework' (2007) 13(2) *Computer and Telecommunications Law Review* 52.

101 Directive 2006/24/EC on the retention of data generated or processed in connection with the provision of publicly available electronic communications services or of public communications networks and amending. Directive 2002/58/EC (2006) OJ L 105/54.

102 The Article 29 Data Protection Working Party was set up under the original Data Protection Directive (95/46/EC). It has advisory status and acts independently of the European Commission. See generally <http://ec.europa.eu/justice/data-protection/article-29/index_en.htm> accessed 30 September 2020.

103 Vilasau, 'Traffic Data Retention v Data Protection: The New European Framework' (n100) 52.

truly huge scope of data relating to fixed, internet, and mobile telephony (including services such as SMS, MMS, voicemail, call forwarding, and call transfer) as well as internet access and email, including data necessary to identify the source of the communication; the destination of the communication; the date, time, and duration of a communication; the type of communication; user communication equipment (including, for mobile telephones, the International Mobile Subscriber Identity and the International Mobile Equipment Identity of the calling and the called party and, in the case of pre-paid anonymous services, the date and time of the initial activation of the service and the cell ID from which the service was activated); and the location of mobile telecommunication equipment.[104] The rationale underpinning the DRD to ensure CD was available for the investigation, detection, and prosecution of serious crime, with the definition of 'serious crime' left to be defined by the Member States.[105] In adopting the DRD on 3 May 2006, the EU effectively adopted a policy analogous to that advocated in the UK in the NCIS Joint Submission.

Direct effect: the Data Retention (EC Directive) Regulations 2007

As one of four countries that had long since been seeking EU approval for such wide-ranging CD retention powers, despite their proposal having been heavily criticized,[106] the UK gave effect to the DRD in the form of the Data Retention (EC Directive) Regulations 2007,[107] but availed of an option to defer the implementation of the Directive's provisions in relation to internet telephony, internet access, and email data until 15 March 2009.[108] A detailed Explanatory Memorandum preceding the 2007 Regulations outlined that Part 11 of the ATCASA 2001 already provided a legal basis for the retention of CD in the UK for certain purposes and that Parliament had approved a voluntary code in connection with this in 2003.[109] For fixed-line and mobile telephony, the Regulations would move retention of CD to a mandatory basis, with the ATCASA CoP remaining in place

104 Stuart Goldberg, 'Data Retention Regulations 2007 come into force' (2007) 12 (5) *Communications Law* 165.

105 ibid.

106 See Article 29 Data Protection Working Party, Opinion 9/2004, on a draft framework decision on the storage of data processed and retained for the purpose of providing electronic public communications services or data available in public communications networks with a view to the prevention, investigation, detection, and prosecution of criminal acts, including terrorism. (Proposal presented by France, Ireland, Sweden, and Great Britain [Document of the Council 8958/04 of 28 April 2004]) 11885/04/EN WP 99 <http://ec.europa.eu/justice/policies/privacy/docs/wpdocs/2004/wp99_en.pdf> accessed 3 August 2020.

107 Data Retention (EC Directive Regulations) 2007, SI 2007/2199.

108 Goldberg, 'Data Retention Regulations 2007 come into force' (n104) 165.

109 Home Office, 'Explanatory Memorandum to the Data Retention (EC Directive) Regulations 2007, 2007 No. 2199' 6.

until completion of the transposition.[110] It also contained a clear statement of the direction of Home Office policy:

> Clearly, a key driver for this work is the need to implement the European Directive. However, even in its absence, Government intervention would be required because of the need to evolve the voluntary code into a mandatory framework to ensure that this essential data is available regardless of providers' policies towards our voluntary approach.[111]

There was therefore a clear policy aim at this time to compel the various types of CD for investigative access. How to best achieve this was still not a settled question.

A centralized state database for all communications data?

It appears that in May 2008, during the deferral period, or perhaps because of it, the Home Office contemplated legislating for the construction of a purpose-built database wherein all internet-usage CD would be centrally stored.[112] This would have completed the DRD's implementation by an alternative route. The plan never received Ministerial approval and remained a proposal. However, it was publicized, prompting the then Assistant Information Commissioner to state:

> If the intention is to bring all mobile and internet records together under one system, this would give us serious concerns and may well be a step too far…We are not aware of any justification for the state to hold every UK citizen's phone and internet records.[113]

Whilst the proposal was undoubtedly dystopian, Chris Pounder articulated why it was even entertained by policymakers. He outlined that the advantage for the government was that it would have control of costs and thus not have to pay the CSPs for CD retention, avoiding 'contentious arguments about retention costs'. The downside would be 'the risk of weakened supervision'. Where at that point, CSPs were able to query excessive requests under RIPA after evaluating them, the proposed database would remove this 'limited independent evaluation of each request'.[114]

110 ibid para 4.3.

111 ibid, Annex A – Regulatory Impact Assessment para 2.7.

112 JCDCDB, *Final Report 2015* (n2) 5.

113 'Privacy Watchdog Opposes Giant Telecoms Database' (*OUT-LAW News,* 27 May 2008) quoting then Assistant Information Commissioner Jonathan Bamford <https://www.pinsentmasons.com/out-law/news/privacy-watchdog-opposes-giant-telecoms-database> accessed 23 November 2020.

114 ibid, quoting Chris Pounder, Pinsent Masons <https://www.pinsentmasons.com/out-law/news/privacy-watchdog-opposes-giant-telecoms-database> accessed 23 November 2020.

'Mission Creep': Data Retention (EC Directive) Regulations 2009

Full transposition of the DRD was completed in the UK with the enactment of the Data Retention (EC) Directive Regulations 2009.[115] This took effect on 6 April 2009. These ensured the implementation of the stated policy intention of 'ensuring communications data is available for one year within communications companies for the prevention, investigation and prosecution of crime and protection of national security'.[116] The scale of mandatory internet CD retention put in place by the 2009 Regulations in addition to the fixed and mobile telephony details in the 2007 Regulations was incredible.[117] Part 3 of Schedule 1 to the 2009 Regulations addressed data obtained from internet access, internet email, or internet telephony and includes: data necessary to trace and identify the source of a communication; data necessary to identify the destination of a communication; data necessary to identify the date, time and duration of the internet communication; and data necessary to identify the internet service used and data necessary to identify users' communications equipment.[118]

The Interception Modernisation Programme (IMP)

At the same time as these new regulations entered force, the 'centralized database' plan, one of three 'options' in an April 2009 consultation document entitled 'Protecting the Public in a Changing Communications Environment' was abandoned therein, as was a second option of doing nothing to stop what was seen as degradation in the capabilities of the UK Intelligence Community (UKIC).[119]

The purpose behind the consultation seems unclear, given that the 2009 Regulations entering force only days earlier virtually covered the field as regards the CD categories that could be retained. The only meaningful third 'option' it offered was legislation compelling UK CSPs to retain all CD deemed of potential investigative value, including third-party data traversing their networks, and to make this available on request.[120]

In yet another example of state disingenuousness, it appears that despite the consultation, secret plans were being pursued regardless. On Sunday 3 May 2009 however, 'days after' the public cancellation of the centralized database plan, in another scoop for investigative journalism, *The Register* and *The Sunday Times* published allegations that

115 Data Retention (EC Directive) Regulations 2009, SI 2009/859.

116 Home Office, 'Explanatory Memorandum to the Data Retention (EC Directive) Regulation 2009'.

117 Data Retention (EC Directive) Regulations 2009, Sch 1.

118 For an expansion on the type of detail this reveals see Andrew Sparrow, *The Law of Virtual Worlds and Internet Social Networks* (Gower, 2010) 172–173.

119 Home Office, *Protecting the Public in a Changing Communications Environment* (Cm 7586, April 2009).

120 ibid.

> Spy chiefs are already spending hundreds of millions of pounds on a mass internet surveillance system…under a GCHQ project called Mastering the Internet (MTI). *It will include thousands of deep packet inspection probes inside communications providers' networks*, as well as massive computing power at the intelligence agency's Cheltenham base, 'the concrete doughnut'.[121]

The news was neither confirmed nor denied. However, the 'Protecting the Public' consultation made reference to a 'cross-government Interception Modernisation Programme to examine how to maintain our communications data capability in the light of the challenges arising from the rapidly changing communications environment'.[122] This meant the transition from circuit-switching telephony to VoIP.[123] The consultation was not well received. A useful indicator of the concerns surrounding it, and containing prescient views on some of the issues that would dog later retention and acquisition legislation, appeared in a 'Briefing on the Interception Modernisation Programme' published by the London School of Economics and Political Science.[124] Without citing an official source, the briefing stated that GCHQ 'had announced' that it was engaged in an internal MTI project, apparently corroborating *The Register* and *The Sunday Times*.[125] Although not a consultation response, the IMP Briefing directly challenged it. It was questioned whether the Home Office fully understood the extent to which they were recommending changes to surveillance authorization processes.[126] The 'efficacy of the supposed oversight mechanism' (IOCCO) was also questioned.[127] In a reference to *The Register/The Sunday Times* allegations, concern was expressed that inadequate consideration had been given to 'the practical and financial challenges in the "black boxes" that would provide deep packet inspection (DPI)', and that if the boxes fell to be controlled by CSPs, 'significant new costs to them' would be incurred. If control fell to GCHQ, 'then the entire existing fabric of warrants, authorisations and judgments over "necessity" and "proportionality" would collapse'. In finding the 'Protecting the Public' consultation exercise 'seriously misleading and misrepresentative of the issues and choices', the LSE team recommended a 'comprehensive review of the UK government's communications surveillance regime'.[128] This would not occur until 2015. Despite the IMP's

121 Christopher Williams, 'Jacqui's Secret Plan to Master the Internet' (*The Register*, 3 May 2009). <https://www.theregister.com/2009/05/03/gchq_mti/> accessed 20 November 2020.

122 Home Office, 'Protecting the Public' (n119) 7.

123 ibid.

124 London School of Economics and Political Science, 'Briefing on the Interception Modernisation Programme' (2009) (*LSE IMP Briefing 2009*). <https://www.statewatch.org/media/documents/news/2009/jun/uk-lse-briefing-state-interception-prog.pdf> accessed 23 November 2020.

125 ibid, 3.

126 ibid, (n125) 4.

127 ibid.

128 ibid.

'cross-governmental' status, discussion of it ceased after the change in UK government from Labour to the Conservative/Liberal Democratic coalition in 2010.

The Draft Communications Data Bill 2012

Conservative Home Secretary Theresa May introduced the draft Communications Data Bill 2012 (draft CDB 2012) to both houses of the UK Parliament on 14 June 2012.[129] Had consensus been achieved during scrutiny and the CDB enacted, Chapter II's CD acquisition and disclosure provisions would have been repealed and replaced.[130] The (relatively new) practice of placing draft legislation for public consultation was welcomed by the Joint Committee established two weeks later and tasked with scrutinizing the CDB.[131]

The Draft Communications Data Bill 2012 final report

Packed with what were now commonplace illustrative case vignettes, their report, published on 11 December 2012, opened with thinly veiled critical references to the stalled 2008/9 IMP initiative and 'Protecting the Public' Consultation.[132] Reference was made to the Cameron/Clegg Coalition Agreement's 'promise' to 'end the storage of internet and email records without good reason' and that no action had been taken in that regard in the first parliamentary session.[133] The coalition's statement appears either disingenuous or to have been made in ignorance, as the only reasons for storage then existing were those of national security, the prevention or detection of crime, and the UK's economic wellbeing. The *known* legal frameworks for storage were the ATCASA 2001, section 11, or the Data Retention Regulations (DRR) 2009.[134] No evidence that the latter lacked efficacy appears in the report despite the Committee having explicitly sought views on how the DRR and draft CDB would interrelate.[135] The paragraphs outlining the Committee's procedure attest to the consultative rigour and to the engagement of the broad spectrum of interested perspectives.[136] There had been no dispute amongst those tendering written and oral evidence to the Committee that the volume of CD had grown, and was continuing to grow exponentially.[137]

129 Home Secretary, *Draft Communications Data Bill 2012* (Cm 8359).
130 JCDCDB, *Final Report 2012* (n2) 13.
131 ibid, 1.1
132 ibid, 5–6.
133 ibid.
134 There are no references to Telecommunications Act 1984, s94 directions.
135 JCDCDB, *Final Report 2012* (n2) 86 (Appendix A).
136 ibid, the Committee held 20 meetings, and took oral evidence from 54 witnesses. Their call for written evidence necessitated the publication of a separate, 609-page document publishing 150 submissions. A separate additional tranche of confidential submissions and more than 19,000 Open Rights Group template emails outlining the publics' concerns were also received.
137 ibid, 13.

However, a key Home Office assertion that at that point, 25% of CD required by investigators was unavailable and would grow to 35% without the CDB was discussed in detail and was ultimately found to be 'misleading and unhelpful'.[138] The Home Office had been slow to publicly identify, or even tell the Committee, the three principal CD types that were frequently unavailable: IP address subscriber data; service/website identifying data; data from overseas-based CSPs providing webmail and social networks to UK users.[139] Their reluctant concession provides a key indicator as to the direction of travel government policy was taking, namely to bring as much web-related data within the definition of CD as possible, and to compel retention of that CD by CSPs.

The JCDCDB Final Report is generally remembered for its dismissal of the draft CDB and ensuring the Home Office returned to the drawing board.[140] It was much more than that. Such was its inherent quality it would be revisited by those charged with reviewing communications and data investigation law in 2014. Its questions were intelligent and its analyses of the many interlinked challenges for this area of law were objective and cogent. Its numerous critiques were scathing, and the Home Office was admonished on more than one occasion. Space precludes a full discussion, however some common threads merit restatement: an apparent failure in Home Office circles to meaningfully consult;[141] to take meaningful cognizance of consultation evidence;[142] to provide credible evidence to support assertions;[143] and to undertake credible costings.[144] As regards the future scope and direction of CD retention, the Report's relevant recommendations included: a review of the controversial issue of web addresses as CD;[145] a statutory commitment that 'no CSP would be asked to store or decrypt encrypted third party data';[146] that any request filter be operated by the National Crime Agency rather than the Secretary of State and be overseen by the IOCCO to prevent 'fishing expeditions';[147] all public authorities to make a 'convincing business case' for accessing CD before being listed on the CDB with changes only possible by a super-affirmative resolution procedure;[148] that the number of purposes for which CD could be sought was already covered in RIPA Chapter II

138 ibid, 18.
139 ibid.
140 ibid, 3.
141 ibid, 20–22 and 75.
142 ibid.
143 ibid, 70.
144 ibid, 76.
145 ibid, 76–77.
146 ibid, 77.
147 ibid. On Request Filters, see Allison M Holmes, 'Automated Investigations: The Role of the Request Filter in Communications Data Analysis' (2018) 2 *Journal of Information Rights, Policy and Practice 2.*
148 JCDCDB, *Final Report 2012* (n2) 77.

and that the proposed Ministerial power for the Secretary of State to add further purposes by secondary legislation be removed.[149]

The Report also provided influential analysis and recommendations in respect of RIPA's Part I, Chapter II provisions on the acquisition and disclosure of CD. These are explored in the next chapter.

The DRD and an Irish problem

Konstadinides asserts that the EU's pre-emptive response to cross-border crime altered our 'constitutional ecosystem' by transferring competence to supranational institutions with limited accountability, and that, as regards the DRD, national judges came under enormous pressure to uphold constitutional values in light of the fact that the Directive had allowed Member States to transpose it using divergent rules in terms of the retention and availability of CD. This was clearly demonstrated in the various national challenges against the DRD.[150] Noting that Ireland had initially, but unsuccessfully, tried to have the DRD annulled on the ground that it was not adopted on an appropriate legal basis,[151] he described how civil rights advocacy group, the appropriately named Digital Rights Ireland, brought a case against the Irish government in the High Court of Ireland seeking, *inter alia*, a CJEU preliminary ruling addressing the validity of the DRD.[152] He noted that the pending case would tackle the problem at its root; i.e. the Directive's interference with the right to privacy of all citizens living in the EU and the permissible degree of EU involvement in the Area of Freedom, Security, and Justice through restrictive regulation to the right to privacy.[153] The Digital Rights referral was conjoined with that of Seitlinger and others, who were requesting the annulment of Austrian domestic provisions which required the retention of personal data, on grounds that such provisions were contrary to their fundamental rights, namely the CFREU, article 8.[154] The Austrian Constitutional Court simultaneously referred the question of the compatibility of the Data

149 ibid.

150 Theodore Konstadinides, 'Destroying democracy on the ground of defending it? The Data Retention Directive, the surveillance state and our constitutional ecosystem' (2011) 36(5) *European Law Review* 722, 727.

151 Case C-301/06 *Ireland v European Parliament and European Council* (2009) E.C.R. I-593.

152 Konstadinides, 'Destroying Democracy' (n150) 722. Under Article 267, Treaty on the Functioning of the EU. *Digital Rights Ireland v Minister for Communications, Marine and Natural Resources* 5 May 2010 High Court, Record No: 2006/3785.

153 Konstadinides, 'Destroying Democracy' (n119) 730.

154 CFREU, art 8 (Protection of personal data).

> Everyone has the right to the protection of personal data concerning him or her. Such data must be processed fairly for specified purposes and on the basis of the consent of the person concerned or some other legitimate basis laid down by law. Everyone has the right of access to data which has been collected concerning him or her, and the right to have it rectified. Compliance with these rules shall be subject to control by an independent authority.

Retention Directive with the CFREU to the CJEU, in particular the sheer volume of data to be retained and the period for which data may be retained.[155] The Austrian legislative position at the point of referral mirrored that created in the UK as a consequence of the Data Retention (EC Directive) Regulations 2009. The CJEU would not deliver their findings in this regard until after the 2013 Intelligence Shock, the consequences of which contributed directly to the finalized structure and scope of the IPA 2016, discussed in the next chapter.

References

Kamal Ahmed, 'Secret Plan to spy on all British Phone Calls' *The Observer* (4 December 2000) <http://www.theguardian.com/uk/2000/dec/03/kamalahmed.theobserver> accessed 26 September 2020

Katrina Dick, 'The Emergence and Regulation of VoIP' (2004) 10 (7) *Computer and Telecommunications Law Review* 157

Electronic Privacy Information Centre (EPIC) 'Origins of the EU Directive 2002/58/EC' <https://epic.org/privacy/intl/data_retention.html#history> accessed 30 July 2020

European Parliament, 'Report on the Existence of a Global System for the Interception of Private and Commercial Communications (ECHELON Interception System)' (2001/2098(INI)) <http://cr.yp.to/export/2001/09.07-europe.html> accessed 30 July 2020

Foundation for Information Policy Research (FIPR), 'FIPR Response to the Retention of Communications Data Consultation' (2003) <https://www.fipr.org/030530retention.html> accessed 3 August 2020.

Roger Gaspar, 'Looking to the Future: Clarity on Communications Data Retention Law' (NCIS Submission to the Home Office on Communications Data Retention Law, 21 August 2000) <https://cryptome.org/ncis-carnivore.htm> accessed 30 September 2020

Stuart Goldberg, 'Data Retention Regulations 2007 Come into Force' (2007) 12 (5) *Communications & the Law* 165

Gloria González Fuster, *The Emergence of Personal Data Protection as a Fundamental Right of the EU* (2014 edn, Springer, 2014)

Eloïse Gratton, *Internet and Wireless Privacy: A Legal Guide to Global Business Practices* (CCH Canadian Ltd, Toronto, 2003) 55

Steve Hedley, *The Law of Electronic Commerce and the Internet in the UK and Ireland.*

Home Office, *The Interception of Communications in the United Kingdom, A Consultation Paper* (Cm4368, 1999)

Home Office, 'Consultation Paper on a Code of Practice for Voluntary Retention of Communications Data' (March 2003) <http://www.statewatch.org/news/2003/mar/atcs.pdf> accessed 30 September 2020

Home Office, *Protecting the Public in a Changing Communications Environment* (Cm 7586, April 2009)

Home Office, Draft Investigatory Powers Bill (Cm9152, November 2015).

155 Sarah Tracey, 'The Fall of the Data Retention Directive' (2015) 20(2) *Communications Law* (Case Comment) 53–55.

Home Secretary, *Reconciling Security and Liberty in an Open Society: A Discussion Paper* (Cm 6147, February 2004).

Joint Committee on the Draft Communications Data Bill, *Legislative Scrutiny: Draft Communications Data Bill* (Final Report) (2012–13, HL79, HC 479)

Joint Committee on Human Rights, *Draft Voluntary Code of Practice on Retention of Communications Data under Part 11 of the Anti-terrorism, Crime and Security Act 2001* (2002–03, HL 181, HC 1272)

Theodore Konstadinides, 'Destroying Democracy on the Ground of Defending It? The Data Retention Directive, the Surveillance State and our Constitutional Ecosystem' (2011) 36 (5) *European Law Review* 722, 727

Quinten Kroes, *E-Business Law of the European Union* (2nd edn, Kluwer Law International BV, 2010)

Liberty, 'Written Evidence to the Joint Committee on the Draft Investigatory Powers Bill (IPB0143)' para 30, emphasis added <http://data.parliament.uk/writtenevidence/committeeevidence.svc/evidencedocument/draft-investigatory-powers-bill-committee/draft-investigatory-powers-bill/written/26430.html#_ftnref35> accessed 21 September 2020

London School of Economics and Political Science, *Briefing on the Interception Modernisation Programme* (LSE IMP Briefing, 2009) <https://www.statewatch.org/media/documents/news/2009/jun/uk-lse-briefing-state-interception-prog.pdf> accessed 23 November 2020

Nóra Ní Loideáin, 'Judicial Review of Mass Metadata Surveillance in the Post-Snowden Era' (2015) University of Cambridge Faculty of Law Legal Research Paper 32/2015, 2 <http://papers.ssrn.com/sol3/papers.cfm?abstract_id=2613424> accessed 30 September 2020

Pinsent Masons *OUT-LAW News 'Privacy Watchdog Opposes Giant Telecoms Database'* (OUT-LAW, 27 May 2008) quoting then Assistant Information Commissioner Jonathan Bamford <https://www.pinsentmasons.com/out-law/news/privacy-watchdog-opposes-giant-telecoms-database> accessed 23 November 2020

Privacy International, 'National Data Retention Laws since the CJEU's Tele2/Watson Judgment: A Concerning State of Play for the Right To Privacy in Europe' (*Privacy International*, September 2017) <https://privacyinternational.org/sites/default/files/2017-12/Data%20Retention_2017.pdf> accessed 3 November 2020.

Privy Counsellor Review Committee, *Anti-Terrorism, Crime and Security Act 2001 Review: Report* (HC 2003–04, 100-I)

Julian Richards, 'Intelligence Dilemma? Contemporary Counter-terrorism in a Liberal Democracy' (2012) 27 (5) *Intelligence and National Security* 761.

Andrew Sparrow, *The Law of Virtual Worlds and Internet Social Networks* (Gower, 2010) 172–173

Statewatch, 'NCIS Communications Data Retention Law (1)' (*Statewatch*, 3 December 2000) <https://www.statewatch.org/news/2000/december/ncis-submission-on-communications-data-retention-law-1/> accessed 26 October 2020

Statewatch, 'EU Surveillance of Telecommunications: The Vote in the European Parliament to Accept Data Retention and Surveillance by the Law Enforcement Agencies: An Analysis' *Statewatch* (15 May 2002) <http://www.statewatch.org/news/2002/may/15epvote.htm> accessed 29 July 2020.

Statewatch, 'Government Trying to Slip through "Voluntary" Data Retention Rejected by Consultation Process' (2003) <https://www.statewatch.org/news

/2003/september/uk-government-trying-to-slip-through-voluntary-data-retention-rejected-by-consultation-process/> accessed 3 August 2020

Sarah Tracey, 'The Fall of the Data Retention Directive' (2015) 20 (2) *Communications & the Law (Case & Comment)* 53–55

US President George W. Bush, Address to the Joint Session of the 107th Congress September 2001, in 'Selected Speeches of President George W. Bush 2001–2008' Whitehouse Archives, <http://georgewbush-whitehouse.archives.gov/infocus/bushrecord/documents/Selected_Speeches_George_W_Bush.pdf> accessed 28 July 2020

Monica Vilasau, 'Traffic Data Retention v Data Protection: The New European Framework' (2007) 13 (2) *Computer and Telecommunications Law Review* 52

Jody R Westby, *International Guide to Privacy* (American Bar Association, 2005) 102

Christopher Williams, 'Jacqui's Secret Plan to Master the Internet' (*The Register*, 3 May 2009) <https://www.theregister.com/2009/05/03/gchq_mti/> accessed 20 November 2020

Russell B Wilson, 'A New Balance: National Security and Privacy in a Post 9-11 World' (Honours Thesis, Paper 729, 2014) 14–15 emphasis added <http://digitalcommons.colby.edu/cgi/viewcontent.cgi?article=1738&context=honorstheses> accessed 30 September 2020

8 Disingenuous statutory regulation

Obtaining retained communications data

Introduction

The acquisition or disclosure of communications data (CD) equates to stage 3 in the CD lifespan outlined in Chapter 2. The previous chapter illustrated the perennially controversial evolution of CD retention regulation at EU and UK level. It also illustrated the intelligence and evidential utility of CD and thus *why* EU and UK lawmakers have, since that utility was made clear to them, been so keen to enact legal frameworks that enable the maximum 'tolerable' amount of personal data (which includes CD) to be retained for potential investigative access. 'Tolerable' means tolerable by the polity, generally 'represented' by civil liberties advocacy, and tolerance has been generally measurable by the responses of civil liberties advocates to personal data-related legislation.

Related to the question of a tolerable amount and type of CD to retain for potential investigative access are questions that include identifying which bodies with investigative functions should be enabled in law to access that CD; for what purposes access should be permitted; whether or not applications to obtain CD should require independent authorization (e.g. from a judge); whether applications should merely require independent scrutiny from persons independent of the investigation; and who should oversee the practical operational efficacy of whole legislative framework. EU and state-level responses have required legislatures to draft the requisite provisions so as to comply with the ECHR and the CFREU and to fall within the parameters of necessity and proportionality established in the jurisprudence of the ECtHR and the CJEU. The UK has additionally had to draft provisions enabling the fulfilment of intelligence-sharing obligations under UKUSA and to enable the protection of national security to the maximum tolerable degree.

This chapter explores the relatively short history of the UK's efforts to regulate applications by a broad range of public and local authorities to obtain CD. Entities requiring access to retained CD for investigative purposes ranged from the UK Intelligence Community (UKIC) and law enforcement agencies (LEAs) through to the UK's local councils. Drafting a single statute that was flexible enough to meet their varied operational purposes would be complex. It should additionally be kept in mind that the UKIC had already become empowered to acquire CD on a bulk basis (albeit for the limited purposes of national security or relations with the government of a country or territory outside the United Kingdom) by virtue of secret Ministerial directions made under the Telecommunications Act 1984, section 94.[1] Of course, at the point in history where the UK was *overtly* consulting on its first dedicated statutory provisions regulating access to retained CD, the existence of section 94 directions remained a closely guarded secret.

History of the acquisition of communications data by investigators

It is unclear when investigators first began seeking to acquire CD, its 'metering data' predecessor, or simple billing and subscriber information from CSPs for use as evidence or for intelligence purposes. A written answer provided to Labour MP Robin Corbett dated 23 February 1978 by then Home Secretary Merlyn Rees stated that 'such factual information may be provided in response to a request from the police if the information is vital to police inquiries in a matter of serious crime, and cannot be obtained from other sources'.[2] This indicates that voluntary cooperation between law enforcement and CSPs was well-established by at least that date and aligns with the longstanding culture of cooperation in the interception domain. There is less clarity as to when the UKIC began acquiring and analyzing CD. CD was originally retained by CSPs principally for business purposes, meaning that its *intelligence* value through data analytical processes was not yet being fully exploited, although the now publicly available evidence of course demonstrates that this was changing rapidly by 2000.[3] GCHQ would certainly have had the ability to access CD as well as content as part of their remit for probably as long as the organization had existed, and their support for the NCIS Joint Submission indicates that the utility of CD for intelligence purposes was well established by August 2000.

CD and data protection legislation: European governance

By that year, data protection in the UK was already subject to a number of EU-level, supranational influences. These include the Charter of Fundamental Rights of the European Union (CFREU),[4] the European Convention on Human

1 Independent Reviewer of Terrorism Legislation, *Report of the Bulk Powers Review* (Cm9326, August 2016) (IRTL, *Bulk Powers Review 2016*) 29–30. See Chapter 7 of this volume and Roger Gaspar, 'Looking to the Future: Clarity on Communications Data Retention Law' (NCIS Submission to the Home Office on Communications Data Retention Law, 21 August 2000) (NCIS Joint Submission) <https://cryptome.org/ncis-carnivore.htm> accessed 30 September 2020.
2 HC Deb, 23 February 1978, vol 944, col 761W.
3 NCIS Joint Submission 2000 (n1).
4 CFREU, Articles 7 and 8.

Rights (ECHR),[5] the Council of Europe (CoE) Convention 108,[6] and other CoE instruments,[7] as well as the EU legislature. The UK's ratification of Convention 108 had resulted in the UK's first data protection legislation, the Data Protection Act (DPA) 1984.[8] The EU legislature followed on 23 November 1995 with the promulgation of 'Directive 95/46/EC of the European Parliament and of the Council of 24 October 1995 on the protection of individuals with regard to the processing of personal data and on the free movement of such data' (Data Protection Directive [DPD]).[9] Its stated object 'was to ensure that the level of protection of the rights and freedoms of individuals with regard to the processing of personal data is equivalent in all Member States'[10] and 'to ensure free movement of personal data while guaranteeing a high level of protection for the rights and interests of the individuals to whom such data relate'.[11] The DPD explicitly referred to the importance of data privacy and its relationship with the ECHR, Article 8(1) right to respect for private and family life, home, and correspondence.[12] However, as a consequence of EU policy, the scope of the DPD excluded:

> the processing of personal data in the course of an activity which falls outside the scope of Community law...and in any case to processing operations concerning public security, defence, State security (including the economic well-being of the State when the processing operation relates to State security matters) and the activities of the State in areas of criminal law.[13]

This complemented the Consolidated Version of the Treaty on the European Union which purports to respect 'essential state functions, including...maintaining law and order and safeguarding national security...[meaning that]...national security remains the sole preserve of each Member State'.[14] These broad exemptions at EU level effectively limited meaningful data protection for UK residents

5 ECHR, Article 8 as it affects private and family life, home, and correspondence.
6 Convention for the Protection of Individuals with regard to Automatic Processing of Personal Data Strasbourg, 28.1.1981 <www.conventions.coe.int/Treaty/en/Treaties/Html/108.htm> accessed 30 October 2020.
7 European Union Agency for Fundamental Rights & Council of Europe, *Handbook on European data protection law* (EU Publications Office, Luxembourg, 2014) 11.
8 Data Protection Registrar, 'Response of the Data Protection Registrar to the Government's Proposals for Revising the Interception of Communications Act 1985' para 2.1. <http://webarchive.nationalarchives.gov.uk/20130128103514/><http://www.homeoffice.gov.uk/oicd/dpr.pdf.> accessed 29 September 2020 (DPR, *IOC Consultation Response*).
9 (2002) OJ L 281/31.
10 Joined cases C-468/10 and 469/10 *Asociación Nacional de Establecimientos Financieros de Crédito (ASNEF) & Federación de Comercio Electrónico y Marketing Directo (FECEMD) v Administración del Estado* [2011] ECR I-12181 (28).
11 Case C101/01 *Lindqvist* [2003] ECR I-12971, (79).
12 Data Protection Directive, Recitals 9, 10, and 11.
13 ibid, Article 3(2).
14 Consolidated Version of the Treaty on European Union, Article 4(2).

where the state's public authorities exercising investigative functions required their personal data. Although later European Court judgments would 'trim' the extent of the exemptions, it is plain in the text that from the outset, at EU level, there was a desire to ensure that Member States' intelligence and law enforcement entities could access personal data (and thus CD) for national security and investigative purposes without disproportionately infringing the purported protection for personal data provided in EU law. As such, rationalizing the UK's regulatory approach to the acquisition and disclosure of CD necessitates factoring in the reality that it was required to align with the EU's approach by virtue of its membership between 1972 and 2020.

CD as a specific category of personal data

Following on from the enactment of the DPD, the EU enacted the first dedicated Telecommunications Privacy Directive (TPD),[15] which sought to apply the DPD's general rules to the provision of public telecommunications services over public electronic communications networks.[16] This complementary Directive outlined rules regarding the confidentiality of communications;

> Member States shall ensure via national regulations the confidentiality of communications by means of a public telecommunications network and publicly available telecommunications services. In particular, they shall prohibit listening, tapping, storage or other kinds of interception or surveillance of communications, by others than users, without the consent of the users concerned, except when legally authorised, in accordance with Article 14 (1).[17]

Article 14(1) policy-based 'restrictions' enabling less fettered personal data investigation by EU intelligence services and law enforcement entities;

> Member States may adopt legislative measures to restrict the scope of the obligations and rights provided for...when such restriction constitutes a *necessary measure* to safeguard national security, defence, public security, the prevention, investigation, detection and prosecution of criminal offences or of unauthorised use of the telecommunications system, as referred to in Article 13(1) of Directive 95/46/EC.[18]

15 Directive 97/66/EC of the European Parliament and of the Council of 15 December 1997 concerning the processing of personal data and the protection of privacy in the telecommunications sector (1998) OJ L 24/01 (Telecommunications Privacy Directive).

16 Quinten Kroes, *E-Business Law of the European Union* (2nd edn, Kluwer Law International BV, 2010) 13.

17 Telecommunications Privacy Directive, Article 5(1).

18 ibid, Article 14(1).

It thus left the question of whether a measure was 'necessary' to Member States and, interestingly, omitted an express requirement for proportionality. The TPD was given effect in the UK when the Telecommunications (Data Protection and Privacy) Regulations 1999 entered into force on 1 March 2000.[19] The then UK Data Protection Registrar (DPR) (created under the Data Protection Act [DPA] 1984) noted that these 'laid down rules...regarding traffic and billing data and also sought to safeguard the privacy of the individual'.[20] This reinforced the conceptualization of CD as a *sui generis* category of personal data. In view of this, the question arises as to why the acquisition (and indeed CSP retention) of CD was not provided for in data protection regulation (the acts of 1984 and 1998). A related question is why independent oversight of its acquisition and disclosure was allocated to the Interception of Communications Commissioner (IOCCO) rather than the DPR (now Information Commissioner's Office [ICO]).

The Data Protection Act (DPA) 1998

As regards the first question, the DPD was given legal effect in the UK via the Data Protection Act (DPA) 1998, the provisions of which relating to national security, crime, and taxation, entered force on 1 March 2000.[21] It replaced not only its 1984 predecessor, but also the Access to Personal Files Act 1987 and certain parts of the Access to Health Records Act 1990.[22] In line with EU policy and law, it exempted 'personal data'[23] from its Data Protection Principles (DPP)[24]

19 Telecommunications (Data Protection and Privacy) Regulations 1999 SI 1999/209. These were privacy-centric and compelled the destruction, in line with the Telecommunications Privacy Directive, of traffic and billing data (regs 3 and 4) with provisions analogous to the DPA 1998 regarding the release for processing of data on national security and crime prevention/detection grounds (regs 32 and 33).

20 DPR, *IOC Consultation Response* (n8) para 2.1. See also Parts 2, 3, and 4 of the Regulations. <http://webarchive.nationalarchives.gov.uk/20130128103514/http://www.homeoffice.gov.uk/oicd/dpr.pdf.> accessed 29 September 2020 para 2.3.

21 Much of the DPA 1998 entered force on 16 July 1998.

22 Robin Callender Smith, 'Private Fire from the Gods: The Protection of Personal Data: The Data Protection Act 1998 as a Celebrity Privacy Remedy' (2 015) <http://papers.ssrn.com/sol3/papers.cfm?abstract_id=2596029> accessed 23 October 2015. The DPA 1998 has since been replaced by the DPA 2018, which gives effect to the EU's General Data Protection Regulation (GDPR).

23 DPA 1998, s1(1). Data relating to a living individual who can be identified from those data, or from those data and other information which is in the possession of, or is likely to come into the possession of, the data controller, and includes any expression of opinion about the individual and any indication of the intentions of the data controller or any other person in respect of the individual.

24 ibid, Schedule 1.

> 1. The Data Protection Principles are that: Personal data shall be processed fairly and lawfully and, in particular, shall not be processed unless...at least one of the conditions in Schedule 2 is met... 2. Personal data shall be obtained only for one or more specified and lawful purposes, and shall not be further processed in any manner

if such data was required for processing in the interests of national security[25] and a Ministerial Certificate certifying that such personal data is exempted was issued. Such a Certificate amounted to conclusive evidence of that fact.[26] This aligned with the Ministerial certification regime in RIPA 2000 for the interception of communications and assists in demonstrating the firm grip the executive maintained on the full spectrum of national security-related data processing. Furthermore, the DPA 1998 maintained its 1984 predecessor's 'crime and taxation' exemption which allowed personal data either to be processed or withheld from the data subject for the purposes of the prevention or detection of crime or the apprehension or prosecution of offenders.[27] CD, once generated, fell to be controlled and processed by the relevant service user's CSP (as data controllers under the DPA) prior to its acquisition by a public authority. CD was thus subject to the DPP unless exempted as described.

CD in the 1999 pre-RIPA consultation

It was against this EU and UK legislative backdrop that the 1999 Labour government circulated its 'Interception of Communications in the United Kingdom' consultation paper that preceded the Regulation of Investigatory Powers Bill

incompatible with that purpose or those purposes. 3. Personal data shall be adequate, relevant, and not excessive in relation to the purpose or purposes for which they are processed. 4. Personal data shall be accurate and, where necessary, kept up to date. 5. Personal data processed for any purpose or purposes shall not be kept for longer than is necessary for that purpose or those purposes. 6. Personal data shall be processed in accordance with the rights of data subjects under this Act. 7. Appropriate technical and organisational measures shall be taken against unauthorised or unlawful processing of personal data and against accidental loss or destruction of, or damage to, personal data. 8. Personal data shall not be transferred to a country or territory outside the European Economic Area unless that country or territory ensures an adequate level of protection for the rights and freedoms of data subjects in relation to the processing of personal data.

The Schedule 2 Conditions are: The data subject has consented; or the processing relates to the entry into a contract with the data subject; or for compliance with any legal obligation on the part of the data controller; or to protect the data subject's vital interests; or for the administration of justice, for the exercise of any functions of either House of Parliament, for the exercise of any functions conferred on any person by or under any enactment, for the exercise of any functions of the Crown, a Minister of the Crown or a government department, or for the exercise of any other functions of a public nature exercised in the public interest by any person.

25 ibid, s28(1).
26 ibid, s28(2) subject to a right of appeal to the Information Tribunal under s28(4).
27 ibid, s35 and see generally Danby G, 'Data Protection and the Police' (House of Commons Library, Standard Note SN/HA/5831, 18 January 2011).

(RIPB).[28] In addition to its 'interception' subject matter (examined in the previous chapter), a succinct Chapter 10 outlined how policy on access to CD would be implemented;

> The Government proposes to introduce a statutorily based framework to regulate access to communications data by investigating bodies. This will lay down the purposes for which an application ...may be made, the minimum standards of information which must be included...and the factors which must be taken into account by the authorising official. We also propose to introduce strict statutory requirements regarding the handling, storage and retention of communications data. It is intended that these measures will be laid out in detail in the publicly available Code of Practice.[29]

Their intention was based on the prevailing regulatory reality as highlighted by the DPR that,

> telephone companies...[were *providing*]...a great deal of communications data to the police and other investigatory bodies by virtue of s28 of the DPA 1984...[*allowing*]...*them, but not compelling them* to release personal data where they are satisfied that to not do so would be likely to prejudice crime prevention/detection, the apprehension/prosecution of offenders or tax assessment /collection. Though they could refuse to release personal data voluntarily and insist that the bodies concerned obtain production orders they are clearly under considerable moral pressure to cooperate.[30]

As such, CD *was* falling within the regulatory ambit of data protection legislation (the DPA 1984), but as will be demonstrated, on a very tenuous legal basis. Section 28 fell within Part IV of the DPA 1984, which provided that reference in any provision in Parts II and III to 'personal data' did not include references to data exempted by virtue of Part IV.[31] As previously outlined, 'personal data' included 'information relating to a living individual identifiable from that information (or from that and other information on the possession of the data user)', meaning that subscriber information and other data held by CSPs that could identify a particular service user fell within the ambit of the Act. Part II of the DPA 1984 included a prohibition on the disclosure of personal data other than in strictly limited circumstances.[32] However, returning to Part IV, section 28(3) provided that personal data was exempted from the non-disclosure provisions

28 Home Office, *The Interception of Communications in the United Kingdom, A Consultation Paper* (Cm4368, 1999).
29 ibid, (n28) 26.
30 DPR, *IOC Consultation Response* (n8) para 8.1, emphasis added.
31 DPA 1984, s26(1).
32 ibid, s5(2)(d) and s15, listed at s26(3).

in any case where it was being *held for the purposes of s28(1).* These purposes related to data held for the prevention or detection of crime; the apprehension or prosecution of offenders or the assessment or collection of any tax or duty.[33] Section 28(3) further provided a defence for a person proceeded against for breaching the non-disclosure provisions if that person (for example, a CSP employee) could prove that not making the disclosure would have been likely to prejudice the three section 28(1) matters. From a legal certainty standpoint, this arrangement was extremely tenuous. CSPs at that point were not holding customers' CD for any or all of the s28(1) purposes as provided for in s28(3). They were holding CD solely for the purposes of their businesses. Consequently, there was no basis in UK law for requesting it (although it was not unlawful to request it), but more importantly, as the government recognized, there was no credible lawful basis for disclosing it. It is thus unsurprising that the Blair administration sought to change this.

The sidelining of the DPR

As regards the second question regarding who was to oversee the acquisition of CD, the role of DPR, at that point held by Elizabeth France, included promoting the observance of, and considering complaints alleging breaches of, the DPP established in the DPA 1984 and a requirement to report annually to Parliament.[34] Although the 1984 Act was in the course of being replaced by that of 1998, the DPR role was still in place at the time of the 1999 consultation.[35] As might be expected, she provided a detailed and measured response. In welcoming the proposed CD acquisition framework, she opined that it 'should not simply provide a statutory basis for investigating bodies to gain easy access' to CD.[36] She also stated that 'the grounds for wishing to obtain certain types of communications data should be subject to prior external scrutiny, ideally by a judge'.[37] What attracted less attention was her reference to the possible use of production orders (presumably under the Police and Criminal Evidence [PACE] Act 1984) as a solution for acquiring CD deemed relevant in a criminal investigation.[38] This would have been a logical step given the extensive use and value of CD in criminal

33 ibid, s28(1).
34 ibid, ss3 and 36.
35 The DPA 1998, ss6, and 51 replaced the role and duties DPR with a Data Protection Commissioner DPC, effective 1 March 2000. This would change name again in 2001 to the Information Commissioner's Office (ICO) to embrace the Commissioner's expanded remit added by the Freedom of Information Act (FoIA) 2000. See generally, Information Commissioner's Office, 'Our History' (*ICO.org.uk*) <https://ico.org.uk/about-the-ico/our-information/history-of-the-ico/our-history/> accessed 20 November 2020.
36 DPR, *IOC Consultation Response* (n8), para 8.2.
37 ibid.
38 ibid, this was provided for in PACE 1984, Schedule 1.

proceedings. Her views on judicial scrutiny appear, on the available evidence, to have set her at odds with the Blair government.

Having expressed them, however, she compounded her sin by touching on the issue of CD retention. On any objective assessment, she was only doing her job by trying to secure the implementation of EU law. She reminded the government that the TPD recognised the importance of safeguarding traffic and billing data and provided strict rules as to its retention and use.[39] She strongly advocated for governmental implementation of strict controls to regulate access to CD and to 'avoid the introduction of lengthy statutory retention periods' for CD.[40] Her views on CD retention are particularly interesting, because as the then principal 'enforcer' and supreme overseer of European data protection legislation as implemented in the UK, she was better placed than most to advise on a CD retention framework. As the previous chapter demonstrated, however, her views were ultimately ignored in the final drafting of the RIPB. In addition, her role was abruptly excised from involvement in overseeing CD acquisition and processing.

The IOCCO takes over

The excision is of historical interest because the 1999 consultation expressly envisaged that it *would* be the DPR overseeing the new acquisition and disclosure of CD regime. The Home Office had rationalized this by stating that, as 'the disclosure of data falls within the remit of [data protection legislation]… the oversight and complaints mechanisms will continue to be provided under this legislation'.[41] However, a subsequent Home Office analysis of consultation responses asserted that there had been 'an almost equally balanced split between those who welcomed the inclusion of powers to acquire CD *in the interception regime* and those who felt it should be left separate and in the DPA regime'.[42] This author's analysis of the same responses failed to locate any expressions of a preference regarding an oversight mechanism, except in the submission of the Foundation for Information Policy Research (FIPR).[43] They opined that the proposal to put access to CD on a statutory basis, while welcome, abolished 'existing Data Protection safeguards…on access whilst relying on present oversight

39 ibid, para 8.3. However, she did not mention the government's right to limit the scope of application of the Directive under Article 14(1).

40 ibid.

41 Home Office, *Interception of Communications in the UK Consultation* (n28) para 10.7.

42 National Archives, 'Details of responses received to the Interception of Communications Act consultation exercise' *National Archives* (snapshot of 16 October 2002), emphasis added <http://webarchive.nationalarchives.gov.uk/20130128103514/http://www.homeoffice.gov.uk/oicd/conslist2.htm> accessed 30 October 2020.

43 FIPR, 'Executive Summary of Response to Consultation Paper Cm 4368' (1999) <http://webarchive.nationalarchives.gov.uk/20130128103514/http://www.homeoffice.gov.uk/oicd/fipr.pdf> accessed 30 October 2020.

and complaints mechanisms with swingeing Executive exemptions'.[44] As the RIPB passed through Parliament, concern was repeatedly expressed regarding the lack of consultation with the Data Protection Commissioner (DPC) as the DPR was now termed under the DPA 1998 now in force. Indeed, at one stage, Harry Cohen MP asked for an assurance that the DPC would be fully consulted with regard to the proposed Code of Practice governing the acquisition of CD.[45] This simply never happened. The change of policy appears to have taken place in unrecorded (or unpublished) discourse between the RIPB Second Reading on 6 March 2000 and the cross-party Standing Committee F scrutiny that commenced in April 2000. It was acknowledged in committee that the DPC's interests 'clearly relate[d] most closely' to the acquisition of CD, but that the oversight role constituted a 'natural extension' of the IOCCO's existing remit.[46] As that remit embraced communications content and related communications data (RCD) acquisition, it is possible to assert that the change of policy was not irrational. Another possibility is that the perennial 'wicked problem' (explored in Chapter 2 of this volume) of practically distinguishing communications content, RCD, and CD mean that it was deemed easier to simply include CD oversight within the IOCCO's remit. This too would represent a rational explanation for the change as it was presciently observed during Standing Committee F scrutiny that the 'dividing line between content and communications data [would] likely…blur rather than strengthen'.[47] Replacing DPC oversight of the Chapter II regime with that of the IOCCO was thus a logical decision that could perhaps have been better handled.

The privacy impact rationale at the core of RIPA 2000

Having side-lined the involvement of the very 'official…tasked to protect individual privacy'[48] Charles Clarke, then Minister of State at the Home Office, reasserted the view at RIPB Second Reading that the acquisition of CD for investigative purposes involved a significantly lesser degree of privacy intrusion than the interception of a communication.[49] This contravened the views expressed in evidence by the seemingly out of favour DPR[50] and in a second submission she made as the new DPC;

44 ibid, 9.
45 Rt Hon Harry Cohen, HC Deb, 6 March 2000, vol 345, col 792.
46 Parliamentary Secretary Jane Kennedy, SC Deb (F), Regulation of Investigatory Powers Bill, 6 April 2000, cols 413–414.
47 Rt Hon Richard Allan SC Deb (F), Regulation of Investigatory Powers Bill, 28 March 2000, col 247.
48 Rt Hon Harry Cohen, HC Deb 6 March 2000 vol 345, col 792.
49 Rt Hon Charles Clarke, Minister of State at the Home Office (Lab) SC Deb (F), Regulation of Investigatory Powers Bill, 28 March 2000, cols 244, 246, and 256.
50 DPR, *IOC Consultation Response* (n8) para 8.2. Cited by the Rt Hon Oliver Heald (Con) SC Deb (F), Regulation of Investigatory Powers Bill, 28 March 2000, col 249.

> The Commissioner questions the distinction made…between the requirements for gaining access to data contained within an intercepted communication…[RCD]…and those for gaining access to other communications data such as traffic and billing information. *Both sets of data provide insight into the private lives of individuals and should therefore be subject to equivalent controls and safeguards.* [51]

The civil libertarian disagreement was articulated by Liberty, who urged the government 'to accept that the grounds on which access to this material may be sought, and the authorisation and supervision procedures applicable, should be no less strict than those…in relation to interception proper'.[52] Opposition members within the Standing Committee also vehemently disagreed.[53]

The privacy impact rationale within Chapter II

The controversial Privacy Impact Assessment was again in evidence when Chapter II of the RIPB progressed to scrutiny. In equating the acquisition of CD with 'surveillance in a public place that gives information about lifestyle, contacts and movements', thereby constituting 'normal day-to-day policing activity', Charles Clarke reasserted his government's view that the 'significantly lower' level of intrusion inherent in the acquisition of CD made internal authorization 'right'.[54] Judicial authorization was dismissed as 'inappropriate' on the grounds that it would, on account of the expected number of acquisition applications, 'place unacceptable strains on the court service'.[55] Given that, in the first IOCCO Annual Report to publish relevant statistics (2007), there were 439,054 requests to acquire CD, the latter statement undoubtedly carried weight.[56] In another example of the cross-party consensus usually reached in this area of law, there was little meaningful resistance expressed to internal authorization of applications to access CD during the passage of the RIPB. Consequently, internal authorization of applications to acquire CD,[57] or to serve a notice to a CSP requiring its

51 Data Protection Commissioner, 'Response of the Data Protection Commissioner to the Government's Regulation of Investigatory Powers Bill-Briefing for Parliamentarians' (March 2000), available at Foundation for Information Policy Research (FIPR) <www.fipr.org/rip/DPCparlRIP.htm> accessed 30 October 2020, emphasis added.

52 Liberty, 'Response by Liberty to Home Office Consultation Paper: *Interception of Communications in the United Kingdom*' (August 1999) para 3.3 <www.fipr.org/ioca/liberty.pdf> accessed 30 September 2020.

53 See particularly the representations of the Rt Hon Oliver Heald (Con) and Rt Hon Richard Allan (Lib Dem) SC Deb (F), Regulation of Investigatory Powers Bill, 28 March 2000, cols 242–250.

54 SC Deb (F), Regulation of Investigatory Powers Bill, 28 March 2000, col 246.

55 ibid, col 247.

56 IOCCO, *Report of the Interception of Communications Commissioner for 2005–06* (HC 315, 19 February 2007) para 82.

57 RIPA 2000, s22(3).

disclosure,[58] remained in the Act as assented to. The question of judicial oversight in obtaining CD was not, however, consigned to history.

RIPA 2000, Part 1, Chapter II as enacted

Chapter II as finally enacted marked the first dedicated statutory governance of investigative access to CD by providing a mechanism whereby an application could be made to *acquire* CD from a CSP, or alternatively, enabling a notice to be given to a CSP to require its *disclosure*. The Chapter II provisions were implicitly reserved within the meaning of the Scotland Act 1998[59] and the Northern Ireland Act 1998,[60] meaning they extended to the whole of the UK.[61] As previously explored, *ex post facto* independent oversight of Chapter II was, as for Chapter I, made the responsibility of the RIPA's newly reconstituted IOCCO.[62]

In line with the typically opaque terminology used throughout RIPA 2000, Chapter II's five sections governing 'the acquisition and disclosure of CD' opened as follows:

> *any conduct* in relation to a postal service or telecommunication system for obtaining communications data, *other than conduct consisting in the interception of communications in the course of their transmission* by means of such a service or system...[and]...the disclosure to any person of communications data...shall be lawful for all purposes if...it is conduct in which any person is authorised or required to engage by an authorisation or notice granted or given under this Chapter.[63]

This drafting thus excluded 'related communications data' (RCD) obtained 'in the course of interception of a communication's transmission' from CD that was to be obtained by applying to a CSP.[64] RCD therefore became distinguishable

58 ibid, s22(4).
59 Scotland Act 1998, Schedule 5, s2(4), B8 and C10. There are some overlaps in legislative competence, however the nascent Scottish Parliament deferred to its Westminster parent in this area in the interests of human rights protection.
60 See Northern Ireland Act 1998, Sched 2 (Excepted Matters), para 17 and Sched 3 (Reserved Matters) para 29. An explicit reservation was proposed for the Northern Ireland Act 1998 in the Draft Communications Data Bill, however this was never enacted. See Home Secretary, *Draft Communications Data Bill* (Cm 8359, June 2012).
61 RIPA 2000, s83(3).
62 ibid, s57(2). Although there existed a single Interception of Communications Commissioner, the fact that he had staff working for him means the term IOCCO is more appropriate. References to the IOCCO are to the institution, rather than the Commissioner. Where appropriate, the Commissioner is referred to by name.
63 ibid, s21(1) and 21(2), emphasis added.
64 RCD was discussed in Chapter 6 of this volume. RIPA 2000, s20 (contained at the end of Chapter I) defines 'related communications data' (RCD) in relation to a communication intercepted in the course of its transmission by means of a postal service or telecommunica-

by definition and regulatory framework. The rationale for this was that RCD represented the unavoidable ancillary derivative of a communication intercepted in the course of its transmission (i.e. *contemporaneously acquired* CD), from CD generated or retained by CSPs as a consequence of *all* electronic or telecommunications usage, and which requires to be sought *after the fact* of transmission. From one perspective these distinctions are logical and practical, but from another, perhaps less so, when the analytical processes to which either type of CD can be subjected are considered. Put another way, investigative data analysis techniques applied to both may have yielded equivalent privacy-intrusive results.[65]

'Communications data' defined

Having already distinguished RCD and included it within Chapter I, Chapter II defined 'communications data' as:

1 Any *traffic data* comprised in or attached to a communication (whether by the sender or otherwise) for the purposes of any postal service or telecommunication system by means of which it is being or may be transmitted;[66]
2 Any information which includes none of the *contents* of a communication (apart from any information falling within paragraph [a]) and is about the *use* made by any person – (i) of any postal service or telecommunications

---

tions system, to mean so much of any communications data (within the meaning of Chapter II of Part I of RIPA) as – (a)is obtained by, or in connection with, the interception; and(b) relates to the communication or to the sender or recipient, or intended recipient, of the communication. The power to acquire RCD is found in RIPA 2000, s5(6) (a) and to disclose it, at s5(1) (d).

65 DPR, *IOC Consultation Response* (n8) para 8.2.

66 RIPA 2000, s21(6), emphasis added. 'Traffic data' includes, in relation to 'any communication;' (a) any data identifying, or purporting to identify, any person, apparatus or location to or from which the communication is or may be transmitted, (b) any data identifying or selecting, or purporting to identify or select, apparatus through which, or by means of which, the communication is or may be transmitted, (c) any data comprising signals for the actuation of apparatus used for the purposes of a telecommunication system for effecting (in whole or in part) the transmission of any communication, and (d) any data identifying the data or other data as data comprised in or attached to a particular communication, but that expression includes data identifying a computer file or computer program access to which is obtained, or which is run, by means of the communication to the extent only that the file or program is identified by reference to the apparatus in which it is stored.

Furthermore, section 21(7)(a) references, in relation to traffic data comprising signals for the actuation of apparatus, a telecommunication system by means of which a communication is being or may be transmitted include references to any telecommunication system in which that apparatus is comprised; and (b) references to traffic data being attached to a communication include references to the data and the communication being logically associated with each other; and in this section 'data', in relation to a postal item, means anything written on the outside of the item. As regard the ultimate assertion of this thesis, data can already be seen as being a core concept within this particular investigatory power.

service; or (ii) in connection with the provision to or *use* by any person of any telecommunications service, of any part of a telecommunication system;[67]

3 Any information not falling within paragraph (a) or (b) that is held or obtained, in *relation to persons* to whom he provides the service, by a person providing a postal service or telecommunications service.[68]

As the voluminous footnotes illustrate, the full definition of CD was lengthy and complex. Those examining it broadly summarised it as constituting 'traffic data', 'service use data', and 'subscriber data'.[69] Nóra Ní Loideáin has provided a welcome elucidation:

> the *context* as opposed to the content of a communication...[and]...a rich source of personal information[that] reveals the 'who' (parties involved), the 'when', how long and how often, (time, duration and frequency), the 'what' (type of communication, e.g. phone call, message, e-mail), the 'how' (the communication device used, e.g. landline telephony, smartphone, tablet) and the 'where' (location of devices used) involved in every communication we make.[70]

Ensuring Chapter II entered force: a troubled implementation

Despite many of RIPA's provisions entering force alongside the Human Rights Act (HRA) 1998 on 2 October 2000, Chapter II as assented to was not among them. In fact, it was another three years and three months before it would take effect, meaning the tenuous arrangements under the DPA 1998 continued. Despite only five constituent sections centred on enabling access to CSP-retained CD by the intelligence services, police forces, and other public and local authorities with investigative functions, a media-led furore accompanied the initial consultative draft of the Regulation of Investigatory Powers (Communications Data) Order, promulgated in 2002 seeking to secure its implementation.[71] This had listed 'some 1,039 public authorities as being empowered to request access to

67 Emphasis added.

68 ibid, s21(4), emphasis added.

69 Joint Committee on the Draft Communications Data Bill, *Legislative Scrutiny: Draft Communications Data Bill (Final Report)* (2012–13, HL79, HC 479) 13. (JCDCDB, *Final Report 2012*).

70 Nóra Ní Loideáin, 'Judicial Review of Mass Metadata Surveillance in the Post-Snowden Era' (2015) University of Cambridge Faculty of Law Legal Research Paper 32/2015, 2 <http://papers.ssrn.com/sol3/papers.cfm?abstract_id=2613424> accessed 30 September 2020.

71 Steve Hedley, *The Law of Electronic Commerce and the Internet in the UK and Ireland* (Routledge-Cavendish, 2006) 117.

communications data'.[72] The Home Office took some time to react, and when they did so, Home Secretary David Blunkett conceded that 'the Government had blundered into the issue'.[73] A follow-up consultation exercise was undertaken in March 2003 (2003 Consultation) and it was this, and some of the responses to it, that informed the final structure, scope, and purposes of Chapter II's acquisition and disclosure provisions.[74] The 43-page document was perhaps unusually detailed and candid for the era, probably as a result of the controversy arising from the initial draft. In his foreword, Mr Blunkett observed that:

> it is not often that a piece of secondary legislation attracts the sort of attention that...engulfed the draft Order adding public authorities to the access to communications data provisions of the Regulation of Investigatory Powers Act 2000. In withdrawing the Order, dubbed a 'Snoopers' Charter' by its critics, I admitted that we had got it wrong...[t]wo years had elapsed since...[RIPA 2000]...had been passed by Parliament and there was great pressure for the Government to clarify and regulate better the interchange taking place between public authorities and communications service providers around disclosure of communications data.[75]

The consultation opened with an expressed 'preferred approach', namely to 'to restrict significantly the access of additional authorities producing a radically different proposals [*sic*] to those laid before Parliament last summer'.[76] With a starting figure of 1,039 authorities this would not have been unduly onerous. Readers were offered 'access to detailed information, significantly more than has previously been publicly available about public authorities need for communications data', at a dedicated website, with a footnote adding that this had been collated by the Home Office from data provided by the public authorities or their representative bodies.[77] Under headings entitled 'Traffic Data', 'Service Use Information', and 'Subscriber Information' replete with examples, readers were offered succinct and clear descriptions of what constituted CD in Chapter II.[78]

72 Statewatch UK, 'Data Retention and Access Consultation Farce: Government to Allow Access for Crime Purposes to Records Which Can Only Be Held for "National Security"' (*Statewatch*, April 2003) <www.statewatch.org/news/2003/sep/11Batcs.htm> accessed 1 October 2020.

73 Stuart Millar, Lucy Ward, and Richard Norton-Taylor, 'Blunkett shelves access to data plans' *The Guardian* (19 June 2002) <www.theguardian.com/technology/2002/jun/19/internet.humanrights> accessed 30 September 2020.

74 Home Office, *Access to Communications Data: Respecting Privacy and Protecting the Public from Crime A Consultation* (Home Office, March 2003) available at <www.statewatch.org/news/2003/mar/ripa.pdf> accessed 30 September 2020.

75 ibid, Foreword.

76 ibid, 8.

77 ibid, (n74) 11. The web page <www.homeoffice.gov.uk/ripa/part1/pas.htm> is no longer available.

78 ibid, 7.

These were significantly clearer than the actual section 21 provisions, although telecommunications definitions are, by their nature, complex, technical, and occasionally difficult to deconstruct. The document then focused on making a strong case, supplemented by illustrative case examples, for awarding CD investigation powers to what still amounted to a very broad range of public and local authorities.[79]

The privacy impact rationale in the 2003 CD consultation

The RIPB's passage through parliamentary scrutiny demonstrated that the Privacy Impact Assessments relating to communications content and data investigatory powers can sometimes appear somewhat simplistic and arbitrary. 2003's Chapter II consultation demonstrated some creditable nuance, however, by acknowledging that the three categories of CD created in section 21 did not infringe individual communications service users' right to privacy to an equal degree. Statements such as 'for the majority of additional public authorities, access to traffic data is currently neither necessary nor proportionate to the matters they deal with'[80] and 'some communications data can be more intrusive than other data: mobile phone location data pinpoints the place where a call is made, whereas subscriber data simply links names to phone numbers'[81] indicated that a greater degree of critical analysis of 'non-content' CD had been undertaken in the two years since the first Order. It was frankly conceded that the initial Order had been 'too permissive…allowing a long list of additional public authorities access to the *full range* of communications data'.[82] Although the Home Office claimed ownership of the views expressed in the document, the credits demonstrate that the 2003 consultation was itself based on a consultation with independent experts, the Confederation of British Industry (CBI), and the Trades Union Congress (TUC).[83] The considered approach to proportionality demonstrated in the consultation reflects the influence of privacy expertise among the consultees.

In terms of influence and policy direction that would lead to Chapter II of RIPA entering force, Chapter 3 of the 2003 consultation stands out for its depth of engagement with the issues underlying targeted CD investigation, particularly the spectrum of entities that should be enabled to undertake it and for what purposes. It discussed, in a hitherto jealously guarded area of secretive UK public law, what were becoming more comfortable concepts derived from repeated engagements with EU institutions, those of necessity and proportionality. 'Necessity', derived from the ECHR and relevant jurisprudence, reflected the need for applications to be viewed by the grantor as being for a purpose that was

79 ibid, 10–21.
80 ibid, 25.
81 ibid, 6.
82 ibid, 22.
83 ibid, Annex A.

'necessary in a democratic society'.[84] In this regard, the document outlined the limited, but still extensive range of permitted purposes already listed in Chapter II as assented to, expressly stating there was no intention to add to them.[85] It did not mention that provision remained in place to add or remove purposes by affirmative resolution.[86] The document then outlined the Home Office's agreed perception of 'proportionality':

> if what is proposed has a legitimate purpose but interferes with a Convention right, the interference is not justified if the means to achieve that purpose are excessive, arbitrary or unfair. Any potential collateral intrusion must also be taken into account. Even after all these considerations, interference may still not be justified if the impact on an individual or group of individuals is too severe.[87]

The consultation restated the statutory criteria that had to, 'in practice, be satisfied before any public authority could be considered for inclusion within the RIPA regime for accessing communications data'[88] and also the applicable safeguards.[89] The latter included clearly specifying the persons designated to seek access to data;[90] an accreditation scheme for individuals who would actually access

84 See, for example, ECHR, Article 8(2).
85 Home Office, *Access to Communications Data* (n74) 22. See RIPA 2000, s22(2)

> (a) in the interests of national security; (b) for the purpose of preventing or detecting crime or of preventing disorder; (c) in the interests of the economic well-being of the United Kingdom; (d) in the interests of public safety; (e) for the purpose of protecting public health; (f) for the purpose of assessing or collecting any tax, duty, levy or other imposition, contribution, or charge payable to a government department; (g) for the purpose, in an emergency, of preventing death or injury or any damage to a person's physical or mental health, or of mitigating any injury or damage to a person's physical or mental health; or (h) for any purpose (not falling within paragraphs [a] to [g]) which is specified for the purposes of this subsection by an order made by the Secretary of State.

86 RIPA 2000, s22(2)(h). s22 remained unaltered until the enactment of the Data Retention and Investigatory Powers Act (DRIPA) 2014 enacted after the decision in *Digital Rights* and which, *inter alia*, substituted s22(2) (b) with 'applicable crime purpose' (see s22 [2A]) (serious crime) and also removed (e) and (f).
87 Home Office, *Access to Communications Data* (n74) 22.
88 ibid. These were that the applicant entity had to be a 'public authority' within the meaning of the HRA 1998, s6(3) and that they could demonstrate the necessity and proportionality inherent in their application.
89 ibid, 23–24.
90 RIPA 2000, s25(2)–(5) provided for the making and amendment of secondary legislation using the affirmative resolution procedure of a list of 'individuals holding such offices, ranks or positions with relevant public authorities as are prescribed for the purposes of this subsection by an order made by the Secretary of State'. The consultation acknowledged that such persons needed to be sufficiently senior and accountable, but to have working knowledge in their field.

the CD;[91] compliance with a statutory Code of Practice;[92] IOCCO oversight;[93] and sanctions for the abuse of powers to access communications data under RIPA.[94] The latter made reference to various obliquely applicable sanctions, but despite pointing out that 'no explicit offence existed under RIPA to cover deliberate, criminally-motivated misuse of the access to CD provisions' as an issue that 'may need to be addressed to send a strong signal to those entrusted to use these powers that abuse of an individual's privacy is unacceptable',[95] no remedial action occurred in the lifetime of Chapter II. The lacuna was rectified by the IPA 2016.[96]

The consultation then offered three options to make Chapter II more restrictive, and thus more proportionate in the eyes of the public. The first involved restricting access according to CD type (traffic, service use, and subscriber) *and* the purposes for which it would be sought (although section 22[2] already stipulated this).[97] An additional second option was that, where deemed appropriate, this restricted access option would be supplemented by a 'further significant safeguard (a double lock)' involving prior independent third-party scrutiny of applications.[98] The specifics of an 'appropriate' double-lock context were not specified. Bearing in mind that the document was aimed at public authorities other than the UKIC and police forces, who 'automatically' qualified for Chapter II, adopting one or both of the options would mean that 'only a small number of additional public authorities' would have access to all three CD types. The remainder meeting the criteria for inclusion in the regime would only be enabled to access service use and subscriber data, and, if the double-lock option was availed of, only with third-party independent scrutiny and approval.[99]

A third 'short list' option, to some extent already discarded by the Home Office in the document, involved enabling only a small number of additional public authorities ('police bodies and the other emergency services') access to CD, with no limitation as to type.[100] In fairness to the Home Office team, the benefits and costs of this option were clearly set out, thus providing a rationale for the choices eventually made for Chapter II. The benefits asserted were that

91 Home Office, *Access to Communications Data* (n74) 23. This introduced the idea of the Single Point of Contact (SPoC) already in use in some police forces and discussed later in this chapter. The role and accreditation scheme were not included in either primary or secondary RIP legislation, but in the CDCoP.

92 ibid. The consultation referred to a draft CD CoP out for public consultation published in August 2001 that would be 'laid before Parliament in due course' (discussed shortly). This turned out to mean six years later.

93 ibid, restating the change of policy as regards Information Commissioner oversight.

94 ibid, 24.

95 Home Office, *Access to Communications Data* (n74) 24.

96 IPA 2016, s11.

97 Home Office, *Access to Communications Data* (n74) 25.

98 ibid.

99 ibid.

100 ibid, 28.

a short list would be 'clear and unequivocal; the investigation of serious crime, protection of national security and saving of life in emergencies clearly satisfied the proportionality requirement' and concerns that powers to access CD should not be widely available to public authorities would be directly addressed.[101] The Home Office opined that this option was 'flawed' and in ultimately discounting it, their reasoning rationalizes the final version of Chapter II. It was argued that a 'short list' would adversely affect the ability of many public authorities, expressly empowered by Parliament to investigate certain types of crime instead of the police, to prevent and detect those crimes, thus adversely affecting the public and adding an additional investigative burden to police forces.[102] In addition, if public authorities excluded from the short list in RIPA remained able to use other legislation to access CD, one of the main purposes of RIPA, the creation of a single ECHR compliant regulatory regime for such access, would be undermined.[103]

In terms of influence and policy direction that would lead to Chapter II of RIPA entering force, Chapter 3 of the 2003 consultation stands out for its depth of engagement with the issues underlying targeted CD investigation, particularly the spectrum of bodies with investigative functions that should be enabled to undertake it and for what purposes. From one perspective, it marked a transparent and candid re-evaluation of the relationship between the Home Office and the public. It was honest, forthright, and appeared to seek genuine and meaningful debate on the principal privacy concerns that accompany communications and data investigation. In aligning the policy approach to EU CD categories and to the ECHR necessity and proportionality tests, optimists might have thought that rights had indeed been brought home in this area of law. From another perspective, however, supported by the evidence now in the public domain, the exercise was somewhat disingenuous. In March 2003, this document made reference to the retention of CD being subject to a separate consultation (based on the Anti-terrorism, Crime and Security Act [ATCASA] 2001, Part 11).[104] Whilst truthful, it masked the fact that the UKIC were secretly benefitting from a bulk CD retention and acquisition scheme enabled by secret section 94 directions, albeit on limited grounds.[105] Neither the independent expert panel, nor the CBI or TUC would have been aware of this partial circumvention of the human rights-compliant framework they were contributing to. It seems unlikely that all Home Office personnel were unaware of the existence of the section 94 regime during the consultation. The Home Secretary would certainly have known. As such, it is difficult to avoid the conclusion that the inclusion of the three intelligence services in Chapter II of RIPA was deliberate and disingenuous, in that, to the public, CD acquisition by the intelligence services was governed, like interception, within a

101 ibid.
102 ibid.
103 ibid.
104 Home Office, *Access to Communications Data* (n74) 8.
105 By virtue of the Telecommunications Act 1984, s94 secret directions ultimately avowed on 4 November 2015.

statutory framework purporting to offer compliance with human rights. The factual reality, however, was that CD was being acquired by the UKIC by another legal provision in secret, on a significantly greater scale, and with the secret permission of the very person signing off on a consultation asserting the benefits of

> A single regulatory regime for public authorities to access communications data compliant with human rights legislation, through explicit statutory requirements to take account of necessity and proportionality, statutory oversight of the exercise of powers and duties under the legislation and a statutory complaints mechanism about the exercise of those powers and duties.[106]

It remains a moot point as to whether the UKIC actually ever really needed to be included in Chapter II. Keeping the section 94 regime secret created a rod for the back of governments still to come, as the public reaction to its avowal, and the legal challenges that followed would demonstrate.[107] Whilst appreciating that hindsight has its benefits, it would not have been unduly difficult to intimate to the UK public at the time that there were secret aspects to the interception and access to CD regimes, supplementary to Chapter II regime and undertaken on national security grounds, without having to disclose the details.

The final outcome of the 2003 consultation was a revised statutory instrument which, despite 'more carefully defining the purposes for which data was needed' incorporated 'an even longer list of authorities who could demand data'.[108] It was enacted in December 2003, enabling Chapter II to finally enter into force on 5 January 2004.[109]

Codes of practice: a troubled implementation

Publishing a finalized and broadly acceptable Acquisition and Disclosure of Communications Data Code of Practice (CDCoP) proved even more troublesome than getting Chapter II itself into effect. Despite the 2003 consultation's reference to a draft CoP published in 2001 that would be released 'in due course', it was conceded in a revised consultative draft published firstly in 2005 and again, after further revision, three years later (June 2006), that the initial draft version had been 'shelved when the provisions of Chapter II and their relevance to a wide range of public authorities attracted adverse public and Parliamentary attention in summer 2002'.[110] This meant that the 'release in due course' referred to in the 2003 consultation disingenuously meant a CoP yet to be finalized. In the first

106 Home Office, *Access to Communications Data* (n74) 8.
107 See Chapter 9 of this volume.
108 Home Office, *Access to Communications Data* (n74) 8.
109 By virtue of the Regulation of Investigatory Powers Act 2000 (Commencement No. 3) Order 2003, SI 2003/3140.
110 Home Office, *Acquisition and Disclosure of Communications Data: A Public Consultation* (June 2006) 2.

Annual Report detailing IOCCO inspections and oversight of Chapter II published in February 2007, three years after its entry into force, it was observed that

> The Code of Practice has been through several drafts and much consultation, and will be ready for approval by the Home Secretary shortly. In the initial stages there were some complaints that it was over-bureaucratic, and difficult to manage. It is quite complex, but not difficult and it is designed to ensure that all acquisition and disclosure of communications data is carried out lawfully and that the rights of the citizen are properly protected. Police Forces have acclimatised themselves to the legislation and the Code of Practice, and now find that they are quite simple to comply with.[111]

It appears, therefore, that various drafts of a CoP had guided applications to obtain CD between January 2004 and the release of the Home Office-approved 2007 edition in October of that year (CDCoP (2007).[112] This was not critical to the proper operation of Chapter II but falls short of full professionalism or acceptable best practice. The 2003 consultation appears to have envisaged that a finalized CoP was still some way off, as it had expressly stated that the existence of the 2001 draft did not 'prevent public authorities from maintaining and publishing their own good practice guides'.[113]

The IOCCO's positive assessment appears accurate, as the CDCoP (2007) did not require significant amendment or replacement for the next eight years. In his comprehensive practitioner-focused assessment of it, McKay is also mainly positive, although he noted that it was 'a curiosity of...[it]...that some of the most helpful practical guidance is hidden in the footnotes'.[114] As for other RIPA-based Codes, the CDCoP (2007) stated that that regard was to be had to it in the exercise of powers under RIPA by virtue of RIPA,[115] that it was admissible in evidence in criminal and civil proceedings,[116] and that if any of its provisions appear relevant to a question before any court, tribunal, or RIPA-empowered oversight Commissioners, it must be taken into account.[117] It omitted to mention, however, the fact that the failure of any person to comply with any of its provisions would not of itself render them liable to criminal or civil proceedings.[118] This omission, when considered alongside RIPA's labyrinthine 'non-enforceability'

111 IOCCO *Annual Report 2005–06* (n56) para 23.
112 Home Office, Acquisition and Disclosure Code of Practice (TSO, 2007) (*CDCoP* (2007)) References to a CDCoP are to the CDCoP 2007 unless otherwise stated.
113 Home Office, *Access to Communications Data* (755), 25.
114 McKay, *Covert Policing* (Oxford University Press, 2011) 126.
115 RIPA 2000, s72(1).
116 ibid, s71(3).
117 ibid, s71(4); CD COP (2007) (n112) para 1.6.
118 RIPA 2000, s71(2).

clause (section 80)[119] support McKay's assessment of RIPA 2000 as a whole as being no 'no more than a voluntary code'.[120]

The Chapter II authorization process

The practical mechanics of the Chapter II internal authorization process have been amply explained and critically analyzed elsewhere.[121] Consequently, only a short descriptive summary of the relevant provisions is made here. The process involved an applicant, a designated person (DP), a single point of contact (SPoC), and a senior responsible officer (SRO).

The applicant

The applicant was defined on the face of Chapter II as 'a person conducting an investigation or operation for a relevant public authority who makes an application in writing or electronically for the acquisition of CD'.[122] The CDCoP required applicants to:

> specify the purpose for which the data is required, by reference to a statutory purpose under 22(2) of the Act; describe the communications data required, specifying, where relevant, any historic or future date(s) and, where appropriate, time period(s); explain why the acquisition of that data is considered necessary and proportionate to what is sought to be achieved by acquiring it; consider and, where appropriate, describe any meaningful collateral intrusion – the extent to which the privacy of any individual not under investigation

119 ibid, s80. General saving for lawful conduct:

> Nothing in any of the provisions of this Act by virtue of which conduct of any description is or may be authorised by any warrant, authorisation or notice, or by virtue of which information may be obtained in any manner, shall be construed (a) as making it unlawful to engage in any conduct of that description which is not otherwise unlawful under this Act and would not be unlawful apart from this Act; (b) as otherwise requiring – (i) the issue, grant or giving of such a warrant, authorisation or notice, or (ii) the taking of any step for or towards obtaining the authority of such a warrant, authorisation or notice, before any such conduct of that description is engaged in; or (c) as prejudicing any power to obtain information by any means not involving conduct that may be authorised under this Act. The Explanatory Note to s80 state – Section 80 ensures that nothing in this Act makes any actions unlawful unless that is explicitly stated. The availability of an authorisation or a warrant does not mean that it is unlawful not to seek or obtain one. In this respect, the Act must be read with section 6 of the Human Rights Act, which makes it unlawful to act in a way which is incompatible with a Convention right.

120 McKay, *Covert Policing* (n114) paras 1.24–1.26.

121 ibid, 108–135.

122 Defined in the *CD CoP* 2007 (n112) para 3.3.

may be infringed and why that intrusion is justified in the circumstances, and identify and explain the timescale within which the data is required.[123]

The designated person (DP)

Applicants were required to make their application for CD to an 'in-house' DP.[124] This was a demonstrably lower approval threshold than that for interception of communications and the acquisition of RCD.[125] The DP was required to normally be independent of the investigation to which the application to acquire CD relates' although the 2007 CDCoP acknowledged that 'unavoidable' exceptions were foreseeable; these had to be explicitly justified.[126] The offices, ranks, or positions of DPs empowered to grant or require access to CD were set out in subordinate legislation using the affirmative resolution procedure.[127] These statutory instruments additionally listed every public authority able to use acquisition powers,[128] along with the particular sub-category or sub-categories of CD they were entitled to acquire (i.e. traffic data, user data, or subscriber data).[129] Conceptually, there were similarities in the DP's role with that of a Custody Officer under PACE 1984, however the 'independence from the investigation'[130] requirement stipulated therein was not replicated on the face of RIPA 2000, but in the publicly available CD CoP.[131] DPs were required to possess current working knowledge of 'human rights principles and legislation, specifically those of necessity and proportionality, and how they apply to the acquisition

123 ibid, para 3.5.

124 RIPA 2000, s25(2), individuals holding such offices, ranks, or positions with relevant public authorities as are prescribed for the purposes of this subsection by an order made by the Secretary of State.

125 *CD CoP 2007* (n112). Para 3.7 stated 'it is the DP's responsibility to consider applications for CD and record their considerations at the time (or as soon as is reasonably practicable) in writing or electronically'. If they believe the acquisition of CD is necessary and proportionate in the specific circumstances, an authorization is granted, or a notice is given.

126 ibid, paras 3.12–3.15. The IOCCO should be informed where this has occurred although no timeframe is stipulated.

127 Regulation of Investigatory Powers (Communications Data) Order 2003, SI 2003/3172, replaced by Regulation of Investigatory Powers (Communications Data) Order 2010, SI 2010/480.

128 ibid, the schedule may be varied using the affirmative resolution procedure by a Secretary of State by virtue of RIPA 2000, s25.

129 ibid, schs 1 and 2.

130 PACE 1984, s36(5):

> none of the functions of a custody officer in relation to a person shall be performed by an officer who at the time when the function falls to be performed is involved in the investigation of an offence for which that person is in police detention at that time.

131 *CD CoP 2007* (n112) para 3.12.

of communications data'.[132] Precisely how that working knowledge was to be attained and maintained was not stipulated, however, and would undoubtedly have varied across the large number of public and local authorities entitled under Chapter II to seek CD.[133]

The purposes for which a DP could authorize obtaining CD

RIPA 2000, section 22(2), provided the purposes for which a DP could authorize the obtaining of CSP-retained CD, adjustable by affirmative resolution. These were substantially broader than those for interception and accommodated the reality that local authorities, as well as the UKIC and law enforcement agencies, required communications data investigation powers.

The Single Point of Contact (SPoC)

The SPoC role was not provided for in Chapter II, but was a product of efforts at best practice made between 2004 and the issue of the CD CoP 2007, which defined them as 'an accredited individual trained to facilitate lawful acquisition of communications data and effective co-operation between a public authority and CSPs and issued with a SPoC Personal Identification Number'.[134] Their critically important role in ensuring human rights compliance in the practical operation of Chapter II was to:

> engage proactively with applicants to develop strategies to obtain...[CD]... and use it effectively in support of operations or investigations; assess whether the acquisition of specific ...[CD]...from a CSP is reasonably practical or whether the specific data required is inextricably linked to other data; advise applicants on the most appropriate methodology for acquisition of data where the data sought engages a number of CSPs; advise applicants and designated persons on the interpretation of the Act, particularly whether an authorisation or notice is appropriate; provide assurance to designated persons that authorisations and notices are lawful under the Act and free from errors; provide assurance to CSPs that authorisations and notices are authentic and lawful; assess whether...[CD]...disclosed by a CSP in response to a notice fulfils the requirement of the notice; assess whether...[CD]...obtained by means of an authorisation fulfils the requirement of the authorisation.[135]

132 ibid, para 3.8.
133 IOCCO *Annual Report 2005–06* (n56) para 8 lists a total of 795 entities.
134 Home Office, *CD CoP* (2007) (n112) para 3.15.
135 ibid, para 3.17.

The Senior Responsible Officer (SRO)

The CDCOP (2007) outlined the 'safeguard' role of the SRO within the in-house authorization regime, deeming them responsible for: the integrity of the in-house process for acquiring CD; compliance with RIPA 2000, Part I, Chapter II and the CD CoP; oversight of error reporting to the IOCCO and the identification of the cause(s) of such errors and the implementation of corrective processes; engagement with the IOCCO during inspections; and overseeing post-IOCCO inspection action plans.[136]

Substantive amendments to Chapter II during its time in force

A requirement for judicial authorization for local authority applications for CD

The Protection of Freedoms Act (PoFA) 2012 amended Chapter II to introduce a requirement for local authorities to obtain judicial authority before their in-house applications to obtain CD by authorization or notice would be held valid with effect from 1 November 2012.[137] This followed significant adverse publicity surrounding the outcomes of poor necessity and proportionality assessments relating to RIPA powers undertaken in-house by some local authorities.[138] The efficacy of the new scheme was examined in the annual reports of the IOCCO from 2013 onwards and in the reviews of investigatory powers conducted after the 2013 Intelligence Shock. As such, these are examined in the next chapter.

Reviews of Chapter II prior to the 2013 Intelligence Shock

The Joint Committee on the Draft Communications Data Bill 2012

The previous chapter explored the draft Communications Data Bill 2012 (draft CDB).[139] It is revisited here because the Joint Committee convened to examine not only its controversial retention provisions but also the Chapter II regime, as the draft CD Bill would have seen it repealed and replaced.[140] As was shown,

136 ibid, para 3.31.

137 Protection of Freedoms Act 2012, s37 inserted a new section 23A and 23B to RIPA 2000. By virtue of the Regulation of Investigatory Powers (Communications Data) Order 2010, sch 2, Part II, a local authority means: the Common Council of the City of London in its capacity as a local authority, the Council of the Isles of Scilly, a county council in England or Wales, a county borough council in Wales, a district council in England or NI, a London borough council, or a council constituted under section 2 of the Local Government etc. (Scotland) Act 1994.

138 See for example *Jenny Paton and others v Poole Borough Council* (2008) UKIPTrib 09/01/C (2010). This related to directed surveillance under Part II of the Act.

139 JCDCDB, *Final Report 2012* (n69) 13.

140 ibid, 3.

unproven executive assertions as to the existence of a 'communications capability gap',[141] a lack of consultation with CSPs, ISPs, and the wider public, and the damning criticisms of the 2010–2015 coalition government's methodology preceding the draft CD Bill's introduction ultimately led to its abandonment.[142] Mrs May's advocacy for its overall schema never waned, however, and her aspirations as expressed in it were ultimately largely given effect in her draft IPB.

Despite the draft CD Bill being famously abandoned, the JCDCDB made cogent observations and recommendations regarding aspects of Chapter II that would remain relevant when the IPA 2016 was on the horizon. These included the need for public authorities wishing to be empowered to apply to obtain CD making a 'convincing business case' before being listed. It was expected that this should 'greatly reduce the number' then empowered by virtue of the RIP (CD) Order 2010. Changes to the list should be scrutinized by an 'appropriate Select Committee' under a super-affirmative procedure.[143] As regards the permitted purposes for which a CD application could be made, additions should be added only by primary legislation as it was unlikely that further purposes could 'properly be added'.[144] The Ministerial power to add purposes should be deleted and the government was requested to consult on whether all the current listed purposes are in fact required. [145]

The Report was particularly critical of Chapter II in respect of definitions, holding the language of RIPA as 'out of date' and finding the definitions of 'use, subscriber and traffic data...particularly problematic'.[146] It made oblique reference to what this book has described as the 'wicked problem' of defining content,[147] but asserted that a 'new hierarchy of data types' required development after consultation and taking cognisance of public attitudes and perceived degrees of privacy intrusion.[148]

The Committee recommended the enshrining of the SPoC system in primary legislation and the establishment of a dedicated SPoC service modelled on the then existing National Anti-Fraud Network service currently offering SPoC services to local authorities. It further recommended the abandonment of the Magistrate's Court approval mechanism only recently introduced in the PoFA

141 That is, a gap between the type and quantity of particular CD being retained so as to be available to be accessed for investigative purposes and the type and quantity deemed as being needed.
142 JCDCDB, *Final Report 2012* (n69) 20.
143 ibid, 77.
144 ibid.
145 ibid.
146 ibid, 78.
147 ibid.
148 ibid.

2012.[149] Its other prescient recommendation was for the introduction of an offence of 'wilful or reckless misuse of CD'.[150]

The Parliamentary Intelligence and Security Committee

The UK Parliamentary Intelligence and Security Committee (UKPISC) also analyzed the provisions of the draft CDB insofar as it related to the UKIC. In dismissing the need to calculate any 'capability gap' as a percentage figure and simply accept the existence of such a gap, the Committee found the security and intelligence agencies (as the UKIC were then referred to) 'less directly affected by it', because they are able to work around the problem through the use of other national security capabilities that they 'chose not to detail', almost certainly an oblique reference to the still-secret section 94 regime.[151] The publicized version of what was essentially a bland business case reworking the JCDCDB Report made no recommendations, but echoed many of the latter's criticisms of the draft CDB. There were hints, however, that the redacted version sent to then Prime Minister Cameron contained significantly more policy-influencing material.[152] The report constituted the final 'official' examination of Chapter II prior to the 2013 Intelligence Shock later that year.

Conclusion

The previous chapter demonstrated the depth of public concern and the willingness of civil liberties advocacy to challenge the scope and magnitude of the EU's compulsory CD regulatory provisions. Those concerns 'leaked' into the arena of governance of who could access retained CD and why. Consequently, if the detailed CD CoP is included as a regulatory instrument (and it should be), it took a total of seven years to establish a fully operational statutory framework regulating the acquisition and disclosure of CD that Labour Home Secretary Jack Straw had envisaged in the 1999 consultation. The evidence demonstrates an inordinate amount of public and industry consultation to try and finalise Chapter II's provisions, and yet by 2012, only eight years after its entry into force, the government was endeavouring to replace it, and the committee established to analyze was criticizing the lack of *meaningful* consultation and costings. Although the draft CDB Committee had indeed identified real definitional problems with Chapter II, in an era of exponential CD generation and advances in electronic communications technology, perhaps the most significant driver was the absence of a unitary CD retention *and* acquisition framework by 2012, as discussed in the

149 ibid.
150 ibid, 80.
151 Intelligence and Security Committee, *Access to Communications Data by the intelligence and security Agencies* (Cm 8514, February 2013) 13.
152 ibid, 27; explored in Chapter 9 of this volume.

last chapter. Despite Mrs May having to abandon the draft CD Bill in 2012, she would have to wait less than one year before events would impel further review.

References

G Danby, 'Data Protection and the Police' (House of Commons Library, Standard Note SN/HA/5831, 18 January 2011)

Data Protection Commissioner, 'Response of the Data Protection Commissioner to the Government's Regulation of Investigatory Powers Bill-Briefing for Parliamentarians' (March 2000), Foundation for Information Policy Research (FIPR) <www.fipr.org/rip/DPCparlRIP.htm> accessed 30 October 2020

Data Protection Registrar, 'Response of the Data Protection Registrar to the Government's Proposals for Revising the Interception of Communications Act 1985' <webarchive.nationalarchives.gov.uk/20130128103514/http://www.homeoffice.gov.uk/oicd/dpr.pdf.> accessed 29 September 2020

European Union Agency for Fundamental Rights & Council of Europe, *Handbook on European Data Protection Law* (EU Publications Office, Luxembourg, 2014)

FIPR, 'Executive Summary of Response to Consultation Paper Cm 4368' (1999) <webarchive.nationalarchives.gov.uk/20130128103514/http://www.homeoffice.gov.uk/oicd/fipr.pdf> accessed 30 October 2020

Roger Gaspar, 'Looking to the Future: Clarity on Communications Data Retention Law' (NCIS Submission to the Home Office on Communications Data Retention Law, 21 August 2000) <https://cryptome.org/ncis-carnivore.htm> accessed 30 September 2020

Steve Hedley, *The Law of Electronic Commerce and the Internet in the UK and Ireland* (Routledge-Cavendish, 2006)

Home Office, *The Interception of Communications in the United Kingdom, A Consultation Paper* (Cm4368, 1999)

Home Office, 'Access to Communications Data: Respecting Privacy and Protecting the Public from Crime A Consultation' (Home Office, March 2003) <www.statewatch.org/news/2003/mar/ripa.pdf> accessed 30 September 2020

Home Office, *Acquisition and Disclosure of Communications Data: A Public Consultation* (June 2006)

Home Office, *Acquisition and Disclosure Code of Practice* (TSO, 2007)

Independent Reviewer of Terrorism Legislation, *Report of the Bulk Powers Review* (Cm9326, August 2016)

Information Commissioner's Office, 'Our History' (*ICO.org.uk*) <https://ico.org.uk/about-the-ico/our-information/history-of-the-ico/our-history/> accessed 20 November 2020

Intelligence and Security Committee, *Access to Communications Data by the Intelligence and Security Agencies* (Cm 8514, February 2013)

IOCCO, *Report of the Interception of Communications Commissioner for 2005–06* (HC 315, 19 February 2007)

Joint Committee on the Draft Communications Data Bill, *Legislative Scrutiny: Draft Communications Data Bill* (Final Report) (2012–13, HL79, HC 479)

Quinten Kroes, *E-Business Law of the European Union* (2nd edn, Kluwer Law International BV, 2010)

Liberty, 'Response by Liberty to Home Office Consultation Paper: Interception of Communications in the United Kingdom' (August 1999) <www.fipr.org/ioca/liberty.pdf> accessed 30 September 2020

Stuart Millar, Lucy Ward, and Richard Norton-Taylor, 'Blunkett Shelves Access to Data Plans' *Guardian* (19 June 2002) <www.theguardian.com/technology/2002/jun/19/internet.humanrights> accessed 30 September 2020

National Archives, 'Details of Responses Received to the Interception of Communications Act Consultation Exercise' National Archives (snapshot of 16 October 2002) <webarchive.nationalarchives.gov.uk/20130128103514/http://www.homeoffice.gov.uk/oicd/conslist2.htm> accessed 30 October 2020

Nóra Ní Loideáin, 'Judicial Review of Mass Metadata Surveillance in the Post-Snowden Era' (2015) University of Cambridge Faculty of Law Legal Research Paper 32/2015, <papers.ssrn.com/sol3/papers.cfm?abstract_id=2613424> accessed 30 September 2020

Robin Callender Smith, 'Private Fire from the Gods: The Protection of Personal Data – The Data Protection Act 1998 as a Celebrity Privacy Remedy' (2015) <papers.ssrn.com/sol3/papers.cfm?abstract_id=2596029> accessed 23 October 2015

Statewatch UK, 'Data Retention and Access Consultation Farce – Government to Allow Access for Crime Purposes to Records Which Can Only Be Held for "National Security"' (*Statewatch*, April 2003) <www.statewatch.org/news/2003/sep/11Batcs.htm> accessed 1 October 2020

9 The 2013 Intelligence Shock

Towards a modern and transparent legal framework

Introduction

This chapter traces the key developments across the UK's communications and data investigation legal framework that followed the 2013 Intelligence Shock. Without revisiting it in detail, the publication in selected global media of selected unauthorized disclosures of Edward Snowden, commencing in the UK with a *Guardian* article on 7 June 2013, marked the commencement of a sequence of events, reviews, reports, and legal decisions that would ultimately bring about the enactment of the Investigatory Powers Act (IPA) 2016.[1] Whilst it is commonly asserted that the principal post-2013 reviews shaped the IPA 2016, that is only partially true. As an Act of Parliament that now 'covers the field' of communications and data investigatory powers in the interests of national security (broadly construed), thus restating almost 700 years of state policy and practice, the IPA 2016 represents first and foremost the necessary product of a sunset clause in a data-retention statute (Data Retention and Investigatory Powers Act (DRIPA) 2014) enacted after only three days of scrutiny following the European Court decision in *Digital Rights*. As such, it was the vexed issue of CD retention, rather than allegations of impropriety in the fields of interception or CD acquisition that impelled change of the magnitude that the IPA 2016 represented. As this book endeavours to rationalize UK communications and data investigation regulation by exploring its chronological evolution, a chronology of the key influences that would shape and thus rationalize the ultimate structure and scope of the IPA 2016 now follows. The number and importance of key events in the path from the Intelligence Shock to the IPA 2016 as assented to mean that two chapters are required to effectively cover them. This chapter focuses on events between June 2013 and the evening prior to publication of the initial draft Investigatory Powers Bill (IPB). This allows examination of the main independent reviews of, and legal challenges to, the regulation of investigatory powers that occurred after June 2013, many of which would assist in shaping the draft IPB. The next chapter

1 Glenn Greenwald and Ewen MacAskill, 'NSA Prism Program Taps into User Data of Apple, Google and Others', *The Guardian* (London, 7 June 2013) <http://theguardian.com/world/2013/jun/06/us-tech-giants-nsa-data> accessed 26 November 2020.

examines events from publication of the draft IPB through to enactment, thus finally rationalizing 700 years of British communications and data investigative practice and governance. Rationalizing the regulation of communications and data investigation became much easier after 7 June 2013 because of the gradual emergence of a culture of candour, delivering transparent secrecy, over the three and a half years between the Intelligence Shock and the IPA's enactment. It will be evidenced herein that, without *changing* the 700-year policy of ensuring that regulation enabled the investigation of all known forms of communication on national security grounds, the government became prepared to publish its rationale through statements in consultation documents and, commendably, through the making of an operational case for each of the controversial relevant powers.

From disingenuous statutory governance to candour and transparent secrecy

The central thesis underpinning this book remains that the UK, in seeking to give effect to its UKUSA Agreement obligations, and to protect national security (broadly construed) had a system of broad investigatory powers in place across a range of statutes that 'covered the field' of communications technology. As of 7 June 2013, this might have appeared to be the case.

What powers were available to investigators?

- Communications (and data)[2] *in the course of transmission* using telecommunications systems or services with a UK presence were all potentially accessible for national security purposes (broadly construed) by virtue of powers to intercept on a targeted or bulk basis (RIPA 2000, Part I, Chapter I);
- Communications *in the course of transmission* by wireless telegraphy were all potentially accessible for national security purposes (broadly construed) virtue of powers to intercept in the Wireless Telegraphy Act 1949 (as amended);[3]
- Communications data (CD) (if retained by CSPs) *at rest* was all potentially accessible for national security (broadly construed) and additional purposes by virtue of powers to obtain it (RIPA 2000, Part I, Chapter II);
- Communications Service Providers (CSPs) could be compelled to retain a broad and intrusive range of predetermined categories of CD (*data at rest*) for future investigative access for national security purposes (broadly construed) (The Data Retention Regulations 2009);
- CSPs could, by agreement, voluntarily retain predetermined categories of CD by virtue of the Anti-Terrorism Crime and Security Act (ATCASA) 2001, Part 11.

2 Related Communications Data (RCD) as per RIPA s20, and data of any description forming the content of a communication as per RIPA s81.

3 Wireless Telegraphy Act 1949, s5.

Gaps

However, gaps identifiable at this point were an ability on the part of the state to enable communications and data *at rest* to be accessed on a targeted and bulk basis and powers to acquire CD in bulk for intelligence-related data analytics. There were also question marks surrounding the acquisition of communications and data from extra-jurisdictional sources such as the United States National Security Agency (NSA) supposedly rendered lawful by the Intelligence Services Act 1994.[4] The question the Intelligence Shock provoked within government was whether the existence of hitherto secret powers that filled this gap and ensured the field was covered should be avowed. This was not answered straightaway in 2013. As per the well-known cliché, events would prove influential.

Government reaction

The 2013 Intelligence Shock occurred while the dust was barely beginning to accumulate on Home Secretary Theresa May's 'abandoned' draft Communications Data Bill (DCDB) and the scathing Joint Committee Final Report.[5] It had not yet had its day. On 10 June 2013, Conservative Foreign Secretary William Hague made a statement to the House of Commons. In addition to continuing the policy of Neither Confirm Nor Deny as regards the content of Snowden's published disclosures, he implicitly acknowledged the UKUSA Agreement as well as the rationale for the then-existing legal framework.[6]

UKPISC reaction

This was followed on 17 July 2013 by a public statement from the Intelligence and Security Committee of Parliament (UKPISC).[7] After certifying completion of a detailed investigation involving the taking of evidence from GCHQ, the UKPISC concluded that it was 'satisfied that they conformed with GCHQ's statutory duties. The legal authority for this is contained in the Intelligence Services Act 1994' and that 'in each case where GCHQ sought information from the US, a warrant for interception, signed by a Minister, was already in place, in accordance with the legal safeguards contained in the Regulation of Investigatory

4 Philip Glover, 'Legal Uncertainty Surrounding the Acquisition by UK Intelligence-Gathering Bodies of Communications Content Intercepted outside the UK' (2014) 18 *Edinburgh Law Review*, 114.

5 Joint Committee on the Draft Communications Data Bill, *Legislative Scrutiny: Draft Communications Data Bill (Final Report)* (2012–13, HL79, HC 479) 13. (JCDCDB, *Final Report 2015*).

6 'NSA Prism Programme William Hague Makes Statement on GCHQ' (*The Guardian*, 11 June 2013). <https://www.youtube.com/watch?v=fOI6nVoZTmY> accessed 20 November 2013.

7 The chosen abbreviation avoids conflation with the Intelligence Services Commissioner (ISC).

Powers Act 2000'.[8] However, in a clear sign that the ongoing furore at that point had triggered a degree of introspection as regards 'whether the current statutory framework governing access to private communications remains adequate', the Committee noted that

> in some areas the legislation is expressed in general terms and more detailed policies and procedures have, rightly, been put in place around this work by GCHQ in order to ensure compliance with their statutory obligations under the Human Rights Act 1998,

stating it was 'therefore examining the complex interaction between the Intelligence Services Act, the Human Rights Act and the Regulation of Investigatory Powers Act, and the policies and procedures that underpin them, further'.[9] An inquiry was announced in October 2013, broadening the scope of the Committee's investigation, followed by a call for evidence in December 2013.[10] This process would lead to the publication of an influential and detailed report on the intrusive capabilities of the UK Intelligence Community (UKIC) in February 2015.[11]

NGO reaction

Civil liberties groups were understandably very concerned about the 2013 publications. As such, and despite the UK government's failure to meaningfully react to the adverse decision relating to the maintenance of a bulk interception regime in *Liberty and Others v United Kingdom*, they were not deterred from initiating further legal challenges to the UK's regulation of communications and data investigation. Litigation veterans at Liberty, along with prominent NGO Privacy International, ultimately in conjunction with another eight civil liberties-focused applicants, lodged proceedings before the Investigatory Powers Tribunal (IPT) alleging violations of Articles 8, 10, and 14 of the European

8 UKPISC, 'Statement on GCHQ's Alleged Interception of Communications under the PRISM Programme' <https://b1cba9b3-a-5e6631fd-s-sites.googlegroups.com/a/independent.gov.uk/isc/files/20130717_ISC_statement_GCHQ.pdf?attachauth=ANoY7cpqnDqfloChw29Gow59L15QdmBzKQ2z0QS9EPPBiHhOsJCcGYSJLTrSZVdcXX-eCLmiP0K2JRDKf-tLeHhaJ8l9o-YL_8bRQAzKDf7OwCECiSSNqObzXdhWpFtYd5ndKVbCLu9jYdz1CKfxw9t_1wb-A1kDtHs7W0BrNLN13P3wJa0oURBHT3omE2NLEq0eA-69oXuct91Wvsada9S5HjfAkVYOavSJJvDUFLGsKdXjSFeH0Yg%3D&attredirects=0> accessed 20 November 2020.

9 The ISC website has archived all relevant documentation – see generally <http://isc.independent.gov.uk/committee-reports> accessed 20 November 2020.

10 ibid.

11 Intelligence and Security Committee of Parliament, *Privacy and Security: A Modern and Transparent Framework* (HC 1075, March 2015) (UKPISC, *Privacy and Security 2015*) UKPISC is utilized for this committee to avoid confusion with the Intelligence Services Commissioner (ISC).

Convention on Human Rights (ECHR) as a consequence of the UK's continuation of a bulk interception regime (RIPA 2000, section 8[4]–[6]) and of acquiring foreign intercept from the NSA.[12] This would proceed throughout 2014.

Other reaction: RUSI Independent Surveillance Review

On 4 March 2014, Nick Clegg MP, then Deputy Prime Minister in the Conservative-Liberal Democrat coalition government, announced an independent review of surveillance practices in the UK to be conducted by the Royal United Services Institute (RUSI). This was the Independent Surveillance Review (ISR). Its terms of reference were to:

> Advise on the legality, effectiveness and privacy implications of the UK surveillance programmes, particularly as revealed by the 'Edward Snowden case'; examine potential reforms to current surveillance practices, including additional protections against the misuse of personal data, and alternatives to the collection and retention of bulk data; make an assessment of how law-enforcement and intelligence capabilities can be maintained in the face of technological change, while respecting principles of proportionality, necessity and privacy.[13]

The reference to 'bulk data' is interesting, as bulk data acquisition remained a secret power until 2015. The term must have meant 'related communications data' (RCD) as collected through bulk interception. The ISR would progress through 2014 and 2015, eventually reporting in July of that year.[14]

8 April 2014

As regards rationalizing the structure, scope, and magnitude of the UK's powers to protect national security through communications and data investigation, 8 April 2014 was significant as regards its influence on all the investigatory powers then existing.

IOCCO Review of powers to intercept communications and to acquire CD

The UKPISC had alluded to a separate review of the UK's legal framework to be conducted by the IOCCO in their late-2013 press releases relating to their own

12 *Liberty, Privacy International and Others v GCHQ, Secret Intelligence Service and Secretary of State for Foreign and Commonwealth Affairs (No1)* UKIPTrib (2014) 13/77/H.

13 Royal United Services Institute for Defence and Security Studies, *A Democratic Licence to Operate: Report of the Independent Surveillance Review* (Stephen Austin and Sons Ltd, July 2015) (RUSI, *RISR 2015*) 1.

14 ibid.

inquiry. Annual reports of the IOCCO tended not to be publications about which to become particularly excited. Until the Intelligence Shock, they had followed a fairly consistent pattern established in 2000 of publishing statistics relating to the matters the IOCCO was required in statute (RIPA) to keep under review.[15] The Annual Report for 2013, however, was quite different and has regrettably become overshadowed by some of the other key events and reviews that assisted in scoping the IPA 2016.[16]

In a 21-page Chapter 6 within the Annual Report entitled 'Questions of Concern' the IOCCO frankly and objectively evaluated his own resources and ability to fulfil the office, and also the RIPA framework governing interception of communications (targeted and bulk) as well as the Chapter II regime. The examination was particularly mindful of public concerns, and indeed his examination of the issues was centred around the questions that the public were most likely to be asking after the Intelligence Shock. By way of example, question 5 asked 'is RIPA 2000 Part I fit for its required purpose in the developing internet age?'[17] The Commissioner summarised the practical effects of the RIPA Part I provisions in commendably clear form and by reference to the primary legislation, applicable Code of Practice and associated safeguards. He concluded that, as regards Part I (interception) the regime was fundamentally ECHR-compliant and fit for purpose. More importantly for present purposes, he stated

> It is ultimately a *matter of policy* whether the interception agencies, duly authorised...and subject to... safeguards, should continue to be enabled to intercept external communications, so far as they are lawfully and technically able, *in order to assist their functions of protecting the nation and its citizens from terrorist attack, cyber attack, serious crime* and so forth. If the policy answer to that question is yes (*which I personally should have thought was obvious*), the questions then are whether: (a) the *present safeguards* are sufficient to assure the public that their legitimate privacy is not impaired; (b) the *present structure* should be strengthened *for the greater protection of privacy*. I leave these questions for others to consider as matters of policy...in the light of this report. I would only emphasise here that question (b) above is heavily overlain by matters of sensitive technical possibility, which any changes would need to accommodate.[18]

15 See RIPA 2000, s57(2) and s58(4).

16 Rt Hon Sir Anthony May, *2013 Annual Report of the Interception of Communications Commissioner* (HC 1184, April 2014) (IOCCO, *Annual Report 2013*) 1. He acknowledges 'This report is rather differently presented, both in its form and some of its content, from recent reports of my predecessors'.

17 IOCCO, *Annual Report 2013* (n16) 45.

18 ibid, 55–56, emphasis added.

In an indication of the direction of travel, he (as an independent overseer of these powers with the gravitas of high judicial office experience behind him) thought that UK national security policy might need to take, he added,

> it is, I believe, beyond question *that technological developments relating to the internet may make the public authorities' interception and communications data legitimate activities in the public interest more difficult.* Recent commentary has tended towards *confining* the public authorities' interception and communications data powers and activities. *There is a legitimate policy question whether those capabilities might not need to be enhanced in the national interest. Present public sentiment might not favour that, and changes would obviously need to be very carefully weighed with interests of privacy.* But perhaps that policy question should not be completely overlooked.[19]

As regards RIPA's Part I, Chapter II regime, he had, after noting the U-turn by the Joint Committee on the Draft Communications Data Bill in 2012 from a position of disapproval of the internal authorization and SPoC system to one of approval of it, he concluded that the regime did not permit 'intrusion into privacy to any greater extent than when the legislation was enacted in 2000. Increases in volume have not affected the integrity of the system. Nor has the increase in volume and sophistication of the internet'.[20]

As of this date, therefore, with other inquiries and a significant NGO legal challenge in the background, the RIPA Part I regime, viewed holistically, had largely been endorsed by the chief instrument for independent oversight. On the very same day those endorsements were published, however, the wheels came off the wagon carrying the UK's statutory framework for enabling the retention of CD for future investigative access.

CD retention by CSPs

In the *Digital Rights* legal challenge referred to in the previous chapter, the Court of Justice of the European Union (CJEU),[21] in response to the Irish High Court's preliminary reference, famously annulled the EU's Data Retention Directive (DRD) *ab initio.*[22] The court was highly critical of the EU legislature, finding that the DRD was excessively broad in its scope and failed to provide clear and precise rules governing the extent of the interference with the fundamental rights

19 ibid, 55, emphasis added.

20 ibid, 48.

21 *Digital Rights Ireland v Minister for Communications, Marine and Natural Resources* May 5, 2010 High Court, Record No: 2006/3785.

22 Directive 2006/24/EC on the retention of data generated or processed in connection with the provision of publicly available electronic communications services or of public communications networks and amending Directive 2002/58/EC (2006) OJ L 105/54.

enshrined in Articles 7 and 8 of the CFREU.[23] It further concluded that it entailed a serious interference with the fundamental rights in the legal order of the EU, without such interference being precisely circumscribed by provisions to ensure that it is actually limited to what was strictly necessary.[24] Following the judgment,

> telecommunications service providers providing their services within Member States and hitherto subject to national laws implementing the Data Retention Directive began questioning whether they were still obliged to do so, with some immediately seeking clarification from their national governments. The Belgian Internet Service Providers Association and Sweden's *Bahnhof AB* actually ordered their technicians to stop retaining traffic data and to erase existing data.[25]

14–17 July 2014

The Data Retention and Investigatory Powers Act (DRIPA) 2014

The *Digital Rights* decision had significant consequences for the UK data retention regime. The UK government reacted to the 8 April 2014 judgment by reconvening Parliament in July 2014 in order to 'fast-track' a hastily drafted Data Retention and Investigatory Powers (DRIP) Bill.[26] In the initial extended version of the Explanatory Notes accompanying it,[27] in an apparent effort to comply with recommendations of the House of Lords Select Committee on the Constitution,[28] the UK government provided three reasons why it was 'necessary'[29] to fast-track the Bill, and a further three 'justifications'[30] for fast-tracking the data retention elements and drafting an explicit statement asserting the

23 Joined Cases C-293/12 and C-594/12 *Digital Rights Ireland Ltd and Seitlinger and Others* (n2) (58)–(65).

24 ibid, (65), see also Sarah Tracey, 'The Fall of the Data Retention Directive' (2015) 20(2) *Communications Law* (Case Comment) 53.

25 Claire Francois, 'ECJ's Invalidation of EU Data Retention Directive Creates Confusion Over Telecommunications Service Providers' Data Retention Obligations', *Bloomberg BNA Privacy Law Watch* (13 May 2013) <https://www.huntonak.com/files/Publication/dec9c9bc-0527-4620-9664-ab40152923be/Presentation/PublicationAttachment/39d39846-4efd-473d-81da-ea264bfbb90d/ECJs_Invalidation_of_EU_Data_Retention_Directive.pdf> accessed 30 October 2020.

26 It was introduced to Parliament on Thursday 10 July 2014 as the Data Retention and Investigatory Powers Bill (Bill 73).

27 DRIP Bill Explanatory Notes initial version (14 July 2014) <https://services.parliament.uk/bills/2014-15/dataretentionandinvestigatorypowers/documents.html> accessed 3 November 2020.

28 Constitution Committee, *Fast-Track Legislation: Constitutional Implications and Safeguards* (HL 2008-09, 116-I) para 186.

29 DRIP Bill Explanatory Notes initial version (14 July 2014) (n129) 5.

30 ibid, paras 28–30.

extra-territorial application of RIPA.[31] The 'necessity' reasons were: a necessity to *urgently* make provisions for data retention in UK law as 'the EU obligation… [imposed by the Data Retention Directive 2006/24/EC]…which the [Data Retention (EC Directive) Regulations 2009] implemented had fallen away';[32] the need to clarify certain provisions of RIPA 2000 because 'companies providing services to individuals within the UK, but which are not themselves based in the UK have questioned whether RIPA applies to them'[33] and the importance of

> passing legislation quickly to make it unequivocal that the UK will continue to have a data retention regime and RIPA continues to have extra-territorial jurisdiction [including] clarifying the definition of a 'telecommunications service' to ensure internet-based services, such as webmail are included.[34]

There is little about the Home Office's activity (or lack of it) prior to, and in light of, the judgment that does them credit. As regards their first reason, the CJEU ruling was delivered on 8 April 2014, yet the judgment had been correctly predicted in a preceding Advocate-General's Opinion delivered on 12 December 2013.[35] Whilst the judgment unsurprisingly concurred with that opinion, it did not take up his suggestion that the effect of its ruling could be suspended pending the adoption by the EU legislature of suitable corrective measures.[36] Initial Home Office inaction may simply reflect what Guild and Carrera describe as the initial hush that descended on the EU and other parties that had been following the case, with the enormity of the calamity that had befallen the DRD taking a little while to sink in and the Ukraine situation preoccupying the main institutions.[37] On the day of the ruling, the European Commission had rushed out the following advice in a rapid release [Frequently Asked Questions] memo:

[Q] What happens to national legislation following the decision by the Court?
[A] National legislation needs to be amended only with regard to aspects that become contrary to EU law after a judgment by the European Court of Justice. Furthermore, a finding of invalidity of the Directive does not cancel the ability

31 DRIP Act 2014, s4.
32 DRIP Bill Explanatory Notes initial version (14 July 2014) (n129) para 25.
33 ibid, para 26.
34 ibid, para 27.
35 Cases C-293/12 *Digital Rights Ireland Ltd* and C-594/12 *Seitlinger* (Grand Chamber, 8 April 2014), Opinion of AG Cruz Villalon, (157) and (158).
36 ibid, (159).
37 Elspeth Guild and Sergio Carrera, 'The Political and Judicial Life of Metadata: Digital Rights Ireland and the Trail of the Data Retention Directive' (May 29, 2014). CEPS Liberty and Security in Europe Papers No. 65 <http://papers.ssrn.com/sol3/papers.cfm?abstract_id=2445901> accessed 30 October 2020.

> *for Member States under the e-Privacy Directive (2002/58/EC) to oblige retention of data.*[38]

Given that the UK's Data Retention (EU Directive) Regulations 2009 had effectively implemented the whole offending Directive that was now deemed invalid by the CJEU, the first sentence of this tentative advice suggests that the Regulations as a whole might indeed require amendment. There was, as the government conceded, a lack of legal certainty. However, the second sentence appears to indicate that the earlier e-Privacy Directive would enable the UK to oblige the retention of data. This avenue does not appear to have been pursued and there does not appear to be an explanation. Given the government's acceptance that 'mandatory data retention ceased to have any basis in EU law on the 8th April', it is unclear as to why there was no emergency *as of that specific date.* The first concrete legalistic reaction to the judgment came in the form of (confidential) legal advice as to its potential ramifications from the EU Council Legal Service on 5 May 2014, which noted the retrospective effect of the ruling (it was void *ab initio*) and its implications for massive data retention and transfer arrangements then pending in the EU such as the Passenger Name Record Agreement and the Terrorist Finance Tracking Initiative.[39] Whether or not the Home Office took direct cognisance of this advice is not known but it must surely at least have resonated with the UK legislature. It cautioned that:

> measures that constitute serious restrictions to fundamental rights, however legitimate the objectives pursued by the EU legislature...do not stand a serious chance of passing the legality test unless they are accompanied by *adequate safeguards* in order to ensure that any serious restriction of fundamental rights is circumscribed to what is strictly necessary and is decided in the framework of guarantees forming part of Union legislation instead of being left to the legislation of Member States.[40]

38 European Commission 'MEMO/14/269 Frequently Asked Questions: The Data Retention Directive' (8 April 2014) <http://europa.eu/rapid/press-release_MEMO-14-269_en.htm > accessed 30 October 2020.

39 General Secretariat Council of the European Union,

> Information Note 9009/14. Judgment of the Court of 8 April 2014 in joined Cases C-293/12 and C-594/12 Invalidation of Directive 2006/24/EC of the European Parliament and of the Council of 15 March 2006 on the retention of data generated or processed in connection with the provision of publicly available electronic communications services or of public communications networks and amending Directive 2002/58/EC (the Data Retention Directive) (5 May 2014) (LIMITE).

<www.statewatch.org/news/2014/may/eu-council-note-data-retention-judgment-9009 -14.pdf>accessed 30 October 2020.

40 ibid, para 19.

DRIPA 2014, section 1(1) awarded a Secretary of State the power to issue a 'retention notice' requiring a 'public telecommunications operator'[41] to retain 'relevant communications data'.[42] This included the huge range of fixed-line telephony, mobile telephony, and internet related data in the Schedule to the Data Retention (EC Directive) Regulations 2009.[43] Consequently, the enactment of the Data Retention Regulations 2014 (by virtue of the Secretary of State's power to issue them under DRIPA 2014, s1[3]) would temporarily provide the UK with the necessary legal certainty in relation to mandatory CD retention lost following the judgment in *Digital Rights*. DRIPA 2014, section 1(4) provided that the 2009 provisions ceased to have effect.

DRIPA 2014: commissioning the IRTL Review of investigatory powers

Debate during the three days of whole-House scrutiny was initially tense, but the sting was drawn from the widespread criticism of the fast-track procedure by the introduction of agreed clauses wherein the Secretary of State 'must' appoint David Anderson QC,[44] then Independent Reviewer of Terrorism Legislation (IRTL) to conduct a review of 'the operation and regulation of investigatory powers',[45] with particular consideration of current and future threats to the United Kingdom; the capabilities needed to combat those threats; safeguards to protect privacy, the challenges of changing technologies; issues relating to transparency and oversight and the effectiveness of existing legislation (including its proportionality); and the case for new or amending legislation.[46] The IRTL Review was to be completed, as far as practicable, before 1 May 2015, with a report to the Prime Minister after the May 2015 election to be published as soon as practicable.[47] Another concession was that the IOCCO was to move from annually reporting to Parliament on the matters he kept under review to half-yearly reports.[48] The additional consensus reached on a sunset clause mandating the expiry of DRIPA 2014 on 31 December 2016 meant that the coalition government ultimately succeeded

41 DRIPA 2014, s2(1) a person controlling or providing a public telecommunication system, or providing a public telecommunications service.
42 ibid, s2(1) (meaning communications data of a kind mentioned in the schedule to the Data Retention [EC Directive] Regulations 2009 so far as such communications data is generated or processed in the UK by public telecommunications operators in the process of supplying the telecommunications services concerned).
43 Andrew Sparrow, *The Law of Virtual Worlds and Internet Social Networks* (Gower, 2010) 172–173.
44 Now Lord Anderson of Ipswich.
45 DRIPA 2014, s7(1).
46 ibid, s7(2).
47 ibid, s7(4). This would be the acclaimed Independent Reviewer of Terrorism Legislation, *A Question of Trust: Report of the Investigatory Powers Review* (Williams Lea Group, June 2015) (IRTL, *RIPR 2015*).
48 ibid, s6.

in securing the enactment of the Data Retention and Investigatory Powers Act (DRIPA) 2014.[49] Critics asserted that the Act marked a 'huge power grab under false pretences'[50] while the UK government held that it was merely 'retaining the status quo'[51] and introducing 'no additional investigatory powers'.[52]

October–December 2014

Operation Alice and Operation Solar

With the reverberations from the 2013 Intelligence Shock centred around RIPA's Part I, Chapter I bulk interception provisions and the receipt of foreign intelligence, the ongoing practical operation of RIPA's Chapter II regime had so far avoided meaningful scrutiny, having only recently received a 'generally fit for purpose' endorsement from the Joint Committee on the Draft Communications Data Bill (JCDCDB).[53] However, events in the latter half of 2014 conspired to have it placed under the microscope prior to any conclusions regarding it being drawn in the principal three reviews then ongoing (UKPISC, RUSI, and IRTL). Throughout September and October 2014 several press pieces expressed concern that CD relatable to journalists had been sought and acquired as part of the Metropolitan Police Service's 'Operation Alice' and Kent Police's 'Operation Solar' in order to identify anonymous press sources. Operation Alice had followed an allegation that then Conservative Party Chief Whip Andrew Mitchell had called PC Toby Rowlands a 'pleb' during an altercation at 10 Downing Street in 2012. There existed concern in police circles that information was being leaked to the press that might constitute misconduct in public office.[54] As regards Operation Solar, *The Daily Mail* alleged that

> Detectives sidestepped a judge's agreement to protect the source for our stories...Instead they used far-reaching powers under the controversial Regulation of Investigatory Powers Act (RIPA) – originally intended to safeguard national security – to hack...[Mail on Sunday]...phone records and identify the source. They trawled through thousands of confidential numbers called by journalists from a landline at the busy newsdesk going back an entire year, covering hundreds of stories unrelated to the...case.[55]

49 ibid, s8(3).

50 Rt Hon Caroline Lucas MP, HC Deb. 15 July 2014, vol 584, col 695.

51 Home Secretary Theresa May, HC Deb, 15 July 2014, vol 584, col 705.

52 House of Commons, 'Data Retention and Investigatory Powers Bill Explanatory Notes [referring to the Bill] as introduced in the House of Commons on 14 July 2014 (Bill 73)' (14 July 2014, The Stationery Office Limited) para 3.

53 JCDCDB, *Final Report 2015* (n5) 48–51.

54 '"Plebgate" Row: Timeline' (*BBC News*, 27 November 2014) <https://www.bbc.com/news/uk-24548645> accessed 29 May 2020.

55 Nick Craven, 'How Police Hacked Mail on Sunday Phone: Officers Used Anti-Terror Laws to Track Down Judge-Protected Source Who Exposed Chris Huhne's Speeding Points Fraud'.

Press concerns were such that a 'Save our Sources' campaign had been initiated by the National Union of Journalists. This included a petition to the IOCCO.[56] Demonstrating the assertiveness, independence, and transparency commensurate with almost 15 years as RIPA's oversight and reporting body, acting Interception of Communications Commissioner Sir Paul Kennedy, of his own motion,[57] initiated an inquiry on 6 October 2014 aspiring to 'identify the extent to which police forces...[had]...used their powers under ...[Chapter II]...to identify journalistic sources, to examine the appropriateness of...[that]...use... and to contribute to any future amendments to the legislation'.[58] In addition to the press concerns, two additional imperatives underpinned the inquiry. The first was the CJEU Grand Chamber's observation in *Digital Rights* that the Data Retention Directive it annulled applied 'even to persons whose communications are subject, according to rules of national law, to the obligation of professional secrecy'.[59] The second was the Cameron/Clegg government's note of response to that finding, published in the context of their forthcoming emergency Data Retention and Investigatory Powers Act (DRIPA) 2014. In it, an undertaking was provided to amend the CD CoP (2007) to ensure that, 'where there may be concerns relating to professions that handle privileged information (e.g. lawyers or journalists), law enforcement should give additional consideration of the level of intrusion'.[60]

(Daily Mail, 8 October 2014) <https://www.dailymail.co.uk/news/article-2780809/How-police-hacked-Mail-Sunday-Officers-used-anti-terror-laws-seize-phone-records-identify-source-exposed-Chris-Huhne-s-speeding-points-fraud.html> accessed 29 May 2020.

56 'Save Our Sources: *Press Gazette* Campaign to Stop Public Authorities Spying on Journalists' Phone Records' (*Press Gazette*, 11 September 2014) <http://pressgazette.co.uk/save-our-sources-press-gazette-campaign-stop-uk-public-authorities-secretly-obtaining-journalists> accessed 23 October 2020.

57 RIPA 2000, s58(5) The Interception of Communications Commissioner may also, at any time, make any such other report to the Prime Minister on any matter relating to the carrying out of the Commissioner's functions as the Commissioner thinks fit. Sir Paul was deputizing for Sir Anthony May, who had sustained serious injuries in a road traffic collision.

58 *IOCCO inquiry into the use of Chapter 2 of Part 1 of the Regulation of Investigatory Powers Act (RIPA) to identify journalistic sources* (IOCCO, 4 February 2015) para 2.1 (IOCCO, *Journalist Sources Report 2015*).

By virtue of RIPA 2000, s58(5) The Interception of Communications Commissioner may also, at any time, make any such other report to the Prime Minister on any matter relating to the carrying out of the Commissioner's functions as the Commissioner thinks fit.

59 ibid, para 3.1 and see joined cases C-293/12 *Digital Rights Ireland Ltd* and C-594/12 *Seitlinger* (Grand Chamber, 8 April 2014) (58).

60 IOCCO, *Journalist Sources Report 2015*, para 3.2 and see Anonymous, 'Data Retention and Investigatory Powers Bill Government Note on the European Court of Justice Judgment' <https://assets.publishing.service.gov.uk/government/uploads/system/uploads/attachment_data/file/331106/DRIPgovernmentNoteECJjudgment.pdf> accessed 20 November 2020.

December 2014

The IPT judgment in Liberty/Privacy and Others (No. 1)

Having taken substantial evidence, and unusually conducting a five-day public hearing during July 2014, the IPT, proceeding on the basis of assumed facts due to the state's maintenance of a 'Neither Confirm Nor Deny' (NCND) position on both issues complained of ruled on the 'lawfulness of the alleged receipt by the Security Services of intercept from two interception programmes operated by the Security Services of the United States, Prism and Upstream', and the RIPA 2000, section 8(4) bulk interception regime. The 5 December judgment is not only important for its findings as to the lawfulness and European Convention on Human Rights compliance but also for its 'rationalising' of national security policy in the area of communications and data investigation. The IPT held that the then-existing regime, both in relation to foreign intercept receipt and bulk interception under RIPA 2000, s8(4) was largely 'lawful and human rights compliant'.[61] The Court then stated,

> The *legislation* in force and the *safeguards* to which we have referred are intended to recognise the importance of, and the need to maintain, an acceptable balance between (a) *the interests of the State to acquire information for the vital purposes of national security and the protection of its citizens from terrorism and other serious crime*, and (b) the vital interests of all citizens to know that the law makes effective provision to safeguard their rights to privacy and freedom of expression, *together with appropriate and effective limits upon what the State does with that information.*[62]

This marked an excellent summation of the longstanding UK national security policy as it involves information (data). It did not limit information by category, implicitly recognising the British state's right to acquire information available anywhere, or on any medium, in transit or at rest for national security purposes (broadly construed).

The Home Affairs Committee Report on RIPA 2000

Despite the report's broad title, the UK Parliament's Home Affairs Committee (HAC) had initiated a separate 'inquiry into police forces' use of RIPA powers to acquire communications data in the course of investigations' shortly after that of the IOCCO.[63] It heard oral evidence from relevant witnesses on 4 and 11 November 2014, including the temporary Interception of Communications Commissioner Sir Paul Kennedy, senior police representatives and Michelle

61 *Liberty, Privacy International and Others* (n12) (156).

62 ibid, (157).

63 House of Commons Home Affairs Committee, *Regulation of Investigatory Powers Act 2000* (HC711, 6 December 2014) 3 (HAC, *RIPA Report 2014*).

Stanistreet, General Secretary, National Union of Journalists. Publication of the HAC's findings (6 December 2014) preceded the IOCCO Report (4 February 2015).

HAC findings on access to journalists' CD via Chapter II

These provide a useful illustration of the context in which communications and data investigation regulation was operating after the June 2013 Intelligence Shock. The committee noted the three 'inquiries in relation to RIPA' then in progress (UKPISC, RUSI, and IRTL) and the broader question of whether or not RIPA Part I as a whole required replacement forming part of the IRTL's inquiry.[64] After examining the IOCCO's staffing levels it urged the provision of additional resources to him in order to complete his then ongoing inquiry into journalists' sources.[65] As regards the CD CoP (2007), now eight years old, it noted the IOCCO's concerns surrounding statistical information and record-keeping on CD acquisition and also a commitment made by the Home Secretary in a speech to the College of Policing on 5 October 2014 that had indicated a draft CD CoP was on its way.[66] It was observed that, during the passage of the DRIPA 2014, it had been made clear in the debate that a new CD CoP would cover 'confidence, professional positions and matters such as legal professional privilege'.[67] A firm recommendation was made that 'the Home Office should hold a full public consultation on an amended RIPA Code of Practice, and any updated advice should contain special provisions for dealing with privileged information, such as journalistic material and material subject to legal privilege'.[68] The HAC Report is more often cited for its ultimate conclusion that 'RIPA is not fit for purpose',[69] however, that statement, and indeed the whole Report, faded in influence throughout 2015, effectively usurped by the impact of the three major reviews that followed it that year. When rationalizing the IPA 2016, however, it deserves its place for the conclusions and recommendations that did have an impact and that were acted upon. These were that the section 94 regime be reviewed and reported upon, and that a public consultation on a new CD CoP should be initiated. On the evidence, the Home Office anticipated the latter, as its public consultation via a draft CD CoP opened less than a week after publication of the HAC Report.[70]

64 *HAC CD Report 2014* (n61) para 14.
65 ibid, para 22.
66 ibid, para 27 – despite it being October, the Home Secretary had stated the *CD CoP* would be published 'this Autumn'!
67 ibid, para 24. Despite the use of quotation marks in this paragraph of the HAC Report, no source is provided.
68 ibid, para 28.
69 ibid.
70 Home Office, 'Acquisition and Disclosure of Communications Data Code of Practice', draft for public consultation (9 December 2014) <https://assets.publishing.service.gov.uk/

DRIPA 2014: judicial review

Permission was granted for judicial review proceedings of DRIPA 2014 on 8 December 2014 to Conservative MP David Davis and Labour MP Tom Watson, aligned with veterans Privacy International, the Law Society of England and Wales, and the Open Rights Group.[71]

Counter-terrorism and Security Bill: CD definition creep

A day later, the Home Office finally released an online-only draft Acquisition and Disclosure Code of Practice for public consultation in an effort to incorporate adjustments to the practical operation of the RIPA Chapter II regime identified as being required since 2007.[72]

The same day, a whole House debate scrutinizing the Counter-Terrorism and Security (CTS) Bill heard James Brokenshire (then-Conservative Minister for Security and Immigration) reassert that, while DRIPA 2014 had maintained the UK's lawful data retention regime, it had not created any additional powers or addressed any of the previously asserted gaps in capability.[73] He re-emphasized that 'Internet Protocol (IP) address resolution', previously explained as 'the ability to identify who in the real world was using an IP address at a given point in time'[74] remained a gap in communications data capability having a serious impact on the ability of law enforcement to carry out their functions.[75] Capability gaps, if genuine, represent a weakness in national security and gaps in the ability to police critical communications infrastructure are as significant a threat as gaps in the ability to police air, sea, and borders. Using her powers under DRIPA 2014 to make further provision about the retention of relevant communications data by regulations,[76] then Home Secretary Theresa May introduced clause 17 as part of the CTS Bill. This became section 21 in the CTS Act 2015. It inserted into DRIPA 2014, section 2(1) an extended definition of 'relevant communications

---

government/uploads/system/uploads/attachment_data/file/383548/DraftCDAcquisitionCodeofPracticeforconsultation.pdf> accessed 24 November 2020.

71 *R (Davis and Others) v Secretary of State for the Home Department* (2015) EWHC 2092 (Admin).

72 Home Office, *Acquisition and Disclosure of Communications Data Code of Practice: Draft for Public Consultation* (9 December 2014) <https://assets.publishing.service.gov.uk/government/uploads/system/uploads/attachment_data/file/383548/DraftCDAcquisitionCodeofPracticeforconsultation.pdf> accessed 30 November 2020.

73 HC Deb, 9 December 2014, vol 589, col 822.

74 Home Office, 'Counter-terrorism and Security Bill: Factsheet – Part 3 – Internet Protocol (IP) Address Resolution (GOV.UK, 3 December 2014) <https://gov.uk/government/uploads/system/uploads/attachment_data/file/388035/CTS_Bill_-_Factsheet_5_-_IP_Resolution_v2.pdf> accessed 30 October 2020.

75 ibid.

76 DRIPA 2014, s1(3) (3). The Secretary of State may by regulations make further provision about the retention of relevant communications data.

data'.[77] Up to this point that definition had included the extensive categories of data present in the original schedule to the Data Retention Regulations 2009 that DRIPA 2014 had been hastily enacted to preserve.[78] This schedule had been subsequently transposed *verbatim* into the schedule to the Data Retention Regulations 2014, originally enacted under DRIPA 2014 section 1(3).[79]

This amendment permitted the Secretary of State to include 'relevant internet data' within a data retention notice being issued to a public telecommunications operator[80] under the Retention Notice Regime set out in the Data Retention Regulations.[81]

As ever, the devil was in the detail of the extended definition, and in the tradition of investigatory powers legislation that detail was complex. The Explanatory Notes accompanying the CTS Act 2015, section 21, stated that 'subsection (3) defines the 'relevant internet data', (as defined in subsection 2) as that which is necessary to reliably attribute internet protocol (IP) addresses to a person or device',[82] adding that subsection (3)(a) 'limits this to communications data relating to an internet access service'[83] or an 'internet communications service'.[84] It was further explained that subsection (3)(b) describes the data that can now be

77 Counter Terrorism and Security Act 2015 s21 (now repealed)

> communications data which – (a) relates to an internet access service or an internet communications service, (b) may be used to identify, or assist in identifying, which internet protocol address, or other identifier, belongs to the sender or recipient of a communication (whether or not a person), and (c) is not data which – (i) may be used to identify an internet communications service to which a communication is transmitted through an internet access service for the purpose of obtaining access to, or running, a computer file or computer program, and (ii) is generated or processed by a public telecommunications operator in the process of supplying the internet access service to the sender of the communication (whether or not a person).

78 i.e. the Data Retention (EC Directive) Regulations 2009/859.

79 Data Retention Regulations 2014, SI 2014/2042. Sch 1 is entitled 'Communications Data of the kind mentioned in the Schedule to the 2009 Regulations'.

80 Defined in DRIPA 2014, s2(1) as a 'person controlling or providing a public telecommunication system, or providing a public telecommunications service'. Public telecommunication system is defined in RIPA 2000, s2(1) as

> any such parts of a telecommunication system by means of which any public telecommunications service is provided as are located in the UK. Public telecommunications service is defined at RIPA 2000, s2(1) as 'any telecommunications service which is offered or provided to, or to a substantial section of, the public in any one or more parts of the United Kingdom'.

81 Data Retention Regulations 2014, regs 2–14.

82 Explanatory Note to Counter-Terrorism and Security Act 2015, para 126.

83 ibid. This can include a home broadband connection, mobile internet, or publicly available wireless internet (Wi-Fi).

84 Explanatory Note to Counterterrorism and Security Act 2015, para 126. This can include internet telephony (e.g. Skype) and internet email (e.g. Gmail and instant messaging services such as Facebook Messenger).

required to be retained is that which may be used to identify, or assist in identifying, the IP address or other identifier belonging to a communication's sender or recipient. This could include data required to identify the communication's sender or recipient (which could be a person or a device), data identifying a communication's time or duration, its type, method, or pattern (e.g. the protocol used to send an email), the telecommunications system used or its location. They explain that an IP address can often be shared by hundreds of people at once; therefore, to resolve an IP address to an individual other data ('other identifier' in this clause)[85] would be required. Data necessary for the resolution of IP addresses could include port numbers[86] or MAC (media access control) addresses.[87] It is therefore this 'other identifying data' that became critical to effectively resolving user identification for intelligence or evidence purposes, but this was not made overly clear. The Explanatory Notes asserted that subsection (3)(c) specifically prevents the retention by a telecommunications operator providing an internet access service of data explicitly identifying the internet communications service or websites[88] (weblogs) accessed by a service user.[89] Yet this was not made clear in the provision itself. Shadow Home Secretary Diana Johnson (Labour) originally sought an amendment (later withdrawn) that would have made it explicit that the extra data retention provided for in what became subsection 3(c)[90] 'did not extend beyond that necessary for the purpose of identifying a user from the IP address'.[91]

Weblog data retention had been a controversial issue since at least the time of scrutiny of the draft Communications Data Bill (CDB) 2012. The JCDCDB set out one aspect of the content/data distinction by outlining that, as the law currently stood, 'anything before the first "/" in a website address is considered to be communications data, and anything after the first slash is considered to be content'.[92]

85 Counter-Terrorism and Security Act 2015, s21(4) (b) means an identifier used to facilitate the transmission of a communication.

86 Bauer explains ports as

> virtual pathways on which Internet data flows…are like telephone number extensions as they allow multiple pieces of data to flow back and forth on a single IP address. In fact, port numbers are appended to the end of IP addresses just as extensions are appended to telephone numbers.

Jason Bauer, 'What Is a Port?' (*portforward.com*) <http://portforward.com/networking/whatisport.htm> accessed 30 October 2020.

87 MAC technology provides unique identification and access control for computers on an Internet Protocol (IP) network. See Bradley Mitchell, 'Media Access Control' (*about-tech*) <http://compnetworking.about.com/od/networkprotocolsip/g/bldef_mac.htm> accessed 30 October 2020.

88 Normally referred to as weblogs.

89 Explanatory Note to Counter-Terrorism and Security Act 2015, para 126.

90 Originally Clause 17 of the Counter-Terrorism and Security Bill.

91 HC Deb, 9 December 2014, vol 589, cols 804-805, Amendment 5.

92 JCDCDB, *Final Report 2015* (n5) paras 73–88.

They viewed this distinction as a 'key issue' and a 'fundamental question at the heart of the proposed legislation'.[93] A useful example they provided was that if the website 'www.nhs.co.uk' is visited by an internet service user, the data referring to that visit would be communications data, but that it would not be permissible to record the fact that a person visited 'www.nhs.co.uk/conditions/depression'.[94] The difficulty of course arises in ensuring that visits of the latter type are not recorded, or where they have been recorded either inadvertently or for business reasons, in ensuring that acquisition of the retained data is denied to any potential enquirer. The JCDCDB outlined the Home Office's eventual concession to them that the 'Communications Data Act 2012' would enable them to access 'two specific types of data: subscriber data relating to IP addresses and web logs'.[95] Despite the fact that the draft CD Bill never made it to the statute book, it is worth noting that, having weighed the extensive evidence submitted to them, the JCDCDB concluded that IP address resolution did not raise particular privacy concerns.[96] It was therefore unsurprising to see its return and inclusion in the CT&S Act 2015.

As regards the far more sensitive issue of weblogs, it is also noteworthy that the JCDCDB heard 'considerable evidence expressing concern at the idea of weblog data being more widely retained and made available to public authorities'[97] and also acknowledged that 'significant inferences could be drawn about a person's interests and, perhaps, activities'.[98] Having done so, they felt 'confident that the safeguards in the draft CD Bill, together with the recommendations…[they were making]…to strengthen those safeguards…[provided]…a high degree of protection against abuse of communications data or inadvertent error by public authorities'.[99] Although they abdicated a final decision on whether the retention of weblog data should be mandated in legislation to Parliament,[100] it was clear that the issue was not going to disappear. The whole-House debate on the CTS bill was additionally noteworthy in flagging the future cross-party policy direction in the area of mandatory data retention. Although all parties were at pains to point out the value of waiting for the findings of what were then-forthcoming reviews of relevant legislation and the fact that DRIPA 2014 and the Regulations enacted under it were subject to sunset clauses,[101] the Shadow Home Secretary articulated Labour Party policy as follows:

93 ibid, para 84.
94 ibid, para 77.
95 ibid, para 73.
96 ibid, para 74.
97 ibid para 80.
98 ibid, para 82.
99 ibid, para 86.
100 ibid.
101 DRIPA 2014, s8(3) provided that 'sections 1 to 7 (and the provisions inserted into the Regulation of Investigatory Powers Act 2000 by sections 3 to 6) are repealed on 31 December 2016'.

> the change in the rules on data retention is a response to the increasing use of floating IP addresses by communications service providers…[t]he extra data retention, as provided for…is to ensure that the data required to allow the relevant authorities to see who is the recipient of a communication…is retained by the CSP…*the Opposition broadly accept the need for this extra category of data*. It has always been the case that phone companies have kept records of phone calls made. People understand and generally accept that their phone company keeps a record of these calls and that they may be used by the police. *We feel that the same principle should apply to electronic communication*.[102]

James Brokenshire (Home Office Security and Immigration Minister) stated the following:

> This…[capability gap]…issue is not going away, and we need to make further changes...While this …[CT&S Bill amendment to DRIPA]…plugs an element, there is still more to be done…The…[CT&S] Bill does not incorporate provisions on weblogs, but apps and weblogs can be directly instructive…and the House will need to confront that in, I hope, an informed way. The… [UKPISC and Anderson] …reviews will inform that debate rather than its being completely informed by belief or emotion, important as those elements are to ensure that it is properly reflective of the view of our communities and the public. We must ensure that the facts are there…when the House considers the legislation it will need to pass before December 2016.[103]

February 2015

The IOCCO findings as regards access to journalists' sources

On 4 February 2015, the IOCCO published the findings from the inquiry into police use of the RIPA 2000, Part I, Chapter II in-house authorization scheme to obtain CD potentially identifying journalists' sources and other 'privileged' material such as that normally subject to legal professional privilege. The IOCCO found that 19 UK police forces had undertaken 34 investigations wherein CD was sought 'in relation to suspected illicit relationships between public officials (sources) and journalists'.[104] It was thus demonstrated that police 'were not randomly trawling communications data relating to journalists in order to identify their sources' and had not circumvented other legislation, such as PACE.[105] However, the use of Chapter II powers to seek journalists' CD, wherein the necessity and proportionality of applications had been assessed 'in house' on

102 HC Deb 9 December 2014, vol 589, col 806, emphasis added.
103 ibid, col 825, referring to what would become the IPA 2016.
104 IOCCO, *Journalist Sources Report 2015* (n58) 29.
105 ibid, 35.

34 occasions was held to undoubtedly provide the potential for violations of ECHR Article 10 of the Convention.[106] The Commissioner expressed dissatisfaction regarding the consideration given to necessity, proportionality and potential for collateral intrusion, also observing that the legislation tended to focus on ECHR Article 8 considerations of privacy rather than Article 10.[107] Unsurprisingly, he recommended, as with the Police and Criminal Evidence Act (PACE) 1984, that judicial authorization 'must be obtained' in cases where CD was being sought as part of an investigation to determine the source of journalistic information' and that where CD was being sought in relation to journalists but in other circumstances (for example, where they were a victim of crime or suspected of committing one unrelated to their occupation) Chapter II could be used 'so long as the designated person gives adequate consideration to the necessity, proportionality, collateral intrusion, including the possible unintended consequence of the conduct', cautioning that 'the revised Code contains very little guidance...and that absence needs to be addressed.[108]

With the benefit of hindsight, the Commissioner's points appear glaringly obvious, and it is curious that those drafting Chapter II and its derivative CoP appear not to have given due regard to the implications of ECHR Article 10 as well as Article 8 upon privileged materials, given that RIPA 2000 purported to ensure 'the relevant investigatory powers were used in accordance with human rights'.[109] The failure seems exacerbated in light of the fact that the PACE 1984, a significantly older statute, recognized the sensitivity of 'privileged' material on its face and in its derivative Codes of Practice, a fact explicitly acknowledged in the HAC Report.[110] The lacuna as identified by the IOCCO in Chapter II lends weight to Spencer's criticism of the failure to include covert investigatory powers in the overall PACE 1984 framework following the 1981 Philips Commission.[111] The new statute envisaged to replace DRIPA 2014 would need to include special provision for sensitive professions and privileged material.

Equipment Interference avowed

In addition to the known powers to intercept communications in the course of transmission by all known means of communication, and powers to retain and subsequently acquire CD, the gap referred to in the introduction to this chapter was filled in on 6 February 2015. It transpired that for a number of years, data at rest other than CD in the custody or control of CSPs, but including

106 ibid, 35–37.

107 ibid.

108 ibid, 37 referring to the draft consultative Acquisition Code of Practice published on 9 December 2014.

109 Explanatory Note to RIPA 2000, 2.

110 HAC, *RIPA Report 2014* (n63) 5.

111 J R Spencer, 'Prosecution Powers to Gather Evidence: The Case for Reform' (2005) *Archbold News* 6.

communications at rest, was accessible to the UKIC, and that there was an opaque legal basis for it.

On that date, counsel acting for the UK government in yet another legal challenge involving Privacy International and being heard in the IPT on the basis of assumed facts, filed an Open Response.[112] Proceedings had been initiated in 2014 on the basis of published unauthorized disclosures of Edward Snowden that GCHQ was involved in 'invasive state-sponsored hacking'.[113] The Open Response conceded the following as regards Computer Network Exploitation (CNE):

1 GCHQ carries out CNE within and outside the UK;
2 In 2013 about 20% of GCHQ's intelligence reports contained information derived from CNE;
3 GCHQ undertakes both 'persistent' and 'non-persistent' CNE operations, namely both where an 'implant' expires at the end of a user's internet session and where it 'resides' on a computer for an extended period;
4 CNE operations undertaken by GCHQ can be against a specific device or a computer network
5 GCHQ has obtained warrants under s.5...[Intelligence Services Act 1994 Property Interference warrants]...and...[Intelligence Services Act 1994]...authorisations under s.7,[114] and in relation to the latter had five s7 class-based authorisations...[suggesting class interference as opposed to targeted person interference]...in 2014.[115]

The disclosure referred only to GCHQ, and despite the reference to section 7 of the ISA 994 was silent on SIS (MI6) involvement. A clear inference was provided that MI5 had undertaken similar conduct between 1989 and 1994,[116] but that disclosure was officially prohibited and in any event any relevant product had been destroyed.[117] The IPT findings in relation to the agreed assumed facts and abandonment of NCND as regards the avowal are discussed later in this chronology. On the same day as the IPT avowal, the Home Office published a

112 See generally *Privacy International, Greennet and Others v Secretary of State for Foreign and Commonwealth Affairs* UKIPTrib (2016) 14/85/CH and 14/120-126/CH

113 Privacy International, 'UK Government Claims Power for Broad, Suspicionless [*sic*] Hacking of Computers and Phones' (*Privacy International*, 18 March 2015) <https://privacyinternational.org/press-release/1350/uk-government-claims-power-broad-suspicionless-hacking-computers-and-phones> accessed 29 November 2020.

114 *Privacy International, Greennet and Others* (n73) (5).

115 The so-called 'James Bond' provision, rendering acts considered unlawful in the UK lawful if undertaken outside the British Islands.

116 ibid, see reference to Security Service Act 1989, s3, subsumed into s5 of the ISA 1994 in that year.

117 ibid, note reference to Official Secrets Act 1989 and to Data Protection Act 1998

draft 'Equipment Interference Code of Practice for public consultation'.[118] An accompanying 'factsheet' stated that 'Equipment interference (EI), sometimes referred to as computer network exploitation, is the power to obtain a variety of *data* from equipment'.[119] The *data* obtainable includes communications not in the course of transmission.[120] This was an interesting initial draft. In addition to outlining the objects of the power and thus align it with the theory that the state-required data at rest and data in transit to be accessible for national security purposes wherever located (this included anywhere in the world much to the chagrin of Privacy International et al.),[121] it attempted to retrospectively 'link' the newly avowed practice to 'property interference more generally (as provided for in Part III of the Police Act 1997, as well as the Intelligence Services Act 1994 and relevant (RIPA Part II) Covert Surveillance and Property Interference Codes of Practice.[122]

In making sense of the power, the plainly worded draft EI Code defined EI as,

> (i) any interference (whether remotely or otherwise) *by the Intelligence Services, or persons acting on their behalf or in their support*, with equipment producing electromagnetic, acoustic and other emissions, and (ii) information derived from any such interference, which is to be authorised under section 5 of the 1994 Act, in order to do any or all of the following: a) obtain information from the equipment in pursuit of intelligence requirements; b) obtain information concerning the ownership, nature and use of the equipment in pursuit of intelligence requirements; c) locate and examine, remove, modify or substitute equipment hardware or software which is capable of yielding information of the type described in a) and b); d) enable and facilitate surveillance activity by means of the equipment. 'Information' included 'communications content, and communications data'.[123]

Privacy International's headline inadvertently lent support to the central thesis of this book. The avowal of EI meant that it was now explicit, for the first time since at least 1324, that the British state was assuming (claiming) powers to access data, in addition to communications data and communications, thus covering the field

118 Home Office, Draft Equipment Interference Code of Practice for Public Consultation (February 2015). <https://www.statewatch.org/media/documents/news/2015/feb/uk-ho-draft-equipment-interference-code-of-practice.pdf> accessed 29 November 2020 (Draft EICoP).

119 *GOV.UK*, Investigatory Powers Bill Factsheet. 'Targeted Equipment Interference' <https://assets.publishing.service.gov.uk/government/uploads/system/uploads/attachment_data/file/473740/Factsheet-Targeted_Equipment_Interference.pdf> accessed 1 October 2020, emphasis added.

120 ibid, emphasis added.

121 Privacy International, 'UK Government Claims Power for Broad, Suspicionless [*sic*] Hacking of Computers and Phones' (n74).

122 Home Office, draft *EICoP* (n118) para 1.2.

123 ibid, para 1.6.

as regards investigative access to data at rest as well as to signals, communications and data in transit. The EI Code went on to describe the rationale for the power, namely the longstanding historical imperatives of

> national security, with ***particular reference to the defence and foreign policies*** of Her Majesty's Government in the United Kingdom, or in the interests of the economic well-being of the United Kingdom in relation to the actions or intentions of persons outside the British Islands, or in support of the prevention or detection of serious crime.[124]

The EI Code would experience several revisions, but the February 2015 avowal signalled the government's intention to include some form of express primary provision for EI alongside the older powers of interception (targeted and bulk), CD retention, and targeted CD access. Whatever form the new statute might take, it was clear by this stage that powers to investigate *data*, in addition to communications were of primary importance.

March 2015

Following the end of the consultation period, the Home Office published the long-awaited and revised Acquisition and Disclosure Code of Practice (CD CoP [2015]). This incorporated the Protection of Freedoms Act 2012 requirement wherein local authorities were to seek judicial approval for their CD applications and new instructions regarding accessing CD potentially 'privileged material' in sensitive professions.[125] It specifically included the IOCCO recommendation that judicial authorization must be obtained in 'privilege' contexts, holding that LEAs, including HMRC, must use the procedures of PACE to apply to a court for a production order pending 'specific legislation'.[126]

UKPISC Privacy and Security Report

Published on 12 March 2015, the same day as the IOCCO Annual Report for the previous year, the UKPISC Report signposted its key finding in its choice of title 'modern and transparent framework'.[127] Its principal recommendation was that the current 'piecemeal' framework be replaced by a new Act of Parliament governing the intelligence and security Agencies' and which should 'clearly set out the intrusive powers available to the Agencies, the purposes for which they may

124 ibid, drawing on the Intelligence Services Act 1994, s3(1)(a), emphasis added.
125 Home Office, *Acquisition and Disclosure of Communications Data Code of Practice* (TSO, March 2015) (CD CoP [2015])
126 ibid, para 3.78. LEAs in NI were required to apply for a production order under the PACE (NI) Order 1989 and in Scotland were to use the appropriate legislation or common law powers to ensure judicial authorization.
127 UKPISC, *Privacy and Security 2015* (n11) 2.

use them, and the authorization required before they may do so'.[128] This echoed Gordon Walker's lonely dissent almost 60 years previously in the Birkett Report, but the exclusion of law enforcement from any future new statute was a strange choice, not least given the statutory duty of MI5 'to act in support of the activities of police forces, the National Crime Agency, and other law enforcement agencies in the prevention and detection of serious crime.[129] It is thus unsurprising that the IPA 2016 did not follow the recommendation. The report was widely criticized, and even ridiculed (on account of the significant redactions).[130] The JUSTICE response exemplifies civil libertarian reaction,

> The recommendations...go nowhere near far enough to restore common sense to the confused, opaque and unworkable framework for surveillance that we currently have in RIPA and its new sibling, the Data Retention and Investigatory Powers Act 2014 ('DRIPA'). We particularly regret the ISC conclusion that 'bulk interception' of communications and communications data by security services is lawful and justified. JUSTICE provided a full response to our concern that data retention, like interception, must be properly targeted, in our submissions on the Draft Communications Data Bill. Since the Draft Bill – widely called the Snoopers' Charter – was shelved; the Court of Justice of the European Union has also called for an end to untargeted, blanket data retention in Europe. The legality of our response in DRIPA is yet to be tested.[131]

The criticism was to some extent unfair. As the UKPISC itself acknowledged, the report contained a hitherto 'unprecedented amount of information' about the various intrusive capabilities relating to the UK intelligence community, the relevant law, authorization processes, and oversight and scrutiny.[132] 33 pages were devoted to the agencies use of interception and CD.[133] Whilst the criticism focused on this, 'quieter' parts of the report restated that EI and CNE were undertaken in the UK and overseas, although, somewhat comically, the statement outlining techniques used to interfere with wireless telegraphy, and an illustrative case example, were fully redacted.[134] As regards rationalizing any future

128 ibid, 2.

129 Security Service Act 1989, s1(4).

130 Ruchi Parekh, 'UK Parliament's Intell and Security Committee: Intelligence Agencies "Do Not Seek to Circumvent the Law"' (*JustSecurity*, 13 March 2015) <https://www.justsecurity.org/21052/uk-parliaments-intelligence-security-committee-bulk-collection-mass-surveillance/> accessed 29 November 2015. The piece carries Tweets displaying redacted pages.

131 JUSTICE, 'JUSTICE Responds to ISC Privacy and Security Report'. <https://justice.org.uk/justice-responds-to-isc-privacy-and-security-report/> accessed 29 November 2020.

132 UKPISC, *Privacy and Security 2015* (n11) 1.

133 ibid, 17–50.

134 ibid, 63–67.

legislation, the UKPISC, acknowledging the 'the growth in, and intrusiveness of…[EI]' recommended consideration of a specific authorization for it.[135] The Report also, after weighing the costs and benefits, recommended retention of authorising powers for the intrusive techniques to Ministers as it was them, and not judges who should, and do, justify their decisions to the public.[136]

Whilst the IRTL would, after critical analysis, amalgamate the most cogent and workable findings in the UKPISC report into his own report, meaning that the UKPISC's work would become somewhat overlooked with the passage of time, it is worth remembering that it was the UKPISC who made public the Agencies' acquisition and use of bulk personal datasets (BPD) for the first time.[137] Despite the objections of civil liberties advocates, it is unsurprising that all three agencies, whether by overt or covert means, used their broad enabling provisions to obtain information in the interests of national security (broadly construed) to acquire BPD.[138] It was also unsurprising that civil liberties advocates almost immediately brought a legal challenge to the acquisition and use of BPD in the IPT.[139] As regards rationalizing UK national security policy, the UKPISC found BPD's 'relevant to national security investigations' whilst SIS and GCHQ made a tentative operational case for them as 'people identifiers and to enrich information obtained through other techniques'.[140] Despite being concerned that there had been no prior public or parliamentary consideration of privacy considerations or safeguards, and that there were no legislative provisions relating to the acquisition, storage, retention, sharing and destruction of BPD, and that access was internally authorized, the UKPISC implicitly recognized the state's 'right' to claim powers to acquire and access CD on the longstanding grounds, recommending that 'in the interests of transparency' the BPD capability should be acknowledged and 'put on a specific statutory footing, as should the then-existing non-statutory oversight of the Intelligence Services Commissioner (ISC)'.[141]

Rationalizing the legislative position as of March 2015

The UKPISC Report helpfully set out the then-existing legal framework governing the range of intrusive capabilities of the UKIC. Although their report was, by definition, restricted to the UKIC, parts of the legal framework were also relevant to law enforcement. It covered the interaction between the Security Service Act 1989, the Intelligence Services Act 1994, and mentioned additional

135 ibid, 67.
136 ibid, 76.
137 ibid, 55–59.
138 ibid, 55, 'large databases containing personal information about a wide range of people'.
139 *Privacy International v Secretary of State for the Home Department, Secretary of State for Foreign and Commonwealth Affairs, Secret Service, Secret Intelligence Service and GCHQ* (2016) UKIPTrib 15/110/CH. The challenge is discussed later herein.
140 UKPISC, *Privacy and Security 2015* (n11) 55.
141 ibid, 59.

intrusive powers set out in other legislation including: Telecommunications Act (TA) 1984; Terrorism Act 2000; Regulation of Investigatory Powers Act (RIPA) 2000; The Wireless Telegraphy Act (WTA) 2006; The Counter-Terrorism Act 2008 and The Data Retention and Investigatory Powers Act 2014.[142] The use of powers under any of these statutes was also governed by aspects of the Human Rights Act (HRA) 1998 and Data Protection Act (DPA) 1998. The Committee found this interaction 'absurdly complicated'.[143] This informed their case for a new, single statute as ultimately concluded.

Reference to these statutes implicitly acknowledges the availability provided by the state at that point to enable access to data in transit (RIPA and WTA) as well as data at rest (RIPA, DRIPA and the remaining statutes). This coupled with the references to EI and BPD provides a clear signal of the powers any new statute would have to encompass. A rationale for the 'Part' structure of the IPA 2016 was starting to appear.

The reference to the Telecommunications Act 1984 is interesting. The Committee obviously had no qualms in restating the terms of what was an innocuous, but public-facing provision, albeit one rarely referred to in the discourse. The Committee 'recognised' concerns expressed to them over a 'lack of transparency' over the use of the powers as well as the lack of RIPA equivalent safeguards.[144] It appears to accept for the time being, Agencies assertions that 'providing detailed information publicly about their capabilities derived from Directions under the TA 1984 would be significantly damaging to national security'. However, they again signposted the need to include all available investigatory powers in any new statute and also rationalized the provision,

> Given the *nature of current threats to the UK*, the use of Directions under the Telecommunications Act is a *legitimate capability* for the Agencies. However, the current arrangements in the Telecommunications Act 1984 lack clarity and transparency and must be reformed. This capability must be clearly set out in law, including the safeguards governing its use and statutory oversight regimes.[145]

The references to clarity and transparency are interesting. 'Clarity' is a term normally associated with 'foreseeability' in leading European jurisprudence in this area of public law, for example, the *Weber* Principles.[146] Indeed a footnote to the UKPISC recommendation referred to the 'question of transparency as a matter

142 ibid, 84.
143 ibid, 85.
144 ibid, 100.
145 ibid.
146 *Weber and Savaria v Germany* Application 54934/00 (93)–(95). See also Rita Esen, 'Intercepting Communications "in Accordance with the Law"' (2012) 76(2) *Journal of Criminal Law* 44.

of policy and 'foreseeability' as a matter of law.[147] Civil liberties advocates often challenge the degree of cognisance the government takes of ECtHR principles. It appears that in this report, the UKPISC quietly recognizes that the forthcoming new statute would require to meet standards of clarity and foreseeability.

July 2015

The beginnings of the IPA 2016: Report of the Investigatory Powers Review (RIPR)

Despite the broad provision in DRIPA 2014, section 7 mandating his review, the IRTL had clarified that focus would be on the objective of 'reviewing the use of legislation governing the use of communications data (CD) and interception' by reference to RIPA and other relevant statutes.[148] This approach, avoiding review of 'the full range of investigatory powers' also principally governed in RIPA 2000, hints at possible foreknowledge on the IRTL's part that policy preference was to regulate communications and data investigation in a distinct unitary statute, leaving the comparatively uncontroversial 'HUMINT' and overt decryption powers in RIPA Parts II and III undisturbed.

The final report represents a masterclass in research and writing that it is frankly impossible to do justice to in this work. In fact, on one view, it is possible to 'rationalise' the IPA 2016 purely on the basis of a thorough reading of the RIPR and discounting this work. Its structure was logical and its analysis sharp. It made 124 recommendations (Chapter 15), and it is these that are often cited as underpinning certain provisions of the IPA 2016. While this is undoubtedly true, the real utility of the RIPR is that, prior to making the recommendations (and grouping them) he publicly examined and weighed the evidence he heard from the Agencies (Chapter 10); CSPs (Chapter 11); Civil Society (Chapter 12). The recommendations were then prefaced in Chapter 14 by *explanations.* These are key in rationalizing the IRTL's recommendations as to the final structure and scope of the Bill that would be required by December 2016. A *clear* new statute constructed essentially from scratch was his first requirement.[149] Indeed, he encouraged the Office of Parliamentary Counsel who would be drafting it to 'produce a clear, effective and readable text...ensuring that the new law can be understood by all those who debate it, apply it or are likely to be affected by it, in the UK or abroad'.[150]

However, the focus in this work is on whether the evidence the IRTL took, and indeed his own views formed on the basis of weighing that evidence, provide a cogent rationale for what would be a new public-facing, transparent statute, wherein every known *form* of communication or data either in storage or transit

147 ibid, at footnote 283.
148 IRTL, *RIPR 2015,* 19.
149 ibid, 285.
150 ibid, 258, Recommendation 4.

could be lawfully accessed by virtue of provisions drafted to meet commonly accepted European standards. Put another way, would the IRTL accept the view that the state could and should assume investigatory powers that enabled access to any form of communications and data at rest or in transit? This would not make the IRTL any less independent. Quite the opposite. It would demonstrate that the independent arbiter of the ECHR-compliance of some of the UK's most sensitive and intrusive legislative provisions had reached an independent conclusion as to the *operational case* for the suite of investigatory powers that the new statute would be required to regulate. In this regard, the Agencies priorities bear restatement. Agencies needed the law to enable them to 'share each other's information and to maintain their position as part of an international community in the exchange of intelligence', an implicit, but clear reference to a requirement for a legal framework that would enable UKUSA Agreement obligations to continue to be fulfilled. An additional requirement was to maintain a flexible and agile global reach (presumably cyber-reach) commensurate with the government's foreign, security and defence policies. Given that their enabling provisions (not the subject of review) covered this, it was uncontroversial. The final two requirements were interlinked and relate directly to the IRTL's terms of reference. The Agencies needed 'to maintain their abilities to access the content of communications and communications data', 'to collect communications in bulk where targeting was not possible' and 'to use bulk collection where necessary to discover new threats and targets'.[151] The agencies provided evidence as to their capabilities, challenges faced, and most importantly sought to argue their case for bulk collection of communications content and RCD. The IRTL described himself as being left 'in no doubt...that the ability to intercept technical elements of communications, such as cookies and weblogs (sometimes described as content-derived metadata) which fall outside the definition of CD in RIPA and so must be treated as content (despite being less sensitive than content as ordinarily understood) was essential to GCHQ's target discovery work'.[152] A clear operational case was beginning to be made for the new statute to enable and oversee not only communications and data investigation powers enabling *targeted* access to material in transit or at rest, but also, as regards the UKIC, enabling *bulk* acquisition of such material so as to enable analysis. It was unsurprising that the case for bulk content and data acquisition was followed by paragraphs detailing international intelligence-sharing relationships, including, but not limited to, the 'Five Eyes'.[153]

Independent rationalization of the IPA?

Space precludes descriptively restating the IRTL's recommendations, particularly those relating to longstanding powers in RIPA Part I, the Wireless Telegraphy

151 ibid, 193.
152 ibid, 197.
153 ibid, 198.

Act or the enabling statutes for the UKIC. It becomes clear in the latter chapters of the RIPR that the IRTL himself has become convinced of the operational case for some of the more recently avowed techniques and for 'bulk' powers. His views would assume even greater importance in 2016. In the RIPR, he rationalizes the state's assumption of a 'right' to conduct EI, by analogising 'the digital sphere' with the 'physical sphere';

> There may be all sorts of reasons- not least, secure encryption- why it is not physically possible to intercept a particular communication, or track a particular individual. *But the power to do so needs to exist*, even if it is only usable in cases where skill or trickery can provide a way round the obstacle. Were it to be otherwise, *entire channels of communication* could be reduced to lawless spaces in which freedom is enjoyed only by the strong, and evil of all kinds can flourish.[154]

Despite the rhetorical finishing flourish befitting of an acclaimed QC, or perhaps because of it, this *independent* rationalisation of state power brilliantly encapsulates the rationale for seven hundred years of state practice, namely the belief that powers enabling the investigation of potentially lawless spaces are required in the interests of national security (broadly construed). This articulation of the rationale for state power carries significantly greater weight than anything the state's spokespersons (e.g. the Home and Foreign Offices) or agencies (e.g. the UKIC) can ever offer. There is firstly an *operational case* (a rationale) being made for CNE (or EI more broadly), namely the belief in a need to combat the lawless nature of the 'dark web' so-called and thus the need, or belief in the need, to add EI to the already existing suite of communications and data investigative *capability*. This is *justified* on account of the nature of the subject(s) of interest and the *technological channel* of communication.[155]

Furthermore, the IRTL extends this independent validation of the state's right to maintain a potentially infinite suite of communications and data investigative powers to incorporate not only their availability to users in law, but also to use skill and subterfuge (e.g. the manipulation of computer software) in their deployment. The conduct avowed by GCHQ in the Open Response in the IPT on 6 February 2015 is thus endorsed.[156] The IRTL has by no means fallen victim to regulatory capture, however. He has rightly recognized that covert surveillance in the physical sphere (whether via directed or intrusive methods, or indeed through the use of covert human intelligence sources [CHIS]) is rendered lawful

154 ibid, 247, emphasis added.

155 ibid, 247. In a footnote, the IRTL states that he does not suggest that law enforcement or intelligence should 'govern' the internet. From a cynical standpoint, this puts him inadvertently, at odds with GCHQ's Mastering the Internet (MTI) Programme alleged in the Sunday Times and discussed in Chapter 7.

156 *Privacy International, Greennet and Others* (n73).

in RIPA, Part II, and may well of necessity involve some degree of subterfuge or disguise.[157] EI and CNE represent covert surveillance in the digital sphere and can thus be justified in any new statute, subject to safeguards, a relevant Code of Practice, and effective oversight.

The RIPR contains enough material to warrant a book on its own. For present purposes, the key takeaway is that the UK governments' rationales for enabling broad communications and data investigative powers were now being endorsed *independently.* The RIPR was submitted to the Prime Minister as provided for in DRIPA in June 2015.

July 2015

RUSI's independent surveillance review (ISR), although independent, had not benefitted from the IRTL's statutory backing and the UK government were not mandated to take cognisance of any findings. It had been instigated by then Deputy Prime Minister (DPM) Nick Clegg (Liberal Democrat) and had very similar terms of reference to the IPR as regards 'communications and related data'.[158] Its report offers no explanation as to why a separate, approximately identical exercise was required. It is thus difficult to avoid concluding that it was a political exercise on the DPM's part to appease Liberal Democrat elements who perceived the IPR as a potential Tory whitewash or doubted the objectivity of the IRTL. With no disrespect intended to any of its participants, the ISR was probably always doomed to comparative obscurity by the very fact of the IPR's existence and Prime Ministerial and Conservative coalition majority backing. Despite attempting to plough a distinctive furrow adopting the 'perspective of the British citizen' (whatever that meant),[159] and being well and written cogently analysed, it assured its ultimate consignment to obscurity by publishing its report one month after the IPR (July 2015), three months after its principal sponsor had lost office in the general election, and unoriginally concurring with most of the IRTL's recommendations while offering little of its own.[160] That stated, it made cogent findings in the still to be settled area of bulk powers that merit revisiting.

Drawing on both the UKPISC and IRTL findings, the ISR recommended:

> two warrant types for the interception of communications in the course of transmission; (a) a specific interception warrant which should be limited to a single person, premises or operation and (b) a bulk interception warrant which would allow content data and related communications data to be obtained.[161]

157 See generally RIPA 2000, Part II.
158 *RUSI Review 2015* (n13) 1.
159 ibid, xi.
160 ibid, xv–xviii.
161 ibid, xvi–xvii, Recommendation 9.

Like the IRTL, they recommended a 'bulk communications data warrant' which would be limited to the acquisition of CD rather than along with content, and that authorization by a DP continue as at present for the acquisition of CD other than in bulk.[162] Their 'composite approach to the authorization of warrants which…does not discriminate between [UKIS and LEA] applications' is worth revisiting:[163]

> Where a warrant…is sought for a purpose relating to the detection or prevention of serious and organised crime…[it]…should always be authorised by a judicial commissioner. Most police and other law-enforcement warrants would fall into this category. A copy…should be provided to the home secretary…Where a warrant…is sought for purposes relating to national security (including counter-terrorism, support to military operations, diplomacy and foreign policy) and economic well-being…[it]… the warrant should be authorised by the secretary of state, subject to judicial review by a judicial commissioner…[which]…should take place before implementation…[in urgent cases]…the secretary of state should be able to direct that…[it]… comes into force immediately…the judicial commissioner…notified straight away and the judicial review conducted within fourteen days. The judicial commissioners in charge of the authorisation of warrants should… remain independent.[164]

Similar to the IRTL therefore, the RUSI took an oblique approach to prioritizing the degree of potential CFREU and ECHR rights infringements, but nevertheless prioritised them. Both reports adopted a 'tiered' approach as regards the perceived necessity of real-time independent scrutiny of executive CD acquisition powers. The IRTL tiered the necessity against whether what was being sought constituted 'content', 'bulk CD' or non-bulk CD with the requirement for judicial intervention greatest for content and least for 'targeted' CD. RUSI 'tiered' the necessity of acquisition against the purpose(s) for which any particular data (content or CD) is sought. Both schemes, intentionally or otherwise, were analogous to a scheme that explicitly adopts a tiered approach towards the perceived necessity for judicial scrutiny based on proportionately increasing degrees of infringement upon individual CFREU and ECHR rights that the use of *any* investigative technique for data acquisition (whether content, CD, or encrypted) entails. This was proper, rights-centric proportionality, and was a reminder of the original conceptual approach towards authorising CD acquisition put forward during pre-enactment scrutiny of RIPA 2000 but which was ignored.[165] The

162 ibid, Recommendation 10.
163 ibid.
164 ibid.
165 Rt Hon Richard Allan MP, SC Deb (F), Regulation of Investigatory Powers Bill, 28 March 2000, cols 247, and repeated at 248.

IRTL and RUSI both deserve credit for arriving at findings that, if implemented, would finally consign to history the now untenable proportionality assessment relating to CD acquisition originally set out by Charles Clarke.

DRIPA 2014 unlawful

In addition to the publication of RUSI's ISR, the judicial review of DRIPA 2014 initiated by UK Parliament MPs Tom Watson and David Davis and others was ultimately successful. In a judgment published on 17 July 2015, just short of one year after DRIPA's entry into force, the England and Wales Court of Appeal (Admin) Division held that DRIPA 2014, section 1 existed in breach of EU law because:

1. It does not lay down clear and precise rules providing for access to and use of communications data retained pursuant to a retention notice to be strictly restricted to the purpose of preventing and detecting precisely defined serious offences or of conducting criminal prosecutions relating to such offences; and
2. Access to the data is not made dependent on a prior review by a court or an independent administrative body whose decision limits access to and use of the data to what is strictly necessary for the purpose of attaining the objective pursued.[166]

In short, the UK legislation, as with the DRD that had inspired it, was found to be too broad and indeterminate in scope. The court further admonished the legislature by stating that: 'the courts do not presume to tell Parliament for how long and in what detail Bills should be scrutinised, but it is right to say (to put it no higher) that legislation enacted in haste is more prone to error, and it would be highly desirable to allow the opportunity of thorough scrutiny in both Houses'.[167]

The Court of Appeal in *R (Davis and Others)* made it clear that any new statutory framework for the retention and subsequent acquisition of CD for processing for investigative purposes will require 'clear and precise rules' providing for *access* to and use of retained CD.[168] More importantly for present purposes, the initial (CSP) retention of such CD:

> will be required to be strictly restricted to the purpose of preventing and detecting precisely defined serious offences or of conducting criminal prosecutions relating to such offences, and that access to such CD will not be

166 *R (Davis and Others) v Secretary of State for the Home Department* (2015) EWHC 2092 (Admin) (114).

167 ibid, (121).

168 ibid, (85), emphasis added.

possible without prior review by a court or an independent administrative body whose decision limits access to and use of the data to what is strictly necessary for the purpose of attaining the objective pursued.[169]

The UK government sought, and was granted, leave to appeal that decision. In the latter part of 2015, the new Conservative majority focused on bedding in and the Office of Parliamentary Counsel set about fulfilling the IRTL's instructions.

References

BBC News, '"Plebgate" Row:Timeline' (*BBC*, 27 November 2014) <https://www.bbc.com/news/uk-24548645> accessed 29 May 2020

Jason Bauer, 'What Is a Port?' (*portforward.com*) <http://portforward.com/networking/whatisport.htm> accessed 30 October 2020

Constitution Committee, *Fast-track Legislation: Constitutional Implications & Safeguards* (HL 2008–09, 116-I)

Nick Craven, 'How Police Hacked Mail on Sunday Phone: Officers Used Anti-Terror Laws to Track Down Judge-Protected Source Who Exposed Chris Huhne's Speeding Points Fraud' (*Daily Mail*, 8 October 2014) <https://www.dailymail.co.uk/news/article-2780809/How-police-hacked-Mail-Sunday-Officers-used-anti-terror-laws-seize-phone-records-identify-source-exposed-Chris-Huhne-s-speeding-points-fraud.html> accessed 29 May 2020

'Data Retention and Investigatory Powers Bill Government Note on the European Court of Justice Judgment' <https://assets.publishing.service.gov.uk/government/uploads/system/uploads/attachment_data/file/331106/DRIPgovernmentNoteECJjudgment.pdf> accessed 20 November 2020

Rita Esen, 'Intercepting Communications "in Accordance with the Law"' (2012) 76 (2) *Journal of Criminal Law* 44

European Commission, 'MEMO/14/269 Frequently Asked Questions: The Data Retention Directive' (8 April 2014) <http://europa.eu/rapid/press-release_MEMO-14-269_en.htm> accessed 30 October 2020

Claire Francois, 'ECJ's Invalidation of EU Data Retention Directive Creates Confusion Over Telecommunications Service Providers' Data Retention Obligations', *Bloomberg BNA Privacy Law Watch* (13 May 2013) <https://www.huntonak.com/files/Publication/dec9c9bc-0527-4620-9664-ab40152923be/Presentation/PublicationAttachment/39d39846-4efd-473d-81da-ea264bfbb90d/ECJs_Invalidation_of_EU_Data_Retention_Directive.pdf> accessed 30 October 2020

General Secretariat Council of the European Union, 'Information Note 9009/14-Judgment of the Court of 8 April 2014 in Joined Cases C-293/12 and C-594/12 Invalidation of Directive 2006/24/EC of the European Parliament and of the Council of 15 March 2006 on the Retention of Data Generated or Processed in Connection with the Provision of Publicly Available Electronic Communications Services or of Public Communications Networks and Amending Directive 2002/58/EC (the Data Retention Directive)' (5 May 2014) (*LIMITE*) <http:/

169 ibid.

/www.statewatch.org/news/2014/may/eu-council-note-data-retention-judgment-9009-14.pdf>accessed 30 October 2020

Philip Glover, 'Legal Uncertainty Surrounding the Acquisition by UK Intelligence-Gathering Bodies of Communications Content Intercepted Outside the UK' (2014) 18 *Edinburgh Law Review* 114

Glenn Greenwald and Ewen MacAskill, 'NSA Prism Program Taps in to User Data of Apple, Google and Others' *Guardian* (London, 7 June 2013) <http://theguardian.com/world/2013/jun/06/us-tech-giants-nsa-data> accessed 26 November 2020

GOV.UK, Investigatory Powers Bill Factsheet, 'Targeted Equipment Interference' <https://assets.publishing.service.gov.uk/government/uploads/system/uploads/attachment_data/file/473740/Factsheet-Targeted_Equipment_Interference.pdf> accessed 1 October 2020 added

The Guardian, 'NSA Prism Programme William Hague Makes Statement on GCHQ' (*Guardian*, 11 June 2013) <https://www.youtube.com/watch?v=fOI6nVoZTmY> accessed 20 November 2013

Elspeth Guild and Sergio Carrera, 'The Political and Judicial Life of Metadata: Digital Rights Ireland and the Trail of the Data Retention Directive' (29 May 2014). CEPS Liberty and Security in Europe Papers No. 65 <http://papers.ssrn.com/sol3/papers.cfm?abstract_id=2445901> accessed 30 October 2020

Home Office, 'Acquisition and Disclosure of Communications Data Code of Practice, Draft for Public Consultation' (9 December 2014) <https://assets.publishing.service.gov.uk/government/uploads/system/uploads/attachment_data/file/383548/DraftCDAcquisitionCodeofPracticeforconsultation.pdf> accessed 24 November 2020

Home Office, 'Counter-Terrorism and Security Bill: Factsheet – Part 3 – Internet Protocol (IP) Address Resolution' (*GOV.UK*, 3 December 2014) <https://gov.uk/government/uploads/system/uploads/attachment_data/file/388035/CTS_Bill_-_Factsheet_5_-_IP_Resolution_v2.pdf> accessed 30 October 2020

Home Office, *Draft Equipment Interference Code of Practice for Public Consultation* (February 2015) <https://www.statewatch.org/media/documents/news/2015/feb/uk-ho-draft-equipment-interference-code-of-practice.pdf> accessed 29 November 2020 (Draft EICoP)

Home Office, *Acquisition and Disclosure of Communications Data Code of Practice* (TSO, March 2015) (CDCoP [2015])

House of Commons, 'Data Retention and Investigatory Powers Bill Explanatory Notes [referring to the Bill] as Introduced in the House of Commons on 14th July 2014 [Bill 73]' (Stationery Office, 14 July 2014)

House of Commons Home Affairs Committee, *Regulation of Investigatory Powers Act 2000* (HC711, 6 December 2014)

Independent Reviewer of Terrorism Legislation, *A Question of Trust: Report of the Investigatory Powers Review* (Williams Lea Group, June 2015) (IRTL, RIPR 2015)

Intelligence and Security Committee of Parliament, *Privacy and Security: A Modern and Transparent Framework* (HC 1075, March 2015) (UKPISC, Privacy and Security 2015)

IOCCO Inquiry into the Use of Chapter 2 of Part 1 of the Regulation of Investigatory Powers Act (RIPA) to Identify Journalistic Sources (*IOCCO*, 4 February 2015)

Joint Committee on the Draft Communications Data Bill, *Legislative Scrutiny: Draft Communications Data Bill* (Final Report) (2012–13, HL79, HC 479) 13. (JCDCDB, Final Report 2015)

JUSTICE, 'JUSTICE Responds to ISC Privacy and Security Report' <https://justice.org.uk/justice-responds-to-isc-privacy-and-security-report/> accessed 29 November 2020

Rt Hon Sir Anthony May, *2013 Annual Report of the Interception of Communications Commissioner* (HC 1184, April 2014)

Bradley Mitchell, 'Media Access Control' (*abouttech*) <http://compnetworking.about.com/od/networkprotocolsip/g/bldef_mac.htm> accessed 30 October 2020

Press Gazette, 'Save our Sources: Press Gazette Campaign to Stop Public Authorities Spying on Journalists' Phone Records' (*Press Gazette*, 11 September 2014) <http://pressgazette.co.uk/save-our-sources-press-gazette-campaign-stop-uk-public-authorities-secretly-obtaining-journalists> accessed 23 October 2020

Privacy International, 'UK Government Claims Power for Broad, Suspicionless (*sic*) Hacking of Computers and Phones' (*Privacy International*, 18 March 2015) <https://privacyinternational.org/press-release/1350/uk-government-claims-power-broad-suspicionless-hacking-computers-and-phones> accessed 29 November 2020

Royal United Services Institute for Defence and Security Studies, *A Democratic Licence to Operate: Report of the Independent Surveillance Review* (Stephen Austin and Sons Ltd, July 2015) (RUSI, RISR, 2015)

Ruchi Parekh, 'UK Parliament's Intell and Security Committee: Intelligence Agencies "Do Not Seek to Circumvent the Law"' (*JustSecurity*, 13 March 2015) <https://www.justsecurity.org/21052/uk-parliaments-intelligence-security-committee-bulk-collection-mass-surveillance/> accessed 29 November 2015.

Andrew Sparrow, *The Law of Virtual Worlds and Internet Social Networks* (Gower, 2010) 172–173

JR Spencer, 'Prosecution Powers to Gather Evidence: The Case for Reform' [2005] *Archbold News* 6

Sarah Tracey, 'The Fall of the Data Retention Directive' (2015) 20 (2) *Communications & the Law (Case & Comment)* 53–55

UKPISC, 'Statement on GCHQ's Alleged Interception of Communications under the PRISM Programme' <https://b1cba9b3-a-5e6631fd-s-sites.googlegroups.com/a/independent.gov.uk/isc/files/20130717_ISC_statement_GCHQ.pdf?attachauth=ANoY7cpqnDqfloChw29Gow59L15QdmBzKQ2z0QS9EPPBiHhOsJCcGYSJLTrSZVdcXX-eCLmiP0K2JRDKf-tLeHhaJ8l9o-YL_8bRQAzKDf7OwCECiSSNqObzXdhWpFtYd5ndKVbCLu9jYdz1CKfxw9t_1wb-A1kDtHs7W0BrNLN13P3wJa0oURBHT3omE2NLEq0eA-69oXuct91Wvsada9S5HjfAkVYOavSJJvDUFLGsKdXjSFeH0Yg%3D&attredirects=0> accessed 20 November 2020

Part IV

Candid statutory governance

2016–?

10 Avowal, transparency, and a modern and transparent framework

Rationalizing the Investigatory Powers Act 2016

Introduction

This chapter examines the period between the publication of the initial draft Investigatory Powers Bill (IPB) through to Royal Assent. The initial draft IPB would change substantially over the course of a single year, although its constituent investigatory powers did not. Many of the amendments made over the course of scrutiny would be technical or procedural in nature. These are not discussed herein, as the purpose of this penultimate chapter remains to test the original thesis outlined in Chapter 1, namely whether the IPA 2016 as enacted represents the latest statutory restatement of almost 700-years practice, wherein the state seeks to ensure that a capability to access communications in transit or at rest, or data in transit or at rest is maintained, and that it grants its agencies with sufficient investigative functions (principally the UK intelligence community (UKIC) and law enforcement) broad investigatory powers to give effect to that capability.

The focus of this chapter therefore is on the powers contained in the draft IPB and what the principal scrutineering bodies, whether parliamentary committees or independent reviewers, concluded in relation to the rationale for the IPB, and ultimately the IPA 2016. For the sake of completeness, the chapter does touch on changes that the new statute would bring to the existing oversight regime, however the nature of the relevant provisions and their practical reach are examined more thoroughly in other academic works.

The initial draft Investigatory Powers Bill

The Home Secretary acknowledged the 'three independent reviews' (those of the UKPISC, IRTL, and RUSI)[1] and their 'nearly 200 recommendations', stating that 'the Government has paid attention' and that attached draft IPB

1 Intelligence and Security Committee of Parliament, *Privacy and Security: A Modern and Transparent Framework* (HC 1075, March 2015) (UKPISC, *Privacy and Security 2015*); Independent Reviewer of Terrorism Legislation, *A Question of Trust: Report of the Investigatory Powers Review* (Williams Lea Group, June 2015) (IRTL, *RIPR 2015*) and Royal United Services Institute for Defence and Security Studies, *A Democratic Licence to Operate: Report*

> published for pre-legislative scrutiny and public consultation builds on their recommendations to bring together *all of the powers* available to law enforcement and the security and intelligence agencies to acquire communications and communications data and make them subject to enhanced, consistent safeguards.[2]

The choice of 'acquire' at this stage is as interesting as it is imprecise. Whilst reflecting a definitive policy decision to excise regulation of communications and communications data (CD) investigation from the 'surveillance'-focused RIPA 2000, there was no explanation for leaving the RIPA Part III powers to investigate encrypted data out of the draft IPB. The fact that Equipment Interference often *accesses* data without any requirement to acquire it also render the policy statement inaccurate.

The avowal of bulk communications data acquisition

Her point regarding '*all* of the powers' reflected the fact that her initial draft will probably be best remembered for its 'avowal' of powers to acquire CD in bulk through the authority of secret Ministerial directions issued under section 94 of the Telecommunications Act 1984 (section 94 Directions). This marked the state's full and final disclosure of the last of its hitherto secretly exercised communications and data investigatory powers. This is evident from the IRTL's oblique reference to them (he was still not authorized to publicly disclose them) in the Report of the Investigatory Powers Review (RIPR) 2015, wherein he stated, 'I am not aware of any sensitive capabilities *which have not been avowed to the Secretary of State*. Indeed I have been assured there are none'.[3] The avowal meant that the full suite of communications and data investigative enabling powers were now outlined in the draft IPB, reflecting the IRTL's recommendation that they all be

> promptly avowed to the Secretary of State...publicly avowed...at the earliest available opportunity and used 'only if provided for in statute and/or a Code of Practice in a manner that is sufficiently accessible and foreseeable to give an adequate indication of the circumstances in which, and the conditions on which, communications may be accessed by public authorities.[4]

The question as to how widely known the existence of these directions were whilst the Regulation of Investigatory Powers Bill (RIPB) was being finalized remains open. Prime Ministers Blair (Labour 1997–2007) Brown (Labour, 2007–2010), and Cameron (Conservative, 2010–2016), along with their

---

of the Independent Surveillance Review (Stephen Austin and Sons Ltd, July 2015) (RUSI, *RISR 2015*).

2 Home Office, *Draft Investigatory Powers Bill* (Cm 9152, November 2015) Foreword.

3 IRTL, *RIPR 2015*, 258.

4 ibid, 286, Recommendation 9.

respective Home and Foreign Secretaries, must surely have known of them but elected to keep their existence secret. Chris Pounder corroborates this assertion, observing that in 2003, Labour Home Secretary David Blunkett failed to take up an opportunity to provide a full explanation to Parliament of the intended impact of Section 94 when a consequential amendment to it replaced the words 'requisite and expedient' with 'necessary' as part of the implementation of the Communications Act 2003.[5] Indeed as recently as December 2014, a Home Affairs Committee (HAC) inquiry into law enforcement's use of powers to obtain CD, which included a number of 'veteran' Parliamentarians, stated:

> Section 94 of the Telecommunications Act 1984 gives extensive powers to the Secretary of State…There is no public disclosure of how this is used, and *none of our witnesses has been aware of anyone who considers it their role to scrutinise it or have any oversight powers.* We believe this should be reviewed, and one of the Commissioners specifically tasked with oversight of this power, and for them to be given the information and access needed to fulfil this role. We also recommend that the government publish on an annual basis the number of times this power is used. We further suggest that the Intelligence and Security Committee conduct an inquiry into the use of this power.[6]

Witnesses to the inquiry had included the Interception of Communications Commissioner, the very person appointed to oversee the acquisition and disclosure of CD. He subsequently was asked to oversee the section 94 regime on a non-statutory basis in March 2015. The secrecy even extended to the then Independent Reviewer of Terrorism Legislation (IRTL). He confirms his prohibition on disclosing their existence his RIPR his Bulk Powers Review (BPR) conducted in 2016.[7] The main consequence of secrecy, as Pounder has observed, was an absence of independent oversight in the public domain.[8]

Rationalizing the nature, scope, and structure of the initial draft IPB

Publicly avowing the bulk CD acquisition power meant the Home Office could simultaneously publish the draft IPB inclusive of what constituted the full suite of

5 Chris Pounder, 'Section 94 of the Telecommunications Act 1984: A Warning From History' (*Hawktalk*, 6 November 2015) <https://amberhawk.typepad.com/amberhawk/2015/11/section-94-of-the-telecommunications-act-1984-a-warning-from-history.html?utm_source=feedburner&utm_medium=feed&utm_campaign=Feed%3A+HawkTalk+%28Hawk+Talk%29> accessed 6 November 2020.

6 House of Commons, Home Affairs Committee, *Regulation of Investigatory Powers Act 2000: Eighth Report of Session 2014–15* (HC711, December 2014) 3 (*HAC CD Report 2014*) para 15.

7 IRTL, *Bulk Powers Review 2016* (n4) 11.

8 Pounder (n5).

national security protective communications and data-focused investigatory powers. In addition to a Part I that set out 'General Privacy Protections', these powers were;

1 To secure the lawful interception of communications and data *in the course of transmission* (in transit) on a 'targeted' or 'bulk' basis;[9]
2 To secure the acquisition of 'communications metadata' as retained by CSPs (data at rest) on a 'targeted' or 'bulk' basis (to including internet connection records (ICR));[10]
3 To compel the retention of relevant communications metadata by CSPs (data at rest) to enable 'as and when required' access by investigative agencies (including ICR);[11]
4 To enable lawful interference with equipment to secure access to equipment data (including communications) stored (at rest) within equipment on a 'targeted' or 'bulk' basis;[12]
5 To acquire and use Bulk Personal Datasets (BPD) (data at rest) for investigative purposes.

The draft IPB included a 'Guide to powers and safeguards' section, reinforced by the now-common use of illustrative case examples. Arguably, however, the inclusion of flow-charts addressed to a notional 'you', with an option for 'Stop: You must not access data', was overly condescending.[13] Sections headed: 'oversight';[14] 'interception';[15] 'CD';[16] 'Equipment Interference'[17] and 'Bulk Powers'[18] each set out the prevailing regulatory *status quo*, and proposed changes. Perhaps most importantly for public perception purposes, a statement as to *why* change was needed was included. This is very helpful in rationalizing the structure and scope of the initial draft IPB and in setting the context for the scrutiny-based jousting that would take place as the IPB passed through Parliament.

Overarching documents

A hitherto unprecedented amount of additional explanatory material in series of 'overarching documents' was published alongside the initial draft IPB.[19] These

9 IPA 2016, Part 2 and Part 6, Chapter 1 (read in conjunction with the General Privacy Protections in Part I and the relevant interpretative provisions in Part 9), emphasis added.
10 ibid, Part 3 and Part 6 (also read with Parts 1 and 9) ICRs were a controversial extension of Communications Data and are discussed later in the chapter.
11 ibid, Part 4 (also read with Parts 1 and 9).
12 ibid, Parts 5 and 6 (read in conjunction with Parts 1 and 9).
13 Home Office, Draft IPB (n2), 24.
14 ibid, 6.
15 ibid, 8.
16 ibid, 12.
17 ibid, 16.
18 ibid, 20.
19 See generally Home Office, 'Draft Investigatory Powers Bill, Overarching Documents' (*GOV.UK*, 4 November 2015) <https://www.gov.uk/government/publications/draft-investigatory-powers-bill-overarching-documents> accessed 30 November 2020.

are worth closer analysis in a rationalization exercise because they assist in demonstrating the government's pre-consultation views on the structure and scope of the initial draft IPB, and the necessity, proportionality, clarity, and foreseeability of its enabling provisions.

Individual factsheets

Individual factsheets summarizing in clear terms the nature of changes to, and brief operational case for, the targeted and bulk powers within the IPB were provided. The targeted powers had been relatively uncontroversial throughout the lifespan of RIPA 2000, but the Home Office was going to have to rationalize what were still highly controversial 'bulk' powers (of which one had only been avowed the same day!) that would now be expressly, rather than implicitly regulated in the new legislation.

Internet connection records

Prior to examining these, the single 'new' power in the proposed statute merits discussion. The draft IPB revisited the utility of extending the definition of communications data (CD) to include internet connection records (ICR). The question of their retention as a form of useful CD had remained unresolved due to a lack of cross-government agreement during the debates on the Counter-Terrorism and Security Act (CT&SA) 2015.[20] A separate factsheet thus sought to rationalize the inclusion of a power to compel CSPs to retain ICRs in the new draft IPB.

> The Counter Terrorism and Security Act 2015 provided...[at s21]...for the retention of certain data to resolve IP addresses. However, without the retention of ICRs, resolving an IP address back to a single user will often not be possible as multiple users may be associated with that IP address. ICRs therefore provide the unique identifier to distinguish between different users of a shared IP address.[21]

In addition, the 'Communications data' factsheet stated:

> CD is essential for the investigation of cyber-crime and the protection of children online, where it is often the only investigative lead that will identify

20 Home Office, 'Operational Case for the Retention of Internet Connection Records' (*GOV.UK*, 4 November 2015) <https://assets.publishing.service.gov.uk/government/uploads/system/uploads/attachment_data/file/473769/Internet_Connection_Records_Evidence_Base.pdf> accessed 30 November 2020.

21 Home Office, 'Internet Connection Records' (*GOV.UK*, 4 November 2015) <https://assets.publishing.service.gov.uk/government/uploads/system/uploads/attachment_data/file/473745/Factsheet-Internet_Connection_Records.pdf> accessed 30 November 2020.

> offenders. *As the way we communicate changes, the data needed by the police is no longer always available. While data is available for traditional forms of communication, such as telephony, it is not always held for internet communications because CSPs do not retain all the relevant data.* This means that while the police can identify all of the phone numbers called by a missing person before their disappearance, they are unable to tell what apps or social media services that person was using to communicate. This is an increasing problem for law enforcement.[22]

In spite of the needless and marginally distasteful over-reliance on public revulsion at child exploitation and paedophilia, the factsheets repeat the necessity of being able to access communications and data *wherever in transit or at rest*, the policy being one of minimizing 'capability gaps'. A 26-page specific 'Operational Case' for the retention of ICR's was also published, supplementing the factsheets.[23]

Selling the bulk powers: no easy task

Factsheets were provided for bulk interception, bulk Equipment Interference (EI), bulk personal datasets (BPD), and the newly avowed bulk communications data (BCD) regimes.

Selling the bulk interception provisions

Bulk interception, having been found not to be ECHR-compliant in its Interception of Communications Act (IOCA) 1985 form in *Liberty and Others v UK*,[24] but lawful in its later RIPA 2000, s8(4) guise in *Liberty Privacy and Others v Secretary of State for Foreign and Commonwealth Affairs, Security Service and GCHQ* was thus probably the easiest of the four bulk powers to 'sell'.[25] The Home Office quoted the 'favourable' findings in the IRTL, UKPISC, and RUSI reviews and the IPT *Liberty* judgment to legitimize the practice, adding the ancient national security 'necessity' rationale, wherein bulk collection of foreign-focused communications was 'crucial to identify new and emerging *threats to the*

22 Home Office, 'Communications Data – General' (*GOV.UK*, 4 November 2015), emphasis added <https://assets.publishing.service.gov.uk/government/uploads/system/uploads/attachment_data/file/473747/Factsheet-Communications_Data_General.pdf> accessed 30 November 2020.

23 Home Office, 'Operational Case for the Retention of Internet Connection Records' (*GOV.UK*, 4 November 2015) <https://assets.publishing.service.gov.uk/government/uploads/system/uploads/attachment_data/file/473769/Internet_Connection_Records_Evidence_Base.pdf> accessed 30 November 2020.

24 See 'Capenhurst Tower' and the analysis of the case in Chapter 6.

25 *Liberty and Privacy International and Others v Secretary of State for Foreign and Commonwealth Affairs, Security Service and GCHQ UKIPTrib* [2014] 13_77H (157)–(159).

UK'.[26] The perennially more difficult question of proportionality was addressed by highlighting the many safeguards for collected material and the 'double lock' whereby a Judicial Commissioner would review any Ministerial decision to grant a bulk interception warrant.[27]

'Selling' the bulk Equipment Interference (EI) provisions

Emphasis on safeguards was also prominent in the factsheet for bulk EI, described as a foreign-focused activity 'that collects data relating to a number of devices (for example, devices in a particular area) in order to identify potential targets of interest'. As for the other bulk powers, they were to be available only to the UKIC and would be subject to 'double lock' authorization. The rationale for it was stated thus,

> EI operations may provide information that would *otherwise be unobtainable*...[e.g.]...when a key piece of information is only transmitted to another device when encrypted...[it]... allows agencies to take receipt of large quantities of foreign-focussed material and then filter it in order to identify only the data of intelligence value...Access to this data is *crucial* to monitor known and high-priority threats and uncover other identities or communications methods targets may be using...*crucial* to *discover new and emerging targets*...[and]...*essential* to enable fragments of communications or other data relating to subjects of interest to be identified and subsequently pieced together in the course of an investigation.[28]

'Selling' the bulk personal dataset provisions

Enabling the UKIC to acquire and investigate BPDs was rationalized as follows:

> an *essential* way for the security and intelligence agencies to focus their efforts on individuals or organisations *that threaten our national security*. The agencies acquire and use BPDs to: help *identify subjects of interest*, or unknown individuals who surface in the course of investigations (and eliminate those who are innocent and unconnected to the investigation without the use of more intrusive techniques); establish links between individuals and groups,

26 Home Office, 'Investigatory Powers Bill Factsheet: Bulk Interception' (*GOV.UK*, 4 November 2015) <https://assets.publishing.service.gov.uk/government/uploads/system/uploads/attachment_data/file/473751/Factsheet-Bulk_Interception.pdf> accessed 30 November 2020, emphasis added.

27 ibid.

28 Home Office, 'Investigatory Powers Bill Factsheet: Bulk Equipment Interference' (*GOV.UK*, 4 November 2015) <https://assets.publishing.service.gov.uk/government/uploads/system/uploads/attachment_data/file/473753/Factsheet-Bulk_Equipment_Interference.pdf> accessed 30. November 2020, emphasis added.

> or else improve understanding of a target's behaviour and connections; and verify information obtained through other sources e.g. via agents.[29]

An additional effort at public reassurance was evidenced by a separate, detailed publication of handling arrangements for BPD as part of the overarching documents.[30]

'Selling' the bulk CD acquisition provisions

Factsheets are thankfully incapable of blushing, meaning that any in the Home Office were spared when they candidly acknowledged that they were following the IRTL's recommendation to avow their BCD acquisition power in the interests of transparency. Following an implicit reference that dated MI5's use of section 94 directions back to 2005, with the 'approval of successive governments' (thus correlating it with Gordon Corera's reference to it as assisting the London bombings investigations in that year),[31] the rationale for including a BCD capability was that

> Access to large volumes of data is essential to enable the identification of communications data that relates to subjects of interest and to *subsequently piece together the links between them.* Carefully directed searches of large volumes of data also allow the agencies to identify patterns of activity that significantly narrows down the areas for investigation and allows them to prioritise intelligence leads. Identifying the links between individuals or groups can also help the agencies to direct where they might request a warrant for more intrusive acquisition of data, such as interception. It allows agencies to search for traces of activity by previously unknown subjects of interest who surface in the course of an investigation in order to identify them.[32]

As with BPDs, a separate document outlining handling arrangements was also published.[33] A common thread in the rationales provided for each of the bulk

29 Home Office, 'Investigatory Powers Bill Factsheet: Bulk Personal Datasets' (*GOV.UK*, 4 November 2015) <https://assets.publishing.service.gov.uk/government/uploads/system/uploads/attachment_data/file/473750/Factsheet-Bulk_Personal_Datasets.pdf> accessed 30 November 2020, emphasis added.

30 Home Office, 'Handling Arrangements for Bulk Personal Datasets' <https://assets.publishing.service.gov.uk/government/uploads/system/uploads/attachment_data/file/473782/Handling_arrangements_for_Bulk_Personal_Datasets.pdf> accessed 30 November 2020.

31 Gordon Corera, *Intercept, the Secret History of Computers and Spies* (Weidenfeld and Nicolson, 2015) 332.

32 Home Office, 'Investigatory Powers Bill Factsheet: Bulk Communications Data' (GOV.UK, 4 November 2015).

33 Home Office, 'Handling Arrangements for Bulk Communications Data' <https://assets.publishing.service.gov.uk/government/uploads/system/uploads/attachment_data/file

powers is the implied use of significant computing power, data analytics, and AI to examine massive tranches of data in the search for new leads or to identify subjects of interest in the interests of the UK's national security. On one view, the impression is given that the powers enable threat-identification 'patrols' of communications infrastructure and wider cyberspace that are analogous to marine and airspace patrols in the physical sphere for the same objective. When the fact that the UKIC simply are not resourced to 'patrol' all communications networks or cyberspace more broadly, their use of bulk powers appears more rational and less sinister than civil liberties advocates portray. In fact, given the duty to protect the UK, anything less than the proportionate use of bulk powers, accompanied by legal safeguards and meaningful independent accountability, verges on state negligence or a dereliction of duty.

Other important overarching material

Henry VIII clauses

In addition to the factsheets, the Home Office published a legal memorandum to the Delegated Legislation and Regulatory Reform Committee identifying the provisions within the draft IPB enabling the Secretary of State to make delegated legislation, with reasons and a statement of which parliamentary procedure would be used.[34] McKay makes reference to the 'vast' power given to the Secretary of State and the Treasury power to avail of these Henry VIII clauses, noting the measured concern regarding them as expressed by the Select Committee on the Constitution.[35]

ECHR compliance

An additional memorandum set out the Home Office's view that 'in the event that the Bill is introduced into Parliament, the responsible Minister could make a statement under section 19(1)(a) of the Human Rights Act 1998 that, in the Minister's view, the provisions of the Bill are compatible with the Convention rights'.[36] This was a bold assertion at that point in time, not least because the assertion that the provisions on CD retention still complied with the ECHR

/473780/Handling_arrangements_for_Bulk_Communications_Data.pdf> accessed 30 November 2020.

34 Home Office, 'Delegated Powers and Regulatory Reform Committee: Draft Investigatory Powers Bill Memorandum by the Home Office' <https://assets.publishing.service.gov.uk/government/uploads/system/uploads/attachment_data/file/473760/Delegated_Powers_Memorandum.pdf> accessed 30 November 2020.

35 Simon McKay, *Blackstone's Guide to the Investigatory Powers Act 2016* (OUP, 2017) 17. Henry VIII clauses are those in primary legislation that authorise the making of secondary legislation that amends or repeals primary legislation.

36 Home Office, 'Investigatory Powers Bill: European Convention on Human Rights Compliance Memorandum' <https://assets.publishing.service.gov.uk/government/uploads/syste

despite the decision in *Digital Rights*,[37] and the fact that the *Davis, Watson and Others* litigation remained unresolved.[38] That said, the use of the ECtHR's jurisprudence relating to investigatory powers throughout the enclosed outlines of the targeted and bulk powers demonstrates that the Home Office appeared more seriously engaged with the European views of concepts of necessity, proportionality, clarity, and foreseeability for the new statute than had been the case at RIPA 2000's enactment. An example is the reference to the *Weber* Principles as they relate to bulk interception of communications.[39]

Privacy Impact Assessments and state investigative capability

As part of the tranche of 'overarching documents' published online on 4 November 2015, the Home Office took the unusual step of publishing impact assessments for the whole draft IPB and for each of the investigatory powers to be included in it.[40] There was an additional assessment of the introduction of a right of appeal on points of law from the IPT.[41] The provision of impact assessments was on the recommendation of the Information Commissioner's Office, marking something of an about turn since the summary dispensing of the Data Protection Registrar's services some 18 years previously.[42] These are of great assistance in rationalizing the IPA 2016 as they contain clear statements of government policy options, objectives, and decisions not often articulated as clearly in parliamentary debates or scrutiny. They also contain succinct evidence bases allowing an understanding of what actually informed the relevant policy decisions. Their publication in this area of public law represents a significant step forward in transparency.

Space precludes illustration or analysis of each assessment, however the one provided for the IPB as a whole is instructive. The policy problem was described as follows:

> The legislation that governs the use of investigatory powers by the security and intelligence agencies and law enforcement is spread out over a number of statutes and *has not kept pace with technology*. New legislation is required to update and modernise the use of investigatory powers, apply greater safeguards and oversight and to *prevent the degradation of capabilities* of law

m/uploads/attachment_data/file/473763/European_Convention_on_Human_Rights_Memorandum.pdf> accessed 30 November 2020.

37 Joined cases C-293/12 *Digital Rights Ireland Ltd* and C-594/12 *Seitlinger* (Grand Chamber, 8 April 2014).

38 *R (Davis and Others) v Secretary of State for the Home Department* [2015] EWHC 2092 (Admin).

39 *Weber and Savaria and Others v Germany* Application 54934/00 (93)–(95).

40 Home Office, 'Overarching documents' (n19).

41 ibid.

42 Chapters 7 and 8 discuss how the Data Protection Registrar was effectively excised from any oversight role in the retention and acquisition of communications data.

> enforcement and the security and intelligence agencies *necessary to protect the public* and keep us safe. The Data Retention and Investigatory Powers Act 2014 is sunsetted to 31 December 2016 and legislation is necessary to ensure a legislative basis for these powers and oversight arrangements.[43]

To the next question, 'what are the policy objectives and the intended effects?' the response was:

> To provide a clear and transparent framework for the exercise of investigatory powers by the security and intelligence agencies and law enforcement, with greater oversight and safeguards. To consolidate existing legislation into a concise and comprehensive Act that will improve public understanding of the need for, and the use of, these *important and sensitive capabilities.* To modernise and update the legal framework to ensure the security and intelligence agencies and law enforcement can continue to exercise *the capabilities they need to maintain public safety and protect us from terrorism, and serious crime* including cyber-crime, human trafficking and child sexual exploitation.[44]

The aforementioned referred to one of two policy choices. The other was 'to do nothing and leave the *capability* gap *for* law enforcement in place and legislation spread over a number of statutes'.[45] The absence of a reference to a capability gap on the part of the security and intelligence agencies here is noteworthy. However, the key rationale for the IPB was, as had been asserted in the ill-fated Communications Data Bill 2012, the existence of a capability gap, on occasion phrased as a degradation in capability.

This restates the rationale for communications and data investigative powers down the ages, namely the state aspires to *maintain the capability* to access communications and data irrespective of where it is stored or being transmitted. The point was well made by the IRTL:

> If the State is to discharge its primary duty of protecting its population, *it needs the power* to do the most sensitive things that can be imagined: bug a bedroom, search a safe, trick a person into a relationship, read a personal diary, eavesdrop on a conversation between lawyer and client or journalist and source. None of those things will be appropriate save in exceptional and occasional circumstances. Even then, they may well be completely

43 Home Office, 'Investigatory Powers Bill Overarching Privacy Impact Assessment' <https://assets.publishing.service.gov.uk/government/uploads/system/uploads/attachment_data/file/473771/Impact_Assessmen-Overarching-Impact-Assessment.pdf> accessed 30 November 2020.

44 ibid.

45 ibid, (n43).

impracticable to implement. *But the issue is when it should be lawful to exercise such powers, not whether they should exist at all.*[46]

Initial draft IPB, conclusion

4 November 2015 is probably best remembered as 'avowal' day, the day the government finally 'came clean' about the use of section 94 directions some 16 years after the NCIS Joint submission recommended their use. It might be fairer to remember the date as that on which the Home Office demonstrated a palpable transition from 'need to know' to 'transparent secrecy' in the area of communications and data investigation governance. At the close of the command paper introducing the initial draft IPB, it was stated that a Joint Committee would scrutinize the draft bill, 'issue its own call for evidence and will invite views from the public and interested parties', adding that 'the Government welcomes views on the issues covered in the draft Bill and will continue to engage with industry, academia and civil liberties groups throughout the pre-legislative scrutiny period'.[47] Whether the engagement or consultation represented a genuine listening exercise remains a moot, participant-dependent point, but there could be no doubting the Home Office's efforts to be seen to be consulting.

Revised draft IPB 15 March 2016

Prior to its reintroduction to the House of Commons for Second Reading on 15 March 2016, the initial draft IPB was scrutinized in depth by three committees, all of which produced final reports. The first was the House of Commons Science and Technology Committee, which reported on 19 January 2016.[48] The second was the Joint Committee on the Draft Investigatory Powers Bill (JCDIPB), which published its report and recommendations on 3 February 2016.[49] The Intelligence and Security Committee also produced a relevant report the same week.[50] Whilst none of the three objected to the broad targeted and bulk investigatory powers contained in the draft IPB, the thorny question of Internet Connection Records (ICR), which remained unresolved since the debates in the Counter-terrorism and Security Bill in early 2015, was revisited by the Science and Technology Committee and the JCDIPB. The former's scrutiny of the case for ICRs is unsurprisingly scientific and technical in nature, but a useful summary

46 IRTL, *RIPR 2015*, 247.

47 Home Office, *Cm 9152* (n1) 34.

48 House of Commons Science and Technology Committee, *Investigatory Powers Bill: Technical Issues: Third Report of Session 2015-16* (HC 573, January 2016).

49 House of Lords, House of Commons Joint Committee on the Draft Investigatory Powers Bill: *Draft Investigatory Powers Bill Report* (HL 93, HC 651, February 2016) (JCDIPB, *IPB Report 2016*).

50 Intelligence and Security Committee of Parliament, *Report on the Draft Investigatory Powers Bill* (HC 795, February 2016).

of the case for and against ICR retention (and thus later investigative acquisition) appears in the Report of the JCDIPB. Perhaps unsurprisingly, the case for ICR retention, and thus the maintenance of a state capability to access internet-browsing histories, was made by the Home Office in support of their published operational case, supplemented by representatives of law enforcement.[51] Important independent support, however, came from the charity National Society for the Prevention of Cruelty to Children (NSPCC) and BCS, the Chartered Institute for Information Technology. The former viewed the proposals to enable the retention of ICR as a 'necessary expansion of existing capabilities' and the latter asserting that 'accessing ICR is essential for identifying the sender of an online communication, identifying which ISP is being used and where and when illegal content has been accessed'.[52]

Opposition to the expansion of investigative capability to include ICR's included, but was not limited to, civil liberties advocates such as Big Brother Watch, Liberty, and Privacy International. Leading public law experts (Tom Hickman) and academics (Dr Paul Bernal and Dr Julian Huppert) as well as a collection of informed internet expertise articulated the view that ICR retention was disproportionately intrusive with the potential for disproportionate profiling.[53] Despite this, and the very real technical problem of how to honour subject access requests to CSPs made under the Data Protection Act 1998, section 7 'that might allow customers to potentially see data relating to the browsing habits of a spouse or housemate',[54] the Joint Committee concluded that,

> on balance, there is a case for Internet Connection Records as an important tool for law enforcement. We have concerns about the definitions and feasibility of the existing proposal, which the Home Office must address...It is also important for ICRs to be properly authorised and overseen, and these issues will be considered in subsequent chapters. We recommend that the Government should publish in a Code of Practice alongside the Bill advice on how data controllers should seek to minimise the privacy risks of subject access requests for ICRs under the Data Protection Act 1998. While we recognise that ICRs could prove a desirable tool for law enforcement agencies, the Government must address the significant concerns outlined by our witnesses if their inclusion within the Bill is to command the necessary support.[55]

51 JCDIPB, *IPB Report 2016* (n49) paras 93–96.
52 ibid, para 97 citing submissions from NSPCC and BCS respectively.
53 ibid, paras 98–102.
54 ibid, para 103, submission of CSP TalkTalk.
55 ibid, paras 106–108. See now Home Office, 'Communications Data: Code of Practice' (Home Office, November 2018) 19–20.

Draft IPB Second Reading

On the same day as the Second Reading, the Home Office published its response to the initial three reports. It was observed that the three committees had 'received over 1500 pages of evidence and took oral evidence from Government, industry, civil liberties groups and many others', and that the 'revised bill, along with the supporting material we are publishing alongside it, give effect to the vast majority of...[their]...recommendations'.[56]

An important inclusion was the promised publication of six Codes of Practice to provide greater detail on the operation of each of the principal powers and their respective oversight arrangements.[57] Space precludes repetition of every recommended change, however some merit mention.

As regards the interception of communications and intelligence-sharing, the revised IPB clarified that an interception warrant had to be in place 'before asking an international partner to undertake activity in the UK on behalf of a public authority'.[58] A much-needed improvement on the 'content/non-content' wicked definition problem was signalled with the announcement that the RIPA 2000 term 'related communications data' (RCD) was to be replaced by 'secondary data'.[59] The Home Office clarified that

> the Bill renames data, other than content, that can be obtained under a targeted or bulk interception warrant as 'secondary data'...[and]...sets out the definition of secondary data, making clear that it is broader than communications data. This clarifies the distinction between this type of data and the narrower class of data available under a communications data authorisation...[the IPB also creates]...central definitions of systems data and identifying data...[ensuring]...consistency when the same data is being referred to in different contexts.[60]

As explored in Chapter 2, the bill also introduced, for the first time, a definition of what would constitute the 'content' of a communication.[61] The 'meaning'-centred approach was not unproblematic, but represented a 'least-worst' approach to delineating the content/non-content dilemma.

As regards revisions to the IPB framework regulating the acquisition of communications data, an initial exemption from the requirement to seek judicial authorization for acquiring communications data to identify a journalistic

56 Home Office, *Investigatory Powers Bill: Government Response to Pre-Legislative Scrutiny* (Cm9219, March 2016), Foreword.
57 ibid, 5.
58 Home Office, *Government Response to Pre-Legislative Scrutiny* (n56) 14.
59 See Chapter 2 of this volume.
60 Home Office, *Government Response to Pre-Legislative Scrutiny* (n56) 15.
61 Draft IPB, clause 193(6).

source for the security and intelligence agencies was removed.[62] In addition to many other technical or procedural modifications in the revised bill, the Home Office also published separate 'Operational Cases' for each of the four bulk powers, providing 'greater information' about them and setting out why they were 'essential'.[63]

The inclusion of bulk powers in the IPB, despite their restriction to use by only the security and intelligence agencies, was not proving universally acceptable. Shadow Home Secretary Andy Burnham MP (Labour) observed that, although 'the operational case for the individual bulk powers was published by the Government alongside the Bill…it is fair to say that the detail has failed to convince everyone'.[64] In addition to misgivings regarding bulk powers consistently expressed by Joanna Cherry (SNP), he added

> important concerns were raised by the Intelligence and Security Committee about scope, oversight and the more generic class warrants, and I do not believe that they have been adequately answered. One of the Joint Committee's recommendations was that the Government should establish an independent review of all the bulk powers in the Bill. Given the complexity and sensitivity of the issue, I think that the House would benefit from that, so my specific ask is for the Home Secretary to commission such a review, to be concluded in time for Report and Third Reading.[65]

The IRTL Bulk Powers Review 2016

This was ultimately agreed to, and following agreement on terms of reference, the IRTL, whose initial 2015 Investigatory Powers Review was widely acclaimed, undertook a 'consideration and discussion of the operational case for the [four bulk] powers' including a view as to the strength of the case, but without opining on appropriate safeguards or the question of their proportionality in ECHR compliance terms.[66] As was the case in his 2015 exercise, the IRTL's final Report of the Bulk Powers Review (RBPR) exhibits a detailed and considered examination of the merits of the Operational Case for bulk interception of communications, bulk acquisition of communications data, bulk equipment interference and bulk personal datasets. The IRTL had a clear methodology with expert support.[67] A complete chapter was devoted to explaining: the nature of each power; the operation of each power (how it works); the 'potential intelligence product obtained; and the relevant safeguards for such product'.[68] He examined the relevant over-

62 Home Office, *Government Response to Pre-Legislative Scrutiny* (n56) 20.
63 ibid, 31.
64 HC Deb, 15 March 2016, vol 607, col 833.
65 ibid, col 835.
66 IRTL, *Bulk Powers Review 2016* (n4) 4–5.
67 ibid, 12–18.
68 ibid, Chapter 2, 21–46.

sight mechanisms (the Interception of Communications Commissioner's Office, the Intelligence Services Commissioner, and the Intelligence and Security Committee of Parliament), and made reference to their assessments of the utility of the powers they oversaw.[69] He also undertook detailed comparative analysis with the US framework and the jurisprudence of Europe's Courts.[70] Perhaps the defining masterstroke in the bulk Powers Report is Chapter Four, wherein he identified that

> A frame of reference is needed for the purposes of evaluating the utility or otherwise of the powers under review. Such a framework is not provided by the Operational Case, which categorises the purposes served by the powers under review in ways which lack coherence and consistency.[71]

The security and intelligence agencies provided this,[72] and set out three stages of intelligence work ('identify', 'understand', 'action') followed by a short list of specific activities (e.g. target discovery) wherein bulk data was stated to be of importance.[73] Central to the IRTL's decision-making were the individual 'Statements of Utility of Bulk Capabilities' from MI5,[74] the SIS,[75] and GCHQ[76] annexed to the final report. All three outlined the critical importance of each of the four bulk powers in the identification, understanding, and action phases of their work, with GCHQ also making a compelling case by reference operational areas such as counter-terrorism.

The IRTL formed his conclusions 'on the analysis of some 60 case studies, as well as on internal documents in which the UKIC offered frank and unvarnished assessments of the utility and limitations of the powers under review'.[77] He generously noted 'the strongest defenders of the utility of the powers', namely 'successive Commissioners who bring to their task the dispassionate and forensic qualities of a senior judge, the additional independence that accompanies retirement and, in the case of the IOCCO, a substantial team of skilled inspectors'.[78]

The IRTL described how the powers under review 'contribute (or, in the case of bulk EI, may be expected to contribute) not only to target discovery, but to target development and to the direction of operations and disruptive action, adding that 'they are used resourcefully: not mechanically, or in isolation, or for distinct tasks, but in combination with each other and with other types of overt

69 ibid.
70 ibid, Chapter 3.
71 ibid, 72.
72 ibid.
73 ibid, 73.
74 ibid, Annex 5.
75 ibid, Annex 6.
76 ibid, Annex 7.
77 ibid, 122.
78 ibid, 121.

and covert intelligence'.[79] In endorsing the asserted utility of all four bulk powers (although bulk EI had not yet been used) the IRTL reinforced his conclusions by finding that the contribution they make 'could not have been replicated by other means'.[80] This was a crucial independent finding as regards not only the necessity of the powers in question, but the proportionality of their use in pursuing a legitimate aim, provided of course that their use would be subject to adherence to safeguards and effective independent oversight. It echoed the views expressed in the Report of the Joint Committee on Human Rights.[81] Consequently, the published Bulk Powers Review was delivered to Parliament in August 2016, with four months remaining until scheduled enactment of the revised IPB.

In the interim period, the clauses in the revised IPB had undergone detailed scrutiny by the appointed public bill committee over sixteen separate sittings between March and May 2016. In addition, as the IRTL later reported, three further parliamentary committees (Human Rights, Constitution, Delegation and Regulatory Reform) reported on the IPB in June and July 2016, rendering the final IPA one of the most carefully scrutinized laws of recent times.[82]

Relevant judicial determinations on the powers within the IPB

Scrutiny also extends to the judiciary. As the IPB progressed from initial draft towards final act, a number of legal challenges were brought in relation to the legality, clarity, foreseeability, necessity, and proportionality of aspects of the investigatory powers included within it, with findings publicized prior to Royal Assent.

Equipment Interference

On 12 February 2016, around one year after the avowal of Equipment Interference, or more specifically Computer Network Exploitation (CNE), the Investigatory Powers Tribunal held, in relation to proceedings based on assumed facts, that the Intelligence Services Act property interference warrant regime was ECHR Articles 8 and 10 compliant both prior to, and after February 2015.[83] In relation to the specific issue of the adequacy of dealing with legal and professional privilege, the IPT concluded that the CNE regime had been compliant with the

79 ibid, 125
80 ibid, 124.
81 House of Lords, House of Commons Joint Committee on Human Rights, *Legislative Scrutiny: Investigatory Powers Bill First Report of 2016–17* (HL6, HC 104) 35.
82 David Anderson QC, 'The Investigatory Powers Act 2016: An Exercise in Democracy' (*David Anderson QC*, 26 June 2017) <https://www.daqc.co.uk/2016/12/03/the-investigatory-powers-act-2016-an-exercise-in-democracy/> accessed 29 November 2020.
83 *Privacy International, GreenNet and Others v Secretary of State for Foreign and Commonwealth Affairs and GCHQ* [2016] UKIPTrib 14/85/CH (89).

Convention since the February 2015 avowal.[84] The IPT's finding allowed what would become Part 5 of the IPA 2016 (Equipment Interference) and Part 6, Chapter 3 (Bulk EI warrants) to proceed through Parliament on the basis the conduct was lawful, necessary, and proportionate, supplementing the IRTL's findings in relation to the operational case.

Bulk CD acquisition (hitherto section 94 directions) and bulk personal datasets

On 17 October 2016 the IPT delivered their 36-page judgment in a separate *Privacy International* challenge to the holding and use of Bulk Personal Datasets (BPD) and the bulk acquisition of CD (BCD) under secret Ministerial directions issued under section 94 of the Telecommunications Act 1984. It was held firstly that it is lawful at domestic law to use section 94 to obtain BCD.[85] In an important finding for historical purposes, however, and in validating civil libertarian concerns, the IPT also held that 'subject to the issue of transfer of data', and to resolution of the issue of proportionality (on which parties were invited to make further submissions following the publication of the IRTL's BPR)[86] the s94 BCD regime had not complied with Article 8 of the ECHR until 4 November 2015 (draft Investigatory Powers Bill publication and avowal day) but did thereafter. They also found that the BPD regime did not comply with Article 8 until 12 March 2015 (when published in the UKPISC, *Privacy and Security Report 2015*).[87] An additional 34 pages publicised the relevant law, potential criminal liability, and internal handling arrangements for BPD and BCD. The IPT findings meant that Part 7 (BPD Warrants) and Part 6, Chapter 2 (BCD Acquisition warrants) could proceed towards enactment on the basis that the conduct authorized was lawful, necessary, and proportionate.

Communications data retention provisions

On 20 November 2015, the England and Wales Court of Appeal had stayed its proceedings reviewing the CD retention provisions in DRIPA 2014 in *Davis, Watson and Others* and referred the following question to the CJEU:

> Does [the *Digital Rights* judgment] (including, in particular, paragraphs 60 to 62 thereof) lay down mandatory requirements of EU law applicable to a Member State's domestic regime governing access to data retained in

84 ibid (90).

85 *Privacy International v Secretary of State for Foreign and Commonwealth Affairs, Secretary of State for the Home Department, GCHQ, Security Service and Secret Intelligence Service* [2016] UKIPTrib 15/110-CH (58).

86 ibid.

87 ibid (101).

> accordance with national legislation, in order to comply with Articles 7 and 8 of [the Charter]?[88]

Over the course of 13 paragraphs, the CJEU reflected on the existing EU law, ultimately declaring that,

> Article 15(1) of Directive 2002/58, read in the light of Articles 7, 8, and 11 and Article 52(1) of the Charter, must be interpreted as precluding national legislation governing the protection and security of traffic and location data and, in particular, access of the competent national authorities to the retained data, where the objective pursued by that access, in the context of fighting crime, is not restricted solely to fighting *serious crime*, where access is not subject to prior review by a court or an independent administrative authority, and where there is no requirement that the data concerned should be retained within the European Union.[89]

The judgment was made public on 21 December 2016, ten days before DRIPA's expiry date and the enactment of the IPA 2016.

In the interim period, neither the Court of Appeal and CJEU proceedings nor the CJEU's eventual preliminary ruling had prevented the introduction of the CD retention regime in the IPA 2016, Part 4. This entered force on 30 December 2016, largely replicating and replacing the impugned DRIPA 2014 provisions which expired the following day. This provided for CD to be retained by any CSP issued with a Ministerial Data Retention Notice for a maximum of 12 months.[90] The scope of the notices introduced in the initial regime was accurately described as 'vast' in that it related to 'a particular operator or description of operators, require the retention of all data or any description of data, and identify the period or periods for which data is to be retained'.[91]

All the aforementioned judgments, including that in Liberty regarding the RIPA 2000, s8(4) bulk interception warrant provisions,[92] assist in rationalizing the IPA 2016 as finally assented to. The act explicitly acknowledged the state's aspiration to maintain the capability to access communications and data in transit over all forms of networks or means of transmission, communications, and data at rest wherever stored. Avowals meant that there were no more secret powers, although the practice remained unchanged. Following a relatively trouble-free passage through the House of Lords, the IPB received Royal Assent on 29 November 2016, thus becoming the Investigatory Powers Act 2016.

88 Joined Cases C203/15 and C698/15 *Tele2 Sverige AB v Post: och telestyrelsen and Secretary of State for the Home Department v Tom Watson and Others* (59).

89 ibid, (125), emphasis added.

90 The provisions of the IPA 2016, Part 4, are outlined and analyzed in Simon McKay, *Blackstone's Guide to the Investigatory Powers Act 2016* (OUP, 2017) 103–111.

91 ibid, 105 citing IPA 2016, s87(2)(a)–(c).

92 *Liberty* (n25).

Conclusion

Given the significance of his contribution to the content of the IPA 2016, and indeed his endorsement of the case for its targeted and bulk investigatory powers, it seems appropriate to turn to Lord Anderson's views of the act as assented to.

> [The IPA 2016]...introduces ***world-leading standards of transparency*** (for example in relation to 'equipment interference' or Government hacking, a widespread practice which few countries even acknowledge in their law). It gives ***legal sanction to a range of powers which have already proved their worth***, whether in warfare, cyber-defence, counter-terrorism or the fight against sexual exploitation and serious and organised crime...It provides ***much enhanced safeguards***, including the requirement of judicial approval before warrants enter into force, additional protection for privileged or sensitive material and new penalties for the wrongful examination of data. It is couched in ***technology-neutral language*** which, notwithstanding the breakneck pace of change, should last – with judicious amendment – for 10 or 15 years...it provides both the powers that are needed to keep us safe, and the mechanisms that are needed to verify that those powers are properly exercised...***it deserves our trust.***[93]

References

David Anderson QC, 'The Investigatory Powers Act 2016: An Exercise in Democracy' (*David Anderson QC*, 26 June 2017) <https://www.daqc.co.uk/2016/12/03/the-investigatory-powers-act-2016-an-exercise-in-democracy/> accessed 29 November 2020

Gordon Corera, *Intercept, the Secret History of Computers and Spies* (Weidenfeld and Nicolson, 2015) 332

Home Office, 'Communications Data- General' (*GOV.UK*, 4 November 2015) <https://assets.publishing.service.gov.uk/government/uploads/system/uploads/attachment_data/file/473747/Factsheet-Communications_Data_General.pdf> accessed 30 November 2020 (emphasis added)

Home Office, *Draft Investigatory Powers Bill* (Cm 9152, November 2015)

Home Office, 'Draft Investigatory Powers Bill, Overarching Documents' (*GOV.UK*, 4 November 2015) <https://www.gov.uk/government/publications/draft-investigatory-powers-bill-overarching-documents> accessed 30 November 2020

Home Office, 'Internet Connection Records' (*GOV.UK*, 4 November 2015) <https://assets.publishing.service.gov.uk/government/uploads/system/uploads/attachment_data/file/473745/Factsheet-Internet_Connection_Records.pdf> accessed 30 November 2020

Home Office, 'Investigatory Powers Bill Factsheet: Bulk Equipment Interference' (*GOV.UK*, 4 November 2015) <https://assets.publishing.service.gov.uk/gove

93 David Anderson QC, 'The Investigatory Powers Act 2016: An exercise in democracy' (n82), emphasis added.

rnment/uploads/system/uploads/attachment_data/file/473753/Factsheet-Bulk_Equipment_Interference.pdf> accessed 30. November 2020 (emphasis added)

Home Office, 'Investigatory Powers Bill Factsheet: Bulk Communications Data' (*GOV.UK*, 4 November 2015)

Home Office, 'Investigatory Powers Bill Factsheet: Bulk Interception' (*GOV.UK*, 4 November 2015) <https://assets.publishing.service.gov.uk/government/uploads/system/uploads/attachment_data/file/473751/Factsheet-Bulk_Interception.pdf> accessed 30 November 2020 (emphasis added)

Home Office, 'Investigatory Powers Bill Factsheet: Bulk Personal Datasets' (*GOV.UK*, 4 November 2015) <https://assets.publishing.service.gov.uk/government/uploads/system/uploads/attachment_data/file/473750/Factsheet-Bulk_Personal_Datasets.pdf> accessed 30 November 2020 (emphasis added)

Home Office, 'Operational Case for the Retention of Internet Connection Records' (*GOV.UK*, 4 November 2015) <https://assets.publishing.service.gov.uk/government/uploads/system/uploads/attachment_data/file/473769/Internet_Connection_Records_Evidence_Base.pdf> accessed 30 November 2020

Home Office, *Investigatory Powers Bill: Government Response to Pre-Legislative Scrutiny* (Cm9219, March 2016)

Home Office, *Communications Data: Code of Practice* (Home Office, November 2018)

Home Office, 'Delegated Powers and Regulatory Reform Committee: Draft Investigatory Powers Bill Memorandum by the Home Office' <https://assets.publishing.service.gov.uk/government/uploads/system/uploads/attachment_data/file/473760/Delegated_Powers_Memorandum.pdf> accessed 30 November 2020

Home Office, 'Handling Arrangements for Bulk Communications Data' <https://assets.publishing.service.gov.uk/government/uploads/system/uploads/attachment_data/file/473780/Handling_arrangements_for_Bulk_Communications_Data.pdf> accessed 30 November 2020

Home Office, 'Handling Arrangements for Bulk Personal Datasets' <https://assets.publishing.service.gov.uk/government/uploads/system/uploads/attachment_data/file/473782/Handling_arrangements_for_Bulk_Personal_Datasets.pdf> accessed 30 November 2020

Home Office, 'Investigatory Powers Bill: European Convention on Human Rights Compliance Memorandum' <https://assets.publishing.service.gov.uk/government/uploads/system/uploads/attachment_data/file/473763/European_Convention_on_Human_Rights_Memorandum.pdf> accessed 30 November 2020

Home Office, 'Investigatory Powers Bill Overarching Privacy Impact Assessment' <https://assets.publishing.service.gov.uk/government/uploads/system/uploads/attachment_data/file/473771/Impact_Assessmen-Overarching-Impact-Assessment.pdf> accessed 30 November 2020

House of Commons, Home Affairs Committee, *Regulation of Investigatory Powers Act 2000: Eighth Report of Session 2014-15* (HC711, December 2014)

House of Commons Science and Technology Committee, *Investigatory Powers Bill: Technical Issues: Third Report of Session 2015-16* (HC 573, January 2016)

House of Lords, House of Commons Joint Committee on the Draft Investigatory Powers Bill, *Draft Investigatory Powers Bill Report* (HL 93, HC 651, February 2016) (JCDIPB, IPB Report 2016)

House of Lords, House of Commons Joint Committee on Human Rights, *Legislative Scrutiny: Investigatory Powers Bill First Report of 2016–17* (HL6, HC 104) 35

Independent Reviewer of Terrorism Legislation, *A Question of Trust: Report of the Investigatory Powers Review* (Williams Lea Group, June 2015)

Intelligence and Security Committee of Parliament, *Privacy and Security: A Modern and Transparent Framework* (HC 1075, March 2015)

Intelligence and Security Committee of Parliament, *Report on the Draft Investigatory Powers Bill* (HC 795, February 2016)

Simon McKay, *Blackstone's Guide to the Investigatory Powers Act 2016* (Oxford University Press, 2017) 17. Henry VIII Clauses Are Those in Primary Legislation That Authorise the Making of Secondary Legislation That Amends or Repeals Primary Legislation

Chris Pounder, 'Section 94 of the Telecommunications Act 1984: A Warning From History' (*Hawktalk*, 6 November 2015) <https://amberhawk.typepad.com/amberhawk/2015/11/section-94-of-the-telecommunications-act-1984-a-warning-from-history.html?utm_source=feedburner&utm_medium=feed&utm_campaign=Feed%3A+HawkTalk+%28Hawk+Talk%29> accessed 6 November 2020

Royal United Services Institute for Defence and Security Studies, *A Democratic Licence to Operate: Report of the Independent Surveillance Review* (Stephen Austin and Sons Ltd, July 2015)

11 Postscript

Introduction

At the time of writing, it is over four years since the Investigatory Powers Act (IPA) 2016 received Royal Assent and the whole Act is now in force. The Act requires the Secretary of State to report on its operation of the Act no later than 29 May 2022.[1] The terms of reference for any review have yet to be publicized, although given the efficacy and widespread favourable reception afforded to both Independent Review of Terrorism Legislation (IRTL) reviews of 2015 and 2016, it may be awarded to the current incumbent to undertake it.[2]

Without prejudice to that review, it is suggested that the state's approach to regulating access to communications and data, both at rest and in transit, as expressed in the IPA 2016, is cogent. Perhaps most importantly, however, the IPA 2016 is transparent. The long history of secrecy, 'need to know' and disingenuous governance has passed and we now have Rachel Noble's transparently secret era.[3] This is probably the best it can get, as operational secrecy will always be required to protect the protection of national security.

Despite residual concerns regarding the conceptual interpretation of communications 'content', the IPA's principal definitions can be read and understood by laypersons. The nature of the powers awarded to intelligence agencies and law enforcement are candid and clear. As Lord Anderson put it, the IPA 2016 'gets the big things right'.[4]

Despite residual concerns as to the scope and magnitude of its constituent powers, the highest courts of the UK and Europe have assisted in neutering the

1 Investigatory Powers Act 2016, s260.
2 Currently Jonathan Hall QC.
3 Rachel Noble (Director-General Australian Signals Directorate), 'Long Histories, Short Memories – the Transparently Secret Australian Signals Directorate', (presentation to the National Security College, Australian National University, Canberra 1 September 2020) <https://www.asd.gov.au/publication/speech-transparently-secret-asd> accessed 20 September 2020.
4 David Anderson QC, 'The Investigatory Powers Act 2016: An Exercise in Democracy' (*David Anderson QC*, 26 June 2017) <https://www.daqc.co.uk/2016/12/03/the-investigatory-powers-act-2016-an-exercise-in-democracy/> accessed 30 November 2020.

most disproportionate aspects of investigative access to communications and data for national security and broadly related purposes.

Communications data retention

The vexed question of constructing a necessary and proportionate legal framework enabling the retention of communications data by communications service providers remained unsettled following the adverse ruling in *Tele 2 Sverige*.[5] Almost two years later, in *Secretary of State for the Home Department v Watson MP & Ors*, the England and Wales Court of Appeal found that where the purpose of legislation is the prevention, investigation, detection, and prosecution of criminal offences, access to and use of retained CD should be restricted to the objective of fighting *serious* crime and that access to retained CD should be dependent on a prior review by a court or an independent administrative body.[6] As such, they were unanimous in finding that, in the context of preventing and detecting crime, DRIPA 2014, s1(1) was inconsistent with EU law and that declaratory relief was appropriate.[7]

Despite the existence of that legal challenge to the DRIPA 2014 CD retention framework, the government had pressed ahead with drafting Part 4 of the IPA 2016 that would replace the DRIPA 2016 on its expiry on 31 December 2016.[8] This did not settle the question of the legality, scope, magnitude, necessity or proportionality of the UK's CD retention regime. It was thus unsurprising that it almost immediately after entering force, the government became subject to a new legal challenge in the English High Court seeking judicial review of the power given to the Secretary of State by section 87(1) of the IPA to issue 'retention notices' to telecommunications operators requiring the retention of data.[9] This had been initiated on 28 February 2017 by litigation veterans Liberty, who sought an 'order of disapplication' in respect of it insofar as it is incompatible with EU law.[10] By 7 July 2017, the UK government had conceded that Part 4 of the IPA 2016 as then existing was indeed inconsistent with the requirements of EU law in two respects and that they had commenced a consultation process.[11] On 27 April 2018, in finding for Liberty, but not going so far as to

5 Cases 203/15 and 698/15 *Tele2 Sverige AB v Post-och telestyrelsen and Secretary of State for the Home Department v Tom Watson and Others.*

6 *Secretary of State for the Home Department v Watson MP & Ors* (2018) EWCA Civ 70 (9). The judges noted a number of circumstances that had delayed the hearing of the case.

7 ibid, (27).

8 *R (National Council for Civil Liberties [Liberty]) v Secretary of State for the Home Department* (2018) EWHC 975 (admin).

9 ibid, (3).

10 ibid (10).

11 Home Office: 'Investigatory Powers Act 2016: Consultation on the Government's Proposed Response to the Ruling of the Court of Justice of the European Union Regarding the Retention of Communications Data' <https://assets.publishing.service.gov.uk/government/upl

disapply Part 4, the High Court found as they had in *Davis, Watson and Others*, and gave the government until 1 November 2018 to make the requisite amendments.[12] This was achieved via secondary legislation amendment that created and inserted a definition of 'serious crime' to section 87 with effect from 1 November 2018.[13] As such, there is now a settled and legally certain communications data retention regime for the first time since *Digital Rights.*

Bulk interception of communications, acquisition of communications data, and receipt of foreign intelligence

Although a final European Court of Human Rights Grand Chamber determination remains outstanding in the long-running proceedings in *Big Brother Watch and Others v UK*, the First Section judgment of 13 September 2018, despite adverse findings as regards the legality and efficacy of safeguards and oversight, will have been encouraging for the UK government.[14] Its ringing endorsement of the Investigatory Powers Tribunal and its 'elucidatory' role will have been particularly pleasing.[15] Although the proceedings relate to the IPA 2016's statutory predecessor RIPA, the overall findings as regards a state's 'right' to maintain a legal framework enabling the impugned communications and data investigation powers indicate that, as Vermeulen ruefully observed 'Big Brother may continue watching you'.[16]

Rationalizing the range of investigative powers in the IPA 2016

Rationalizing the IPA 2016, as a legislative instrument giving effect to national security policy, requires firstly a rationalisation of that policy. A government's duty to look after its citizens has been asserted to be 'one of its primary functions and (arguably) a condition of its legitimacy.[17] The UK government has articulated its national security policy by stating that 'in a world of startling change, the *first duty* of the Government remains: the security of our country'.[18] This was reiterated in the most recent (as of 2020) National Security Strategy and Strategic

---

oads/system/uploads/attachment_data/file/663668/November_2017_IPA_Consultation_-_consultation_document.pdf> accessed 20 November 2020.

12 *R (National Council for Civil Liberties [Liberty]) v Secretary of State for the Home Department* (2018) EWHC 975 (Admin) (186)–(187).

13 See Data Retention and Acquisition Regulations 2018, regs 5-8, which amended s87 of the IPA 2016

14 *Big Brother Watch and Others v UK* (Applications Nos 58170/13, 62322/14 and 24960/15.

15 ibid, (250)–(265).

16 Judith Vermeulen, 'Big Brother May Continue Watching You' (*Strasbourg Observers*, 12 October 2018) <https://strasbourgobservers.com/2018/10/12/big-brother-may-continue-watching-you/#more-4225> accessed 30 November 2020.

17 David Miller, 'The Responsibility to Protect Human Rights' in Lukas H Meyer (ed) *Legitimacy, Justice and Public International Law* (Cambridge University Press, 2009) 232.

18 Home Office, *A Strong Britain in an Age of Uncertainty: The National Security Strategy* (Cmnd 7953, 2010), emphasis added.

Defence and Security Review (2015); 'the Government's most important duty is the defence of the UK and Overseas Territories, and protection of our people and sovereignty'.[19] National security remains undefined, but in introducing a national security strategy for the first time in 2008, the UK government stated that national security was

> the traditional focus of foreign, defence and security policies, and...understood as dealing with the protection of the state and its vital interests from attacks by other states. Over recent decades, our view of national security has broadened to include threats to individual citizens and to our way of life, as well as to the integrity and interests of the state.[20]

This has actually aged quite well, as has the view that the UK needs 'to maintain *a set of capabilities*...to deal with those threats and risks and the underlying drivers to understand them better, act early to prevent them where we can...[ensuring that] we minimize and manage any harm they might cause'.[21] In preparing the ground for public acceptance of the IPB (and the IPA 2016) the IRTL stated

> Only in a society whose institutions are protected from attack and in which there is an expectation that laws will be enforced is it possible for people to trust strangers, live without the fear of attack or intimidation, participate fully in the economy and society and develop to the full their own interests, personalities and quality of life. The libertarian view that the State has no business snooping on the private affairs of the individual, and that some places or channels of communication should enjoy guaranteed immunity, has its attractions for some. But those attractions wane once it is recognised that there are individuals who will take advantage of *any unpatrolled space* to groom, abuse, blackmail, steal secrets from, threaten, defraud and plot destructive acts of terrorism against others. *Any State that claims to protect its citizens must have the ability effectively to detect, disrupt and prosecute such behaviour.* The central issue is how that ability can be combined with the expectation of privacy which law-abiding people have and deserve.[22]

19 HM Government, *National Security Strategy and Strategic Defence and Security Review* 2015 (Cm 9161, 2015) 23.

20 Cabinet Office, The National Security of the United Kingdom: Security in an Interdependent World (Cm 7291, 2008) 3–4.

21 HM Government, *National Security Strategy and Strategic Defence and Security Review* 2015 (Cm 9161, 2015) 24:

> the Royal Air Force protects our airspace and is ready at all times to intercept rogue aircraft. The Royal Navy protects our waters and deters terrorist and criminal activity. Our NATO Allies provide us with early warning of approaching ships and aircraft, or deal with them before they reach our territory or airspace, as we do for our Allies.

22 Independent Reviewer of Terrorism Legislation, *A Question of Trust: Report of the Investigatory Powers Review* (Williams Lea Group, June 2015) 247, emphasis added.

The reference to unpatrolled space is telling. Any rational national security strategy involves defending airspace, maritime, and territorial boundaries. It is thus entirely rational that the UK would seek to patrol cyberspace in the same way, to identify threats to national security at the earliest possible opportunity.[23] It is also entirely rational that as communications technology developed, and the means by which communications and data could be stored or transmitted evolved, the maintenance of a capability to access communications and data, wherever stored or transmitted is of critical national security importance. Leaving aside the aforementioned judgments of the proportionality of aspects of the UK's communications and data investigation regime, or any perceived deficiencies in safeguards, the necessity, or *rationale* for, the UK's position is actually supported by the European Courts. They have had no difficulty finding that 'the existence of some legislation granting powers of secret surveillance over the mail, post and telecommunications…[is]…necessary in a democratic society in the interests of national security and/or for the prevention of disorder or crime',[24] and that the margin of appreciation afforded to Member States in this respect is a wide one.[25] However, the same courts have held that the interest of states in protecting their national security 'must be balanced against the seriousness of the interference with the applicant's right to respect for his private life'.[26] Consequently, the interests of national security marginally assume primacy over the ECHR, Article 8 right to privacy, meaning that in any national security-critical balancing exercise, the protection of lives should assume marginal primacy over the protection of rights. This is not least because as a consequence of ECHR's Article 2, states are under a positive duty to all required of them to prevent lives being put at risk.[27]

Conclusion

This book has examined the British state's governance of investigative access to communications over its traceable 700-year history. Throughout that period, the state has followed its unshakeable and justifiable belief in the right to defend its domestic national security and to enter into alliances with other like-minded nations to assist in delivering national security protection. That belief has extended to a belief in the right to undertake macro-surveillance of all known *means* of communication and data transfer, and, increasingly, communications and data at rest, as well as in the right to investigate communications and data in transit or at rest on a more targeted basis. Whilst there has been a transition from secrecy to candour in the regulation of this state practice, and, since RIPA

23 HM Government, *National Security Strategy and Strategic Defence and Security Review* 2015 (n21) 15.

24 *Klass & Others v Germany* (n113) (48).

25 *Leander v Sweden* (1987) 9 EHRR 433 (59).

26 ibid.

27 *LCB v UK* (1998) 27 EHRR 212 (36).

2000, cognisance of human rights implications and the need for appropriate safeguards, the rationale for the state practice has never changed. Consequently, the IPA 2016, containing as it does only five investigatory powers (broadly defined) can indeed be rationalized as an entirely logical progression in formerly secretive British state powers, assumed or granted in the interests of national security (broadly construed), aimed at enabling the capability to lawfully access communications and data at rest or in transit wherever located.

Thank you for reading.

References

David Anderson QC, 'The Investigatory Powers Act 2016: An Exercise in Democracy' (*David Anderson QC*, 26 June 2017) <https://www.daqc.co.uk/2016/12/03/the-investigatory-powers-act-2016-an-exercise-in-democracy/> accessed 30 November 2020

Cabinet Office, *The National Security of the United Kingdom: Security in an Interdependent World* (Cm 7291, 2008)

HM Government, *National Security Strategy and Strategic Defence and Security Review 2015* (Cm 9161, 2015)

Home Office, *A Strong Britain in an Age of Uncertainty: The National Security Strategy* (Cmnd 7953, 2010)

Home Office, 'Investigatory Powers Act 2016: Consultation on the Government's Proposed Response to the Ruling of the Court of Justice of the European Union Regarding the Retention of Communications Data' <https://assets.publishing.service.gov.uk/government/uploads/system/uploads/attachment_data/file/663668/November_2017_IPA_Consultation_-_consultation_document.pdf> accessed 20 November 2020

Independent Reviewer of Terrorism Legislation, *A Question of Trust: Report of the Investigatory Powers Review* (Williams Lea Group, June 2015)

David Miller, 'The Responsibility to Protect Human Rights' in Lukas H Meyer (ed) *Legitimacy, Justice and Public International Law* (Cambridge University Press, 2009)

Rachel Noble (Director-General Australian Signals Directorate), 'Long Histories, Short Memories – The Transparently Secret Australian Signals Directorate', (presentation to the National Security College, Australian National University, Canberra 1 September 2020) <https://www.asd.gov.au/publication/speech-transparently-secret-asd> accessed 20 September 2020

Judith Vermeulen, 'Big Brother May Continue Watching You' (*Strasbourg Observers*, 12 October 2018) <https://strasbourgobservers.com/2018/10/12/big-brother-may-continue-watching-you/#more-4225> accessed 30 November 2020

Index

shock 235–236; Codes of Practice 230–232, 254; communications 155; Communications Commissioner 135; Home Affairs Committee report 253–254; independent oversight 179; intelligence raw material 154–155; intercepted material 162; interception 29, 161–162; interception warrants 162; military investigations 178–179; NTAC (National Technical Assistance Centre) 160–161; Part I, Chapter I 150; Part I, Chapter II 222–224, 245–246; Privacy Impact Assessment 153–154; privacy impact rationale 220–221; rationalizing 151; RCD (related communications data) 37, 155–156; thematic warrants 164–166; UKUSA Communications Intelligence Agreement 157–160; warrants 164

For Product Safety Concerns and Information please contact our EU
representative GPSR@taylorandfrancis.com
Taylor & Francis Verlag GmbH, Kaufingerstraße 24, 80331 München, Germany

www.ingramcontent.com/pod-product-compliance
Ingram Content Group UK Ltd.
Pitfield, Milton Keynes, MK11 3LW, UK
UKHW020019200926
475702UK00014B/1969
* 9 7 8 1 0 3 2 0 4 0 4 2 4 *